# The Vickers Papers

# The
# Vickers
# Papers

## *edited by Open Systems Group*

**Harper & Row, Publishers**
London

Cambridge
Hagerstown
Philadelphia
New York

San Francisco
Mexico City
São Paulo
Sydney

First published 1984

Harper and Row Ltd
28 Tavistock Street
London WC2E 7PN

British Library Cataloguing in Publication
Data

Vickers, G.
    The Vickers papers.
    1. Social sciences
    I. Title        2. Open Systems Group
    300        H5
    ISBN 0-06-318270-X


Typeset 11/12 Sabon, printed and bound by
Butler & Tanner Ltd, Frome and London

# Acknowledgements

We would like to thank all the people who have helped to make this volume possible. Jeanne Vickers, Sir Geoffrey's literary executor, helped to initiate the project and has been unfailingly supportive throughout. Pamela Miller, Sir Geoffrey's daughter, has provided invaluable guidance to the papers in her possession and supplied other biographical information. Sheila Seymour, Sir Geoffrey's last secretary, has been indefatigable in locating papers and assisting our research. Lyn Jones, of the University of Edinburgh Department of Community Medicine, provided illuminating comments on Vickers' contribution to medical debate in the 1960s. Marianne Lagrange, of Harper and Row, has helped to smooth our path since the first conception of the volume. Finally, we are grateful for the collaboration of our colleagues in the Open Systems Group, John Hamwee, John Martin, Bill Mayon-White, John Naughton, and Joyce Tait.

Margaret Blunden
Geoff Peters
*April 1984*

# Preface

The field called the 'systems approach' seems to be rather fragmented, as each author tries to take one theme and convert it into the whole topic. Perhaps this is how matters should be, given the enormity of the systems task: to make sense out of human destiny.

To me, the most interesting and valuable writers base their work on tradition, because they realize that the systems approach is not a brand new idea of the latter part of the twentieth century, but rather has its roots in a long history of endeavor. Vickers was an important contributor to this genre of systems writings. The tradition he selected could be called 'the law,' but with an emphasis on the ethical implication of legal processes.

Ethics is a slippery subject and also one that most systems writers attempt to ignore. They prefer to say 'given these objectives, here is how we should proceed,' even though the objectives might be reprehensible, or illegal, for that matter. Vickers called the systems which can be studied in an ethical manner 'appreciative,' a rather difficult concept even for a philosopher like myself who has been steeped in ethical writings for well over a half century.

Instead of repeating themes from the excellent Introduction to this book, I'd like to choose one which has had a profound influence on my own ethical conversations, namely, responsibility. A number of systems writers have expressed their ideas in terms of freedom of choice, the desirable ability of systems inhabitants to choose their own options. They have pointed out many groups of humans who have been denied certain freedoms, e.g., the freedom of women to become full fledged citizens, or of children to eat nourishing food, or of all of us to be able to vote significantly. But most writers on 'causes' fail to point out that freedom implies not only the ability to make choices but also to assume the ethical responsibility of the choice one makes.

Vickers wrote in his own way about responsibility, and it is up to each of us to translate what he told us into our own terms. My translation runs somewhat as follows: a person is responsible for the choice he/she has made, if she/he tries very hard to recognize the moral significance of the choice. This is not a definition, of course, but I can add to its meaning by including Kant in the conversation: the responsible person tries to understand how the choice produces benefits and harms both for the choicemaker and for others. Since we humans are making many choices these days which will harm future generations, then I'd say that our chief responsibility is to them.

I realize I might assume, as Vickers himself did according to his biographer, that few people will pay any attention to these remarks, because they imply that most political leaders, educators, workers, even 'concerned citizens' are irresponsible. Perhaps the most tragic implication to people like Vickers and myself who are lovers of science, is that most of today's so-called scientists are irresponsible.

But I learned another important theme from Geoff: it doesn't matter so much whether people agree with you; the important point is to get them talking.

C. West Churchman
*University of California*
*Berkeley*
*California*

# Contents

## Level IV—The Individual

# Introduction

This collection of papers is intended as a tribute to the late Sir Geoffrey Vickers, V.C., who in the last years of his long life made a valuable contribution to the work of the Open University Systems Group. He was a regular guest speaker at our annual Summer Schools, one of the Core Group of Scholars at the Silver Jubilee meeting of the Society for General Systems Research for which the Open University acted as UK organizer, and his last book, *Human Systems are Different*, was originally commissioned as an Open University set book.

We have produced this selection of papers because of the growing interest in Sir Geoffrey's work, and the lack of readily available publications. Although there are now two more of his books in print than when he died, much of his output was in papers in a wide range of publications. Some of the publications would usually only be encountered by specialists. Even readers familiar with some of Sir Geoffrey's work may be surprised by the diversity of his interests and contributions. For example, he contributed fourteen papers to *The Lancet* and other medical journals, four articles in *Futures*, five papers to professional psychology or psychiatry journals, as well as contributions to journals of management, policy sciences, ecology, education, communication, and, of course, systems. Much of this work has not been readily accessible. We have been fortunate in being able to put together a collection of papers which testifies to the breadth of his contribution and in having access to his private papers for our biographical introduction.

The audience for this book will include some specialists, as well as the professionals in management, medicine, psychology, planning, and the policy sciences. But all Sir Geoffrey's writings bear on questions of general relevance, notably the urgent need to develop appropriate ways of thinking about our current problems at all levels, from the personal to the planetary, and particularly to develop ways of thinking which can cope with the important and neglected ethical dimension in human judgement.

Although Vickers' contributions are made in diverse fields, they represent a coherent body of thought, linked by continuing concerns, a characteristic epistemological stance, and the creative use of systems ideas. It has been difficult to group the papers. The approach we have taken has been to select the articles that in our opinion most deserve a wider audience and at the same time to try to reflect the range of his contributions and avoid duplication with books in print. We rejected a categorization by topic – Vickers on planning, health, education, management, and so on; this scheme seemed to do violence to the systemic quality of Vickers' writings, which constantly draw parallels across different academic and professional boundaries and exploit cross-disciplinary insights. We also rejected a categorization by concept: Vickers' most important concept, the appreciative system, for example, recurs in slightly different form in very many of the articles reproduced here. The categorization we have adopted, that of *system levels*, most closely reflects the systemic quality of Vickers' own thinking. The bulk of the book is arranged into four parts in which the articles are predominantly concerned with issues at the following levels:

Level I—Planetary

Level II—Society

Level III—Organizations

Level IV—The Individual

The first chapter, *Geoffrey Vickers - An Intellectual Journey*, has been specially researched by Dr Margaret Blunden. It traces Vickers' intellectual development in the context of an exceptionally rich and varied professional life; it draws heavily on Vickers' private papers. The second chapter, *A Classification of Systems*, is one of the few articles he wrote which was purely concerned with the development of that subject, and shows Vickers after his discovery of the work of Ross Ashby et alia offering his own contribution.

We do not expect the readers of this book to start at the beginning and read it right through to the end. Rather it is intended as a much abridged Vickers library and we hope that many people will wish to read further. To this end we have included at the back of the book a select bibliography of books and papers based upon one prepared by Sir Geoffrey a couple of years before his death.

# I

# Geoffrey Vickers – an intellectual journey

In March 1955 Geoffrey Vickers gave up his membership of the British National Coal Board, left London and moved with his wife to a cottage at the foot of the chalk downs in Berkshire. Sir Geoffrey – who had already had three major occupations, as soldier, lawyer, and administrator – did not see the move as a retirement:

> I wanted to keep in touch with public and private affairs sufficiently to remain in circulation (and hopefully to sustain solvency at a not too acute level of austerity). But what I most wanted was to contribute to what I believed to be a revolution in human thinking which had been reaching and exciting me for the previous ten years.[1]

Vickers had just encountered systems ideas in the writings of Von Bertalanffy, Norbert Wiener, and Ross Ashby. He had close contacts with scientists engaged in medical and psychiatric research and had written and thought a great deal about management. He was soon to establish mutual interests with a wide variety of academics, especially in the professional schools spanning academic and applied areas, such as government, planning, policy sciences, architecture, and social work. His own writings, addressed to widely diverse audiences, rested on a single coherent theme – the inadequacy of the dominant modes of thought in the Western world for addressing our complex and dangerous predicament. His central concerns were epistemology and ethics, and he was essentially a professional, seeking knowledge to guide action. His concept of the *appreciative system* was an important contribution both to academic epistemology and to what Vickers called 'the art of human governance'.

Publicly, Sir Geoffrey's para-academic career was an apparent success. He published 87 papers between 1955 and 1982, wrote nine books, lectured at universities in North America and Britain, and carried on an impressive intellectual debate by correspondence with academics from many different disciplines throughout the English-speaking world. In 1980 a group of well-known American scholars began to prepare a Festschrift.

Privately, Sir Geoffrey felt 'hugely ambivalent'[2] about his achievements. What he identified as centrally important concerns were, he believed, eliminated from enquiry by the prevailing 'culture of the natural sciences' which 'continues to erode and debunk all human insights, especially ethical ones which lie at the heart of culture'.[3] He became aware of what he called 'a huge and growing impoverishment which has so far been implicit and often explicit in what is commonly understood as a "scientific" approach to human affairs'.[4]

His own ideas were, he felt, essentially ignored. In February 1980 he wrote to Guy Adams, one of the American scholars preparing his Festschrift, that:

> I am nearing the end of my capacity for output, am slowly realizing that most of my assumptions are heresies or worse to most academics today and that what I have to say, however obvious to me, is truly shocking to most readers – so much so that they won't even notice it unless it is expressed in a much more challenging way than comes easily to me.[5]

Vickers died in March 1982. *The Times* obituary (18 March) dwelt at length on his fine military record and his achievements in public affairs, but barely recognized that he was a serious thinker.

This first chapter attempts to chart Geoffrey Vickers' intellectual journey. It is written in the belief that Vickers' distinctive development of systems thinking and its application to the human rather than technological questions of organization, government, and survival, are deserving of much wider attention.

Geoffrey Vickers was born in 1894, the youngest child of Jessie Lomas and Charles Henry Vickers of Nottingham. Charles Vickers ran the family lace manufacturing business built up by his grandfather, a former Lord Mayor of Nottingham. Lace manufacturers were going through difficult times and the family lived simply in a small house with two small rooms on each of three floors. Charles Vickers was a man of great vitality and intellectual curiosity; in particular, he loved poetry, science, and philosophy. He had an unselfconscious disregard for class divisions. From the age of nineteen until his death at seventy-three, Charles Vickers held a weekly discussion meeting he called 'The Class', originally intended for the down-and-out but coming to include men of different types and fortunes.

> 'The Class' illustrated but by no means exhausted my father's gift for combining sympathy for those less fortunate than himself with the capacity for friendship, on absolutely level terms, with all sorts and conditions of men.[6]

Geoffrey, the youngest of three children, was a child of unusual sensitivity and intellectual awareness. His earliest memory, from the age of three, was of the moving into their new house of an immense wardrobe, which had previously stood in their earlier house and had seemed to be as fixed and immovable as the house itself:

> It seems to me in retrospect that as I watched the wardrobe edge through the door, I caught my first glimpse of the fact that human order and disorder are largely made by men, consciously or blindly, compulsively or deliberately, with understanding or with grotesque misunderstanding of the delicate medium in which they work and of the endless repercussions of everything they do.[7]

This was an early foretaste of a lifelong concern with identity:

> From an age not older than ten (perhaps much younger) I have been fascinated by identity and by time. When does a familiar something, when repaired, altered,

or renovated, become something new rather than its familiar self though changed?[8]

Until the age of twelve Geoffrey lived at home, educated first by a governess and then at local schools. His family life was both happy and cultivated: 'If I could have my life again my parents and my childhood home are among the few things that I would not wish to change in any way or for any alternative.'[9] His parents, both of them Baptists, created an atmosphere that encouraged confidence, curiosity, and originality and the family shared a love of poetry.

At the age of twelve, he was sent away, first to preparatory school and then to public school at Oundle, a Church of England foundation in the tradition of Thomas Arnold. Typically, the emphasis was on the humanities and the classics – though fond of mathematics, Vickers was taken off mathematics early:

> I was educated almost wholly in the humanities, that is to say, in the study of human experience. The subjective domain was assumed to be paramount in importance for human subjects such as we. Mathematics and logic were honoured though perhaps not adequately stressed. They were important intellectual tools in the ordering of experience. But the Word was paramount.[10]

The academic curriculum was only a part of a total educational experience including the school chapel, the Officers' Training Corps, and organized team games, designed to imprint certain attitudes and a distinctive kind of character. As Vickers reflected much later (1940):

> At the turn of the century the public schools offered something which was supposed to be 'pure' education but which was in fact a subtle blend of vocational and cultural training, well suited to the ruling class of that particular place and time. It was a preparation for the Government services and the professions; and at the same time it developed in the individual a set of attitudes, towards himself, his fellows and authority so constant and so pronounced as to constitute one of the most recognisable human types in the world. The most determined experiments of the totalitarian states in standardising human attitudes by education still look amateurish when compared with the effortless and unconscious achievement of the Thring–Arnold tradition.[11]

Vickers did not fit into the public school system and spent four unhappy years at Oundle. He was not good at sport. He had always been acutely anxious in the company of adults, other than his parents, and felt excluded by their 'incommunicable code'.[12] The experience of school reinforced these anxieties. He spoke later of 'the anguish reserved both for non-conformists who long to conform and for the awkward who long to excel in dexterity'.[13]

But the prevailing ethos meant that his unhappiness, along with other impulses or feelings, had to be repressed. There is little indication of it in his letters home. Vickers was later to reject many of the assumptions of the turn of the century public school – particularly its defence of privilege, its social divisiveness and its religion – but he was profoundly affected by it. His lifelong concern for order and stability reflected partly the interests and world view of the upper middle classes in Edwardian Britain. Above all, Vickers internalized the idea that membership of a community, whether family, school, or country, involved commitments, responsibilities and obligations.

Early in 1913, in an interlude between school and university, Vickers spent a few months in Germany, where his father had contacts. The ease of the experience, taken for granted at the time, seemed remarkable in retrospect:

> When I first visited the continent, no frontier asked to see my passport, and a golden sovereign (there were no pound notes) was exchangeable at a fixed rate for any currency from Antwerp to Athens. My standards of stability were set in a world which still looked and felt far more stable than it was or ever has been since that glorious sunset.[14]

In October 1913 Vickers went up to Merton College Oxford to read 'Greats' – classical languages and civilization. He joined the Officers' Training Corps, a popular branch of university life; 1200 officer cadets turned out for review by General Lord French the year before the war. But Vickers and his contemporaries were unaware of the dangerous political developments in Europe:

> Most of my co-evals even at Oxford were as unpolitical and as naive as I. This negative memory constantly reawakens in my mind an uneasy awareness of what may be the greatest of human limitations – the distinction between all that they believe to be real and that tiny part of it which to us individually is actual, able to awake sympathy or indignation as a fact, not a generalisation, to become a matter of personal concern.[15]

On 4 August 1914 Britain entered the war against Germany. Vickers immediately enlisted; he was one of 2000 volunteers from the university during the first two months of the conflict. War was not the occasion for a crisis of conscience or even of political doubts:

> War was still almost universally accepted as the normal instrument of last resource in international politics and by no means necessarily as self-defeating or signalling a bankruptcy of policy.[16]

He was immediately given onerous military responsibilities:

> At Oundle and Oxford I had been in what was then called the Officers' Training Corps, so I was deemed fit, without further screening, to command in battle men of whom many were much older than I. I was given a commission in our local territorial battalion, the 7th (Robin Hood) Battalion of the Sherwood Foresters, without even a medical examination. I was with them before the end of 1914 and in France in February of the next year.[17]

His brother Burnell, who had been to a Quaker School and had no military training, took a few months longer to get to France.

During the spring of 1915 Vickers' battalion was involved in heavy fighting in Flanders. Life in the trenches, barely endurable to some men, seemed to Vickers to have been essentially uncomplicated: 'A fight is a refreshingly simple and supportive situation; in few other circumstances do we have so many comrades and so few doubts'.[18]

On 13 October 1915, his twenty-first birthday, Vickers showed exceptional gallantry in defending, wounded and almost single-handed, a barrier against enemy attack, and was awarded the Victoria Cross. The episode reproduced in almost identical form an incident in his childhood when, at the age of eight or nine, he and his gang had fought a mock battle with crab apples against a rival gang. On that occasion Vickers, left to guard a gap in the hedge, had retreated under attack. His gang leader had given him a dressing-down on the disgrace of deserting his post, and had forcefully reminded him of Horatius and Thermopylae.

Later, Vickers was to argue that courage was a learnt response, the outcome of expectations which have been internalized:

> If, then, an individual who has thus accepted courage as one of those qualities which are to be expected of him is impelled to run away from a present danger, the image which the impulse evokes – the image of 'himself-running-away' – comes into instant conflict with the other image which the circumstances evoke, the image of himself as a person of whom courage is expected. If his acceptance of the imposed characteristic is sufficiently complete, cowardice will have become impossible for him.[19]

It took Vickers twelve months to recover from his wounds. During his convalescence, his brother Burnell was killed at Ypres. In October 1916 he returned to France to command a company in his old regiment. He knew hardly anyone in the battalion, since those he had left the previous year had nearly all been killed or wounded on the Somme. At the age of twenty-two, he commanded four subalterns, three even younger than himself, and one twenty years older. One incident, in March 1917, long reminded him of the importance of belonging, and the strength of human relationships:

> One day, just before we were due for a week out of the line, I received a chit from Battalion H.Q. It said simply – 'You will proceed to London on the – (the next day) and report to War Office room so-and-so. You will be struck off the strength of the battalion.' No explanation. Some home job presumably. Utter darkness fell. I passed it round the dugout in silence. It was read in silence. We came out of the line that night. Next morning after a silent breakfast the mess cart came round (horse drawn, two wheeled, with a tilt and one cross seat). My things were stowed in, I shook hands with the other four, I couldn't speak but otherwise I kept up appearances until we drove away. Then sitting with my back to the horse to hide my face from the driver, I wept all the way to railhead. Never, in a life full of many partings, have I felt so diminished and lost from the ending of a relationship (except once by death).[20]

Vickers spent nine months galloping round Salisbury Plain training officer cadets and two months at the Senior Officers' school. Early in 1918 he married Helen Newton, whose family lived in the Hertfordshire village where his unit had been billeted for a time. He returned to France in March 1918. He was involved in more active fighting and received the Croix de Guerre. At the end of the war he held the rank of Major.

After his discharge Vickers returned to Oxford. The freshmen he had gone up with six years before had been decimated by the war. Some of his contemporaries who had survived, particularly the exceptionally sensitive and intelligent, had come to see the war as senseless slaughter, a tragic waste which nothing could justify. The poets Siegfried Sassoon and Robert Graves, for example, regarded the continuance of the war after 1915 as 'merely a sacrifice of the idealistic younger generation to the stupidity and self-protective alarm of the elder'.[21]

Vickers, however, emerged from the war with his belief in the nobility of fighting – the conventional belief of the Imperial ruling class – intact. He had written poetry since childhood and on his return to Oxford he read a paper to the Bodley Club of Merton College on 'Poetry and War'. War, he insisted, brought out many qualities:

> The love of fighting is an instinct which is still one of man's driving forces, for it is deep set in that pride of strength and joy in mystery which marks the dominant race. The love of killing for killing's sake, however, is but a bastard branch of it. . . . Thus war is a paradox from the beginning; and war poetry is a reflection of that paradox; its discovery, its development and its partial solution in the mind of man.[22]

Vickers would not concede that poets had been disillusioned by the Great War:

> There are some – it were strange indeed if it were not so – to whom a world at war is still a contradiction and a lie. But nowhere – save once or twice – despair; everywhere, the feeling of release, and quickened life.

He quoted lines from Siegfried Sassoon which seemed to express his own feelings:

> The anguish of the earth absolves our eyes
> Till beauty shines in all that we can see
> War is our scourge; yet war has made us wise
> And fighting for our freedom we are free.[23]

In 1921 Vickers took his degree in classics. He was always happy to have been educated at a time when the humanities had a pre-eminent place:

> People were still primarily interested in people – not because they thought that man was the dominant species, not even because they still thought that men were of especial interest to God – though many still held this useful belief – but simply because this was the species to which they happened to belong. If it was for that very reason the species which human science was least likely to illuminate for human beings, so much the worse. It remained none the less – all the more – the prime concern of men and they screened new knowledge for the

value which it might have for them as men, in dealing with and understanding men. I am glad that I spent my youth in a culture where this obvious scale of priorities had not been overlaid.[24]

Vickers' first two children, a daughter Pamela and a son named Burnell after his brother, were born in the early 1920s. Their father's strong human values are apparent in a remarkable letter which he wrote in 1924 at the age of thirty to his son then aged two – the letter was to be kept for him to read when old enough to understand it:

> Every contact which you make with a human being (or even with an animal) is an experiment and a dangerous and therefore important experiment. It is danger-ous because it can never be repeated. However serious, however trivial it may be, though you will afterwards make many others, perhaps more unusual, more intimate or more complete – that chance will not come again.
>
> Human contacts are dangerous, too, because they matter so much, and no one knows how much they matter. Even the most trivial meeting makes a difference, slight but lasting, to one or both. Intimate contacts make heaven and hell, they can heal and tear, kill and raise from the dead.
>
> These contacts are the fields in which we succeed or fail. I believe that they matter far more than anything else in life. What we are is written on the people whom we have met and known, touched, loved, hated and passed by. It is the lives of others that testify for or against us, not our own.[25]

An implicit systems thinker, Vickers thought naturally in terms of processes and relationships rather than entities. The value he attached to success in human relationships was to make his separation from his wife and children, and subsequent divorce, ten years later, harder to bear.

On leaving Oxford, Vickers was articled to the legal firm of Godfrey Warr and Co. He qualified as a solicitor in 1923 and three years later became a partner in the City of London firm of Slaughter and May. Donald Hall later recalled:

> When he arrived at Slaughter and May in 1926, I was still only an articled clerk. In that prestigious firm there were then only four partners; he was 33, had won the Victoria Cross on his twenty-first birthday, and was already reputed to be an almost dangerously brilliant lawyer.[26]

Of his four careers – lawyer, soldier, public administrator, and aca-demic – only one, the law, was in Vickers' own eyes a Class A success.[27]

At Slaughter and May, Vickers was involved in the legal aspects of large financial operations, often with an international dimension. In 1927 he worked on the financial launching of the International Wagonlits Trust. As corporation lawyer, he had exceptional opportunities for travel. In 1930 he made a five-day flight to India during the first year of the commercial airline service between Britain and India. The experience prompted him to write a semi-autobiographical story, 'Ambrose', and an article on British rule in India entitled 'The Man on the Elephant'. Professionally, he was struck by the different expectations and assumptions engendered in managers and business men in the Indian culture. Politically, he accepted the received thinking on Imperial questions current in Britain – 'England had no need to apologise either for her position in India or for the avowed goal of her policy[28] – but he was sensitive to the psychological costs of British rule to the Indians. The British pretended that careers were open to all by merit; in practice they had established a new caste. They had given the Indians a permanent sense of inferiority.

Vickers had little political awareness until well into the 1930s: he accepted with little question the liberalism in which he had grown up. However, as a number of typescripts written at this time indicate, he was giving considerable thought to philosophical questions. One of these, 'The Divine Animal', indicates why he moved away from the accepted Christian beliefs of his childhood:

> So long as strong spirits can be broken, straight spirits twisted, and clean spirits defiled by the ruthless pressure of inconscient fact; so long as human creatures can be *born* broken, twisted and defiled for no apparent reason save that the wheel of circumstances has passed over generations of their forbears; it is hard to see how a courageous and logical mind can believe in a God who is a benevolent controller of events with reference to the individuals whom such events affect, and at the same time can retain any idea of good and evil.[29]

Vickers' separation from Helen in 1932 and subsequent divorce marked another break with the past. In 1935 he married Ellen Tweed; their son Hugh was born in 1939.

Vickers' most demanding legal work during the 1930s involved the extension of the German debt, a task which took him to Berlin many times, as part of an international team of bankers and lawyers. In 1923, in a few weeks of runaway inflation, the German currency had 'eerily disappeared, leaving notes, coins, and money symbols with no meaning'.[30] Now the future stability of Western and world economies seemed to depend on their effective collaboration with their German counterparts.

One particular occasion in 1935 long remained in Vickers' mind: it testified to a shared professional ethic which spanned national boundaries:

> Round a huge table in the Reichsbank in Berlin sit 31 bankers representing the banks of 14 countries, and opposite them 3 German bankers. They are renegotiating an agreement by which the volume of bank credits available to finance international trade in and through Germany was maintained through the years of the depression. It had been suggested that some of these might be used for another purpose which would in effect allow them to be reduced. The German delegation had just expressed its agreement but coupled it with a plan for giving effect to the proposal – a plan which seemed to every creditor banker so plainly unworkable that not one of them doubted it had been devised to frustrate the scheme. The atmosphere of the meeting changed suddenly to intense hostility and mistrust.
>
> The Germans observed that it was not their plan but the Reichsbank's. It was for the Reichsbank to defend it. The creditors should express their views to Dr Fuchs.*

---

* President of the Reichsbank.

And so they did, abrasively, to the small, tired man who arrived, after an icy, silent pause, to hear what the creditors thought of his plan.[31]

Dr Fuchs was able to secure support by appealing to shared, professional standards:

Looking round the hostile faces, he said 'Gentlemen, you do not like my plan. Many of my colleagues do not like my plan either. They all think I am wrong. So perhaps I am wrong. But I have thought it all over again. And I still think I am right. So I hope you will now accept my plan – because I am responsible for the mark and you are not.'

All traces of anger and suspicion, Vickers recalled, passed away. He, like the thirty other professionals in the room, identified with Dr Fuchs, accepted his professional judgement and thanked God he had not Dr Fuchs' job to go back to.[32]

Vickers and his associates observed only superficially the broader political framework in Germany, the rise to power of the Nazis. Donald Hall, his colleague at Slaughter and May, later recalled discussing the question with him: 'When I naively remarked that their worst trait seemed their awful tactlessness, he said severely and forever memorably, "My dear Donald, tactlessness implies an absolute inability to understand other human beings; it is one of the most terrifying sins against the spirit." '[33]

The political dimensions of the Nazi movement, and their international implications, escaped Vickers' attention. He failed to notice what was going on. The great selectivity of human consciousness in general and his own astonishing lack of political awareness until middle age in particular, much exercised Vickers' mind in later life. He was to define the *appreciative setting* as a predisposition to notice some aspects of reality and not others. Vickers' own appreciative system at this time was set in the context of collaborative work with fellow German professionals whom he respected; and in what he later called 'the comfortable, even pampered, life of the self-employed professional, who need not talk to anyone not willing to pay for the privilege'.[34]

Vickers became politically conscious, with the shock of a revelation, only when the British Prime Minister Neville Chamberlain returned from Munich in September 1938, having agreed to Hitler's demands for the cession of the Sudetenland to Germany and promising 'peace in our time'. What was now at issue was a national decision about the legitimacy of force, about national unity and national purpose, the kinds of issues to which Vickers' earlier life had sensitized him. He suddenly perceived a threat. It was more a threat of internal confusion than of foreign invasion. It stemmed from what he now saw as a lack of national coherence in his own country; there was no consensus about what people wanted. There was no agreement about the kind of order people wanted to create, no sense of national purpose, and a lack of national will or thought out views on the legitimacy or otherwise of force.[35] The importance of generating agreement about what to want was to be a lasting preoccupation.

Within a month of Munich Vickers started a political movement in the City of London which he called 'The Association for Service and Reconstruction'. A manifesto, written by himself and another, was issued on 21 October 1938. The opening paragraph said:

> We believe that this country is in danger from without and from within.
>
> The danger from without lies in the policies of those nations whose Governments accept war as an instrument of policy and approve it as a stimulus to virility. The danger from within lies in the confusion both in our moral and in our material resources; in the sluggishness of our over-burdened Government; in our acceptance of fear as a dictator of policy; and in our smugness. . . .
>
> The national effort needed will evidently require citizens to accept both sacrifices and opportunities . . . on the one hand, a reduction in the standard of living of the wealthier classes and perhaps temporarily for all; a tolerance of far reaching regulation of life; a weakening of the power of vested interests . . . on the other, a more vital social relationship, a sense of responsibility springing from the realisation that all work is public as well as private; greater opportunities for service.[36]

The Association for Service and Reconstruction attracted a lot of support. Vickers wrote two handbooks for it which reveal a move away from conventional liberalism towards a mild form of social democracy.[37] He advocated the acceptance of restraints on personal and institutional freedom, especially for the rich and privileged, and of greater state action and control. Vickers was, however, embarrassed by the support which the Association attracted, as he was not certain what to do with it. Its greatest value to him was to introduce him to J. H. Oldham, Secretary of the International Missionary Council, and through Oldham to a group of distinguished men who met regularly for discussions which they called 'The Moot'. The Moot, made up for the most part of committed Christians like Oldham, had grown out of an ecumenical conference held at Oxford in 1937. Its members included Karl Mannheim, sociologist and epistemologist, Reinhold Niebuhr, Professor of Ethics and Theology, the poet T.S. Eliot, Michael Polanyi, then a Professor of Physical Chemistry and subsequently an epistemologist, and Adolph Lowe, economist, emigré from Nazi Germany and recent author of a pamphlet, *The Price of Liberty*, which Vickers much admired. The Moot provided Vickers with intellectual stimulus and opportunities for political debate: at this time he was particularly influenced by the views of Mannheim, while Polanyi and Lowe were to be both influential intellectually and lifelong friends.

The political position which Vickers adopted was both nationalist and mildly socialist or social democratic: national unity could only be based on more equitable distribution, which in turn involved the subordination of private interests and traditional liberties. In an article published in *The Spectator* in January 1939 he argued that:

> An important section of the nation will require assurance that a community which learns to produce and distribute guns will not fail afterwards to produce and distribute butter. Many in all classes will require assurance that their effort

and sacrifice will be used to support a policy which offers at least a hope of creating a nobler and more significant world for the generations to come.[38]

A typescript written just before the war broke out reveals how strongly he rejected pacificism:

Nearly all so called 'pacifist' propaganda in this country is misconceived and pernicious serving only to befog the issue and weaken the will to face it. How futile to suppose that the cause of peace is served by depicting the horror of war. How futile to suppose that science has made war something other than it was, something formerly supportable but now too dangerous a game to play. Wars are not fought because men are insufficiently careful of their skins. Men are not ruled by fear.[39]

Vickers' justification of force in international relations rested on a legal basis, as an article written for the Royal Institute of International Affairs (April 1940) makes clear:

Any rule of law is a qualification of some pre-existing rule of force. It is an exception, like a clearing in the jungle. Force fills social space, just as air fills terrestrial space whenever it is not displaced by something else. Thus it is vain to inveigh against 'violence' as such; it can only be excluded by the growth of something else – and this something else can only be a system of mutually consistent expectation. Beyond the scope of such a system, force necessarily prevails.[40]

At this point in 'history' coherence and integration was only possible within the framework of the nation state, but it was important, he argued, to maintain communication between people who wanted to keep alive a spirit of internationalism. This was the purpose of *The Christian News-letter*, edited by J. H. Oldham, for which Vickers wrote a long open letter in the spring of 1939. In this letter he condemned the 'hateful gangster rule' of Hitler in revolutionary Germany and its idolatrous worship of the state – 'a sin against the spirit of man' – but argued that there were other aspects of National Socialism which Britain and the Western world could well learn from. He had in mind the 'state-socialising element', based on conceptions of social responsibility and the common will:

This is an attempt to answer a crying need of the whole Western world. I have no doubt that within a generation we in Britain will be much farther along this road than the Germans and it will be a very good thing. The slogans of the revolution in this field – 'Gemeines vor Eigenes', 'Kraft durch Freude' – do not shock us and might well interest us more than they do. And the entire totalitarian machinery which is used for the purpose is in part an experiment in the use of powers which every state is learning to use for good though it runs counter to our liberal traditions.[41]

Britain, he argued in a significant passage, was in the difficult position of fighting against a movement which in some essential aspects was ahead of her in the historical process and which she ought to want not to resist but to overtake and pass:

> Everyone realises this when they say that our greatest danger is to go totalitarian like the enemy. Few realise that the vital question is not whether we go totalitarian – or to use less distorted words, whether we shall become a completely socialized state – but by what spirit we shall be animated when that has occurred. This is a question of purpose.[42]

The immediate practical measures of state control required in Britain were spelt out in a typescript, dated April 1940, and entitled 'A Bill of Duties for Men in England'. First of all, distribution should reflect need, not ability to pay:

> It is not tolerable that any of this island's deep fertility should be left unused, that the distribution of its products should be left to chance or that the way in which its land is used should be determined by consumers' purchasing power, instead of human need.

Private rights to the ownership and use of land needed to be restricted to whatever extent was necessary by this criterion. Indeed, fundamental concepts and traditional values needed rethinking. In particular, Vickers argued in a passage reflecting his intellectual quality and as relevant today as when it was written forty-three years ago, Englishmen needed to think deeply about their ambiguous use of the term 'freedom':

> 'Freedom' is ... ambiguous. ... To some it means 'freedom from interference'; to others 'opportunity'. The negative concept of freedom which expresses itself by 'let me alone' is characteristic of the comfortably situated. The others express their demand for freedom by 'give me a chance'. The comfortable take opportunity for granted, but their illusion only reflects their good fortune. Between these conceptions of freedom there is a great gulf.[43]

The industrial age distributed 'opportunities for living' very unequally, Vickers argued in 1940, and the defence of 'freedom' was often a cloak for self-interest:

> The extreme aversion from allowing the central Government to use certain sorts of power has in the past been due not so much to a passion for freedom as to the natural and often unconscious desire of the ruling industrial class to keep the prerogative for themselves.[44]

By the spring of 1940 Vickers had substantially broken with liberalism. In eighteen months of intense political awareness he had come to reject the 'free' market as a distributive mechanism, and to associate the ideology of liberty with the self-interest of the privileged. He now supported a greater measure of state control and saw increasing state regulation as part of a continuing historical process. Above all he stressed the importance of shared national purposes, a national consensus about what to want. These concerns endured throughout his lifetime. Although the outbreak of the 'hot' war in 1940 brought public political debate to an end for Vickers – and scattered the members of the Association for Service and Reconstruction to a variety of wartime jobs – his prewar political thinking had a lasting effect. It was to influence his decision not to stay long in the City when the war ended, but to enter the public service.

In 1940, at the age of forty-six, Vickers reenlisted in his old regiment as an infantry lieutenant. He spent six weeks training in Scotland, practising with explosives and expecting to be parachuted into battle. He was, however, assigned a quite different mission: he was given the subterfuge rank of Colonel and sent on an intelligence mission to South America, overtly to put the British Government's case before the English-speaking communities, covertly to assess the potential for fifth columnists. He found it hard to accept being sent on a safe and secure posting while his second wife Ellen and baby Hugh were left to face the threat of bombs in England. The flavour of his activities during his three months' journey, and his longing to be home, are apparent in a letter to his wife from Buenos Aires:

I have been in this town one week during which time I have addressed two theatre audiences, one Scottish congregation in Church, one cocktail party of 500, two official lunch parties, one British Legion meeting (half in French, for the benefit of the Free French men) three sewing guilds and one Seamen's Mission. I have two more speeches to make tomorrow, two on Tuesday, one on Wednesday and then thank God I go. I have been kept on the go all the time with left-handed hospitality and I am fed up and full of hatred for B.A. The impression it makes after the other places is simply awful. However perhaps like S. Paulo it will suddenly thaw and come alive or something just before we go.[45]

Vickers returned home late in 1940. Forty-one years later he reread his official report:

The message is confident and clear. Wonderful things are happening in beleaguered Britain. Britons abroad must be kept in touch or they will be as clueless as foreigners.[46]

The 'wonderful things' which were happening in Britain flowed from what he later described as the 'manifestation of spontaneous consensus'[47] engendered by the threat of war. His recollection of wartime Britain, as a country with its unity of purpose, acceptance of constraint and sacrifice, and comparative fairness of distribution, was to exert a lasting hold on him. In 1972, for example, he described wartime Britain to members of a new and uncomprehending generation: they would be startled to be reminded, he said, that, Britain

turned almost overnight into a society of 50 million people in which the Government exercised personal control over the activity of everybody; physical controls over all the essentials that anybody personally enjoyed, controls over the activities of all businesses, and total financial control. They will also be surprised, if they were not there to appreciate it, to hear what a very human, even unstressful, world it produced. It was a world in which almost everybody could afford what they needed to have, and nobody, however rich, could get any more. It was a world in which the necessities of life were probably distributed more surely and more equitably than they had ever been before or since. But it was a world of Government, a government which was highly sensitive to its public image.[48]

Vickers himself spent the war, not on active service as he had expected, but as a civil servant. He was assigned to the Ministry of Economic Warfare where he was to become Deputy Director and then Director, and member of the Joint Intelligence Committee of the Chief of Staff. Vickers had no previous knowledge of intelligence work but his staff soon came to see him as a man of unusual intellectual powers, with a keen nose for muddled thinking and the second rate.[49] Towards the end of the war, he was involved in meetings about the role of Britain in Europe in peace time. There was, he recollected later in a letter to Lowe, 'no doubt anywhere that the only unoccupied West European belligerent would have a leading part to play'.[50]

But the world in which this part would be played was changed beyond recognition. Despite his admiration for the effectiveness of the British wartime state, Vickers was far from confident that stable government could be achieved at home and abroad in the future:

> By 1944 my early assumptions were shaken if not destroyed. Stability could not be taken for granted, could not even necessarily be ensured by even the greatest conscious effort. Still less could either automatic regulation or human design be trusted to achieve 'betterment' by any of the diverse criteria which had emerged.[51]

In 1945 Vickers was knighted for his service in the Ministry of Economic Warfare. The end of the war brought a profound and largely unexpected political change in Britain - the advent of a Labour Government. Vickers was optimistic at the prospect ahead. He was, he told an American correspondent (23 August 1945) impressed by the strength of democracy in Britain which had made this immense change possible and peaceful:

> Englishmen differ in their views of the cause and of the wisdom of this decisive change, but they can agree in being proud that it was possible.[52]

He was confident that, despite the apparently wide differences between the Labour Government and its Conservative opposition, the parties shared those underlying values which he believed essential for the success of two-party politics:

> ... two-party Government demands not merely two - and only two - major parties, but also a certain relation between them, a certain identity in objects and methods, a certain degree of difference in emphasis and tempo. Without a certain identity in objects and methods, policy becomes intolerably discontinuous; no country could endure Government by alternative parties, each pledged to reverse what its predecessors had done.
>
> It is possible to think that the difference in aim between a socialist and a non-socialist party is too great to permit of them forming alternative governments for the same country. Indeed logically a strong argument can be produced

in support of that view. I find it entirely unconvincing. However dramatically extreme views may clash, I believe that the country is broadly divided between exponents of more socialism and less socialism, between more daring and more cautious experiments in public control, between more helpful and more sceptical attitudes towards the relation between social responsibility and personal incentive. I do not believe that the programme outlined in the King's speech of August 1945 seems a whit more shocking even to the diehard than did the programme of the Liberal government which swept the board in 1906. . . .

Vickers himself was soon drawn into the public sector. In 1947 he was asked by a client who had accepted the Chairmanship of the National Coal Board, to become its legal adviser and to help organize the Board. The newly created Coal Board, set up that year, was one of the biggest industrial enterprises in the world, taking into public ownership and assets of some 600 undertakings, consisting of 900 collieries and employing 750,000 men. Vickers immediately accepted the offer. The public sector was, in his view, bound to become so important that large public monopolies of this kind had to be made to work.[53] It was characteristic of him to throw himself with confidence and enthusiasm into whatever came his way and to relinquish it totally and unthinkingly when the next call came.[54]

The Board was instructed to get the coal, organize the industry and satisfy the consumer; duties, he later reflected,[55] never before laid on anyone. It was to cover its costs from its proceeds; but this requirement of financial stability was a condition, not a criterion of success. Success was to be measured by comparing its achievements with what informed opinion thought it might have achieved in the dimensions of its public responsibilities. The newest element in the system was the requirement, imposed by statute, to consult with all the employees on all matters of policy. This involved relationships unfamiliar to most people in the industry. Vickers was thrown into the middle of this when, in 1948, he moved from being legal adviser and organizer of the legal department, to become Board member in charge of manpower, training, education, health and welfare, a seat he was to hold until 1955. Vickers, like his father, had little class consciousness and easily shared a frame of reference with 'trade unionists who came to consciousness in the 1930s'. He once confessed to feeling more at home with the national executive of the Miners' Union than with his fellow Board members.[56]

Life as a functionary was less comfortable than that as a self-employed lawyer. Vickers found what he described as the 'graduation' from private enterprise to public service a curious experience and it drew his attention to some urgent intellectual issues raised by the implementation of socialist ideas. In an article in *The Quarterly Review* entitled 'Personal Incentive and Public Service', he questioned whether a moral revolution was necessary to make a socialist state work. How could personal incentive and public service, self-fulfilment and national needs, be harmonized? Did men and women working in state enterprises feel or behave differently from those in private enterprises?

How could states best combat bureaucratic inefficiency, 'a problem of life and death for socialists and the communities which they govern'? Did the conditions which release maximum individual energy – conditions closely related to group processes – conflict with those permitting the most perfect coordination?[57]

The answering of these questions was, he now believed, hampered by current epistemological difficulties. There was, for instance,

> that haunting inability to conceive 'man-in-society' as the indivisible reality which the intellect can see it must be ... we need more than anything else a more appropriate mental picture of the sort of place which is the world of men.
>
> When we have found it, we shall apprehend more clearly many of the more urgent questions of the day such as why wars happen, what are the conditions in which men work hard and happily together, what can and cannot be done by force and why.

This much-needed knowledge could, he then believed, only be achieved by 'the honest, painstaking method of science'.[58]

Politically, Vickers was still optimistic during this, the period of the Attlee government, when far-reaching social legislation laid down the foundations of the British welfare state. He contrasted these years favourably with the dismal aftermath of the First World War. He saw no sign that the British were not as united and self-confident as during the Battle of Britain.[59] The political unit still seemed to have a coherent identity. The architect of the National Health Service, Aneurin Bevan, he noted approvingly, 'declared that we should thank heaven for having preserved this island as an example of humanity. Statesmen of the left were as proud as statesmen of the right to admit their dedication to the country which they served'.[60]

In February 1950, a Liberal by tradition, a lawyer by training and a surtax-payer by income group, Vickers voted Labour for the first time. He believed it desirable for the sake of the country's political development that the Labour party should continue subject to the strains and responsibilities of office for at least another four years. A Labour Government alone had any chance of getting even the minimum necessary response from industrial workers, and was better able to work out the immensely difficult techniques needed for efficient operation of purchasing, production, and distribution under monopoly conditions. But he had some reservations about the welfare state. Although he had long advocated greater state regulation and control, he was uneasy about the effect of state provided benefits:

> I am not a socialist in that I have a liberal's strong dislike of the state as an agent of positive social action. I suspect that in the set up of the welfare state as now conceived there is a psychological flaw, not yet clearly seen, which will frustrate to some extent the dividend in human happiness and in human efficiency which its sponsors reasonably expect. ...
>
> Our fundamental liberties are no doubt in some danger but it will be our fault if we cannot find a way to preserve them in the radically new and

uncomfortable world into which we are moving. The worst guides in such a search are likely to be those for whom these liberties are inseparably connected with agreeable conditions which are passing away and which in any case were never enjoyed by more than a small minority.[61]

Vickers himself continued to exercise his mind about the distinctive problems of operating nationalized industries. In an address to the Administrative Staff College in 1952, he returned to the issue of how the requirements of a nationalized enterprise and the requirements of the nation could be harmonized. A public corporation not operating for profit had to hold the scales between consumers and work people, and the latter had stronger bargaining power than the former. Nationalization raised a new and difficult question of criteria of success:

> The task of assessing what success the undertaking achieved and what confidence its management deserved – the task of shareholders in a private enterprise – was now that of Parliament. To assess the record of a big nationalised undertaking like the Coal Board, with its extended and not entirely quantifiable objectives, was a much harder task.
>
> The difficulty lies in appraising achievement in new tasks, which can at best be achieved with only relative success; and it is enhanced by the lack of precedent, of accepted standards even of a subjective kind, of any pre-existing background of confidence, the absence, in fact, of that relationship of the two parties to the account without which the most careful explanations may fail to evoke conviction or even understanding.[62]

Within the coal industry itself Vickers, as Board member for manpower and welfare, had continually to combat entrenched and divisive attitudes between colliery managers and miners formed during the last years of private industry, 'that 30 years of decline when men were cheap'.[63] In an address to the National Association of Colliery Managers in May 1953 he asked how individuals and groups of workers with a history of divisiveness could be persuaded to embrace the economic purpose of the pit as their own. The group process was critical, he concluded, and habits were changed not by new arguments but by new experiences:

> ... in making pits more attractive we must think of them both as workplaces and as communities of people. I believe that the second is more important and that the chief significance of the first is as an expression of the second. Good buildings, clean layout, services, amenities get their pull from the fact that they express the attitude of the leaders towards the group and its common task. A hole in the ground, as such, will attract no one but a geologist or a cave explorer; but a pit is more than a hole in the ground. It is a community of men engaged in common enterprise; difficult, challenging, complex, interesting and important. The more that concept is realised, the more attractive the pit will be.

The address to the colliery managers reflects the intellectual influence which was to permeate all Vickers' subsequent thinking. In the late 1940s and early 1950s he discovered systems ideas, then being formulated by Ludwig von Bertalanffy, Norbert Weiner, and Ross Ashby. 'The effect on me was not so much revelation as liberation. The ideas did not seem surprising or even new. But they provided a new language in which to talk about the perplexing experience of my lifetime and a new point of view from which to regard it.'[64]

What Vickers sensed in systems thinking was not only a relevance to the problems of organization and control which so deeply engaged him professionally on the Coal Board, but also an intense relevance to the problems of organizing his own life:

> I had been born in a Victorian age which perhaps expected more responsibility from its young than some of them could achieve and I had been through the various forms of rejection or repression which this engendered on those who could not fully take it. And it seemed to me that these new insights would help me to understand better what could be changed and what had to be accepted – great and timely promises in a world that was just discovering that life was more than the 'rational' solution of problems accepted as given and assumed to be soluble.[65]

Vickers' interest in systems ideas had from the beginning a particular focus. A key idea was the distinction between information and energy as a means of inducing change and preserving form. This suggested a hierarchy of systems: those systems open only to energy exchange – the traditional province of the natural scientist since Descartes – and those systems open to both energy and information exchange, the human systems which were Vickers' essential interest, for which new conceptual approaches were urgently needed. In his last book, written in his mid-80s, Vickers was still grappling with the vital ways in which human systems were different from natural systems. Another key systems idea was the concept of a 'standard', set by the controller in a standard mechanical feedback system. Vickers applied the concept of a standard control model, not in technological contexts as the vast majority of systems thinkers were doing, but at the level of human societies:

> The mere concept of a 'standard' by reference to which match and mismatch signals could be elicited authorised the whole idea of ethical behaviour and linked its positive and negative poles, commitment and constraint. It even provided a sufficiently sophisticated way of thinking about human history.[66]

The idea of system itself – as an organized assembly both more and less than the sum of its parts – seemed crucially relevant at the level of human societies. The organized constituents of human systems can do what they could not do otherwise; but they cannot do some things which, unorganized, they could do.[67] The insight that systems both enable and *constrain* validated much that Vickers had long sensed about the growing need for restraint which modern societies demanded. It provided a coherent framework from which he was to analyse and criticize the development of Western societies during the next quarter of a century.

Vickers' education and experience was different from that of most other people who took up systems ideas. His background in the humanities and his experience in high levels of the civil service and nationalized industry inclined him towards high level problems of the management of human societies over time. It greatly surprised him that no one else 'of my sort' seemed to respond to systems ideas:

> ... it seemed to me that these ideas were ideas that everybody, governors and administrators, should be excited about.[68]

Technologists, on the other hand, took readily to the systems approach, and Vickers was to spend long years resisting the tendency for the very concept of 'system' to have a purely technological flavour:

> While I was pursuing these thoughts, everyone else who was responding at all was busy with man-made systems for guided missiles and getting to the moon or forcing the most analogic mental activities into forms which would go on digital computers. 'Systems' had become embedded in faculties of technology and the very word had become dehumanized.[69]

Vickers' own capacity to contribute to the systems movement, and to apply systems ideas at the level of individual and social learning, was greatly enhanced by his becoming, in 1951, Chairman of the Research Committee of the Mental Health Research Fund, a voluntary position which he was to hold for sixteen years. He acted as lay chairman to a body of about twenty scientists including psychiatrists of different persuasions, representatives of the preclinical sciences, anthropologists, sociologists, psychologists and social psychiatrists, animal ethologists, and specialists in mental retardation. The Research Committee brought together a more comprehensive gathering of medical and social scientists than met regularly round any other table and – of great importance – established a tradition that people spoke on subjects outside their own speciality and listened when others did the same.[70]

Mental health is a highly contentious field but, according to Dr J. M. Tanner, Honorary Secretary of the Committee, so great was Vickers' personal authority that 'psychoanalysts and pharmacologists, clinical psychiatrists and behavioural psychologists, professors of neurophysiology and social science, lay down together in unassuming and devoted amity.'[71]

The exchange of ideas and resultant wide range of reading gave Vickers an exceptionally broad interdisciplinary background. Added to his expertise in the humanities, law, management, and government, he now acquired a new competence – in psychology – and a new interest – the organization and promotion of health from the individual level to that of the health service. His chairmanship of the Research Committee was followed quickly by appointment to the Medical Research Council (1952–1957). During the next ten years he was to be a frequent contributor to the British medical journal *The Lancet* and to academic debate in the fields of occupational and cognitive psychology and to psychiatry. His knowledge of cognitive psychology was fundamental to his development of the concept of the appreciative system.

In 1955 Vickers retired from the Coal Board, though continuing to keep up his voluntary medical positions. His retirement was a great opportunity:

I had time to read and write and think. I already had some experience of the process of decision making and policy making. I had also been concerned with medical research and I knew at least of the existence of biological controls. I had been concerned with psychiatry and had been (sic – 'not seen'?) a model of man which I could recognise as remotely adequate as a description of others or even of myself. I dived into ethology and recognised myself in the behaviour of disturbed sticklebacks and of young chaffinches trying to get their half inherited song right by adult standards (my garden was full of them). But this wasn't enough. It was no surprise to me to find how like we were to other creatures. The puzzle was why some people sometimes were so different not only from chaffinches but even from others of their own kind like me, who admired them but could not match their performance. And this seemed to me a problem which no scientist wished to admit until he had diminished it unrecognisably.[72]

Vickers was impelled to structure his thinking at this important stage by an unexpected invitation from Charles Hendry, director of the School of Social Work at the University of Toronto, to spend three consecutive Michaelmas terms there, advising on a current project. The invitation put him into an academic environment for a sustained period – the first since his undergraduate days nearly thirty years before – and required him to formulate and express his ideas at a time when his intellectual powers were approaching their peak. Hendry was, Vickers later wrote, 'one of the many to whom I shall always be grateful for opening unexpected doors which opened into fascinating places and led on into yet others'.[73]

At Toronto Vickers was faced with a range of challenging assignments. He led three colloquia at the School of Social Work on 'values and decision-taking'; he lectured to the Faculty of Applied Science and Engineering on 'control, stability and choice' and he gave a public address, entitled 'The Needs of Men' on the impact of industrialization on human well-being. What enabled Vickers to make a relevant contribution to the concerns of academics as disparate as social workers, engineers, and applied scientists, was his systems perspective which held out hope of more fruitful interdisciplinary interaction. He told the Science and Engineering Faculty that:

The whole world of experience begins to look like a hierarchy of systems; and the main task of science to formulate the laws by which these systems maintain themselves and by which they interact. These changes seem to me to open the way to a better relationship between physics, biology, psychology and the social sciences, that is, between the concepts which we use in trying to understand the processes of matter, of life, of mind and of society.[74]

New concepts, common to the natural sciences and the humanities would, he believed, soon appear. The idea of control implicit in the theory and design of man-made control devices could help us to understand the underlying principles of control in the brain and in the boardroom. Each involved a continuous matching of what 'is' and what 'ought to be'.

The address to the school of social work[75] took such ideas a great deal further. Faced with the subject of values and decision taking and an audience of graduate social workers, Vickers approached the question from a characteristically broad systemic stance; what principles of organization spanned the different hierarchic system levels of animals, individual human beings, and societies? At what levels did new elements appear? Like other animals man was a goal-seeking animal, he concluded, but the new distinctive attribute apparent at the human level was that man was also a goal-setting animal; and human cultures were also goal-setting. At both the individual and the social level goals were set by a circular causal process, operating over time:

> Thus we can sense, though we cannot yet explain or understand, a circular causal process, by which the goals of a society are set. They are continually under revision; factors which make for constancy are overcome by new demands, resulting from new experiences.... This process cannot be explained without taking into account the verdict of the individual conscious mind. 'I like it', 'I hate it', 'I want it', 'I fear it'. These dynamic value judgments are both a product and a cause of the ceaseless process of goal-formulation.

In this, an early formulation of what was later refined as the appreciative system, the contributory strands are clear: the systems perspective which directed attention to standards and to similarities in the goal-setting process in individuals and cultures; cognitive psychology, which may suggest how, by selection and association from their experience people make patterns which have meaning for them; and cultural anthropology and social psychology which were, he argued, 'beginning to provide a workable model of the process by which the culture is modified and transmitted'. And Vickers' perception of the mutual interaction between the setting of standards and the applying of standards owing something to his legal background: 'Judges to some extent make the rules which they apply; indeed, every new application adds something to the rule which it exemplifies.'[76]

The process of goal-setting, at the individual and the social level was, Vickers argued, an exercise in the creation of form; and such creation could best be understood as an art rather than a science. The development of these ideas, formulated in 1956–1957, was to occupy Vickers' remaining quarter-century.

In November 1957 Vickers was invited to address the School of Public Health at Harvard. Speaking on the subject of 'What sets the goals of public health?', he argued that the setting of major public goals was a historical process, part of the 'process of interaction and mutual adaptation which we call history'.[77] It was characteristic of Vickers to redefine, in passing, the nature of an established scholarly activity. To his regret, historians did not in his lifetime explore the implications of seeing human development as a circular process, consisting 'no less in the redesigning of our own expectations than in the manipulation of our environment'. Nor did they follow up his characterization of historical development as the progressive redefinition of the unacceptable. Vickers' interest in the connection between *what is* – including what is technologically feasible – and *what ought to be* the case, that is, standards and expectations – gave him a fresh insight into some central questions of public health:

> To some extent at least techniques set the goals of public health. For techniques not only enlarge our response, they mould our expectations.
>
> Every new technique, by opening a possibility, awakens a need – at least in our Western culture, where in matters of health we have a highly developed sense that whatever is possible for any should be available to all.

Vickers' understanding of the interaction between technical possibility and expectation enabled him to question some of the central assumptions on which the British National Health Service was founded, and to predict, rightly, what was to prove an increasingly acute problem:

> In Britain the introduction of a national health service has helped to clarify our thinking about health. At one point it was widely, if half-consciously, held that a health service was a self-limiting service. When the demands of health were fully met, there would be nothing more to do. Indeed, better preventive services might in time reduce the total resources needed to provide optimum health for all. It is clear, I think, that health services are not self-limiting in this sense. The amount of effort which can plausibly be devoted to the health of the individual and the community increases with every scientific development and will, I think, increase indefinitely. Thus the services which might be provided may well continue to exceed, perhaps by an ever-increasing margin, the services which can in fact be provided, since the total will be limited by the amount of resources available, having regard to conflicting demands.... These decisions will grow harder, not easier, with the passage of time.[78]

During the first years of his retirement Vickers developed sufficiently his understanding of the principles of systemic interaction to apply them fruitfully in a wide range of fields – medicine, public health, engineering, social work, and management. He had read widely in a variety of different disciplines: and not only was every paper or address now a synthesis of different disciplinary insights but he was able to build bridges and point to gaps in relevant fields. His address to the Annual Conference of the British Psychological Society in 1958 was a case in point. Entitled 'The Role of Expectation in Economic Systems',[79] the paper looked at biological and economic phenomena as systems, with a systemic capacity for self-regulation. An important regulator of economic systems was expectation, a question of concern both to economists and psychologists. Much business activity consisted of deliberately building and moulding these structures of expectation, which interact circularly with the environment. But the human capacity for expectation as a governor of human behaviour had been little studied by psychologists:

> We need a better model of the cognitive process by which the brain abstracts regularities from the stream of experience and uses these abstractions to classify

future experience, a circular process which progressively determines what further experience it can assimilate and in what form.

Psychologists might usefully learn from business: the way in which businessmen control their operations through the projection of estimates and standards could illuminate the less conscious processes of the individual mind. The different meanings which people attached to activities - particularly apparent in business and administration - was of relevance to psychologists' study of cognitive processes:

> For A the proposed development of a housing estate is a way to get people housed. For B it is an addition to the rateable value of the area and to the demands on the rates. For C it is a threat to the Green Belt; for D an increase in the traffic load on a road; for E an attempt by F at empire building; for G a threat to the coherence of his administrative team.[80]

What Vickers was attempting was no less than to persuade psychologists to move on from behaviourism to phenomenology. His concern for a more relevant psychology was taken up again in 'The Concept of Stress in Relation to the Disorganization of Human Behaviour', an article contributed to a volume on *Stress and Psychiatric Disorder*.[81] Stress, he argued, was a form of disorganization. By better understanding disorganization we could increase our understanding of organization, and vice versa. The existing conceptual models of organization - psychological concepts of perception and learning theory - needed to be integrated, and the systems concept of stability might also prove valuable. But another psychological model was needed of the matching process by which men classified and evaluated experience, shaping it and being shaped by it:

> In pursuing, maintaining, and eluding the external relations by which we live and die, we are guided by symbolic representation of what is happening and what ought to be happening. We need a model of this process to understand the working of stress; and contrariwise, in seeking to understand the working of stress, we may well contribute to our understanding of controlled behaviour.

By the early 1960s Vickers' ideas were exciting interest in a number of North American scholars. His association with North America, begun in 1956 with his visit to Toronto, had borne fruit in an extensive correspondence with Americans who shared his concerns and whose fellowship meant much to him. Many American academics were in the early 1960s less locked into their disciplinary specialisms than their British counterparts, more familiar with systems concepts and more responsive to Vickers' focus on interpretation and values. 'I share with them the excitement of a search for meaning', he wrote in 1963.[82] The occasion was a contribution he was invited to make to an American volume, edited by L. J. Duhl, on *The Urban Condition*. His contribution, 'Ecology, Planning, and the American Dream', was another stage in the formulation of the concept of the appreciative system, a concept which Vickers had gradually been evolving in his mind over the previous eight years:

(We must ask) – what causes an individual or a society to see and value and respond to its situation in ways which are characteristic and enduring, yet capable of growth and change. A rational ideology, a professional ethic, an individual personality, resides not in a particular set of images but in a set of *readinesses* to see and value and respond to its situation in particular ways. I will call this an appreciative system.

We know something of the ways in which these readinesses are built up. Even our eyes tell us nothing until we have learned to recognise and classify objects in particular ways; and there is little doubt that our conceptual classifications are built up in the same way. So, equally, are our values and our patterns of action. Our appreciative system grows and changes with every exercise of image formation, a process normally gradual and unconscious; and like all systems, it is resistant to changes of a kind or at a rate which might endanger its coherence.

Behind Vickers' interest in the ways the appreciative system operates over time lay a specific concern with the setting of the appreciative system at this particular point in time. In his judgement:

The last two hundred years have left us with an appreciative system peculiarly ill-suited to our needs.[83]

Vickers was, by the 1960s, increasingly alarmed by many features of Western society. People did not, for instance, notice that increased power to alter the environment meant reduced power to predict or control it, because every intervention produced a host of unintended consequences. The task that he set himself was a mammoth one: first, to direct the energies of scholars in relevant fields to elucidating the processes of appreciation; second, to alter the appreciative setting of contemporary Western society.

The concept of the appreciative system reached maturity in 1963 in an article entitled 'Appreciative Behaviour'[84] which Vickers wrote for *Acta Psychologica*, the European journal of psychology. This article was one of the few to appear in a purely scientific journal, and the first written with the full knowledge that what he was saying was not orthodox.[85] The concept of the appreciative system derived from bringing a systems approach – systems ideas of information, communication and control – to bear on two very different areas of academic enquiry, psychology, and history. The concept has explanatory power at both levels. This was audacious and innovative, an intellectual leap made by a man at the height of his powers, with a uniquely favourable combination of life experience and scholarly range. Development of the concept – what Vickers called 'a model rough and speculative but better, I think, than no model at all' – would come, he hoped, from psychologists and historians taking up the issues which it raised. 'Appreciative Behaviour' contained one of many, largely unheeded, appeals to scholars to address these concerns. Vickers was at this time just becoming aware of intense resistance towards addressing concepts such as appreciation, a resistance which caused psychologists to concentrate on the study of behaviour – which was observable in the sense that rats and stars are observable – to the exclusion of such human processes as thinking and consciousness. The problem was that psychologists desired to be seen as scientific and supposed that certain limitations derived from the scientific method. The resistance he encountered was to draw Vickers more deeply into epistemology in general, and criticism of scientific epistemology in particular.

He returned to these questions when he was invited to give the Maudsley Lecture to the Royal Medico–Psychological Association in November 1963. He began by distinguishing regulation as a relationship extended in time 'not something which can be attained once for all, but something, like a mariner's course, which must constantly be sought anew'.[86]

> I believe that psychology has done a disservice to the study of higher mental function by making goal-seeking the paradigm of rational behaviour. I do not accept the view that all norm-holding can be reduced to the pursuit of an endless succession of goals.

A preoccupation with goal-seeking – reflecting the limitations of research method or even the diseases of an acquisitive society and equally apparent in the 'problem-solving' school of management as in psychology – meant a failure to appreciate relations in time. Vickers' awareness of relationships in time had been fostered by his own work experience concerned with the sustained regulation of organizations over time, not with discrete episodes such as occupied management consultants, engineers, or even researchers:

> Anyone familiar with the papers presented to any governing body will realise how much trouble is taken to present the major variables as flows in the dimension of time.[87]

Psychologists and engineers had done important work in problem-solving but there were prior, more fundamental questions which urgently needed attention:

> Where the norm can be taken as given, much important work has been done both by psychologists and by system engineers in exploring the mechanisms of problem solving and learning: in discovering and imitating the mechanisms by which organisms solve problems, devise alternative means and choose between them and improve their performance by practice. . . .
>
> I, on the other hand, am concerned with . . . the setting of the norms to be followed and hence of the problems to be solved. The norms which men pursue, and hence the problems which they try to solve, are I suggest, largely self-set by a partly conscious process which merits and is susceptible of more study than it has yet received. . . .

Vickers hoped that psychologists, who had contributed so much to understanding of mental disorder, would turn their attention to the skills involved in creating order over time, the skills involved in the appreciative system. This was an urgent practical task, 'at a time when an appreciative system is unstable and under rapid change, as ours is today; most of all when many policy makers and others appear blissfully unaware that any appreciative system has an upper limit to its possible rate of change, which cannot be passed without disaster'.

He seems to have charged psychologists with the responsibility for tackling what would normally be considered to be sociological phenomena. Sociology was a much less familiar field to him. The urgency of the intellectual task he levelled at psychologists derived from what Vickers perceived with an increasing sense of foreboding, as the world's 'accelerating spin into chaos';[88] those leaders and policy makers who should most be addressing necessary changes in the organization and culture of Western societies were committed to resisting them.[89] In two radio talks given in 1965, called 'The End of Free Fall', Vickers put before the general public what he considered to be the most urgent issues needing attention.

These talks were reprinted in *The Listener* nearly twenty years ago and little of them seems irrelevant today. The time of free fall was that of exploding technology and exploding world population. The increasing rate of change and unpredictability of the man-made environment demanded an unprecedented scale of government, and unprecedented revision of culturally induced assumptions. He did not baulk at the radical changes already required; and despite the superficial conservatism of his concern with regulation, he was prepared to follow both the logic of population change and the requirements of equity to their unpopular and radical conclusions:

> In this country the struggle for some place to live has already reached a new level of intensity. The present inequity between the minority who buy and own their homes and the majority who rent them or wait for them can only be remedied by measures more radical than those yet tried. The whole concept of land as an object of private property and profit must, I think, be on the way out in countries like ours which are both developed and crowded. This concept was a product of the agricultural epoch, and it will be as inept in a world where land is over-scarce, as it was in the pre-agricultural epoch, when land was as over-abundant as the sea. Yet what an edifice of prestige and esteem, of security and independence, of speculation and profit-taking, still rests on land ownership; how successfully it has so far defended itself; what political, social, and psychological disturbances have always followed any effective attack on it![90]

Although there was currently a shortage of labour in Britain – a shortage predicted to increase over the next ten years – Vickers foresaw from United States' experience that the overall effect of increasing technological efficiency was unprecedented unemployment, especially of the young. Great political and cultural change would be needed to give the unemployed an acceptable status, acceptable to themselves and to those in employment.

More fundamental still, the world needed now to develop international institutions for keeping the peace and for redistributing income, a task difficult enough even within a single coherent national entity. This could only be accomplished if fundamental cultural change – a revision of man's sense of self – took place. Men had to extend their sense of obligation not only in space – extending beyond neighbours and fellow countrymen to people of other races, colours and religions – but also in time, to encompass generations yet unborn. This demanded a new framework for thought, such as he believed and hoped systems thinking would one day provide:

> When we learn to attach reality to others and to the future, are we not simply enlarging our idea of self to include new relations with others, and deepening the present in which we live to include more of the future which it always comprehends? These ideas may come more naturally to future generations which have learned to think of men and societies as systems of internal and external relations, extended in space and time and increasing in their selfhood, through the extension of these relations.[91]

In 1965 Vickers published *The Art of Judgment*. It marked the culmination of ten years of intellectual advance, the most creative and fruitful of his life. The book was well received. William Robson, Professor of Government at the London School of Economics and editor of *The Political Quarterly*, described it as subtle, original, and profound and called it 'the most important contribution to administrative theory which has been made by a British thinker during the past twenty-five years'.[92] But the follow-up work to develop his concepts for which Vickers had so often appealed was not forthcoming. Sixteen years later he was to write to Guy Adams:

> ... ever since I published the *Art of Judgment* in 1965 I have not read a practical book about administration which took seriously the primacy of human motivation, still less one which questioned the rational model of action which insisted that no action at human level was possible unless it was explicable as the pursuit of a purpose. The attack on rationality and purpose or rather the effort to place these in relation to more subtle forms of human regulation is a mammoth task:[93]

The rest of the 1960s were years of continuing high output. After *The Art of Judgment*, written largely for publication in that form, Vickers published two collections of previously published papers in quick succession. *Towards a Sociology of Management* (1967) contained more recent articles and reflected much more strongly Vickers' growing sense of impending crisis. 'The context', he wrote in the introduction, 'is one of threat, arising from a self-generated rate and direction of change.' He perceived a world crisis impending 'both as the closing of an ecological trap and as a failure of communication between nations, between governments and governed, and between the generations. This crisis is conceived as due not to any lack of means to transmit, store and process information ... but to the absence or breakdown of those shared systems of interpretation by which alone communications have meaning and enable human beings to influence each other'.

The emphasis in *Value Systems and Social Process* (1968) is on the threat to relationships within human societies, threats above all arising because of the conflicting needs for appreciative systems to change sufficiently quickly to interpret a changing world, but yet remain sufficiently stable and sufficiently shared to make possible mutual understanding and common action.

*Freedom in a Rocking Boat* (1970), written in response to a commission from Penguin Books, and the most accessible of Vickers' writings to the general reading public, reflected more strongly the threat to stable relations between human society and the ecological milieu on which it depended.

Vickers continued to write regularly on the topic of health during the 1960s - he remained Chairman of the Research Committee of the Mental Health Fund until 1967. He always emphasized the easily overlooked importance of medicine as a caring activity, involving the management of health and sickness in the world of the well, and partnership with both patient's family or neighbourhood support systems as well as other kinds of health or social work professionals. The central importance of medicine as *caring* was, he believed, threatened by the rapid technological developments which focused so exclusively on the *curing* role. Doctors, like other professionals, threatened to become mere technologists.[94]

He questioned whether a single profession could assimilate the three different dimensions which had expanded so rapidly and which were of urgent relevance to it: that of scientific therapy, public health, and the recognition and study of psychosocial factors. He questioned the suitability of the training of general practitioners, then a matter of debate within the medical profession:

> It is an oddity peculiar to medical training that, whereas the layman first meets his doctor in general practice, the doctor first meets his patients in hospital. A hospital is a splendid place in which to study sick organisms and a correspondingly bad place in which to study the impact of sickness on persons and families, let alone societies.[95]

As always, systemic insights illuminated his approach - the general practitioner was managing and intervening not only in a biological organism but in a social system. This led him to frame what was still an unfamiliar concept in the 1960s - a concept for which he coined the phrase Community Medicine, which he defined as 'managing illness in the community of the well'.[96] This should provide a second stream of medicine, parallel and complementary to the hospital stream, relying on different skills, interests, experience and to some extent training in its doctors and focusing on the patient, not only as a psychobiological but as a psychosocial system - including helping to reinforce the support given by the patient's family and friends. Community medicine would, Vickers foresaw, have to carry an ever increasing load, 'for the transient nuclear family and the fragmented family group are ill-adapted and ill-conditioned to support their own sick, as once they did, and at the same time have developed ever higher standards of what the sick are entitled to expect'.

Many of the individual medical problems which Vickers addressed in the 1960s have since been taken up and acted upon. The training of general practitioners has made tremendous strides and many younger GPs are more sensitive than their older colleagues to 'social factors'.[97] All doctors now learn, in their undergraduate years, some 'behavioural science', and are exposed to the heretical thought that patients are more than defective biological machinery.[98]

Community medicine has emerged as a separate speciality within medicine since 1974; the hospice movement has greatly expanded; and 'community care' is much in vogue. However, as Lyn Jones of the University of Edinburgh Department of Community Medicine points out,[99] Vickers' *systemic* thinking about such issues has not been followed through. Community medicine as it has evolved in Britain operates patchily, rather than as a coherent theme of development based on Vickers' concept of 'the care of the sick in the world of the well'. GPs still do fundamentally the same kind of job they did in 1967, rather than having developed into a new kind of doctor, a 'second stream of medicine'. And the vogue for community care owes more to its apparent cost savings rather than the clinical, humanitarian, and social merits which Vickers expounded. He was dealing with a rather closed medical world, which generally does not take much notice of anything said by a nonmedical voice, however penetrating or cogent.[100]

In the field of public health Vickers was to have the satisfaction of seeing at least some developments of which he approved. In the academic sphere, however, and particularly in epistemology, he felt increasingly isolated. His fear of the potential dominance of technology in medicine was paralleled by a growing concern at the potential dominance of a particular technology, the digital computer, in intellectual life. There was, he commented in 1965, 'a grave practical danger' that myths about computers would encourage the tendency to fit intellectual activity into the pattern which digital computers can handle.[101]

The fundamental problem was an epistemological one. The science of information had made possible a new conception of systems, including lower hierarchical levels such as meteorological systems open to the exchange of matter and energy alone, and systems which were also open to exchanges of information. The formulation and acceptance of his new concept of hierarchy would usher in a post-Cartesian world.

However, physical scientists, trained in lower levels of the hierarchy where human communication was irrelevant, were not equipped to cope with the important higher levels where information operated. There were 'sombre doubts whether the world of men alive today has any hope of surviving the Cartesian world'.

Prevalent scientific culture, he believed, accorded primacy to facts and neglected the underlying role of values. In *The Tacit Norm*, a paper prepared in 1969 for a symposium at the Wenner-Gren Foundation for Anthropological Research, he argued that human understanding was essentially normative: 'Facts, not values, are enigmatic. If we were to put together even those fragments of a scientific epistemology which we already have, we should realise that the challenging study of our day is not ... "the place of values in a world of fact" but rather the nature of fact in a world of values.'[102]

Contemporary scientific culture was though, he feared, quite unsuited to this task:

> ... to rescue our conventional epistemology from its present state, which seems to me purblind and distorted beyond measure, we do well to take as the paradigm of knowledge the process of creation and appreciation not in the field of science or even in the field of ethics but in the field of art, which alone has not yet been buried beneath the mythology of our culture.

'A growing sense of alienation' from the academic and professional world characterized this period of Vickers' life.[103] A powerful academic and professional establishment, committed to traditional scientific paradigms in both physical and social fields, shrugged off epistemological challenges, more by ignoring them than by rebutting them. The guardians of established discipline boundaries resisted holism and cross-fertilization. The systems movement, in which Vickers played a prominent part, was small, struggling to develop its distinctive approach, and poorly understood. A complex of academic, disciplinary, and cultural factors worked together to ensure that Vickers was ignored. He also felt increasingly alienated from the political and social world of the 1960s – the permissive age, with its rejection of responsibility and institutional roles and its insistence on protest, individualism, and doing one's own thing. In 1968 he wrote to Professor Melvin Webber of the University of California:

> There has never been a time in my lifetime when obedience, discipline and responsibility have been such dirty words. Paranoic alarm about individual rights has everyone screaming against being planned for or regulated in any way. Not only participation by everyone in everything but almost a right of veto for everyone on anything seem to be the standard pattern of expectation. Yet whatever else may be inherent in any solution of our governmental problem, the one thing certain, as it seems to me, is that any workable solution will make much greater demands on everyone for mutual support and mutual trust.
>
> I have a theory that all this shrill screaming is not so much a protest against a new despotism as an unconscious protest against the absence of guidelines, standards of mutual expectation without which neither individual nor collective life is livable. If nothing else provides these standards, they will emerge from the disasters into which their absence will precipitate us.[104]

The emphasis on 'obedience, discipline and responsibility' was unfashionable in the political climate of the 1960s: it suggested an authoritarian stance. But Vickers' political views could not easily be categorized: he was critical of prevailing views on the right as well as on the left. As he made clear in paper after paper, the need for constraint was to be expected disproportionately from the well-endowed and the privileged. It was the rich, the landed, and trade unionists with exceptional industrial bargaining power, not the poor and dispossessed, who needed to surrender their unjustifiable claims to 'individual rights'. The mechanisms of the market, which favoured particular classes so disproportionately, were outmoded in an age of increasing scarcity, particularly in the case of land. 'A resource that is inexpansible, indispensable and overscarce can no more be distributed through the machinery of the market than can the places in too few lifeboats on a sinking ship.[105] The Conservative concept of the free market, like the Liberal concept of the autonomous individual, was an anachronism in modern Western society.

Political questions became increasingly prominent in Vickers' writings during the early 1970s, years when his visits to North America remained as frequent as ever. He was increasingly drawn into the emerging academic specialism of futures research, a field in which political choices and political values loomed large. But underlying the political issues there was always a basic epistemological concern - how could more appropriate concepts be developed?

The difficulty of thinking about the future had, Vickers argued, increased proportionately with power to change it. The natural environment had ceased to be an independent variable because of the escalating impact of human technology. Expectations, however, were based on short-term past experience and were shaken if human actions made the future different from the recent past.[106] In one respect, expectations generated by the immediate past were bound to be falsified: a century or so of growth in the West meant that 'human expectations have escalated at a rate and in a direction for which the past has no parallel and the future (I think) no hope of fulfilment'.[107] Three developments in particular convinced him that the future presented difficulties for which the recent past in the West, with its comfortable belief in indefinite growth, was a faulty guide. First, population increase was posing acute problems for all countries, population policy could only be gradual and long term and the traditional avenues of escape from population pressure were being closed in one way or another.[108] Second, the return from natural resources was bound to become more costly as poorer quality resources had to be exploited. Third, mounting pollution, if unchecked, was bound to impose its own limitations.

Vickers predicted that by 1984 'the age-old stabilisers of pestilence and famine, if not also war, will be too manifest for anyone to ignore'.[109] The position, he argued, required that prevailing conceptual frameworks should be rethought:

It invites us to accept a new model of our situation, a systemic model, self-limited in ways never before experienced, and thus questions the validity of familiar experience as a guide to the future.[110]

The position demanded a new scale of redistribution:

It threatens us ... with the need to make changes in our ways of distributing wealth and power which, though only vaguely foreseeable, are frightening and unwelcome, especially to the most favoured beneficiaries of our present system.[111]

The likelihood that 'total real net personal incomes will stabilise or fall

33

... for decades and perhaps indefinitely', whatever mix of conservationist or expansionist policies were adopted,[112] seemed self-evident. It dismayed him that those politicians who shared his concern for redistribution, such as the leaders of the British Labour Party, refused to face the unpalatable fact that redistribution would need to be accomplished in the adverse circumstances of declining living standards:

> Socialists as well as non-socialists have been saying for decades that the answer to inequality and injustice was to generate more stuff, and it was only in that way that these could be relieved. Therefore, the threat that the system may become stable and may even in part recede, not only sets problems of its own but appears greatly, and indeed does greatly, accentuate the distributive problem that we are up against.[113]

He wrote to Adolph Lowe of Anthony Crosland, a leading intellectual in the Labour party, that:

> I was ... dismayed to hear that our Anthony Crosland in one of the latest papers he wrote before he died took as a basic assumption that social justice was out of the question except in the society where everyone was getting more net disposable income every year.[114]

Vickers argued unequivocally that there must be 'a much greater equality of all personal incomes'.[115] The implications of this were stark:

> Since in any shrinking situation existing disparities are bound to grow less rather than more, it seems to me to be quite inevitable that at least the whole top half of the income pyramid is going to be abruptly curtailed.[116]

Equitable redistribution was made even more difficult by the effects of advancing technology which, he believed, inescapably bred mounting unemployment and created extraordinary disparity between what those in technological activities could generate and what others in labour-intensive activities could generate.[117] The increasing rewards of technology should go to produce and benefit everyone, not to reward disproportionately those who happened to work in technological industries.[118]

Not only were British political leaders not confronting the full gravity of the situation in the 1970s; there was, he felt, a general 'collapse of coherence'[119] which proscribed any shared interpretation of the present difficulties or agreed response to them. He personally had a 'sense of being in a country of strangers about whom no assumptions whatever can be made'.

Vickers' growing loneliness was increased by the death of his wife Ellen in 1972, after a long illness during which he had been unfailingly sympathetic. Ellen had not followed his intellectual interests but they shared a love of poetry and he relied greatly on her humour and support, and her skill in human relations which contrasted with his own tendency 'to leave behind ... a trail of mess and apologies'.[120] He was probably thinking of Ellen in particular when he wrote of women in general:

In sense of context, sense of touch, ability to be without doing they far excel.[121]

After his wife's death, Sir Geoffrey spoke to Adolph Lowe, one of his oldest and closest surviving friends of 'the corrosive loneliness of Ellen's absence, which other presences and absences leave quite untouched, though a few of them comfort'.[122] He did not, however, relinquish his para-academic life. In 1975 he accepted an invitation to spend some months at the University of Berkeley in California, a stay which was to prove 'the happiest of my American visits, and also by all accounts, the most successful'.[123] The topic he chose for his lectures was 'culture':

> My concern with culture developed largely through realising that the resistances to what I was trying to say were largely cultural and related to the two elements which we prize most in our contemporary culture. One is the scientific culture, which hates to admit the devastating variable 'culture' either into subject matter or still more into its image of itself in so far as its prized objectivity allows it to have one. The other is the individualist culture which has evolved from the liberal tradition and has given two contradictory meanings to the word 'autonomous'. . . .[124]

Although the lectures were enthusiastically received, the manuscript, originally called 'Western Culture and Systems Thinking', was repeatedly rejected for publication. The dropping of the word 'systems' from the title, and its renaming as 'Autonomy and Responsibility' was of no avail. Every new version which Vickers rewrote made it, he felt, 'more complicated and indigestible' and he eventually came to accept that 'the final result does not deserve to be published'.[125]

In 1977 he told Adolph Lowe that 'since I seem to be better at cooking than writing, I propose to do more of the first and less of the second.'[126]

His sense of failure in the art of communication was heightened by the consciousness that few among his closest family or personal friends could follow his ideas, since what he was saying was subtle, complex, and unfamiliar. He confided to Lowe that:

> No one even among my closest friends outside the academic and professional areas involved can read a word I write, and those who try find it pure anguish. And yet I've spent all my life, not least in the law, trying to write about what anyone can understand.[127]

His writing output was in any case reduced in 1976 and 1977 by bouts of serious illness. He felt his strength diminished. He told Lowe:

> I have less vitality now, less mental nerve and spring, a doubt whether I have any more to say, a greater concern for personal relations and individual lives as against the socio-cultural background in which they grow, a sense of biological and psychological withdrawal from a scene in which I have almost finished playing a part of which I am not proud.[128]

In 1977, unable any longer to cope adequately with living alone, he moved into a nearby residential home for elderly people. Sir Geoffrey, with his unfailing courtesy and thoughtfulness, became a much loved and respected resident. It seemed though, to some of the many scholars who visited him there, an unpromising environment for one whose intellectual powers were undiminished. But he was not starved of intellectual stimulation. Although he gave away most of his library and discarded quantities of personal and professional papers, he continued intense correspondence with scholars, especially in North America, and with friends old and new. Young strangers, affected by something in his writings, came to visit him to talk to him and to express their gratitude. Few people of his age had so many unrelated friends in the two generations younger than his own and he was delighted to bring people together. Although often doubtful about the coherence of his life and about what he had achieved, he had still much to give others, and received a lot in return:

> Nothing, he wrote in some autobiographical notes found after his death, surprises and delights me more than that I should have made more friends in the twenty-five years since I was sixty than at any other time in my life. Nearly all those who befriend and accompany me now are in the generations of my children and grandchildren. Many are abroad, largely in North America. I owe largely to them what insight I have into the huge cultural changes of which my own life has been a tiny ingredient of both cause and effect.[129]

Another pleasure of the 1970s was greater contact with British academic circles. Increasingly British academics from new areas of enquiry such as systems, futures, or policy sciences recognized the relevance and value of his work. In particular he enjoyed a dialogue with two systems departments which had recently come into existence in Britain, the Systems Department at Lancaster and the Open University Systems Group, at whose Summer School he was a regular guest speaker until shortly before his death.

Although no one else in the British systems movement was attempting to apply systems ideas at the high level of politics and history which engaged Vickers, there were others, notably Peter Checkland, much in sympathy with his epistemological stance.

In 1979 Vickers' health revived, if only for another spell of what he called his 'medicated survival', and with it his productivity. It was ethics and morality which featured most prominently in these writings. As he wrote to Guy Adams in September 1979:

> To restore ethics to the centre of the human stage and to explain the ethical imperatives is probably the main focus of all my interests.[130]

The greatest threat to moral behaviour at the individual and political levels which he identified was a lack of coherence and commitment. Coherence was a precondition of both individual and political morality. The individual personality had to be structured by strong, comprehensive and coherent self-expectations. 'He must have a self to which he can be true.'[131] Political morality depended on a shared sense of membership and commitment:

Political units will not act morally unless nearly all the governed as well as the governors feel a profound commitment to them and identify with them. That they should do so will not of itself guarantee that they will act morally. But without such commitment they will have no chance of acting morally at all. For commitment is of the essence of morality and collective commitment is of the essence of collective morality. The quality of their actions will of course depend on the quality of their shared commitment. In what collective character do they take pride? What does their sense of collective identity most impel them to guard? These are moral questions; but they can only be posed in a society sufficiently coherent to have a collective ideal.[132]

He returned often to the definition of human endeavour propounded nearly a century earlier by T. H. Huxley: 'That which lies before the human rise is a constant struggle to maintain and improve, in opposition to the state of nature, the state of Art of an organized polity, in which and by which man may develop a worthy civilization capable of maintaining and constantly improving itself. . . .'

The criteria of success of human societies were ethical standards. In 1979 Vickers wrote:

The art of government is to sustain this set of standards not intolerably unattainable or mutually inconsistent yet real enough and high enough to regulate a society capable of maintaining and constantly improving itself. This involves the constant adjustment of our standards, including our standards of what we can usefully try to do and what means are legitimate. It is a task which grows ever more difficult as numbers and interactions multiply and the rate of change increases. It is a task over which we have only the most limited control. It may be doomed to total failure. But it is a human task, inescapable at the present stage of world colonisation, making ever greater demands on mind but developing mind in the process, as other ecological adjustments have developed new capabilities as well as new relationships. The outcome is uncertain. The instrument is probably inadequate. But it is all we have. We cannot help using it.[133]

In 1980 Vickers embarked on the writing of another book on human systems, originally intended as set book for an Open University systems course. *Human Systems are Different* reiterated what he called 'the elementary facts about systems in general and human systems in particular', still not widely known and recognized although crucial for an understanding of the predicament facing mankind. Apart from a chapter envisaging a new role in an age of conservation for the technologist – traditionally limited to devising means to ends and radically unfitted to understand the dangers and limitations of technology – the book contained little that was new. Rather, it was the last refinement of those concerns, and the means of addressing them, which had occupied him for a quarter of a century.

In January 1981, on returning home from a conference, he found waiting for him a letter from Bayard Catron of George Washington University: he sent warm greetings from a small group of his North American friends who wanted to acknowledge their debt and express their appreciation in a Festschrift:

... we want to acknowledge more than the power of your intellect. The character of the man, his warm and gentle humanity, his indomitable curiosity and zest for life – these have touched us.... None of us has known you throughout your several careers, and many have known you for less than one of your eight-plus decades. But having known you as a person as well as author, we understand ourselves and our culture better.[134]

'No letter', he replied, 'I have ever received has moved and pleased and comforted me more than yours bringing the outline of the Festschrift.... This even exceeds the highest hopes which I privately nourished when in March 1955 we left London and the Coal Board. ...'[135]

On 14 December 1981 Vickers went into hospital for the routine two-day blood transfusions which made possible his 'medicated survival'. Internal bleeding set in and he stayed for three weeks, unable to read and write, reflecting much on his past life. It had often troubled him that his life lacked coherence, a sad reflection for one who believed that the making of a personality, and the living of a life, was an exercise in the creation of form, the making of a work of art. He had told Guy Adams three years earlier that:

I'm the last person to claim that I 'planned my lifework' systematically or at all. No single step was taken more than a few months, sometimes even days ahead of the event which posed some specific choice of which it was a necessary outcome. The older I get, the less I understand how it got even what coherence it has. I'm not sure whether I could have planned it better though I can see lots of ways in which it could have been better planned ... I know and usually admire people who have planned theirs and regard myself as abnormal in the degree of my lack of understanding of the process called me, even after the event.[136]

Now in hospital, at the age of 87, his life seemed more coherent than he had realized. It was important to one who had so valued the process of creating order. He was, he told Lowe, 'glad to be alive'.

He continued working. In March 1982, admitted to hospital again, he continued to dictate letters until the day before he died.

Among his papers were found notes for a projected autobiography started and abandoned in 1979: their keynote is serenity:

I write ... to express my grateful bewilderment at the course which my life has taken. What chose it? Sometimes accident. Sometimes the urge to explore new possibilities, often ones which I see myself in retrospect ill equipped to undertake. Such a career was bound to have its costs, to me and others. I cannot conceive why the costs to me should not have been higher, the irregularities greater and more mutually defeating. So often the timing of events wholly beyond my control has perfectly filled my convenience. So often intriguing assignments have come my way at what was for me precisely the right time. And surely few have received so many invitations to undertake fascinating tasks for which they had no manifest qualifications.

I would think it arrogant to postulate a Providence concerned to regulate my small affairs, when I see around me so many more deserving whom fortune has treated less kindly. But one can be grateful without a specific benefactor. So some of these episodes have found their way into this book because they stand out so vividly in my memory and in the hope that I can share the surprise and delight which they brought.

Behind all this lies the delight which I have always felt in being alive in this astonishing world. . . .'[137]

Margaret Blunden
Open Systems Group

# References

1. Letter to Bayard Catron, 19 January 1981.
2. Autobiographical notes, October 1982 (Vickers papers, Goring).
3. Letter to Guy Adams, 10 April 1980.
4. Autobiographical notes, op. cit.
5. Letter to Guy Adams, 28 February 1980.
6. Geoffrey Vickers, *My Family*, privately printed, 1973, p. 14.
7. Autobiographical notes, op. cit.
8. Foreword, 'Why do I write this book', undated and book not identified (Vickers papers, Oundle).
9. Autobiographical notes, op. cit.
10. Ibid.
11. Geoffrey Vickers, 'The End of the Gentleman'. Typescript dated 20 May 1940 (Vickers papers, Oundle).
12. Autobiographical notes, op. cit.
13. Ibid.
14. Ibid.
15. Ibid.
16. Ibid.
17. S. Sutton, 'Sir Geoffrey Vickers: An Affectionate Portrait', in *Human Systems are Different*, Harper & Row, 1983.
18. Geoffrey Vickers, 'Industry, Human Relations and Mental Health'. An address given at the 17th Annual Meeting of the World Federation of Mental Health 1964, subsequently published by Tavistock Publications, 1965.
19. Geoffrey Vickers, 'The Divine Animal'. Undated typescript (Vickers papers, Oundle).
20. Vickers papers. Undated letter, addressee not known. Probably written after his wife's death in 1972.
21. Robert Graves, *Goodbye To All That*, Penguin edition, 1960, p. 202.
22. 'Poetry and War'. A paper read before the Bodley Club of Merton College, 14 November 1919 (Vickers papers, Oundle).
23. Ibid.
24. Autobiographical notes, op. cit.
25. 'Dear Boy'. Typescript. Written to his son Burnell (Vickers papers, Oundle).
26. Donald Hall. Address given at the memorial service for Sir Geoffrey Vickers, 14 June 1982.
27. Autobiographical notes, op. cit.
28. 'The Man on the Elephant'. Undated typescript, p. 12 (Vickers papers, Oundle).

29. 'The Divine Animal', op. cit. p. 9.
30. Geoffrey Vickers, 'The Changing Nature of the Professions', *American Behavioral Scientist*, Vol. 18, No. 2, November/December 1974, p. 189.
31. Ibid p. 187.
32. Ibid.
33. Donald Hall. Memorial address, 14 June 1982.
34. 'The Changing Nature of the Professions', op. cit. p. 185.
35. Geoffrey Vickers, 'Purpose and Force: The Bases of Order', *World Order Papers*, Royal Institute of International Affairs, p. 163 (written April 1940).
36. S. Sutton, op. cit.
37. Letter to Adolph Lowe, 4 January 1982.
38. 'What National Service Involves', *The Spectator*, 20 January 1939.
39. 'Idols and Ideals'. Undated typescript p. 2 (Vickers papers, Oundle).
40. 'Purpose and Force: The Bases of Order', op. cit. p. 157.
41. Letter to J. H. Oldham, Spring 1939, printed in *The Christian Newsletter*, Supplement No. 2, 8 November 1939.
42. Ibid.
43. 'A Bill of Duties for Men in England'. Typescript dated April 1940 (Vickers papers, Oundle).
44. 'Purpose and Force: The Bases of Order,' op. cit. p. 164.
45. Letter to Ellen Vickers, Sunday 22 (no month) 1940 (Vickers papers, Oundle).
46. Letter to Adolph Lowe, 4 January 1982.
47. Letter to Adolph Lowe, 9 August 1978.
48. Geoffrey Vickers, 'Incomes and Earnings – A Steady State?' An address published in Michael Schwab (ed), *Teach-in for Survival*, London, 1972, pp. 87–88.
49. M.Y. Watson. Memorial address, 14 June 1982.
50. Letter to Adolph Lowe, 4 January 1982.
51. Foreword to *Appreciation, Communication and Education* (prospective collection of Vickers' papers; Guy Adams and Bayard Catron (eds)).
52. Letter to Dr Fritz Kempner, 23 August 1945 (Vickers papers, Oundle).
53. Letter to Guy Adams, 14 March 1979.
54. Autobiographical notes, op. cit. p. 3.
55. Geoffrey Vickers, 'Institutional and Personal Roles', *Human Relations* 1971, Vol. 24, No. 5.
56. Letter to Adolph Lowe, 4 January 1982.
57. Geoffrey Vickers, 'Personal Incentive and Public Service'. Typescript (Vickers papers, Oundle).
58. Ibid.
59. Letter to Adolph Lowe, 4 January 1982.
60. Geoffrey Vickers, 'The Future of Morality', *Futures*, October 1979, p. 380.
61. 'Why Vote Labour?' Undated typescript (Vickers papers, Oundle).
62. Geoffrey Vickers, 'The Accountability of a Nationalised Industry', *Public Administration*, Spring 1952, p. 73.
63. Geoffrey Vickers, 'How Can Pits Be Made More Attractive?' National Association of Colliery Managers, National Coal Mining Conference, Blackpool, 6–8 May 1953.
64. Foreword to *Appreciation, Communication and Education*, op. cit.
65. Letter to Bayard Catron, 19 January 1981.
66. Letter to Guy Adams, 14 March 1979.

67. Taped interview with Sir Geoffrey Vickers, December 1982, Open University media library.
68. Ibid.
69. Letter to Guy Adams, 14 March 1979.
70. Mental Health Research Fund newsletter, June 1965.
71. *The Times*, 29 March 1982.
72. Letter to Bayard Catron, 19 January 1981.
73. Letter to Bayard Catron, 19 January 1981.
74. Geoffrey Vickers, 'Stability, Control and Choice'. The 9th Wallberg Lecture, University of Toronto Press, October 1956.
75. Geoffrey Vickers, 'Values and Decision-Taking'. Paper for circulation before three colloquia to be held at the University of Toronto, November 1956 (Vickers papers, Goring).
76. Ibid.
77. Geoffrey Vickers, 'What Sets the Goals of Public Health?', *The Lancet*, 22 March 1958, p. 599.
78. Ibid.
79. Geoffrey Vickers, 'The Role of Expectation in Economic Systems', *Occupational Psychology*, Vol. 32, No. 3, July 1958.
80. Ibid.
81. Geoffrey Vickers, 'The Concept of Stress in Relation to the Disorganization of Human Behavior'. Reprinted with minor deletions, from *Stress and Psychiatric Disorder*, J. M. Tanner (ed), Oxford, Blackwell Scientific Publications 1959.
82. Geoffrey Vickers, 'Ecology, Planning, and the American Dream', *The Urban Condition*, L. J. Duhl (ed), New York, Basic Books.
83. Ibid p. 385.
84. Geoffrey Vickers, 'Appreciative Behaviour', *Acta Psychologica*, Vol. 21, No. 3, 1963.
85. Letter to Guy Adams, 14 March 1979.
86. Geoffrey Vickers, 'The Psychology of Policy Making and Social Change', *British Journal of Psychiatry*, Vol. 110, 1964.
87. Ibid.
88. 'Industry, Human Relations, and Mental Health', op. cit.
89. Ibid.
90. Geoffrey Vickers, 'The End of Free Fall', *The Listener*, 28 October 1965, p. 648.
91. Ibid.
92. *The Political Quarterly*, Vol. 36, 1965, p. 477.
93. Letter to Guy Adams, 23 February 1982.
94. Geoffrey Vickers, 'Medicine's Contribution to Culture', *Medicine and Culture*, F. N. L. Poynter, (ed). The proceedings of an international symposium sponsored by the Wellcome Trust and the Wenner-Gren Foundation. FNL Wellcome Historical Medical Library, London, 1969.
95. Geoffrey Vickers, 'Medicine, Psychiatry and General Practice', *The Lancet*, 15 May 1965.
96. Geoffrey Vickers, 'Community Medicine', *The Lancet*, 29 April 1967. (Based on a lecture given at the London School of Hygiene and Tropical Medicine, 14 December 1966.)
97. Letter from Lyn Jones to Margaret Blunden, 22 August 1983.

98. Ibid.
99. Ibid.
100. Letter from Lyn Jones to Margaret Blunden, 12 September 1983.
101. Geoffrey Vickers, 'Alchemy and Artificial Intelligence'. A comment on Dr H. L. Dreyfus' paper of that title. Rand Corporation, 1965 (Vickers papers, Goring).
102. Geoffrey Vickers, *The Tacit Norm*, Wenner-Gren Foundation for Anthropological Research, 1969 (Vickers papers, Goring).
103. Letter to Adolph Lowe, 4 January 1983.
104. Letter to Melvin Webber, 6 March 1968.
105. Geoffrey Vickers, 'The Uses of Speculation', *Journal of the American Institute of Planners*, January 1968. Vol. XXXIV. No. 1.
106. Geoffrey Vickers, 'Problems of Distribution', *World Modelling: a Dialogue*, C. West Churchman and Richard O. Mason (eds), North Holland, Vol. II 1976.
107. Geoffrey Vickers, 'Projections, Predictions, Models and Policies', *The Planner*, Vol. 60, No. 4, April 1974.
108. Geoffrey Vickers, 'Population Policy, its Scope and Limits', *Futures*, October 1974.
109. 'Projections, Predictions, Models and Policies', op. cit.
110. Ibid.
111. Ibid.
112. 'Problems of Distribution', op. cit.
113. 'Incomes and Earnings – A Steady State?', op. cit.
114. Letter to Adolph Lowe, 4 April 1979.
115. 'Incomes and Earnings – A Steady State?', op. cit.
116. Ibid.
117. Ibid.
118. Ibid.
119. Letter to Adolph Lowe, 4 January 1982.
120. Autobiographical notes, op. cit.
121. Ibid.
122. Letter to Adolph Lowe, 11 September 1975.
123. Letter to Adolph Lowe, 17 June 1975.
124. Letter to Guy Adams, 14 March 1979.
125. Letter to Adolph Lowe, 7 December 1979.
126. Letter to Adolph Lowe, 14 January 1977.
127. Letter to Adolph Lowe, 5 February 1977.
128. Letter to Adolph Lowe, 14 September 1978.
129. Autobiographical notes, op. cit.
130. Letter to Guy Adams, 14 September 1979.
131. 'The Future of Morality', op. cit.
132. Ibid.
133. Geoffrey Vickers, 'The Ethical Criterion in Human Ecology', April 1979, unpublished (Vickers papers, Goring).
134. Letter from Bayard Catron to Geoffrey Vickers, undated (Vickers papers, Goring).
135. Letter to Bayard Catron, 19 January 1981.
136. Letter to Guy Adams, 12 January 1979.
137. Autobiographical notes, op. cit.

# 2

# A classification of systems*

## I

The words 'general systems theory' imply that some things can usefully be said about systems in general, despite the immense diversity of their specific forms. One of these things should be a scheme of classification. Every science begins by classifying its subject matter, if only descriptively, and learns a lot about it in the process; and systems especially need this attention, because, as I shall suggest, an adequate classification cuts across familiar boundaries and at the same time draws valid and important distinctions which have previously been sensed but not defined.

I find it convenient to classify systems along two dimensions: according to the ways in which they are regulated, and according to the extent to which they are affected by what I shall call the historical process. I adopt this classification partly because it identifies the field of my particular interest, which lies, unhappily, at the extreme end of both these dimensions and which is not commonly distinguished as clearly as I think it should be; but I hope that the classification will prove of some general relevance and usefulness.

## II

The most obvious feature which systems have in common is the attitude they evoke in the mind of an enquirer. That a snake's internal temperature should vary with that of the ambient air is what I should expect. That my own holds constant within a single degree, while the external temperature ranges through a hundred degrees, suggests that some regulative mechanism must be intervening to offset these variations, and directs my enquiry to the regulator. Similarly, if I want to intervene in some present state to secure some enduring and predictable change, I must first understand what regulates its present course and must conceive my intervention as artificial, supplementary regulation. A system is a regulated set of relationships, and the key to its understanding is the way in which it is regulated.

The weather is a system mediated simply by transfers and transformations of energy. Pressure gradients *occasion* the flow of air which will

---

*From *General Systems*, XV, 1970. Originally presented in December 1969 to the first meeting of the London Chapter of the Society for General Systems Research.

reduce them but they do not *invite* it. We do not need the concept of information to explain these balancing movements, any more than we need it to explain the coupling of a Watts governor. By contrast, the simplest signal introduces a radically new regulative mediator and marks the significant distinction between systems regulated simply by the transfer of energy and those regulated also by the transfer of information. A rabbit alerted by the snap of a stick under a predator's foot is responding to a signal, he effect of which bears no relation to the energy which carries it. Not loudness but nearness threatens – so long as the signal is loud enough to be heard. Even where the response to a signal is as rigidly linked to it as any mechanical trigger mechanism, it is a form of mediation different in kind from those which regulate, for example, the movements of the atmosphere.

In fact, regulation mediated by rigid responses is much less common than was once supposed. The rabbit interprets the signal in the light of its context; even nearness does not alarm, when the source is identified as friendly. Cells transplanted in developing creatures or challenged by the need to combine in healing a wound respond in ways equally responsive to context. In interpreting animal and especially human behaviour the innate and conditioned reflex have been worked to death, for lack of the concept next to be discussed. Nonetheless, there are systems, both man-made and natural, in which information plays no more regulative part than to elicit what the enquirer can regard for his purposes as a given response. I will describe such information as the product of a simple signal.

The next staging point along this dimension is marked by the emergence of what I will call the cybernetic signal. The most important general idea inherent in cybernetics is, I suggest, the identification of a special kind of signal, which derives its meaning from the comparison of some input with some standard which awaits it at the receiving end. Of course, this is true even of simple signals; but where the response is given, this dependence can be safely ignored; it is in fact constantly ignored even when there is no such assurance. The idea is deeply rooted that information is a packet complete in itself which only needs to be transmitted.

In fact, information is an incomplete concept. It implies a receiver – in human contexts a mind* – to be informed and its effect is wholly dependent on the interpretative system which structures that mind and which alone determines what meaning, if any, the information shall have. In human societies, no less than in individuals, this system, so far from being a datum, changes constantly with time. Much communication is directed solely to changing it and still more has this for its chief, if undesigned, effect.

The process is most obvious in collective activities. Every city government, for example, contains a number of departments, each concerned to maintain some relationship within acceptable limits, be it the relation of

---

* I use the words 'mind' and 'brain' much as I use the words 'programme' and 'computer'; the second, when the context concerns the assembly which performs the process, the first when it concerns the process which the assembly performs.

roads to traffic, sewers to sewage or schools to school children. In each case the level of what is acceptable has been set by a policy decision, which in turn reflects a social judgment, mediated by the political institutions of the place and time. This standard of comparison gives meaning to all incoming information and even determines what information shall be sought. Match and mismatch signals so generated are the primary mediators of regulative action.

Thus the most conspicuous distinction between human societies and other kinds of systems is their capacity to generate and change the settings of their own systems. This capacity is exercisable only within limits. The town hall contains other departments which are concerned with these limits, notably the need to keep the total demands of all its activities within its total resources of men, money, and materials. It is also limited by even more general factors, such as the conditions of political obedience. The pressure of these limitations on the competing needs of disparate activities makes each limit the others, apart from their inherent tendencies, which may be complementary or conflicting. Thus these standards, which form the setting of the political system, become themselves systematically organized.

So, along my first dimension, systems range from those which are the resultant of forces unregulated by any exchange of information, through those where this is supplemented by simple signals rigidly linked to given responses, up to those which are regulated increasingly by cybernetic signals; these in turn extend through a range of increasing complexity, in which at least three progressions can be discerned. One is the increasing multiplicity of the standards which constitute the 'other half' of the cybernetic signal. A second is increase in the inconsistency of these standards with each other and, collectively, with the stability of the system, which is nonetheless a condition of their realization. A third is increase in the autonomy of these standards, by which I mean the extent to which they themselves become part of a self-maintaining system of concepts and values.

Obviously, this progress is not necessarily in the direction of stability. On the contrary, by multiplying desirable but mutually inconsistent standards of aspiration and unacceptability, it creates the ever present danger that systems at the far end of this dimension, being the societies we know, will jeopardise their stability for the sake of their aspirations and lose both. And although this characteristic distinguishes all human beings and their societies from other systems, it has reached among Western men what may be regarded as a pathological overload. Traditional societies posed no such problems of multi-valued choice, either to their governors or to the governed, such as plague both in our time and place. These reasons are partly historical and lead to a consideration of the second dimension.

## III

All kinds of cyclical changes, however violent, may form part of a recognizable pattern, if they are repeated often enough during the period under review. When they are not so repeated, I will describe the changes as historical, whether the non-repeatable character of the sequence is due merely to the relatively short time span of the observer's interest or to the fact that the object of his attention really does form part of a non-repeating pattern of events.

Historical changes perplex the student of systems when they occur in environmental variables, still more when they occur in variables within the system, and most of all when they affect the setting of the system itself. As an example of progress into these gathering complexities, consider the history of the river Thames, a physical system of a type which has long been a favorite example of form more enduring than substance.

Viewed over a time perspective of a few millennia, the river Thames is the way water originating in a given catchment area finds its way to the sea. If, however, our time perspective needs to be extended to include the end of the last Ice Age, only some ten millennia ago, we observe that the catchment area itself is not a datum but a product of history. For, until the melting ice allowed the contours north of the Chilterns to rise, what is now the upper Thames is believed to have made its way to the North Sea, without making any contact with the lower half of the river. Today's catchment area is itself historical.

Suppose our interest in the river allows us to ignore this long-term view; even on a shorter view, the river itself is a historical process. It made its own bed, and its own daily activities are still potent to scour and to silt, thus changing the physical conditions in which its future stream will do the same.

For two hundred years and more, the human beings who have always lived on its banks have been responsible for much more far-reaching historical changes. They progressively controlled its flow with locks and barrages. They withdrew water from it and returned water to it in increasing volume and at different places. They used it as a sewer. Their manifold demands began to conflict with each other. Now they begin to exceed in total demand the volume of the river. We plan to increase its volume by pumping out the deep reservoirs; perhaps, later, by pumping up desalted water from the sea.

Thus the physical system known as the river Thames is losing its identity, merging in the human socio-technical system which comprises the generation, conservation, utilization, purification and recycling of the water supply of Southeast England. This system lies at the more complex end of both my dimensions. It is mediated by cybernetic signals, and the standards which give these signals meaning are themselves in rapid change. It is for the Water Resources Board to estimate the demand for water which Southeast England will generate over the next fifty years; to consider how, if at all, this demand can be met, and to recommend regulative action which will keep supply and demand in line. Nearly every variable in this equation is subject to historical change, and none more so than the demand which sets the standard for the regulative action and thus defines the problem. A century ago no one dreamed of using water at the rate of thirty gallons per head per day. Fifty years hence, this standard may seem equally absurd, either because it cannot be attained or because it has ceased to be desirable in the light of what its attainment would cost in terms of frustrating the attainment of other standards. Perhaps our children will be scandalized, as well as amazed, that their parents used drinking water to wash away their sewage.

## IV

I choose these two dimensions for the classification of systems chiefly because they distinguish my own interests. I am interested in human and social systems in their present state of rapid historical change. I am especially interested in the systematic organization and historical change of the standards by which these systems are regulated; and this for two reasons. First, I believe that this system – our current value system, or, as I prefer to call it, our current appreciative system – is greatly stressed both by its inner inconsistencies and by the rate of its historical change. This is, I believe, the most acute and dangerous of the systemic breakdowns which threaten us. And further, I am interested in the structure and change of this system, because I believe that its shaping is the noblest and most human, as well as the most important activity of men; and this not only in our present state of self-induced crisis but even more if the abatement of crisis should enable us to give priority to the important over the urgent, and thus to exercise and even develop our limited but not, I think, negligible powers of moral initiative.

It may be objected that these interests, however valid, have no place in scientific discussion, since, being concerned with situations which are not predictable or repeatable, they escape the canons of scientific study. These objections, I think, would be mistaken, but they usefully bring out some peculiarities of this area of study and action.

Prediction and explanation answer different kinds of questions. The behavior of some systems can be predicted with great precision by simple statistical laws, although the behavior itself remains wholly unexplained thereby. Conversely, the behavior of a system can be explained by an understanding of the systematic relations involved, even though uncertainties prevent us from predicting its future course. The second is not only more common but is often more useful.

For example, the 11-year fluctuation cycle in the population of Arctic hares was familiar to the Hudson Bay Company, intent on the fur trade, long before ecologists disentangled, first, the relation between the changing number of hares and the number of lynxes that prey on them, and, later, the biochemical relations between the number of hares and their fertility (which I understand is now regarded as by far the more important explanation). These explanations add nothing to the predictive power of the statistical law, but they most usefully enlarge our understanding of the events behind it. This affects our minds and our powers in three ways. It answers a 'why' question. It develops the mental model by which we represent to ourselves the working of this ecological system and others that seem like it, and affects all the conclusions that we shall draw from those models. And finally, it adds prestige to the successful explanation and makes it more likely to be tested first as a hypothesis in other cases and to be assumed as an explanation in the meantime. (This last effect may sometimes be disastrous but seems inescapable and may be useful, on balance.)

But, it may be argued, prediction, apart from its practical use, is essential to verify our explanations. Is not this the heart of scientific method, the only source of the assurance, always tentative, that we attach to our hypotheses? Prediction is indeed one of the major criteria of scientific truth, though not the only one; but its role in human affairs is less direct and less conclusive than in the simplified conditions of physical experiment. The mental models which we build, representing the situations in which we conceive ourselves as acting, contain (at best) as much verified fact and rational deduction as are relevant and available; but they necessarily contain so many assumptions that, if action based on them should fail to have the result expected, we can seldom say which assumption has failed us. And if the facts behind the assumptions are themselves changing historically, we cannot be sure that a model which works today will work tomorrow – unless we can understand or control the process of change itself.

Even in a dialogue between two friends, each must choose his words to fit his model of the other's interpretative system, which will give them meaning. And if the result is other than he expects, he can only revise his model and try again. There is no finality and seldom any assurance of success. Yet we are likely to get on better if we behave with the patience, the humility, and the attention to the other which are supposed to characterize the scientist.

## V

The social sciences have no direct predictive power; but they have immense explanatory power and thus hugely enrich the models by which we both explain and predict. The sociological concept of role, for example, presenting a society as a net of self- and mutual-expectations, attached to social positions, tells us nothing of the contents of that net at any given time and place. Only culture and history can supply the materials from which the model must be built. But the concept is an incomparable guide to the building of the model – flexible enough even to model a society in revolt against the tyranny of role.

To those whose concepts of explanation and prediction are built on the physical sciences, it may seem inexplicable that in human affairs men understand and predict even with the limited success that they sometimes enjoy. The explanation lies, I think, in two obvious facts which a culture based on the physical sciences tends to underrate. Men act with assurance in human affairs chiefly because they have a source of enlightenment and a source of power which are denied to the physical scientist. Their enlightenment comes (no doubt with much deception also) from their personal experience of being human, without which they could attach no human meaning to anything presented to them either by observation or by communication. Their power comes from the incomparable force of language both as a source of information and as a means of mutual influence.

For men are more predictable than the weather only because they are concerned to be predictable and to make each other predictable. Order and disorder in human affairs are human creations, as well as human discoveries. The standards which define them were made and will be changed by men, consciously as well as unconsciously. The appreciative system is our supreme social artifact. It is not indeed wholly under human control; no social system is. Yet its content, its changes, and its pathologies are much the most important conditions of our lives today and rightly claim by far the greatest part of our attention. We urgently need to understand them better; and I hope that we may find in general system theory a way of thinking about them which will both define and increase the scope of our initiative in shaping and controlling the system which they form.

# LEVEL I: PLANETARY

LEVEL 1: PLANETARY

# Introduction

The sixteen years spanned by the papers in this section were years of fierce controversy between those branded technological pessimists such as J. W. Forrester and Dennis Meadows, whose models predicted an impending world catastrophe, and technological optimists such as the Science Policy Research Unit, confident that technical ingenuity could keep ahead of resource depletion, pollution problems and rising population. Vickers was a technological pessimist but his contribution to the debate, which rested on systems insights and the high valuation of stability, was always a distinctive one. Systems, he argued, both enable and constrain. The greater the enablements made possible by modern technology, the greater the constraints imposed on individuals and societies, the greater the load to be carried by the processes of political choice, and the greater the requirement for political regulation.

In a series of broadcasts in 1965 (*The End of Free Fall*) Vickers spelt out his profound concern about the contemporary technological age and set out the minimum changes which were necessary to stabilize it. 'Exploding' technology had released several critical rates of change: in population growth, in human expectations, and in unpredictability. The environment was now man-made rather than natural and was created largely by the *unintended* results of people's actions. Technology set but could not solve the fundamental problems: the critical problems, such as population growth, were not technological but political and cultural. There had already been a massive and accelerating increase in the scope and volume of regulation of national life. The world was now so unpredictable that it demanded to be regulated, nationally and internationally, by political decisions of increasing scope:

> The regulation of today's and tomorrow's world needs collective decision and collective action on a scale of space and time far longer than has ever been achieved or attempted before; it demands institutions, international as well as national, which do not exist...

Prominent among the new collective responsibilities was population policy, now that decisions on family size had moved from Act of God to act of man. All the traditional avenues of escape from population pressure such as emigration were being closed one by one and the age-old population stabilizers of pestilence and famine would soon be too manifest to ignore. What was needed, Vickers argued in *Population Policy, its Scope and Limits*, was public discussion of the issues of optimum limits of population and governments must take a line in this debate.

*Population Policy* is one instance of the kind of profound cultural changes, involving increased collective responsibility and reduced individual autonomy, which Vickers believed followed inescapably from modern technological developments. In general, he argued in *The Weakness of Western Culture*, the growth of science and technology had led to a world ever less predictable and manageable. Large cultural changes were needed in Western societies if they were to cope with the changed conditions created by two centuries of 'progress'. The most important of these was a change from the current ideal of the autonomous individual to what he believed to have been an earlier concept of the responsible person, who freely chose his own commitments and then was true to them. The immense cultural changes needed if we were to live in the world we had made were not matters of choice or opinion but derived from the behaviour of systems. Linear cultural developments, like all linear developments, ultimately bred their own reversals – no system could tolerate single direct change in one of its variables indefinitely:

> The main value of studying 'trends', especially cultural trends, is not primarily to project them or speculate on how to live with them. It is rather to assess how soon they will breed their own limitations and reversals. This process is indeed only slightly under our control, but the extent of our control depends largely on our understanding of it. . . .

The pronounced cultural trend towards moral inversion – a phenomenon explored at the organizational level by which institutions rather than individuals were held to be morally responsible and morally culpable – was inconsistent with the survival of an increasingly interdependent society. There were now, he argued (*The Future of Morality*), widespread demands for individual rights. These 'rights' could be satisfied only (if at all) by huge institutional efforts. But institutions were widely seen as dehumanizing and oppressive. Only a widespread commitment to political institutions and a broadly based identification with them would enable them to act morally.

Political coherence – including a strong measure of culturally generated shared values – was a precondition of political effectiveness. But, he argued in *Violence, War and Genocide*, most of the 160 'politico-fiscal' units in the world were too incoherent internally to act effectively as organized entities, except perhaps in war. The violent conflicts of today were even more commonly *within* rather than between states. Meanwhile technology had monstrously magnified the power of individual men to kill all forms of life including their own and a new battle for resources had already begun. Only the generation of a common culture – or a set of compatible cultures – could generate sufficient coherence for effective political action in this field:

> I have no idea whether either a common culture or a mosaic of compatible cultures is a possible goal for mankind or any part of it, today, but I have no doubt that without one or other or some combination of the two there is no future for men – or at least for Western men – on earth.

# 3

# The end of free fall*

## I

There is a story of a man who fell from the top of the Empire State Building, and he was heard to say to himself as he whistled past the second floor, 'Well, I'm all right so far'. This story caricatures two absurdities into which we often fall. One is the absurd speed with which we come to accept as normal almost any outrageous condition, once we have actually lived with it, however briefly. The other is the absurd slowness with which we come to accept as real any impending change which has not yet happened, however near and certain it may be. Both tendencies are natural; they were indeed evolved for our protection. They only become absurd when they come to threaten us and all we value – as I think they are doing today.

Within six generations or so we in Britain – and others elsewhere even more quickly – have blown ourselves out of the agricultural into the industrial epoch, out of a rural into an urban way of life, and out of a natural into a man-made environment. The drive was supplied by exploding technology and by the novel institutions with which we exploded it and used its energy; but neither the technology nor the institutions which achieved the explosion are capable of dealing with its results. The main problems of a technological age are not technological but political and cultural; and it is these I want to discuss here.

The explosion released several critical rates of change. Populations began to multiply faster, individuals began to produce and consume more, to travel and communicate more, to expect and demand more. As a result they began to depend more on each other and, soon, to get more and more in each other's way; but these consequences were noticed only later, because the explosion began in a world so under-occupied and under-developed that for a time each change could excite itself and the others without breeding limitations. This is what I call the time of free fall. It grows clearer every day that the time of free fall is coming to an end. For the man-made environment in which the industrial epoch is enclosing us – created as it now is largely by the unintended results of what everyone does – is becoming too unpredictable to live in and may soon become too unacceptable to live with; so if it is to survive, it will have to be controlled – that is, governed

---

*From *The Listener*, 28 October and 4 November 1965. Originally a series of talks on the BBC Third Programme; also in *Value Systems and Social Process*.

- on a scale and to a depth which we have as yet neither the political institutions to achieve nor the cultural attitudes to accept.

So the end of free fall (if we escape nuclear disaster) will probably not be like hitting the pavement but more like falling into a pond. We shall have to live in a much denser political medium. We must take account of the increasing mutual demands and expectations of people and societies who are growing more numerous, more crowded, more mutually dependent - but also, at present, more diverse and more mutually intolerant. This has already been happening, nationally and internationally, for long enough to invite a look ahead.

Let us consider first some of the more obvious trends which cannot go on as they are without defeating themselves and us; and then we can speculate about the changes which are likely to result from them or from the need to control them. The most obvious is the trend of population growth. The figures are becoming familiar, but they are worth repeating. It took about 1,650 years from the beginning of the Christian era for the world's population to double from about 250,000,000 to 500,000,000. With the beginning of the industrial revolution, the next double, to 1,000,000,000, took only 200 years. The next double, to 2,000,000,000, took only seventy-five years, which brings us to 1925. The next, to 4,000,000,000, is due, at present rates, ten years hence. The increase is greatest in those areas which are already most densely populated and least well fed.

Technologists may regard this as a challenge to the technology of food production. If we had free and unlimited power, so they claim, this planet could support - on the products of yeast factories and algae farms - as many as 50,000,000,000 people, a figure which as present rates will not be reached until the early 2100s or five generations hence. But this kind of speculation seems to me uninteresting, because the critical problems set by the trend are not technological: they are political and cultural. Long before food production was defeated, the trend would obviously have set off a new battle for living space on a scale not known before. Indeed, this battle is already on.

## Ambivalent attitude to immigrants

I do not necessarily mean the kind of struggle which submerged the Roman Empire under successive waves of wandering peoples, though there are still some artificially empty preserves where this might happen. What I have in mind runs more like this: The right to deny immigration and to discriminate between immigrants is already becoming notably more important to the countries which attract immigrants and more resented by the others. The attitude of the receiving countries is at present ambivalent, for their economies increasingly depend on colonies of alien labour which their cultures are unwilling or unable to absorb. This reluctance to admit will become even more marked if automation continues to eliminate more and more jobs in the lower grades of the employment pyramid. In any case, it seems inevitable – without some important political and cultural change – that the richer countries should continue for some decades at least to become even richer in relation to the poorer ones and at the some time to close their doors even more closely to immigration; and that in consequence both the pressure to enter and the resistance to entering should mount.

Suppose the barriers hold, and the struggle for the earth remains a national rather than an international one. In this country the struggle for some place to live has already reached a new level of intensity. The present inequity between the minority who buy and own their homes and the majority who rent them or wait for them can only be remedied by measures more radical than those yet tried. The whole concept of land as an object of private property and profit must, I think, be on the way out in countries like ours which are both developed and crowded. This concept was a product of the agricultural epoch, and it will be as inept in a world where land is over-scarce, as it was in the pre-agricultural epoch, when land was as over-abundant as the sea. Yet what an edifice of prestige and esteem, of security and independence, of speculation and profit-taking, still rests on land ownership; how successfully it has so far defended itself; what political, social, and psychological disturbances have always followed any effective attack on it!

But the struggle for the earth is not confined to the fight for a place to live. All kinds of necessary and expanding land uses – for industry, agriculture, transport, amenity – fight with increasing fierceness for diminishing opportunities. This fight is being transferred from the market-place to the political arena, because the conflict of values which is at issue involves the interests of many others beside the parties to a market transaction. But we have still to develop effective political ways of solving the more complex problem.

It could be claimed that medical technology will provide a solution for the problem of increasing population, long before food technology has been overwhelmed. And it is true that medical technology, which has contributed so greatly to the population explosion, has made or will soon make conception much more widely controllable than it has ever been before, at least in those countries where the culture does not oppose the change. But whether the power of potential parents to regulate the size of their families will result in stable population – and, if so, how – is a matter which is uncertain, and wholly beyond the scope of technology.

## Average size of family

The average size of family is an important factor in determining the size of population. It is also a sensitive one; in Britain today an average of three children per family would be far too high for stability and an average of two per family far too low. We do not know what determines the size of families, but if a sense of overcrowding became the effective trigger, it would be likely to work much too late and then too vigorously. The population would oscillate wildly between limits of perhaps increasing amplitude – a behaviour familiar to the engineers who design the control of automatic systems; they call it 'hunting'. But suppose, on the other hand, that at an overcrowded period the needs of unhoused families won overall priority; the best passport to a house would then be a large family and those penalized by overcrowding could escape only by making the over-crowding worse. (The feedback, as system engineers would say, would have become positive.) I offer no prophecy; I am only concerned to show that technological devices to control conception do not of themselves achieve or even make possible the stabilizing of a population.

Moreover, even a population which is stable in numbers would on present form continue to expand in other directions. Today's multiplying millions progressively take up more space and use more stuff per head. An American calculation, already more than ten years old*, showed that in 1950 each individual in the United States was using, directly and indirectly, eighteen tons of stuff each year, a rate not so far short of his own weight, every day, from birth to death; and this was expected to rise by 50 per cent in twenty-five years. Obviously, such a rate must soon run into practical limitations. On the way, it may or may not meet technological limitations; resources of raw materials might become exhausted; or energy supply might fall short of the increasing demand; or we might be stumped by the problem of disposing of waste. But even if we assume, as most technologists do, that every technological problem will always find its answer – and I see no conceivable reason why it should – there remain the political and cultural problems. They are inevitable, for this enhanced activity is taking place on the surface of a planet which is neither expanding nor expansible.

## Planning conurbanizations

One aspect of these problems is urbanization. A hundred years ago only a negligible proportion of the human race lived in cities of more than 100,000. A hundred years hence only a negligible proportion are likely to live anywhere else. Even the United States, a country with an average popula-tion density less than one tenth of ours, has had to coin the word 'megalo-polis' to describe conurbanizations, comprising many tens of millions of folk, united only by the fact that they live in a common warren; and of course we have them too. How are these aggregations to be planned? How governed?

The urbanization of Asia and Africa poses even more intractable prob-lems which technology can set but cannot solve. For in the first half of this century, while the urban population of Europe and America increased two and a half times, that of Asia increased five times; and Africa's explosion may be even faster. The Ivory Coast is a country of only 3,000,000 or

---

* Report of the President's Materials Policy Commission, *Resources for Freedom* (Wash-ington, U.S. Government Printing Office, 1952).

4,000,000 people, speaking sixty-nine native tongues, none written and none mutually understandable; but the Ivory Coast capital, Abidjan, has grown in ten years from 10,000 to 300,000 – partly by a proliferation of multi-storey offices, air-conditioned hotels, and elegant residences, and partly by incorporating in its suburbs mud and straw villages which were traditional rural communities ten years ago.

## Problems of urbanization

We know well enough the social problems which were created here in Britain by the urbanization of the nineteenth century, problems far harder to solve than the physical problems of public health. In Asia, still more in Africa, the disturbance created by this mass transition from rural to urban life is likely to be even greater. Meantime, in highly developed countries, such as ours, as the Buchanan report has shown, continuing urbanization raises new technological problems which can be solved, in turn, only after further political and cultural change. The multiple purposes for which we have used our streets ever since medieval times will mutually frustrate each other within the next twenty or thirty years, unless we replan and rebuild our towns in wholly novel ways. But these new technological solutions are impossible without the new institutions needed to achieve them and the changes in cultural values which would be needed to support planning on such a scale. Even a temporary answer demands innovations more radical and more difficult than the technological innovation that posed the problem in the first place.

Other familiar trends present even sharper challenges. In Britain, already one of the most densely populated lands on earth, current forecasts show that the shortage of labour will increase over the next ten years. But in America, automation, on which our economic future also depends, is already said to be eliminating 2,000,000 jobs a year; and there already exists there a disfranchized class for whom the economy can at present provide support but not work. Nearly half their unemployed are young men who have never yet found a job. If this is to be the overall effect of increasing technological efficiency, what political and cultural change can we devise to give these millions an acceptable status – acceptable either to themselves or to their working fellows?

A related but distinct trend is the scarcity of particular types of skill. We are short of doctors, nurses, teachers, scientists, technologists, craftsmen. All these skills take several years to develop; so the number of those who possess any of them at any point of time depends on individual choices made several years earlier, by a process which is only slightly understood or controlled. And the distribution of these scarce skills between the places where they are needed – including their distribution between the public and the private sector – depends on a labour market which has become far too inflexible for this sort of regulation. This complex bit of political and cultural machinery, so necessary when it comes to maintaining technological momentum, seems clearly to be breaking down. What kind of change would make it work, or replace it with a better?

The general nature of all these political and cultural demands is clear enough. What is needed to keep the system going is a better mechanism for collective choices – both to make the choices and to put them into practice. These choices must commit ever larger numbers of people over wider areas of life and extend further into the future. Even so simple and marginal a matter as the future of motoring depends no longer on providing cars which people can afford to buy, but on providing roads; and hence on collective decisions not only on the pattern of the public road system, but also on how much resources, including land surface, to devote to roads – assessing this one demand against all the other demands that compete not just for public resources but for all resources. Individual choices through the market have generated a society which only political choice can regulate.

## Growth of the public sector

The response to this demand has been visible in Britain for at least three generations. We can measure it roughly by the growth of the public sector. In 1850 the central government had eight departments of which four dealt wholly and one partly with external affairs. Five more departments were added in the next fifty years, eleven more in the first years of this century, four more in the last three years. By 1956 more than one in five of the entire labour force were working for the central government, local government, or public bodies. Eight years later it is nearer one in three. It would be naive to dismiss these figures as an example of Parkinson's Law. They record a massive and accelerating increase in the scope and volume of deliberate regulation of the national life; it has grown despite strong ideological resistance, and it now extends to the distribution of incomes, of services, of jobs and of homes; to education and health and welfare and transport; to economic planning and physical planning and social planning. It grows ever faster, yet few, I would think, would question that it fails ever further to keep up with its problems.

But it is in the international field that the lag in institutional development, by comparison with the growing need, has been most striking. In the past twenty years the number of sovereign states has more than doubled, almost entirely by the emergence of states without previous experience of self-government. In size, wealth, state of development, cultural type, and political ideology they are far more diverse than they were. Their potentiality for mutual destruction has increased immeasurably and their mutual hostility is certainly no less; yet their political and economic interaction has increased many times. Against this huge increase in the need for international regulation we can set little by way of new international machinery. Means have been found, on American initiative, to give something away across national frontiers, a feat unknown on any serious scale before 1946. Yet if we reflect on the difficulties both of keeping the peace and of redistributing income within a single political unit – even one which has been developing a coherent political system for centuries – it seems clear to me that corresponding institutions in the international field do not yet exist and cannot yet be imagined though they are clearly needed now.

These are some of the more obvious trends to which we are so often urged to adapt; but some of those who urge us have naive ideas of what adaptation means. We are men, not rats. It is through our societies that we survive and transmit the skills of survival; and it is equally through our societies that we create the opportunities for human life and the skills to use and value them. Our major instrument of adaptation is government. T. H. Huxley, in a famous lecture sixty years ago*, said: 'That which lies before the human race is a constant struggle to maintain and improve, in opposition to the state of nature, the state of Art of an organized polity in which and by which men may develop a worthy civilization, capable of maintaining and constantly improving itself. ...' Nothing less than this, I suggest, is a worthy definition of human adaptation: and on that course there are cultural limitations and possibilities which I have not yet charted.

## II

In my first talk I described our present state as the last stage in a free fall – the fall from the agricultural into the industrial epoch; from a natural into a man-made world, and so into an increasingly political world, a world so unpredictable that it demands to be regulated, nationally and inter-nationally, by political decisions of increasing scope.

There is nothing defeatist in this conclusion. Government is our major instrument of adaptation. Just as we pride ourselves that through technol-ogy we have learned to shape the natural world to suit us, rather than suiting ourselves to it, so we shall pride ourselves, if we ever succeed in doing it, on shaping the man-made world to suit us, rather than scurrying about in search of ways to live with its vagaries. But we cannot pride ourselves on this yet, because we have not yet achieved it, nor have we evolved either the political institutions or the political ability to achieve it; worse – we are not yet developing this ability fast enough even to keep pace with the course of events. This is not surprising, because political change is limited by the speed at which people can change their ideas of the world they live in, their expectations of it and their willingness to accept its expectations of them; and all of these I regard as *cultural changes*. Culture changes with the generations, but, as with other changes, there is a limit to the rate at which it can change without losing its coherence.

## Re-learning in each generation

It is a fact strange beyond comprehension that the whole corpus of human knowledge is re-learned at least three times each century; and this becomes

---

* Romanes Lecture (1893).

even stranger when we remember that what is re-learned is not only the technological skills and knowledge which serve our common needs, but also the political and cultural ways of thinking and feeling and acting which determine what we shall conceive our common needs to be, and how we should pursue them. Every one of us not long ago lay in a cradle, helpless and speechless, unable to distinguish one thing from another, even self from non-self, equipped only with a few reflexes, a unique genetic code, and a learning potential. Whatever we are now, our readiness to notice this and ignore that, to accept this as a commitment while we dismiss that as having no claim on us, to enjoy or accept relations of one sort and to hate and resent others – all this we have learned from our experience of the culture into which we were born; and it is increasingly this which determines how we shall accept and interpret new experience. This is the process by which each generation is incorporated into and inherits the society into which it is born, and through which alone it is socialized and humanized.

Yet how far from passive is the acceptance of the heritage! How selective are these learners, how much they amplify, change, or reject! For at least a dozen generations now, each generation has had more to transmit, to add, and to change than the generation before. This rate of change cannot increase indefinitely without breeding discontinuity with the past and in-coherence in the present. That it has begun to do so is suggested by the increasing use of the word 'alienation' to describe the imperfect relation of Western man not only with his increasingly man-made world but with his neighbour and himself.

To capture some sense of this accelerating rate of change, we can let our minds run back over the generations. Politically and economically, we are already some way from Beveridge and Keynes; but how far were they from the generation before them which began the first world war with the slogan 'Business as usual', and which set up a committee on reconstruction to plan how best to return, after the war, to the social and economic conditions of 1914? Karl Marx is distant four generations, Bentham five, Adam Smith six. Eight take us to the Declaration of Rights, twelve to the Elizabethans, twenty-seven to William the Norman, 100 to the builders of Stonehenge. About 300 generations have passed since the glaciers melted on what is now the coast of Devon. The linear ancestors of any one of us, back to the last ice age, would barely fill the first ten rows of the stalls in a modest theatre.

## Guardians of coherence: artificers of change

Let us consider only the first of those ten rows, the thirty generations that separate us from the England of Alfred the Great. Measure in imagination the difference in physical state, in institutions, and in culture between his England and ours, and divide by thirty. That is the measure of what, on the average, each of those generations accomplished, both in creation and in conservation. For each of these ancestors, born into his father's world and dying in the world of his children, was both a guardian of coherence and an artificer of change, sometimes sudden and violent change. From their hands to ours has come the triple heritage of environment, institutions, and culture which we are guarding, wasting, and remaking today, as they in their day guarded, wasted, and remade it. For this heritage has no enduring substance unless it constantly be made anew.

This backward glance reveals much to encourage us. Britain twenty years after the second world war seems in most human ways a better and more coherent society than it was twenty years after the first world war or twenty years after Waterloo – and Peterloo. For 150 years the political heritage and the cultural heritage have been growing to meet the demands of the emergent industrial epoch; and they seem to have more than kept pace.

Yet if my earlier analysis is right, we and our children and their children have a task which is harder now in several ways. The regulation of today's and tomorrow's world needs collective decision and collective action on a scale of space and time far larger than has ever been achieved or attempted before; it demands institutions, international as well as national, which do not exist, and cultural changes even faster than those which have already raised the spectre of alienation; and it will have to be done, in Britain at least, in conditions remote from those of free fall. To give more definite content to the cultural challenge, consider how the past generations understood and re-made in their day three ideas which have been dominant in ours – liberty, equality, and fraternity.

## Combating the 'five giant evils'

To at least the earlier half of those thirty ancestors, liberty meant the safeguard of specific rights to which persons of their class were entitled, and the corresponding restraint of other men's power, especially the public power. Of those nearer to us, some, widening the second half of the idea, aspired to make *all* power responsible; others, widening the first part, sought liberty in extending the area in which each could live as he pleased. None but the last would have conceived of including, among the liberties to which he aspired, freedom from the 'five giant evils' which our welfare state was designed to combat – sickness, ignorance, unemployment, squalor, and want. Not even the last generation would have realized that, by this transition, the executive public power, which is still feared as the enemy and yet prized as the guardian of private liberties, had in fact also been acknowledged as their main architect.

And equality? For at least the first twenty of those thirty generations, equality was conceivable only in terms of the individual's place within a social order which was defined by nature and sanctioned by God. Only the last three or four would have conceived these social positions as theoretically open to all alike. Not even the last would have readily conceived the order itself as a human artifact, to be made and re-made, either blindly or knowingly, by the people whom it ordered.

And fraternity? All these generations knew the bond of fellow humanity that underlay differences of status and circumstance; but to earlier generations it had a stronger content within a narrower frontier. The Church might teach the brotherhood of man, but mutual dependence reinforced the lesson only within familiar groupings, bound by accepted ties and common culture and often consolidated by fear and hostility for the 'non-brothers' beyond the pale. Only the last few generations knew the 'mass-fraternity' of large national entities, or even of mammoth trade unions. Only the very last glimpsed the net of world-wide dependence which underlies the mounting alienation of nation from nation. None had become conscious of the still nameless bond which links each generation to its unborn successors.

## Irresponsible power in new forms

We and our children can keep what we value in our heritage only by re-making it even more radically and more quickly than our ancestors had to do. Ever more of our most urgent needs today can be met only through responsible choice made for us by others – not only by institutions and departments of state (as for example in implementing the Buchanan report sufficiently to give us towns in which it is possible to live) but equally by our ordinary fellow citizens, who can block collective action by simply withholding their confidence and support. New forms of irresponsible power dominate our world; for, as a recent writer* has observed, the creations of our own hands and minds have power over us by their very existence – the plant that *must* be used, the newspaper that *must* be filled, the institution that *must* grow – and such power proliferates. Even our present degree of interdependence makes nonsense of the kind of freedom we are still conditioned to prize most highly.

The hierarchy of industrial roles distributes authority between our would-be equal selves at least as unequally, and sometimes less acceptably, than did the structure of traditional society; and this hierarchy depends on a more unequal and specialized spread of skills and abilities. It may even have come to depend on natural abilities which are distributed so unequally that in the name of equality we are making societies in which many people can find no place. We do not know; for we are almost wholly ignorant of human variation, whether biological, psychological, or cultural, and our entrenched misconception of equality prevents us from using even such knowledge as we have. We are seeing only the first stirrings of that respect for human difference on which an adequate concept of equality may some day be based.

Fraternity claims for the first time a bond so wide in space as to lack

---

* Herbert Rosinski in *Power and Human Destiny*, Frederick A. Praeger, 1965.

reinforcement by what it excludes, and so deep in time as to include our responsibility to the future generations that we increasingly commit; and the claim appals us. It is no accident that our age has heard its most contemporary philosophy propound, through the mouth of its prophet, Jean-Paul Sartre, the sombre creed 'Hell is other people'. If that is true, the world into which we are moving will be hell indeed; and it will be true, unless we can give to fraternity an extension in space and time which has never seemed more remote.

In the man-made world beyond free fall, our children's first concern will probably be to establish sufficient authority to create their liberties. This will require them to exact from all an equality of responsibility more nearly corresponding to their equality of rights and to widen their sense of human obligation so that it extends not only across the frontiers of nations but also across the temporal boundaries of the generations, including the unborn. This will be a challenge to innovate and to conserve – a challenge more difficult, as I believe, than any which earlier generations have had to face.

## Two widening gulfs

For the industrial epoch has opened as never before the two gulfs which in the past have always challenged most gravely the adaptability of mankind. One is the gulf between cultures; the other the gulf between generations. Even if within our own nation the ancient cultural gulfs are closing, the gulfs between the national cultures, in the world which technology is making interdependent, are at present so great as to exclude joint action which is even remotely equal to the needs of any of the participants; and the gulf between the generations compounds this cultural division and multiplies the threat to that cultural continuity which is the very medium of change.

In such a world, political and social life is likely to become more collective or more anarchic or, almost certainly, both. Communities, national, sub-national, and supra-national, will become more closely knit in so far as they can handle the political and cultural problems involved – and, in so far as they cannot, they will become more violent in their mutual rejections. The loyalties we accept will impose wider obligations and more comprehensive acceptance and will separate us by wider gulfs from those who reject them. These tendencies multiply around us now. A world in which interaction increases does not thereby necessarily become a more integrated world. On the contrary, these interactions may generate such tensions and pressures as to disrupt it. The worse the strains, the more demanding will be those societies which survive. Technology cannot unify the world. Unification, integration, are the fruits of political action, and the limits of political action are in the character and coherence of the cultures within which that action is taken, and in the rate at which those cultures can grow and change.

For us in Britain, some recent developments could prepare us to live in a multi-cultural world. One is the eclipse of our own once dominant position. Westminster democracy is clearly only one among several imperfect ways of governing a society. Christianity is one among several world religions, which together claim today the loyalty of a diminishing fraction of mankind. White is only one among several widely distributed colours of skin. These facts, which were always true, are no longer obscured, and they challenge us to find a more intelligent basis for loyalty to our own culture and for co-operation with others. This the social sciences can now supply, as they could not fifty years ago. We need no longer lack an understanding of the nature of our commitment to our own culture, and of others to theirs – and of the necessary limitations of them all.

## Present significance of past and future

Even the temporal boundaries of our awareness may be widening a little. It was only at the end of the eighteenth century, say five generations ago, that Western man seems to have awakened to the present significance of his own past. Only in the nineteenth did he become absorbed in the historical record, with ears attuned to hear in every age the persuasive voices of its own dead. Then, just a century ago, Darwin extended the historical perspective so far that recorded time became too brief to notice; and fifty years later Freud opened our eyes to a historical process in each individual life that links each latest development with its earliest past. As we are now so well equipped to sense the present significance of the past, it may be that we are not far from sensing the present significance of the future.

We are accustomed to distinguish so sharply between 'I' and 'not-I' and between 'now' and 'not-now' that any blurring of the dichotomy may seem unnatural to us; but this distinction also differs with the culture, and it is not immune to cultural change. When we learn to attach reality to others and to the future, are we not simply enlarging our idea of self to include new relations with others, and deepening the present in which we live to include more of the future which it always comprehends? These ideas may come more naturally to future generations which have learned to think of men and societies as systems of internal and external relations, extended in space and time and increasing in their selfhood through the extension of these relations.

And there is another way in which we are increasing our understanding of the continuity of life into the future as well as out of the past. Eric Erikson, in a recently published book*, discusses the human virtues. He defines them as those strengths which make humans human; and he describes how these virtues develop at different periods of life, each relying on the successful development of the one before. In infancy and childhood,

---

* *Insight and Responsibility*, W.W. Norton and Co., New York, 1964.

according to Erikson, we have to develop hope, will, purpose, and competence; in adult life, love, care, and ultimately wisdom. In adolescence, linking the two, we have to develop one virtue only, which he calls fidelity, and which he describes as the ability to be true to self-chosen loyalties. I do not think I go beyond his ideas if I say that this stage covers the making of all those choices which lay the ground-plan of a system of values capable of growing for a lifetime without collapsing through incoherence, or becoming a prison through ineptitude.

This concept seems to me of great value, because it points beyond the relativity of particular values to the human quality or virtue which creates, preserves, and re-makes them; and also because it stresses the essential part which the sequence of generations plays in making possible this consistent transcendence of each generation's value system. The infant learns to hope in a milieu formed by the love and care and wisdom of a generation which was itself so nurtured; and only a generation which has learned in childhood hope, will, purpose, and competence to a degree seldom achieved today will be equal to building in adolescence a pattern of fidelities equal to its needs.

So the limits implicit in the rate of cultural change are not tiresome relics of the past for some social technology to eliminate. They are rooted in the most basic reality of our daily lives. They deserve the common allegiance of innovators and conservators alike. Our genetic heritage, as it seems to me, fits us not at all to live in the world which our technology is making; but we are evolving another, a cultural, heritage which, if we can understand it and be true to it, may yet enable us to realize that dream of T. H. Huxley, 'the state of Art of an organized polity....' When the first seed-bearing plants began to release their seeds to the wind's distribution, no mind could have foretold, if mind had been there to speculate, that, rooting and dying on the infertile wastes, their own decay would build up a bed of humus in which unimagined successors would evolve and flourish. We are guardians of a social humus more precious and more vulnerable than theirs – guardians not merely of values but of the soil in which values grow. That seedbed is today menaced by a vastly-increased erosion. Conservators and innovators alike, our paramount duty to the future is to leave it a little deeper for our passage.

# 4

# Population policy, its scope and limits*

Balancing population and food supplies is a problem as old as man, but the population problem today has three new facets. Supplies of food are spread unevenly over the globe without relation to population; medical science brings difficulties with its success in prolonging life and reducing infant mortality but also provides the means of controlling conception. Replacing the conventional picture of a dual world based on the level of development, the author presents here a four-celled matrix according to the ratio of resources to population. The envisaged population stabilizing policies extend far beyond the field of family planning and may include radical changes in population mobility and food rationing in the next decade.

## A problem both old and new

The population problem is the oldest human problem – even older, perhaps, than the problem of human governance. In our day it is transformed by three new factors to which I will return; but it is nonetheless conditioned by all those features which shaped it in Cro-Magnon days.

Any human group must maintain a certain minimum size if it is to survive. There will always be more mouths to feed than there are pairs of hands to hunt and gather food. And the active pairs of hands must be numerous enough to survive accidents to any one of them. But equally such a group cannot exceed a maximum size, originally set by the food potential of the area over which it can range in a day. And this in turn will vary with the natural richness of the area and with the group's skills in using it.

So three critical ratios emerge when we analyse even the simplest human societies. One is the composition of the group, notably the relation of consuming mouths to producing hands. A second is the relation of the group's demands to the resources of the area on which it is effectively free to draw. A third is the extent to which the group can enlarge its use of these resources or extend its access to them. This third element, the relation of its actual to its potential command of available resources, has proved to be the most elastic of all. It includes both the dimension of technology and the dimension of physical expansion, whether by colonisation, rapine or trade.

A very few communities exist today which have maintained a stable

---

*From *Futures*, October 1974. Based on an address given at the invitation of the Population Council in April 1974.

relation with a limited environment for many millennia. One such is the group of tribes in the highlands of New Guinea with whom contact was first made, by air, in the 1950s. Confined to a fertile area by jungles which equally protected them from invasion, endowed with a cultivable grain and domesticable animal, these people have subsisted with no remembered change of technology for countless centuries, any potential surplus population being controlled only by unnoticed and unidentified variations in the birth and death rate. Inter-tribal war, though not unknown, seems to have played no significant part in population control.

Such examples are rare. A few others are to be found which supplement natural controls by infanticide or by the ritual killing of the old, but infanticide has usually been designed to eliminate the potentially unproductive, rather than to maintain a stable population. And even this, though known in Rome and Sparta in classical times, has been rare. Some Cro-Magnon bones in an Anatolian cave tell us that the man they supported some 30000 years ago had from birth a withered right arm as well as other infirmities; and that he died, probably from an accident, at what was then the advanced age of over 40. Human family solidarity is nothing new.

The general pattern of societies which have survived has been one not of stability but of expansion of numbers, accommodated either by getting more food from the same area or by expanding into other areas. The first is the story of man's progress through husbandry to agriculture and industry. The second is the story of emigration and conquest and colonisation. Linking the two is the story of specialisation, division of labour and trade, internal and international.

One significant feature of this last link was the slave trade. From the time when societies became sufficiently large and efficient to generate surplus wealth, and consequently inequalities of wealth, to the time when mechanical and electrical energy became widely available, slaves were perhaps the most precious form of productive wealth. The wealth of Solomon testifies to this, no less than to the wealth flowing along the trade routes which he dominated by conquering the Edomites. Most of recorded history is the history of slave-based cultures or of cultures based on the labour of those who were not enfranchised citizens. This distinction distorted the equation between populations and their ground of subsistence by establishing a class of human beings who were equated with their masters' flocks and herds, whether they were formally slaves or not. It is a distinction not easily eliminated or easily forgotten. Moreover, the substitution of mechanical for human slaves has not removed all the effects which a slave-based culture has on the masters.

That in brief summary is the uneasy story of the process by which the human race has spread over the planet, and the key to its present dilemma. All the traditional avenues of escape from population pressure are being closed in one way or another. These closures are of such varying kinds that they need to be distinguished.

First, there is nowhere to go. There are indeed still areas of the earth's surface which would support larger populations than they support now. But all these are under the sovereign control of governments and in nearly all of them all the cultivable land is already in public or private ownership, individual or collective, and most of it is under some kind of development unless it is of a kind (desert, mountain, jungle) which we do not know how to develop. Immigrants admitted now can no longer be given an area of land to cultivate as they were in North America even a century ago. They can only be assimilated into a more or less integrated economy in which they can be productive only in so far as they can be employed. And this qualification increasingly restricts both the numbers and the character of the immigrants whom such countries are willing to admit.

This is not the only restriction. Even those countries which still admit immigrants are increasingly aware of the difficulties of assimilating people of an alien culture and in consequence are increasingly selective. Since those whom they admit are likely to be those who can least easily be spared by their countries of origin, immigration policies are usually inconsistent with emigration policies.

It is not surprising then, that population increase is posing ever more acute, though different problems to all countries. Population pressure can be relieved only to a dwindling extent by that natural process by which the disadvantaged and the adventurous left their homelands to seek their fortunes elsewhere. Wars of conquest followed by settlement or colonisation, though not unknown, are less tolerated and could not again play their former part without an international cataclysm, which today would almost certainly serve to reduce rather than to redistribute populations. The frontiers of political states are hardening and must continue to harden as each assumes more consciously the responsibility for keeping its members alive. This increasingly heavy national responsibility may be muted, but it may equally be sharpened by whatever international machinery may exist for redistributing across national frontiers populations or resources or both.

## Four types of nations

I find it convenient to consider four typical situations. There are highly developed countries which, like the UK and Japan, have populations larger than they could support if they were not able to import food in exchange for their manufactured products. There are other developed countries, like the USA and Australia, which are net exporters of food. And though they also import food and depend for their prosperity on international trade, the real resources they command in their own territories are sufficient to support their present populations. At the other end of the scale there are relatively undeveloped countries which, like India, are unable today fully to support their growing populations, whilst others, equally undeveloped, more than meet their present needs with their present resources and technologies. Between these extremes are many intermediate varieties, but the four types serve to focus the different policy issues which are dominant in these different situations.

In each of them, whether developed or undeveloped, problems of food production or acquisition are compounded by problems of distribution, within as well as across frontiers. All highly developed societies and many others face the political difficulties of governing huge urban aggregates of high density and low social coherence. Human life cannot be lived acceptably in conditions appropriate to battery hens, even if abundant food could be provided from synthetic protein and processed algae. Food is not the only limit to acceptable human density. These limits are neither known nor knowable in advance. When they are exceeded, they used to become manifest first in plague and pestilence, or in waves of colonisation. Today these ancient regulators are likely to be preceded by the breakdown of services, law and order, and other aspects of governmental regulation.

In the Western world, urban growth is already more intense in smaller cities than in those which set the pace a century ago. This is due partly to deliberate policy as well as to deteriorating quality of life in the largest centres – for example, the combination of policies in the UK designed to limit the growth of London by channelling it to other places, including new towns designed for the purpose. It is hard to find statistics which clearly reflect this process of redistributing urban growth. London, New York, Tokyo, and Calcutta have different stories to tell, each too complex to encourage facile comparisons or contrasts with the others. But all alike emphasise that population problems are not necessarily soluble because they fall within the area of a presently viable national government.

There remains a basic difference, even within the developed countries, between those countries, like the UK and Japan, which are viable only so long as they can buy food and other resources in the international market, and those which are not so dependent. Economies of the former type are based on a 19th century assumption which may fail, which is indeed failing now. This is the assumption that market mechanisms will generate, internationally as well as nationally, whatever increase in real resources is desired sufficiently for the desire to be expressed by a rise in price. Today there is enough surplus food on offer to support all those developed populations which can afford to buy it – not all those which need it. But their ability to buy it depends on their competitive power in world markets, which itself calls in question the ability of the non-competitive to sustain themselves. And the surplus is on offer only because it is surplus and only so long as it is surplus. No country will long sell food when it is hungry.

It is therefore of the greatest significance that the huge grain reserves accumulated in the past decade have already almost melted away and that the number of countries, developed or undeveloped, which are net food exporters has dwindled to a tiny minority.

71

The plight of countries which are undeveloped but overpopulated may be a little less grave since their very lack of development suggests that food supplies may be more readily increased. The 'green revolution' has indeed increased Indian yields over the past years to a notable extent. It depends on fertilisers which require energy and which may depend directly or indirectly on imports; it may have other self-limiting factors which have not yet disclosed themselves. It is nonetheless a notable pointer, not least because its value does not greatly depend on devising new patterns of distribution.

Such countries have also open to them a resource which the West has forgotten, though we may soon have to recall it. In a country where men are plentiful and food is short, what matters is yield per acre rather than yield per man. The Western habit of prizing increased productivity *per man*, even when it is offset by the employment of fewer men, makes sense only when the men thus freed can be otherwise usefully and acceptably employed. This assumption does not hold today for the homeless, workless crowds in Calcutta or for the unemployed of any Western country. It is giving way to the paradox of a Western world in which men are the only abundant resource, but nonetheless the only resource which is too expensive to be fully used. This in turn reflects the process which has already reduced most skilled men to machine minders and which is in process of reducing them still further to the status of consumers, supported only on condition that their rising demands keep the automata fully employed. This nonsense at all events may be expected soon to crumble before the logic of bitter experience.

I have heard of a case, though I have not yet been able to verify it, in which the agricultural yield of 100 acres of farmland was actually increased by using the land for a housing development. A thousand lovingly cultivated gardens more than offset the area lost to roads and buildings, and the supposed advantage of more mechanical power. The product made no visible addition to GNP because it was eaten without the prior formality of being sold and thus assigned a money value. But it was no less nourishing on that account.

There remain the happiest of my four classes, the countries still undeveloped, yet producing with their existing technology all they need to sustain their current rate of population growth. They have, at least in theory, wider options in policy and more time in which to bring policy to fruition. Anyone to be born in 1974, if he could choose his place of birth, would surely choose to be born in such a country.

No such choice is open to us. We have to cope with the problems which history and geography have dealt us, each in our own land, but with due regard for those of others, and for planetary limitations. These problems as I have so far reviewed them include the problems of urban regulation – the governing of huge urban aggregates of people, and the design of the urban environment and its social and political institutions. They include problems of national distribution, both of people over available areas and of resources to people who need them. Both these are problems which market machinery failed to solve acceptably even when the conditions of a free market were far less remote than they are now. Our problems also include immigration policy and for some countries, emigration policy too. They include the even more intractable problems of international distribution of resources, whether knowledge, capital, physical resources or consumer goods and whether by unrequited gift, by political bargain or through the medium of trade. And above all in urgency they include the problem of increasing food production, especially within those countries, developed or undeveloped, which by my definition are already overpopulated. In this context we have also to remember the one great resource which is at present little developed and largely unappropriated, though it is already over-exploited and more than a little polluted – the oceans which cover more than half the surface of the planet.

## Medical science – a new factor

Only against this background can we assess the second and third of those three changes which, as I mentioned earlier, have given a new dimension to a problem as old as man. The first I have already discussed. It is imbalance of food and population, both globally and within many individual countries, on a planet which lacks adequate means to redistribute even what food it has and which is divided by rising barriers against the redistribution of populations. The other two are double-edged gifts of medical science. One is the knowledge needed to prolong life and especially to abate infant mortality – so long of course as food is available. The other is the knowledge needed to control conception.

The first of these poses problems which are still unacknowledged. It is a fact that in many countries today medical science is fostering a growth rate of population which the sciences of food production have no present prospect of sustaining from internal sources or perhaps from any source. Only extremists at present would allow children to die of disease in infancy, in order to save them from dying of starvation later. But a country budgeting limited resources between food production and preventive medicine may well give a larger share to the first, when faced with present famine. Except at that level, today's greater knowledge of how to reduce the ratio of deaths to births is likely to affect policy only in so far as it adds emphasis to medicine's other gift, the power to control conception.

To an extent greater than ever before, individuals now have the power to dissociate conception from sexual intercourse. Next to the control of death – which happily is not yet with us – this is probably the most radical change in the human condition that has ever happened. Its effects seem to me to be highly unpredictable. It is likely to reduce the birth rate; but it might also reduce the death rate. In so far as it reduces populations, it will certainly work differentially, reducing some more than others, perhaps reducing some classes more than others within a single population. It will

73

not necessarily reduce average family size; it might instead multiply an at present unnoticed category, the non-celibate but non-breeding pairs who will leave to the philoprogenitives the task of sustaining the population. It may result in the unwilled extinction of populations. How far will it be within the control of public policy? To Westerners the decision on family size may seem an even more inalienable personal 'liberty' than the right to choose one's employment. Yet even in the West it raises questions of high policy which no makers of policy can afford to ignore.

Whenever some aspect of our lives becomes modifiable by human action, it becomes possible to argue that it ought to be other than it is. Responsibility for its results is attributed, often wrongly but nonetheless irresistibly, to some human agency. The event has passed from the category 'Act of God' to the category 'Act of Man'. The responsibility for having children has long occupied a middle place, an act of man indeed, but a by-product of a biological urge so natural and so powerful that it has been regarded as only marginally within control. Many welcome the fact that parenthood should become more optional and its responsibilities correspondingly more willed. Whether welcome or not, this increase in individual responsibility cannot fail to involve an increase in *collective* responsibility in at least three major fields.

However great or small its powers of control, every society has an intense interest in the size and composition of its population and in the rate of any changes therein. Until recently an increase, especially in competent males, was deemed to be a national asset. From time immemorial men's work has made families and nations rich and strong, whilst younger generations have been the only support of the old. Today attention focuses on stability and on the level at which stability should be sought. There are societies today where the population so far exceeds indigenous food supplies that a rational judgement may aspire to stability at a lower level, even though at present they are able to sustain a much larger population through international trade. There are countries so manifestly underpopulated that a prudent population policy might well aim at increasing numbers before external pressures force a more abrupt and less well-planned incursion. Whatever the situation, it raises two inescapable questions – '*What shall we deem to be the optimum limits of our population?*' and '*What should we regard as the acceptable limits in its rate of change?*'. These questions need to be asked. For the issues affect everyone and their public discussion is the best way to reach some consensus and thus to generate standards to which individuals may in turn respond. No government can escape responsibility for taking a line in this debate.

Its most inescapable choice is in deciding whether and if so to whom and on what terms contraceptive advice and resources should be made available and in what circumstances abortion should be legal. Advocates of family planning have campaigned in both fields, not only on account of exploding populations. Many governments have developed national programmes or changed legislation accordingly. The effects of these vary from the apparently unsuccessful, as in India, to what appears to be the stunning success of China, two countries which between them account for more than half the population of the world. Although it is far too early to assume that India cannot do what China is doing, the present contrast provokes some fruitful reflections. In China it appears that extra-marital pregnancy is exceedingly rare and extra-marital births virtually unknown, whilst the problem of stabilising the population seems to have been solved.

These programmes are themselves contributions to the dialogue which will clarify and change public attitudes and thus help to make population policy. They may and should be backed by advocacy of whatever governments see as the national interest – and also of the international interest, where national governments dare to invoke this criterion.

## Policies for population mobility

Governments cannot fail to contribute further to the debate by the assumptions on which they base other policies, notably those of immigration, emigration and food production. It is hard to think of any area of policy which is not affected by these assumptions. The most dramatic Western example is probably Canada. Here, the current size of the population and its birth rate, coupled with its very high ratio of resources to population makes immigration a key variable. The net increase of population by immigration, over a range between 75 000 and 500 000 per annum – a range not beyond the conceivable scope of immigration policy – would produce results ranging from stability at the present level to escalation at a probably prohibitive rate.

The least controversial but not least relevant contribution of public authority is to monitor change and supply information. Any government today can, if it wishes, collect and analyse information about its population on a scale undreamed even a decade or so ago. Even though the blessings of the computer may be less and more mixed than its more passionate addicts proclaim, it has revolutionary and, I think, beneficent power in classifying, aggregating and presenting data. Population trends, including the projected effects of changes which have already occurred, are among the more reliable of the materials on which it can work. And the wider the services which governments provide, the more they need such information. Changes in the work force, in numbers of schoolchildren and old age pensioners need to be foreseen, even a decade ahead, if the services which deal with them are to be adapted to meet them. It seems, for example, an absurd anachronism that governments so placed should still depend on a decennial census.

It seems to me therefore to be a pathological, if natural, sign of the times, that the so-called free world should be so reluctant to allow its governments to collect the information with which to guide its freedom. Our freedom in the last analysis is only freedom to choose our commitments. And our commitments are becoming increasingly collective, none more so than our commitment to stabilised populations.

## Urgent actions for the long term

Finally one sombre thought should I think be stressed. Although population changes may be sudden and dramatic, the effect of population *policy* can only be gradual and long term. It is concerned with the unborn. During the rest of this century the problems of the living – and the dying – will I believe be more revolutionary and worldwide than ever before in human history. It seems probable to me that within ten years food rationing will be needed in most, or even all of the countries, however developed, which are not self-sufficient in food and that it would be needed in every country, if starvation in the least self-sufficient is to be abated even to the extent that policy permits. I can also envisage a vast switch from fodder grains to food grains to avoid the huge waste of biosynthesis involved by the luxury of being so carnivorous as Western men today. All such changes imply a revolution in expectations, in institutions and in methods of distribution. But these affect us, in the context of population *policy*, only in one respect. We can be sure, as I believe, that within a decade it will no longer be necessary to argue the case for stable populations. The age-old stabilisers of pestilence and famine, if not also war, will be too manifest for anyone to ignore. It is the more important that those who are dedicated to solving the problem of population control should be neither dismayed nor diverted from their task but should on the contrary exploit to the full the more favourable climate in which to pursue it.

Whatever happens to those alive today, our goal is that the unborn shall inherit an earth in which they have at least the possibility of continuing the great adventure of human social and individual life. One of the conditions of such an earth is that its human populations shall have such stability of size and composition as makes it possible for them to live in balance with each other and with their physical home and to look forward to progress along the dimension of a redefined humanity.

Such stability is only one of the conditions which would make that adventure possible. Even if achieved, it does not guarantee that the adventure will succeed. It is nonetheless a noble aspiration and a difficult task – noble and difficult enough to claim the allegiance of dedicated men and women not only in the Population Year of 1974, but for many years to come.

But its implications extend far beyond the field of family planning and they fall with wholly different emphases on countries in different sectors of the four-celled matrix in which, earlier in this article, I arranged the nations of the world. The relative importance of these divisions is itself changing; *differences between high and low 'development' are already, in my view, far less important than differences between a high and a low ratio of resources (especially food) to population.* And over all these broods the problem of distribution and its enigmatic relation to politics. The mind reflecting on this huge problem should not ignore the singular fact that, as it ranges over the enormous spectrum of threat and of distress conjured up by 'the population problem', its few foci of comfort should include both Canada and the People's Republic of China.

# 5

# The weakness of Western culture*

The author describes five characteristics of Western culture which, he argues, have marked the last 200 years. The one which most concerns him is the rise of the autonomous individual as a dominant and acceptable concept, a concept which, he argues, is radically opposed to the concept of the responsible person as this had been understood through several preceding centuries in the West. The future of Western civilization and in particular of Britain – with which he is especially concerned – depends, he argues, on achieving a new ideal of personal responsibility which will subsume both innovators and conservators.

I believe that about 200 years ago British culture entered on a new phase which is abruptly ending now. In this article I examine what seem to me to be the five most salient characteristics of that culture and enquire where they have left us, why they are losing our confidence, and what alternatives are likely to arise from their collapse which we should try to foster with whatever initiative we may have.

The five aspects which I shall examine are the market economy, the utilitarian political philosophy, the narrowing of science as a concept, the explosive interaction of science and technology, and above all the concept of the autonomous individual, as distinct from the responsible person who, I shall argue, was the dominant Western ideal until that time.

This theme demands a book rather than an article.[1] I shall have to be summary, though not, I hope, superficial; I shall invite criticism from many who know this period of history better than I. What I should not need to do is to justify the relevance of such a study to any attempt to forecast or to design Britain's immediate future.

## The impact of culture

Our culture has made the world we live in. It also determines the ways in which we apprehend and value that world and the range of actions which we perceive as open to us, including actions designed to change the culture. It affects both our milieu and ourselves. It is both a major determinant in our field of action and a major variable not wholly beyond our control. It should focus the attention both of forecasters and of planners.

I use the word culture in an anthropological sense, more widely perhaps

* From *Futures*, December 1977.

than all anthropologists would use it. No one can doubt that in this sense we have a culture as distinct as that of any primitive tribe. We have, for example, characteristic ways of making things and of organising action, and a set of still dominant though increasingly questioned norms defining the ways which are appropriate, or even thinkable, in given contexts. These might be other than they are. They are different elsewhere. They were different here not long ago. They are changing now.

Our current ways of making, for example, are not only technological but characterised by technology of a particular kind – high energy, high rate of change, high waste. Some foresee a changed technological pattern, imposed partly by the increasing cost and scarcity of materials and partly by changing cultural patterns of what is desirable (and even accept-able), no less than through a more realistic understanding of what is possible.

We have a culture of distribution which determines who gets what and which also includes our ideas of who should get what. It has three inter-locked constituents – the private household, the market, and what Daniel Bell recently called the Public Household.[2] The relations between the three are changing rapidly, largely through the growth of the Public Household, which is beginning to disclose both its limitations and its demands on its beneficiaries.

We have a regulative culture defining our ways of making rules, settling disputes and sanctioning the distribution of wealth, power, and function. It has a long history of which we used to be proud and should still be proud, though it is at the moment in some confusion and disrepute.

We have a social culture, determining what we should expect of each other and of ourselves in different contexts and what self-expectations we can confidently attribute to others. This is of immense importance, since it is the basis of that net of self-expectations and mutual expectations which we need if we are to interact confidently with each other. We also have an institutional culture, defining what we can expect and what we should be able to expect of those organisations which transcend the interpersonal scale and which are so characteristic of our age and society; and defining, equally, what we accept as their legitimate expectations of us. This field also is today in a state of unusual uncertainty and disturbance.

These are examples only of the cultural web which supports our life, as it supports the life of any aboriginal tribe. It is far less stable. This may be due to the fact that we have outgrown our biological capacity for ordering our social life, even to the minimal extent which any social species needs to do if it is to survive. Alternatively, it may mark one of those phases of cultural confusion which always intervene between the decay of one cul-tural phase and the emergence of another.

In any case it is manifestly essential to planners and to forecasters to understand so far as they can the role of culture in the regulation of society and especially the process of cultural change.

This is an historical study. That, I think, is why it is so notably neglected in our time – especially in governments and among managers, where it is surely needed most. The reason, I believe, is that they aspire to be 'scientific'; and human history is not regarded as a science. So before examining the particular period which concerns me, I feel it necessary to say *something* about the nature of historical knowledge, at least enough to make clear my own assumptions about it.

## The historical process

Human history is clearly a field in which knowledge (*scientia*) and even understanding may be sought. But the historian is not today accorded the title of scientist. He *is* expected to be as rigorous as any scientist in verifying his facts and in arguing from his hypotheses; but his hypotheses have not yet generated that degree of common acceptance to which contemporary philosophers of science have reduced scientific 'truth', even in the natural sciences. On the contrary the historical process is an ideological battle ground.

Yet we know a lot about human history and we use this knowledge whenever we try to forecast or control its future course. I will try in this article to suggest how greatly the forecasting and planning of human affairs is influenced by our knowledge of history and our view of the historical process – and hence our understanding of the present, and our appreciation of possible futures.

### History and the scientific method

The historian fails to qualify as a scientist, at present, for three main reasons. First his subject matter is historical and history is commonly regarded today as a course of irreversible change. Science likes repeatable observations of unchanging and independent variables. But observations of a process of irreversible change are by their nature not repeatable.

Some studies of historical processes are none the less regarded as sciences. Geology is largely historical. So is evolutionary biology. So is ecology. But these are distinguished from human history by a feature still not universally acknowledged. Human history is mediated by culture; and cultures develop under their own partly autonomous laws. Human history is thus doubly historical.

T. H. Huxley, Darwin's champion, was as much at odds with the 'social Darwinists' of his day as he was with those who defended the doctrine of special creation.[3] He insisted with passion that social evolution is a process different in kind from biological evolution and indeed basically opposed to it. Human history, he asserted, is the record of man's effort to create 'in opposition to the State of Nature the State of Art of an organised polity, capable of maintaining and constantly improving itself'. What he called the ethical process is, he insisted, as different from the cosmic process as the process of making and maintaining a garden is different from the process which produced the Amazon jungle. A new selector had set himself up to create form according to new criteria of his own creation.

These are the criteria which give the distinctive character to what anthropologists call a society's culture. Each has its own foci of concern, its own ideas of what those concerns should be, its own ways of interpreting its world, its own repertory of actions and its own standards of what actions are appropriate, required, or even conceivable, in particular circumstances. These together constitute a system of shared assumptions and expectations, which give each society whatever coherence it may have. They are not readily changed, even when they prove inadequate with respect to changes arising either within the society or in its milieu.

The third incorrigibly 'unscientific' feature of human history is that its individual members and the culture and cultural differences which they express are powerful agents in the historical process itself. Marx's theory of history made a difference to human history. Thus the making of historical hypotheses affects the future course of the process which they seek to explain; such hypotheses cannot even in theory be judged simply as true or false.

None the less, as I have already observed, we know a lot about human history. We are part of it. In particular we know a lot about its dialectic nature.

## The dialectic and cultural change

Hegel and Marx have given the words 'dialectical nature' so definite a meaning that I need to free them from some connotations which, whether true or not, are not necessary for my purpose. I do not assume that human history is moving towards a more stable state (though I hope it is). I do not assume that a particular cultural state is bound to generate only one antithesis or that the conflict between the two has only one possible resultant synthesis. Nor do I assume that dialectical change has the regularity of natural law.

What I wish to insist on is simply this. When a society's culture is felt to be inept or inadequate by a significant part of its members, they press for its revision. They disregard its injunctions so far as they dare. They argue its inadequacy or ineptitude. They thus raise to the level of conscious debate what was before a tacit and uncriticised assumption.

Such, for example, was the assumption, virtually unchallenged in England a century ago, that women should not vote.

The target of the reformer or revolutionary may be as limited and as positive as the electoral franchise for women. It may be as unlimited and as negative as the anarchist's assault on government as such. It is usually polarised by specific negative targets. The agent of change does not doubt that things would be better if the element criticised were purged. He can, however, seldom predict with any certainty what else will follow from the change. And even if he is aware that the desired benefit will have its costs, he is more likely to be moved by the desire to be rid of what he knows he hates than to be deterred by fears of ancillary results which may or may not follow.

The culture of a society, however, is a closely associated web of self-expectations and mutual expectations, based on assumptions which are often more closely related than is apparent. To extend the franchise to women, for example, changes the status of women in society and in the home, and invites further enfranchisements. The articulation of protest, even of question, awakens debate. Debate mobilises defenders of the status quo, but also mobilises criticism and alerts the unaware. If the movement is premature, it will be crushed and the culture will affirm the challenged view with even greater rigour, and will be less tolerant than before of criticism in that area. Yet even so the status quo will not have been fully restored. A heresy will have been defined and its existence, however ostracised, will make a difference.

If on the other hand the movement is timely, it will succeed. The culture will assimilate the demand: women will be enfranchised, trade unions will be legitimised, or whatever may be the issue. This, however, is the beginning, not the end of the process. The new concern has wider implications. The new perceptions comprise an ampler view. The change develops a dynamism of its own, supported by its own logic. And every new success leaves the new culture stronger and the old culture weaker.

In time the heresy becomes the faith; assumptions once daring are taken for granted. A new culture has become dominant. The seeds of its decay may be already present, among those whom it least benefits and among those who see most clearly its new inherent dangers. These seeds will not germinate until events outside or within the system sap its self-confidence or challenge its authority. That day will come through changes either in the milieu or in the culture itself. And these changes may well be generated by the culture itself, and by its successes as well as its failures and defects. Then the dialectical process will enter on another round. Meantime the hope for individuals within a culture is that their culture should last long enough to develop its full potential; the proper goal of their activity should be that it generates a worthy successor with the least disturbance.

This at least is what I regard as the optimal course for the dialectical process open to us today. It is not the only possibility. History records three alternatives: changelessness, prolonged instability, and dissolution.

For more than 99% of its existence on earth, our species has subsisted in loose associations of families, usually linked by both actual and mythical kinship. Men, like their hominid predecessors, are social animals. There have always been more mouths to feed than hands to gather and prepare food. The smallest society capable of indefinite survival, even in theory, is one large enough to ensure its own reproduction. And until very recently its maximum size was restricted to the population that could be supported by the territory over which it could rove in a day.

## Change and stability

Many such societies still persist. When untouched by 'development' they are extraordinarily stable. Their technology is not powerful enough to affect their milieu permanently and critically. The life experience of each member is so similar to that of the others that common culture is easily sustained. Given some means to stabilise its population, and sufficient freedom from attack by other human groups, such societies can remain stable for millennia. And although war and population growth have some-times been destabilising factors, they have had less effect than we might imagine today.

At the other extreme, violent changes in culture or in conditions of life or both have often resulted in the extinction of a human society. The surviving aboriginal cultures which have been most affected by Western culture, such as the Eskimo and the prairie Indian, testify more to what has been *lost* than to what has been preserved.

Between the two are many examples of prolonged instability. Most apparent is the political instability of many countries which have gained their independence since the end of the 18th century. Political instability does not of course attest the existence of a cultural vacuum. But it does attest cultural traits inadequate for or even antipathetic to any form of government sufficient to the needs of the society concerned.

According to this summary picture, human societies have always been characterised and regulated by specific cultures; but rapid cultural change is a new phenomenon. So far as we know, it was only in the third or fourth millennium BC, and in a few favoured river valleys, that particular human populations escaped from their previous limitations of size and density; there they began to accumulate wealth, and to display marked disparities amongst their members in the distribution of wealth, power, and function. The resultant civilisations were organised around a governing class, and cultural imperatives expanded to support and enforce the more complex set of mutual relations on which such systems depended for their continu-ance.

The new empires were not so stable as the old tribes, but they endured for centuries; and struggles for power, within the small groups qualified to struggle, often left the main cultural structure unchanged. Few questioned that societal order was any less 'given' than natural order. The ideas that it might develop over time or might be redesigned by human will and power were seldom entertained, and even more rarely acted on. They first erupted as enduring forces only in Western Europe about 200 years ago, following the immense cultural change which is commonly – though perhaps euphe-mistically – called The Enlightenment.

## The character of the last cultural phase

No cultural change can be precisely dated. It is, for example, often said that 'modern man' was born in 'the Renaissance', and there is a sense in which that is true. But the changes with which I am concerned became dominant later. They can even be given a 'precise', though symbolic date, in 1776. For in that year Adam Smith published *The Wealth of Nations*, Jeremy Bentham published his *Fragment on Government* and Britain's American colonies signed the Declaration of Independence.[4] It was about this time also that the word 'science' first began to be used in its present restricted sense, as distinct from knowledge and fields of knowledge which once shared the name *scientia*, but which were now relegated to an area of less authority. (The change is reflected in the wording of the Declaration of Independence itself.[5]) It was a time when the marriage of science and technology was first confidently expected to produce miracles of material abundance. It was a time when the autonomous individual emerged as the paradigm of modern man, economic, political, scientific and technological.

I can trace only briefly these five interlocked changes, their similarities, their mutual inconsistencies, and their current state.

## The market economy

It was a noble and liberating concept that the accumulation of wealth by nations was not a zero-sum game but a cooperative enterprise, indefinitely expansible. Its more visible conditions were freedom of exchange in goods, services, labour, capital, land and foreign exchange, and the indefinite division of labour. Its less visible conditions were political.

For the market economy could flourish only in highly artificial political conditions. It demanded the sanctity of contract, supported by cultural as well as legal sanctions, as well as freedom of contract for all. It demanded the abolition of all constraints other than those imposed by the market and the acceptance of all those which the market imposed. It was far from the 'state of nature' with which social Darwinists in the mid 19th century would compare it. T. H. Huxley was right in comparing it with a garden rather than a jungle.

But a garden implies a gardener and Huxley would have been the last to attribute this function to a philosopher king or a benevolent despot. The human subjects in the garden must do their own gardening, collectively and individually. It was an essential part of the economic faith that a free market would be self-regulating, so that the political load implicit in 'collective gardening' would be limited. But it could not disappear, as Adam Smith clearly perceived. It was in fact to be hugely magnified. And its growth was served by the utilitarian philosophy which emerged at the same time.

## Utilitarianism

This too was a noble and liberating dream. It propounded a new criterion for government. The government of a country was to be judged not by the power or wealth of the state, still less of its rulers, but by the happiness of its people – the greatest happiness of the greatest number.

This was a revolutionary change in a world where Bourbons still ruled France and where London supplied subjects for the drawings of Hogarth. Moreover it was accompanied by an equally revolutionary faith in the power of legislation to design human order. This was as apt to a socialist or communist society as to one dominated by the market. It was at first constrained by the economic faith that inhibited interference with market economies, but it was bound to grow in scope and vigour as the market disclosed its inability to generate the demand for collective goods and services or to convince the 'greatest number' – who were unorganised, unskilled casual labourers – that it provided their greatest happiness.

The aspiration to extend and disseminate knowledge was also noble and liberating. Diderot and his colleagues, preparing the great Encyclopaedia – which was to comprehend and make available to all this expanding body of knowledge – had no doubt that they were liberating the many from one of their greatest enslavements: ignorance. And the achievements of natural science had awakened expectations of enlightenment in the human field which experience had not yet curtailed. Condorcet declared, as he waited for the guillotine, his faith that a day would come when the sun would rise on an earth of none but free men, with no master save reason; and he testified thereby his faith that men free from tyranny, superstition, and ignorance, would need no master save 'reason' to discern where their common interest lay.

Yet the growth of knowledge based on the natural sciences was to have a restricting and distorting effect both on the culture's concept of knowledge and on its idea of the human understanding.

## The concept of science

In mediaeval universities, *scientiae* covered all fields in which knowledge could be sought and all accepted knowledge accumulated in those fields. Rhetoric, no less than astronomy, was *scientia*. Yet the degree accorded to those who satisfied their examiners in these and the other required subjects was the degree of Master of Arts. For art also was an extended term, covering all skills which could be systematically acquired. There was an Art and Mystery of Bricklaying. Moreover the two terms overlapped. For no one had yet forgotten that knowing is a skilled activity, a meaning we preserve today only when we use the verb 'apprehending'. Both science and art comprised process as well as product; skill in apprehending and in making as well as an accumulation both of artifacts (knowledge and institutions as well as works of art) and of standards of excellence in knowing and doing and making.

The narrowing of 'science' to cover only knowledge approved as sufficiently validated by scientific method, downgraded – and even concealed from consciousness – the vast body of assumption and belief on which we are accustomed to act, whether based on personal experience or on conventional wisdom, a treasure which 'science' can criticise and refine but can never replace. It did even more than this. It exalted analysis to such a level as to dwarf or even conceal the separate mental function of synthesis.

Space does not allow me to develop here the argument that synthesis is more than analysis, judgement more than calculation, recognition more than identification, and empathy more than sympathy. But I welcome the recent findings of brain science to support the common experience that we have two 'styles of cognition' the one sensitive to causal, the other to contextual significance.[6] I have no doubt that the cultural phase – which is now closing – restricted our concept of the human reason by identifying it with the rational, and ignoring the intuitive function, and thus failing to develop an epistemology which we badly need, and which is within our reach – if we can overcome our cultural inhibitions.

## The interaction of science and technology

The fourth of the characteristics which I have chosen to examine is the marriage of science and technology. Throughout almost the whole of human history, technology has progressed with an uncanny ignorance of the scientific principles which were guiding it. Japanese swordsmiths, for example, were by the 13th century making steel of a quality never yet made in the West and describable, even in theory, only by the use of concepts developed in the 20th century. Their mastery lay in their complete control of the disposition of carbon in the sword blade they were making – a control vital to the forging of a weapon which needs an edge hard enough to be highly sharpened, a blade soft enough not to shatter, and a back rib stiff enough to prevent it from bending. Yet the Japanese swordsmith had no word for carbon and no concept of it. Refinements like this are to be found elsewhere in early technology. They are not convincingly attributed to trial and error. The metallurgist who told me this example, the fruit of his own researches, spoke of craftsmen communing with their material in language which I should have expected from a Zen Buddhist, rather than from a Professor of metallurgy (which he in fact was).

The craftsman's intuition would continue to keep ahead of scientific guidance in many instances even into the 20th century. But already at the end of the 18th century, prophets of material achievement were building extravagant pictures of the abundance which the approaching partnership between science and technology would create.[7] An unbiased observer today would probably regard technology as the senior partner.

## Common features of the last cultural phase

There are similarities in these four pictures. All consciously envisage a self-regulating system, dependent on individual judgement and powered by individual self-interest; but the emphasis differs significantly in the four cases.

In the economic system it was unquestioned that the blanket maker need not, perhaps *should* not, be animated by the wish to keep his fellows warm. Yet he would prosper and even survive only if he was judged, by buyers as indifferent to his interests as he was supposed to be to theirs, to do so better than his competitors.

In the political system it was less clear why the majority should agree on their common interest (still less why they should acknowledge the claims of posterity) or even why a dissident minority should accept the decisions of a majority, even though the majority be the greatest number. Philosophers differed in their views of human sociality, though they were almost unanimous in ignoring the facts of human acculturability. But so long as societies were organised by the few for the few, it was reasonable enough for reformers to expect improvements when they were organised by the many for the many. And the market place supplied analogies, imperfect but persuasive, to suggest that political consensus was at the worst a product of bargaining and 'trade-off'.[8]

The scientific community claimed, and was accorded, even greater individual autonomy in deciding where each should pursue his enquiries. Knowledge would grow best not by planned concentration on areas of greatest ignorance or greatest importance, but on those areas which individual scientists felt moved to explore. Technology would prosper similarly by inventors following their own bent, rather than by concentrating on those problems which most needed to be solved. Economic man, political man, scientific man and technological man were alike individuals, whose personal motivations and valuations were their own affair. The common good could prosper without common concern. It would prosper *best* without common concern.

## Freedom and the enfranchised individual

The dominant concepts were individual enfranchisement and automatic control. The free entrepreneur was subject to the automatic control of moneyed consumers expressed through the market. The free politician was subject to the automatic control of voters expressed through the ballot box. The free scientist was subject to the automatic control of his peers, expressed through their power to accord or withhold positions, facilities and reputation. The free technologist was subject to the automatic control of the markets in which he sold his skill and his products. And all these fields, it seemed, were not only self-regulating but also self-exciting.

It is well known today, though not well recognised, that no element in any system can develop linearly and indefinitely. For it is bound to change the system of which it is part and to breed its own limitations or reversal in one way or another. These insights were hidden in a world still dazzled by the Enlightenment. And indeed there was time for a great deal of linear development in all these fields before the corresponding limitations began to be felt.

The economic system, for example, responded only to those with buying power. It was not geared to distribute widely the monetary enfranchisement on which it depended. Indeed by defining human labour as a commodity to be bought as cheaply as possible, it ensured extreme disparity of distribution even in a society of increasing productivity.

Though the potentially successful minority might need no more than equality of opportunity, the 'greatest number' were bound in time to demand an equality of enjoyment which could be provided only by increasing intervention of the political will. And this intervention was bound to increase as the political franchise widened – which it was bound to in a political system set to respond only to the politically enfranchised voter. Universal suffrage was implicit in a political system which consciously applied to government the utilitarian criterion of 'the greatest happiness of the greatest number'. Yet it was far from the intention, or even the consciousness, of the Parliament which passed the Reform Act of 1832.

Nor did these developments satisfy the aspirations which they generated. Even a government elected by universal suffrage might be less responsive to its electorate than to the pressure groups which its electorate generated.

Concentrations of wealth and power, in corporations, gave to a few the control of vast wealth and major decisions, irrespective of their personal fortunes. The claim for equality of enjoyment – or at least for the progressive mitigation of misery – could not be met by the public sector without interventions inconsistent with the maintenance of a purely market economy.

Even to supplement the market by public provision of those collective services which few or none could provide for themselves (roads, police, education) involved the interaction of the public and the private sector in a way radically different from anything imagined by classical economists. The result was the mixed economy. Certainly, their structure – or rather, growth – does indeed deliver benefits now beyond most dreams of the 18th century; but it satisfies few of its operators or its beneficiaries, largely because it has bred extravagant and conflicting expectations far beyond its power – or any power – to satisfy.

Similarly the growth of science has generated its own constraints. As research has become more expensive and has involved larger cooperative teams, its paymasters, whether in the public or the private sector, have been forced to choose how to distribute their support. This has been intensified by the need to direct technological enquiry to the solving of problems, such as energy shortage, posed by limitations generated by its own past success.

## The individual in the body corporate

The most important change of the period has been the emergence of the corporate citizen – notably, the business corporation, the trade union, and the public agency. Until the middle of the 19th century the right of private citizens to form corporations of indefinite life, especially profit-making corporations, was a jealously guarded privilege, allowed only rarely by special Act of Parliament or by the granting of a Royal Charter.

The decision to extend this right to any citizen for any lawful purpose was a decision of stunning importance. It did what it was intended to do – to facilitate the concentration, in the control of entrepreneurs, of aggregations of capital far exceeding their own fortunes. But its unintended effects were even greater. It created a means to create corporate entities and to concentrate their control to an extent never dreamed before.

Even more novel and radical was the series of decisions which legitimised that different and even more privileged entity, the trade union, authorised to use its power of collectively withholding labour in the furtherance of an industrial dispute, *but not for political purposes*. In the culture of mid 19th century Britain, it did not occur to any of the minds concerned that there might ever be any difficulty in distinguishing between the two. The difference was potent enough to affect the resolution of the general strike of 1926. Where is it now?

The reversals bred by the cultural phase which became dominant two centuries ago throw light on the historical process and help us to recognise the cultural dynamics of the present and the cultural needs of the future.

The age of the individual has bred collectivities on a scale never dreamed before. The age which exalted individual independence has produced a society of which the constituents are interdependent to an unparalleled degree. In consequence a society dedicated to majority rule has become subject to domination by ever smaller minorities.

The growth of the private sector has bred growth, not a withering in the public sector, and an intimate interdependence between the two. The growth of science has led to a world ever less predictable. The growth of technology has led to a world ever less manageable. The age of progress has bred an overwhelming concern for stability. The age which confidently expected to transcend nationalism by a Great Commercial Republic has become burningly aware of the difference between the internal relations of each sovereign state and its external relations – and the unique position of each. And no Western state has been so sharply confronted with this difference as Britain.

T. H. Huxley, in a lecture published in 1895, observed that life for all Britons had become precarious.[9] For Britain had grown beyond its subsistence base and could survive only so long as it preserved two conditions. One was the ability to buy its food by outselling its technological competitors in world markets; the other was the preservation of its social coherence. He wrote at a time when both conditions seemed well assured. He was not an economist, but his biological insights gave him an understanding which few share 80 years later – when both conditions are in manifest and grave danger. The proud and confident culture which achieved so much, for good and ill, in the two centuries since 1776, is indeed in a trough of dialectical confusion.

## The next cultural phase

None of these changes should surprise us. None should suggest to us that the last cultural phase was futile or without effect, for good as well as ill. None should be regarded simply as a reversal. For although in each particular, what has emerged negates the cultural aspiration which inspired it, none will restore any previous state, and each will leave its mark on the cultural pattern which will replace it. Nor could any of them have done so without the experience which the preceding culture brought.

It remains to ask what the new cultural pattern will be and how we should shape it – so far as we have any initiative to do so.

It is easy to state the characteristics of the culture which will be needed to support Britain in its next phase. Some are common to all the cultures of the West. Some are particularly relevant to Britain, exposed at last for all to see to the hazards which Huxley described 80 years ago.

Professor Lynton Caldwell, in a paper called *Ideas and Counter Ideas* published in 1972, summarises the cultural changes needed by Western societies generally, in the changed conditions created by two centuries of 'progress'.[10] The emphasis on popular rights needs to shift towards social responsibilities, by which alone such rights can be created and maintained, 'Autonomous egoism' should give place to a sense of organic interdependence. Progressive expansion should make way for an ideal of self-sustaining growth. Economic imperatives should give way to ecological imperatives. Technological imperatives should be subordinated to judgements of political need. External constraints which invite efforts to overcome them should give way to self-imposed restraints, supported by a sense of personal commitment to accept them.

These are indeed changes which would be needed to make viable the world which the last cultural phase has created. They are cultural changes, and the chief resistances to accepting them or even conceiving them as possible are cultural attitudes generated in the past, often the recent past. All these attitudes have been known in other cultures: most have been known even in the earlier stages of our own.

### The autonomous individual and personal responsibility

I shall concentrate on only one change – though this subsumes most of the others – the transformation of what Caldwell calls 'autonomous egoism'. I have already singled out 'individualism' as the most important and characteristic feature of the last phase of our culture, and I have distinguished the autonomous individual from the responsible person who, I have suggested, was the ideal of Western culture prior to its last and now closing phase. This distinction I will now emphasise and seek to justify.

Western culture and both its parent traditions – the Judaeo-Christian and the Graeco-Roman – emphasised the responsibility of the human person, and defined this as loyalty to inner standards which might conflict with the standards of society – though they might equally reflect them and use them to condemn the actual practice of others, and even of the supreme authority itself. The great Jewish prophets of the pre-exilic period criticised their rulers with a freedom which was exceedingly rare in the world of 25 centuries ago and which is becoming no less rare today. But the standards to which they appealed were universally accepted in their tribe, which was why their freedom was so unconstrained.

Only a little later, Greek tragedians were articulating the essentially tragic nature of the human predicament; and one element of this was the collision of inconsistent moral responsibilities. Antigone chooses disobedience to the secular power – and its inevitable consequence, death – rather than ignore the moral responsibility to give her brother due burial. Her sister Ismene chooses otherwise. Perhaps she lacks the independence of spirit and of judgement which steeled Antigone to violate the civil law. But in choosing she, no less than her sister, took a responsible, personal moral decision.

Luther, when he nailed his protest to his church door, expressed not an arbitrary decision but an inner judgement, too strong to be ignored. So did the host of 'protestants' (and later of Catholics) who maintained their faith in the face of social opinion strongly directed to persuading them to conform, and indeed in the face of extreme persecution.

Through more than 20 centuries of Western culture, the 'non-conformist' has been admired, often grudgingly, even by those to whom his opinions were anathema. He exemplified the responsible person, true to his own standards, even when these ran counter to standards which were deeply ingrained and passionately held in the culture of which he was part.

These standards, however, were not arbitrary creations of his own, still less biological urges which he alone was having the courage to express. They demanded respect simply because they claimed a 'higher' authenticity than the authority of Church or State. It was this which made their exponents respected as well as feared.

It is this which distinguishes the responsible person from the autonomous individual.

Literally, an autonomous person is one who makes his own rules and sets his own standards. He is at the opposite pole from the responsible person. Luther said of his momentous action that 'he could do no other'. We do not therefore regard him as enslaved or unfree any more than we regard as unfree the 300 who died defending the pass of Thermopylae. They too could 'do no other'. Both were prisoners of their own commitments. Luther and his like are distinguished because their commitments are more obviously self-chosen, since they conflict with, rather than express, the current mores of the society. But both symbolise for us the freedom of the responsible person.

It is safer, perhaps, to say that they used to symbolise the freedom of the responsible person. Over the last two centuries this concept has been not merely overlaid but denied by a different concept of freedom. The economic man was free to seek what he wanted so far as his monetary enfranchisement allowed. What he wanted was his own affair. The political man was free to seek what he wanted so far as his political enfranchisement allowed. If this collided with the wants of others, he, like the economic man, would get what his muscle deserved. His wants also were his own affair. Confrontation and trade-off were the approved instruments of adjustment. The subtle web of ethical convention which constrained both was ignored until it withered from neglect as it is patently withering today.

## The pursuit of ultimate autonomy

To this concept of the autonomous individual, there are only two or possibly three ultimate positions. One is Nietzsche's superman, immoral by definition, 'free' from all the constraints which make human beings human. Another is Sartre's existential man, seeking in purely arbitrary action, such as the killing of a total stranger, the evidence of 'freedom' which this concept of autonomy required. The third, perhaps a variant of the first, is the self-satisfied parasite on a human society which he has defined as worthless and meriting no loyalty of any kind; this type was first described by Diderot in his long unpublished dialogue *Rameau's Nephew*, and echoed to some extent nearly 200 years later by Thomas Mann in his picture of *Felix Krull*.

It is no accident that the homeless Western mind, after two centuries of the culture which I have described, should have articulated these three grotesque inhuman types as the *reductio ad absurdum* of the autonomous individual. It is, equally, no accident that the world which has produced such types as literary constructs and which contain so many partial examples amongst its atomised and alienated members should be marked even more strikingly by the revival of tribal entities, more compelling in their loyalties and fiercer in their mutual hostility than the world has seen since the religious wars of the 16th and 17th centuries – and far more dangerous because of their greater destructive power. Political partitions and secessions multiply. Racial and religious cleavages reappear. The cultures of subgroups (students, ethnic minorities, trade unions) dominate the decaying structures of the societies which they constitute. The autonomous individual is a status tolerable only by those who are able to use its facilities to choose an acceptable and manageable set of personal commitments.

At the beginning of this article I observed that times of dialectical change in human history are not necessarily followed by a new phase of culture confident enough and viable enough to realise its potential and generate its successor. There may follow a long period of cultural instability, an oscillation in which no pattern gains ascendancy for long enough to realise its potential. There may follow ossification, a state in which one set of cultural imperatives is so strongly enforced that the dialectic process is inhibited, perhaps permanently (as in Orwell's *1984*, a picture which does not grow less convincing as its imagined date approaches).

Finally there may follow a dissolution of the society by the creation of a vacuum of loyalties. The old nexus is no longer valid, either because external conditions have changed too radically or because the tacit values latent in the culture have been eroded by the impact of a rival culture, as with the Eskimos and the prairie Indians. This fate could befall 'developed' as well as 'undeveloped' societies, especially societies such as Britain which have suffered both forms of challenge so conspicuously.

So the question which history, including the history of its own culture, has posed to Britain, seems to me to be predominantly the question how and in what form to replace the autonomous individual by the responsible person.

## From autonomy to responsibility

This, like every cultural change, will be no mere reversal. Until two centuries ago the responsibility of the person was commonly seen as personal responsibility to a personal God. Divine rewards and punishments were far less important than the sense of success or failure in shaping an individual life as a work of art, which was to be judged by God and man by moral criteria. It was a culture which overestimated what was to be expected of human responsibility. None the less it made human beings far more responsible than they would otherwise have been. Moreover, it endured long after its metaphysical base had begun to weaken. It was still dominant in the England into which I was born at the end of the 19th century.

Many people regard religious or at least metaphysical belief as essential to moral responsibility. I do not personally believe that this is so. Whatever else may be involved in the sense of responsibility which animates the 'responsible man', it seems to me to be primarily a sense of responsibility to the culture itself, to the immense cultural legacy which each of us inherits and which it is our function to pass on, enriched or impoverished, to the next generation.

## *The illusion of cultural determinism*

This is the heritage which makes us human, and at the same time specifically acculturated in a particular tradition. But we are neither prisoners of that tradition nor automatic transmitters of it. From birth onwards each of us is both socialised into and differentiated out from the society into which we are born, and both processes, complementary rather than contradictory, are necessary to society as well as to each individual member of it. For without the first the society will be too incoherent, whilst without the second it will be too rigid. The individual's claim to discern and act on standards different from those of his society and its institutions is based on his claim to be a contributory artist in the ongoing, never finished task of remaking the culture that made him, of contributing in Huxley's words to 'the state of Art of an organised polity'.

Ethical and aesthetic judgements are closely related, for both depend on appreciating form and contributing to the standards by which form is judged, standards which are themselves changed by their endless exercise. Nor are these judgements basically different in their *modus operandi* from the discrimination of true and false which we have come to regard as 'factual'. All depend on our ability to appreciate form, that tacit partner in our 'reason' which our most recent cultural heritage has led us to neglect, to ignore, or even to deny.[11]

None the less I do not underrate the stunning difficulty of generating what Caldwell calls a sense of systemic interdependence, sufficient to support the manifold loyalties which make their claims on us today. The difficulty, I believe, does not arise from the conflict between these claims and our 'autonomous egoism' – which, as I have made clear, I regard as a cultural deviation rather than a biological datum. It arises rather, in my view, from the multiplication of these claims on our loyalty, the result of the multiplicity of systems on which we have in fact come to depend for our day to day existence.

I do not assert that we are biologically incapable of living in the world we have made. I do assert that we can do so only by an immense cultural change and that the key to that change, if it is to be sufficiently successful to give us another chance, will be both a new emphasis on human responsibility and a new understanding of it. I assert further that this new understanding will restore our faith and re-awaken our interest in, and respect for, the most essential characteristic of social and acculturable man.

## The national and international 'culture'

I think this will be less hard for Britain than for most other developed countries because of our greater vulnerability. As Huxley observed, we are economically vulnerable in real terms. We cannot count on the continuance of food to feed us any more than we could during World War 2. Britain, viewed merely as a fiscal unit, has limitations and makes demands which affect us all, and which I think we shall soon feel far more acutely than we do now.

But membership of land and country is a far more powerful and subtle bond than membership of State, especially in those fortunate countries whose frontiers have been undisturbed for centuries. When reinforced by collective hardship and collective need it can be potent to generate a sense of continuing culture, and of responsibility, both to preserve and to change it.

It is out of fashion. We are accustomed to stress the areas in which membership transcends national boundaries. We tend correspondingly to forget that we can operate as members of a world of populations, however united or divided, only in so far as we ourselves preserve the inner relations which enable us to act effectively as a whole. Huxley's 'social coherence' is a condition necessary for far more than earning a living in an international market.

I have no space here to pursue the implications of these thoughts. I can do no more than stress what seems to me to be the main value of studying 'trends', especially cultural trends. It is not primarily to project them and speculate on how to live with them. It is rather to assess how soon they will breed their own limitations and reversals and thus to take a hand in the dialectic process of history. This process is indeed only slightly under our control, but the extent of our control depends largely on our understanding of it – which makes us not passive but active constituents in it and thus offers us an unfailing meaning and purpose for life, as well as fortifying our capacity for accepting its constraints. These are no small personal gains, even if they offer us nothing which we can judge as collective success.

## References

1. I have nearly completed such a book, under the title *Reshaping Western Culture*. [This book was never published (ed).]
2. Daniel Bell, *The Cultural Contradictions of Capitalism*, New York, Basic Books, 1976.
3. T. H. Huxley, *Evolution and Ethics and other Essays*, London, Macmillan, 1895.
4. Bentham's longer and better known book, *The Theory of Legislation*, was not published until 1789, but the *Fragment on Government* initiated the political debate which will always be associated with his name.
5. That all men are entitled to life, liberty, and the pursuit of happiness is hardly a 'self-evident truth' and was not so described in earlier drafts of that famous clause. The wish to start from a 'self-evident' axiom, rather than from a human aspiration or a divine ordinance, reflects the growing authority of 'objective' scientific thinking as then conceived.
6. The phrase is Dr David Galin's, in 'Implications for psychiatry of left and right hemisphere specialisation', *Archives of General Psychiatry*, Vol. 31, October 1974.
7. For example, Joseph Priestley wrote, '... nature ... will be more at our command, men will make their situation in this world abundantly more easy and comfortable ... and will grow daily more happy ... thus whatever was the beginning of the world, the end will be glorious and paradisiacal beyond what our imaginations can now conceive.'
8. Oliver Wendell Holmes in a famous dissenting judgement in the American Supreme Court in the 1920s said:

   When men have realised that time has upset many fighting faiths, they may come to believe even more than they believe the very foundations of their own conduct that the ultimate good desired is better reached by free trade in ideas – that the best test of truth is the power of the thought to get itself accepted in the competition of the market and that truth is the only ground upon which their wishes safely can be carried out. That at any rate is the theory of our Constitution. It is an experiment, as all life is an experiment. While that experiment is part of our system, I think we should be eternally vigilant against attempts to check the expressions of opinions which we loathe and believe to be fraught with death.

Extract quoted in C. D. Bowen, *Yankee From Olympus*, New York, Little Brown, 1949, p. 170.

9. In *Evolution and Ethics and other Essays*, op. cit.
10. Lynton Caldwell, *Franklyn Lectures in Science and Humanities*, Auburn University, Auburn, Alabama, November 1972.
11. I have developed these ideas further in a paper, 'Rationality and Intuition', *Aesthetics in Science*, Dr Judith Wechsler (ed), Cambridge, Mass, MIT Press, 1978. Article 23 in this collection.

# 6

# The future of morality*

Moral criticism of human institutions is frequent: the acceptance of social constraints by the free individual is rare. This moral inversion is inconsistent with the survival of an increasingly interdependent society. Statements of human rights must be replaced by statements of human responsibility if we are to make the world viable.

The future of morality? The question will seem to some embarrassing, to many irrelevant, to most unanswerable.

What is morality anyway? What impact does it really make on the course of human affairs? And what can be usefully said about its future development? I shall seek to show that it is not irrelevant; that its nature and impact are not obscure; and that any embarrassment which it occasions is evidence of ambivalent feelings and muddled understanding which need to be and can be cleared up.

## Moral inversion

Moral imperatives are out of fashion if and in so far as they imply the acceptance of social constraints by would-be autonomous individuals. But they are not at all out of fashion if and in so far as they power criticism of human institutions and their office bearers. They are taboo in the first field but obsessional in the second. Michael Polanyi drew attention to this apparently contradictory feature of our Western culture in several papers,[1] and christened it moral inversion. Never since the religious wars has moral fervour fired so much strife, bitterness, and brutality.

Dr Johann puts it differently.[2]

> ... these times manage to combine an extraordinary degree of moral activism on the level of practice with an all-but-dogmatic brand of ethical nihilism on the level of theory. On the one hand all our inherited ways, traditions and institutions are being subjected to unrelenting criticism with a view to their radical transformation. Absolutely nothing is sacred. On the other, there is widespread denial of any basis in reality for judging one way of life to be morally superior to another or even for preferring the moral standpoint to some other in evaluating proposed courses of action. The situation is nothing short of absurd.

The situation, if not absurd, is at least paradoxical. But I think Dr Johann

---

* From *Futures*, October 1979.

oversimplifies it in presenting it as an inconsistency between theory and practice. One thing *is* sacred – the 'rights' of the autonomous, self-actualising individual. The UN has produced a Declaration of the Rights of Man and even a Declaration of the Rights of the Child, and these have been subscribed by many though not all of the world's governments. It has set up judicial machinery to determine whether these rights have been infringed. And the rights embody widespread beliefs about the optimal conditions in which men and women should live and in which children should be brought up. Many countries are under political and economic pressure from their neighbours on the grounds that they are failing to secure these rights for their subjects; and these pressures are often carried to a degree damaging to the countries which exercise them because of the vehemence of public opinion within their borders. Many other countries are equally divided internally by feuds which express themselves as the demand for 'justice'.

It is too sweeping, I think, to dismiss all these as without theoretical foundation, in that the social sciences provide abundant though not wholly consistent theories about the optimum conditions for human growth and development. However, as Dr Johann points out, these theories supply no logical reason why desirable objectives should become moral imperatives.

## The freedom spiral

What has happened, I suggest, is that the Western world has come full circle, or more exactly full spiral, in the two centuries since Rousseau declared that man was born free but was everywhere in chains. To the emancipators of Rousseau's generation is seemed that nothing was needed but to strike off the chains. Men freed from tyranny, superstition, ignorance, and want would, in Condorcet's words, need 'no master save reason'.

Two centuries later the passion for emancipation is no less feverish but the perceived cost has hugely risen. These 'rights' can be satisfied only (if at all) by huge institutional efforts. Education, health care, nutrition, shelter (which now includes all the amenities of urban living) are not distributed freely and evenly by nature unless distorted by human institutions. Only human institutions beyond our present compass could supply them even to a proportion of those who demand them. Yet these same institutions have become as suspect, even as hated as they were in the days of the Ancien Regime. They are again widely seen as the chains which bind potentially free men.

Of course Rousseau's slogan, admirable for starting a revolution, was totally untrue. Men are not born 'free'. They are born in total dependence on other men and they perish biologically and never emerge psychologically as human persons unless they are cherished and nourished for years by men and women of the previous generation. Their debt to these they will be able to repay only by their devotion to the generation which follows. Meantime they are kept alive from day to day by the efforts of other people, most of whom they do not know and never even see. And their only possible acknowledgment of this, even where the service is made for payment, is not the money which they pay but the probably quite different contribution which they themselves (one hopes) have made. Of course there is a kind of freedom in interdependence but this is not the kind of freedom which Rousseau was talking about; and it depends on mutual trust to a degree scarcely conceived as possible today.

## Ethical nihilism

Dr Johann is none the less right, I think, to emphasise the influence of what he calls ethical nihilism. Its full force can be realised perhaps only by those old enough to have experienced what preceded it. Less than a century ago in Western countries, certainly in Britain, it was widely believed that the individual was at least potentially equipped with an innate capacity, a 'conscience', which enabled him to distinguish 'right' from 'wrong' and that he had an equally inherent duty to pursue what was right. The duty had a religious origin in the will of God; but there was no lack of rationalists who were prepared to find it in the nature of man. The dimension of right and wrong, good and evil was widely accepted and human excellence was commonly assessed by reference to apparent achievement, both in the discharge of an individual's civic and occupational roles and in meeting those standards of honesty, loyalty, compassion, and so on which were held applicable to human status as such and which were comprehended in 'goodness'.

Then Freud located the conscience in the internalised voice of (primarily) the parent. He asserted the individual's need and right to review such early impositions and to confirm or replace them with criteria of his own choosing. It was a revolutionary change in so far as it threw upon the conscience the burden of proving its own authenticity. But it increased, rather than reduced, the responsibility of the ego for choosing its own standards. Freud was not very explicit about the criteria which the ego could use. He may have been unduly influenced by the pathological aspects of such internalised norms which concerned him so closely as a psychiatrist. But as I understand it, he always allowed the ego some role as an artist as well as a broker in reconciling the demands of its 'three hard masters'; and his followers and deviants have spent much fruitful time in developing this aspect of the ego in a mental atmosphere less rigidly determinist than the one in which Freud wrote.

But Marx long before had insisted that this scope for self-design was limited if not negligible because the individual was too deeply conditioned by his own self-interest to make such choices with any independence. Marx confined his argument to the rich and the propertied but logic and history were bound to widen, even to universalise it. Property is not the only conditioning factor in human life. Marx's insights, propagated as a polemic on behalf of a class, contributed to the suspicion of all moral judgments as rationalised self-interest. And this was confirmed by the very culture which he was attacking. For both the market economy and representative political democracy encouraged the view that the individual knew what was best for himself and acted so as to maximise it. The concept of the self became still further narrowed to the individual (envisaged nearly always as adult and male) and altruism became an anomaly which Freudian analysis was welcome to debunk.

A further stage in the sorry story started when 'science' began to turn its attention to management and government. The evaluation of policy required an analysis of cost and benefit expressed in terms which were at least comparable and preferably quantifiable. The fact that people do constantly weigh imponderables and compare disparates, however well confirmed by experience, was not explicable in terms of any current theory of mental function except a crude dynamics which reduced them all to pushes and pulls. And this model tended to remain dominant even when it had been supplemented by the belated acknowledgment of information as an agency which produced effects otherwise than by transferring energy. We are now allowed to believe that books do not operate like bulldozers; but most of the lessons have still to be drawn.

## The dynamics of moral obligation

This familiar story has its positive side. Its most precious positive contribution is, I think, the understanding that the sense of obligation associated with moral and indeed all ethical thought, feeling, and behaviour derives from expectations which people learn to expect *of themselves* as a necessary part of their identity, a term which includes their image of themselves not only as individuals but as belonging to some admired class or type.

These expectations may be imprinted in earliest childhood. Religious faith and respect for authority used to be familiar examples. They may arise, sometimes no less early, from the *rejection* of some such attempt at imprinting. The child who has been 'turned off' by efforts to 'turn him on' may long find difficulty in conceiving himself as someone who could entertain a religious faith or accept a secular authority without something approaching treason to himself.

The expectations may arise later from social pressures, as when the individual, entering a profession such as medicine, the army, or the law, absorbs the professional ethic into his image of himself. They may arise at any time by an act of conscious artistry on the part of the ego, desiring to emulate some human possibility which experience has revealed to him and which claims his commitment. Such is the response of those who fall under the influence of men whom they recognise as 'great'. However they arise, they provide in my view the source of that sense of personal obligation which is one of the components I am seeking. I will call it commitment.

It is, I think, a source of human motivation different in kind from the prudential calculation of cost and benefit which may lead a man to conform to what standards others expect of him, even though he himself feels no personal commitment to them. This is a difference which should be more familiar to us in these cybernetic days, when we are accustomed to the idea of comparing some incoming or self-generated information with some standard or norm. The 'new' information does or does not match the norm and thus a 'match' or 'mismatch' signal is generated from which flows not only information but meaning.

I have described elsewhere[3] what I think should be the impact of this thinking on theories of human motivation (which many will agree to be badly in need of some refreshing supplement). I need not develop this argument further here and need only point out that control by reference to a standard or norm is now part of our most common conceptual stock in trade.

To make the concept of commitment more precise, I emphasise the following aspects. First, commitment may be more or less intense or wholly lacking. Its presence and state can only be recognised in action or subjectively in imagined action. An individual may have no idea at all of what to expect of himself in a particular context, in which case he will act at random or assume whatever persona seems to be expected of him. He may have a standard, vaguely held in principle, which dissolves when he is faced with the actual cost of living up to it. Or he may find himself more deeply attached to it than he knew. Personalities vary in the strength, comprehensiveness, and coherence of the self-expectations which thus structure them. These are major dimensions of personality.

Second, commitment does not necessarily impel its subject to conduct regarded as moral by anyone else or even by himself. The Marquis de Sade proudly identified himself with a persona so repulsive that his name has come to stand for one of the most widely recognised vices or psychopathologies. Moreover he claimed to have made that persona deliberately by rooting out from his personality anything which could interfere with his 'enjoyment'. Confidence tricksters may take a professional pride in their success, even though it is possible only in a world where trust is sufficiently taken for granted to be betrayed. The world's Napoleons are committed to a personal destiny which neither they nor others necessarily identify with moral good. Less extreme examples are to be found in the distinguishing marks of professions or classes which are internalised by their members with a passion proportionate to their symbolic importance rather than to any imaginable scale of moral values. A breach of good manners may diminish the perpetrator far more than a failure of compassion.

This last example brings me to the third and most difficult aspect of what I am calling commitment. The dimension committed–uncommitted is by no means the same as the dimension inner directed–outer directed. All commitments are formed by accepting (or rejecting) standards with which one is invited to identify. Who can say how far the resulting commitment is due to the invitation of society and how far to the exercise of personal choice? Even where personal choice is at its highest it may owe its power to a society whose culture encouraged it from the beginning by making the individual expect of himself that he would bear the burden of assessing and accepting or rejecting the imperatives which that same culture pressed upon him. Contemporary Western culture is obsessed by the urge to claim individual credit for the shape of the personality and to deny to society anything but the power to suppress and distort it.

But in fact this inflamed distinction between the individual and society cannot be sustained. It is basically untrue that the individual must be either a mere cell in an organism or an entity free to make its own relations with its environment and entitled to ignore any which are not voluntarily assumed. Fishes are not free to live out of water.

Finally, commitment may be positive or negative. The individual may expect of himself action in some circumstances, constraint in others. He would be ashamed, for example, not to go to the help of another who was drowning or under attack and equally ashamed if he lost his temper with a subordinate. Sometimes the same commitment can be described either negatively or positively but it is convenient to distinguish the two, especially at a time when negative commitments are so out of fashion. Self-accepted constraints are commitments no less than self-accepted obligations to act.

## Mutual expectations

It remains to consider the other side of the coin, the expectations which each entertains of all the others. Human societies cohere only in so far as their members can entertain reliable expectations of each other: they sustain this net of mutual expectations by means which we may fail to notice only because we take them for granted.

At their most visible, every law court in the land is busy applying to particular cases rules, usually of long standing, and defining and trying to correct deviance. Schools at all levels are seeking to transmit the culture's heritage, its approved ways of thinking, expressing, valuing, and behaving. Men in organisations take for granted that others on whom they depend will perform their roles in the ways expected of them and management is largely concerned with correcting deviance from the expected. Social relations are structured by a similar net of mutual expectations and those who violate it are made aware of their offence in culturally determined ways. The basic problem of supporting life in community is to allow variety, criticism, and innovation to an extent sufficient to permit growth and adaptation to change without so disrupting the tissue of mutual expectation as to destroy people's trust in it and each other and therewith the possibility of social order. And this is everyone's interest and everyone's business though it usually requires also the exercise of some central authority.

There has been much argument about the extent to which 'force' is needed to enforce 'order' in human societies but I question whether such general discussions are useful about subject matter so idiosyncratic and so context bound as particular human societies. In Moscow, I understand, bus passengers serve themselves with tickets and pay for them without the supervision of a conductor. An attempt to enjoy a free ride would be frustrated by the outrage of the other passengers. But so would the attempt to jump a London bus queue, though the second, unlike the first, would not be a breach of the formal law. It may be significant that the second would be an infringement of personal 'right' whilst the first would be 'only' a fraud on a public body. The consciousness of a Soviet citizen would seem to be differently structured from that of most Westerners.

The significance of mutual expectations is best seen in their simplest manifestations, such as forms of greeting and dress. In socially stratified societies these serve to assure the parties that each knows his place and concedes the place of the other. The touched cap, the raised hat, the nod, the bow all have their place. In egalitarian societies they serve equally to assert and to accord equality of status. Both can be used also to assert a claim which the other does not admit or otherwise to make a communication of an antagonistic kind. In either case they are communications and usually unambiguous. When they are ambiguous, as when a greeting is ignored, they produce disproportionate anxiety. (Am I being cut or censured or did he simply not notice?) A response so bizarre as to be outside the common repertory of both greeting and insult would be even more disturbing. What other common expectations can no longer be safely made about this particular person?

Clothes used to serve a similar purpose. At one extreme, uniform defines clearly at least one aspect of what a person is - policeman, soldier, air-force pilot - often with added details of rank and status. Within the uniformed organisation the uniform serves to make members aware of each other and of their common service. Externally it invites others to attach to any wearer of the uniform the expectations which they are accustomed to attach to members of the force and to accord whatever its members are regarded as entitled to expect. But 'uniformity' is a matter of degree. A century ago in England, the clothes a person wore and the way he spoke conveyed a great deal of information about him - largely about his occupation, his income, and his social class, each of which had an associated subculture, more or less defined. Today these indices are more blurred and this is usually welcomed as showing that these differences have decreased or are regarded as less important. But other differences can be expressed in the same media and our current subcultures often seize on them and use them as symbols. I know a young man, gifted, intelligent, and humane, who threw up his job rather than obey a company rule and wear a tie.

## Mutual reassurance

Wordless communication is a huge subject, not to be pursued here. I am concerned only to make the case that a vast amount of human communication is devoted simply to *mutual reassurance*. Small talk and social ritual serves little other purpose. By such means each party assures the others that it belongs to their group (or to some other sufficiently known and trusted to be acceptable) and thereby invites the assumption that it knows and will observe the code of mutual expectations common to the group. Each member must give the others the benefit of the shared cultural assumption, to be withdrawn only if experience disproves it. And this I think explains why confidence tends to be an integrated attitude, vulnerable as a whole to evidence that even a part of it is undeserved.

Mutual reassurance is important primarily because it makes possible inter-relations *more human* than they would otherwise be. In some cultures the outer doors of houses are fitted with grilles through which a visitor may be inspected before the door is opened. In others even lone women in isolated houses feel no need to lock their doors. Obviously the mutual expectations expressed by the latter state invite far readier communication between strangers than do those of the former state. Examples can be multiplied and suggest that there is a transcultural, though not an acultural, dimension of humanity or humaneness which helps to determine how far men in society can develop their peculiarly human capacity for using communication to build relations of high 'quality' between them. There is here the nucleus of a theory not merely of commitment but of *moral* commitment. I have no space to pursue it here. But obviously if it exists – and it is widely recognised – it will need constant reinforcement even to maintain itself in a world ever more crowded with mutual strangers. The example is one of many but it is of sombre significance that 'security' is a fast-growing activity in Western countries.

Perhaps the most important assumption that anyone can extend towards another is that that other has himself internalised the responsibilities expected of him and will obey them because he expects them of himself; they are for him commitments and increasingly include constraints.

## Complementary expectations

I have used the expression mutual expectations reluctantly because, although it serves to distinguish such expectations from self-expectations, it conceals the fact already mentioned that they are nearly always not mutual but complementary. Doctor and patient, teacher and taught, judge and litigant, buyer and seller, administrator and administered, husband and wife, parent and child do not entertain the same expectations of each other, except for those most general and fundamental ones such as honesty, respect, and compassion which we regard as 'obligations' due to humanity as such. This perhaps explains why role-governed relations are today so distrusted and despised. We cannot logically derive this pathology from moral inversion; for even in a world of ideally organised institutions (whatever be the ideal) role-governed relations would be not only inescapable but a major factor in life's significance and a major field for human excellence. We must attribute it to that concept of equality which, as de Tocqueville foresaw long ago, is likely to erode both sides of the complementary relations which hold any society together. In fact both kinds of mutual expectation are needed. Role-governed relations may well become rigid and inhuman unless the parties also acknowledge the truly mutual responsibilities which spring from their common humanity. But equally these, however universally shared, will not replace the huge nexus of precise role-defined responsibilities which is due from each of us and on which we all depend from day to day.

But with the appearance of such words as compassion and respect we are clearly in the realm of quality, not merely stability, in human systems.

## Ethics and morals

Murder, theft, and arson are commonly regarded as more than breaches of good manners. Yet the division between manners and morals is hard to draw partly because manners are the basis of stability and stability is itself a value – if not a moral value, at least the soil in which moral values can grow. I have discussed in an earlier paper the relation between stability and quality in human systems.[4]

I seek in this article to give this distinction more precision in terms of contemporary Western culture and to consider what if anything might succeed the state of moral inversion from which we now suffer, a state manifestly unstable and not to my mind convincingly progressive in the direction of quality however defined. It would be convenient as well as logical to keep the word ethics for all those patterns of thought, concern, and behaviour which characterise a particular culture and to keep the word morals for those among them which can be commended, however controversially, on grounds of quality.

Qualitatively it does not matter whether we drive on the left of the road or the right but it does matter that we should all obey the same convention. When we refine the rule by giving priority to ambulances and fire appliances we express a value judgment that this inequality is on balance in the general interest. No doubt we shall have to ration the use of the road far more than we do now, either because of traffic congestion or because of fuel shortage. And we ration it already by requiring tested competence to drive, compulsory third party insurance, a licence fee (which as I write is under discussion) and ability to pay the price of petrol (which can be raised or lowered by taxation or subsidy) as well as by other factors. All these forms of rationing derive from conscious public decisions and express views of what is qualitatively best among the courses seen to be available.

These judgments express some degree of moral preference but they are debatable in a sense that the simplest interpersonal moral judgments are not. It is widely agreed in most cultures that it is more congenial to live in a society in which members are relatively free from the fear of violence, fraud, and other acts of malevolence by their neighbours. They vary in their standards of what is to be expected. Some enjoy standards which others do not conceive as possible. And they change with time.

Isabella Bird was free to ride alone round the Colorado Rockies in the 1870s, accepting any hospitality she was offered, exciting admiration for her horsemanship but no surprise at her trust in her fellow humans.[5] A few decades later MacMullen, an early English yachtsman, excited more surprise for his daring in sleeping alone in his boat in an English port than for his remarkable exploits at sea – and this despite the fact that unlike Isabella Bird, he was, as he put it: 'not dependent on any man's forbearance'. There are – or were – Bedouin tribes where stealing is unknown. A comparison of cultures discloses a wide difference in the level of their interpersonal moral expectations but a fair degree of conformity in the dimensions in which these are measured. The question: 'Who is my neighbour?' admits a far wider range of answers than the question: 'What are my duties to him?' however commonly neglected the duties may be.

## Political morality

When we move from interpersonal duties to political morality we run into difficulties which have beset the human mind since before Plato wrote his *Republic*. Broadly they are of two kinds.

One concerns the characters of the men who are selected and preselected by the struggle for public power. The Guardians who were to run Plato's Republic were to be of a type least likely to seek power for its own sake, men who would carry for the public weal an office which was a burden to them. It is a question whether this would not have ruled out some of the world's most successful and honoured statesmen. But history records that the struggle to get and keep political power does not always lodge it in hands most likely to use it responsibly in the long-term interest of the governed. Hereditary monarchy has the merit of vesting it in those who did not seek it and who usually have had some training in using it; though this does not guarantee their competence. No doubt all countries have in their records governors who are honoured as Guardians. Englishmen need not go back a thousand years to Alfred of Wessex and Cuthbert of Lindisfarne. The long struggle to make power accountable without emasculating it has had results of which we can be moderately proud. But I doubt whether our present methods or any other methods can themselves be sufficient for the needs of the future.

The second set of difficulties concerns the nature of the political choice. The governor, individual or collective, decides for others who may themselves be divided. To satisfy the conditions which I have described as necessary for individual moral judgment there must be a collective commitment, justifiable as a move in the direction of greater humanity. This means that not the decider only but substantially all those for whom he decides must be committed to a common idea of their collective self and a common consciousness that the step which they are taking is consistent with that ideal and needed for its realisation. Such things are not impossible. The last occasion when it happened in Britain was I think the passing in 1946-1951 of the legislation giving effect to the Beveridge report. An interparty unity in and out of Parliament marked this occasion in a way seldom seen in Parliamentary activity, at least when this is devoted to internal relations. There was a widespread feeling that this was 'right'.

If this argument is right, a precondition of political morality is that the political unit shall be coherent at least in the field involved by any particular decision. This is not surprising. The individual also must be coherent, at least in the relevant area. He must have a self to which he can be true. The idea of a similar collective self is out of fashion today but only through a recent eclipse. Aneurin Bevan, architect of the National Health Service, declared that we should thank heaven for having preserved this island as an example of humanity. Statesmen of the left were as proud as statemen of the right to admit their dedication to the country which they served.

A further conclusion follows. Political units will not act morally unless nearly all the governed as well as the governors feel a profound commitment to them and identify with them. That they should do so will not of itself guarantee that they will act morally. But without such commitment they will have no chance of acting morally at all. For commitment is of the essence of morality and collective commitment is of the essence of collective morality. The quality of their actions will of course depend on the quality of their shared commitment. In what collective character do they take pride? What does their sense of collective identity most impel them to guard? These are moral questions; but they can only be posed in a society sufficiently coherent to have a collective ideal. 'Lords and Commons of England consider what manner of man it is whereof ye are and whereof ye are the governors.' We may give a new answer to Milton's question but the question itself needs to be asked anew not only by Lords and by Commons but by every man in the street. It is not out of date. Its answer determines what impact these 56 million people will have, not only on each other but on the billions beyond their shores.

## The moral frontier

Thus we come to what is undoubtedly the most difficult field of political morality. From the dawn of time human culture, and with it all ethics and morality, has grown within specific populations. The relation of these populations to each other has been generally one of mutual hostility unqualified by any moral constraints or commitments. When they have collided, in pursuit of land or resources or slaves, or mere adventure, the weaker has suffered accordingly; and where the incursion has been permanent these have been driven out or exterminated or subordinated or absorbed. The cultured Athenians in democratic debate decided to slaughter all the males in the neighbouring Greek-speaking island of Melos and enslave the women and children in the service of an Athenian colony to be planted there. Constraint and commitment stopped at the frontier.

Cultural provision for the succour of strangers and trade, supported by trust based on treaty or custom, barely qualified this pattern of mutual hostility. J. H. Seeley, a well informed historian writing in 1865, counted it a major achievement (which he attributed to Christian morality) to have outgrown endemic hostility between all nations not bound by a specific treaty.[6] A specific declaration of war was needed to terminate the relations of peace. Even this applied only to 'civilised' nations and was to be eroded in the 100 years following his death. Yet each of these peoples which raided and destroyed each other so mercilessly in the human colonisation of the planet had an internal code of mutual obligation and a net of shared commitment and constraint often far more effective and accepted than our own.

Since statecraft is much concerned with external relations, it faces in this area moral problems far greater than in any but the most bitterly divided internal relations. And these problems are likely to grow much worse. The quest for resources and living space is no longer eased by the existence of huge land areas sparsely occupied by people ill equipped to resist the colonising West. The West itself begins to feel the limitations generated by its own expansion, and it can no longer count on the rest of the world to supply its raw materials. Much of the rest of the world and part of the Western world has already outgrown its indigenous food supplies. Already more people are starving than ever before. Pressure for immigration mounts and so, predictably, does well founded resistance to it. The surface of the planet is not everywhere equally supportive of human life and those peoples who still enjoy a viable relation between population and resources have everything to fear from those who do not.

Yet the dimensions of political morality, even of international morality, are the same as those of personal morality.

## What future for morality?

Faced with this awesome prospect, few would dare to forecast the probable future structure of morality, whether interpersonal, intranational, or international, or the extent of its influence on the course of human affairs. But it is possible to make some statements about what is needed even with no assurance whether or how far the need will be met.

First, moral inversion is inconsistent with social survival and must be corrected. Its existence is explicable as a by-product of the last two centuries in the West but it is none the less a lethal danger. It is significant that it has been a central target in every major revolution of this century.

Second, ethical nihilism is an absurdity which needs to be stamped out. Moral standards are cultural artifacts without which no society can survive in the stresses of social life, especially those which await us now. Cultural artifacts are facts just as real as any other facts and even more important for a social species now dependent on a net of interdependent relations which it has no other means of sustaining.

Third, the problems of intercultural stress have to be faced in full recognition of the relation between political coherence and effective political action, whether intranational or international. Opinions doubtless differ as to the extent to which the populations of the world today show any cultural convergence, but the question is less important than the question of what culture they share.

Most important of all, perhaps, statements of human rights need to be replaced by statements of human responsibility, defining as clearly as possible on whom these responsibilities rest. They will be found to rest not only, often not chiefly, on governments. They will often be found to be unattainable and never to be attainable except at the cost of some prized alternative 'right'.

The world of the future, if viable at all, will be a world in which people know when to say 'no' and when to take 'no' for an answer. But it will not on that account be a less moral world. On the contrary it will be a world in which both personal and collective commitments and constraints will be developed to a level known to only a few societies today and least of all to the pampered West. It may even be a world nearer than today's to Aneurin Bevan's aspiration.

## References

1. Notably in Michael Polanyi, 'Beyond Nihilism', Eddington Lecture 1960, Cambridge, Cambridge University Press, 1960; and in M. Polanyi, 'History and Hope', *Virginia Quarterly Review*, Spring 1962, Vol. 30, No. 2.
2. Robert O. Johann, 'Person, Community and Commitment', *Person and Community*, Robert J. Roth, (ed), New York, Fordham University Press, 1975.
3. Geoffrey Vickers, 'Motivation Theory – a Cybernetic Contribution', *Behavioral Science*, July 1973, Vol. 18, No. 3.
4. Geoffrey Vickers, 'Stability and Quality in Human Systems', a paper prepared for an Open University Summer School.
5. Isabella Bird, *An English Lady's Life in the Rocky Mountains*, Norman, OK, University of Oklahoma Press, 1960.
6. J. H. Seeley, *Ecce Homo*, London, Everyman's Library, J. M. Dent, 1970. Originally published 1865.

# 7

# Violence, war and genocide*

I do not regard violence as a problem; only as a symptom common to a wide variety of problems. These range from baby battering to genocide, but there is a significant difference between acts of individual and collective violence.

The former, though more common within human societies than within societies of other primates, have hitherto proved to be containable within most human societies at most times by four familiar cultural constraints, namely (1) the cultural consensus of the society, exerting positive and negative pressures on the individual from birth on; (2) the political constraints and sanctions of the society's executive, legislative and judicial machinery; (3) religious imperatives and sanctions reinforcing (1) and (2); and (4) internalized constraints generated in the individual by the three pressures previously mentioned.

The latter, intersocietal violence, has far exceeded anything observed between other societies of primates throughout recorded time and its current escalation is the main contemporary focus of concern about violence.

I take it as given that human beings are prone to violence, firstly to express rage, secondly to get what they want when it seems most easily obtained by force, and thirdly to resist violence offered by others; and that it can only be constrained by cultural imperatives. Though these may be expressed in the nature and conduct of a society's institutions, I do not share the belief, common in the Enlightenment, that man freed from tyranny, superstition, ignorance and want will have no quarrel that 'reason' cannot resolve without the aid of any of the cultural constraints mentioned at the beginning of this paper. I regard 'reason', at least in the restricted sense now given to it, which is barely if at all more than rationality, as a merely instrumental human faculty useful in applying these constraints to actual situations. Common values are the product of common culture, though some may be common to several cultures. But cultures are divided by their areas of acceptance far more than by their content. The question, 'Who is my neighbour?' is far more contentious than the question, 'What are my duties to him?'. Professor Blacking quotes a delightful Zulu saying which he translates as, 'a human being is a human being because of other human beings'. But it was none the less a Zulu tribe which invaded what is

---

* Originally a paper presented to a conference on the Study of Violence and Peace, organized by the Dag Hammarskjold Information Centre in January 1981.

now Zimbabwe only a generation before Rhodes. When is a human being not a human being to other human beings?

I am therefore not surprised that even the most civilized states have so commonly killed their murderers and, with even more signs of repugnance, their traitors and heretics but have loaded with honours the leaders who have most effectively destroyed their national enemies and other individuals who are thought to have served them conspicuously in war. I am not surprised that throughout recorded time whenever populations have collided in search of land, resources (including slaves) booty or mere adventure, the weaker has usually been driven out, exterminated, subordinated or absorbed. The dreary record is not confined to the past or to 'uncivilized' peoples. The classical Athenians decided in democratic debate to slaughter all the males of Melos and to enslave the women and children in the service of a colony to be planted there. The Romans dealt similarly with an already defeated Carthage to remove the fear of a possibly renewable threat to their dominance in the Mediterranean. The settlers in Tasmania exterminated the aborigines there no less deliberately and efficiently and much more recently, though for less obvious reasons. Yet the Athenians, the Romans and the British had at the time a high degree of cultural control over the use of violence within their homelands.

Obedience to the claims of the 'patria' have always been honoured whatever form or size the dominant concept of patria has taken – as is I think to be expected in societies of creatures which are not only social but also acculturable and which consciously share the legacy of a shared and remembered common past.

Nor am I surprised that these genocidal tendencies are more threatening now than ever before. Technology has monstrously magnified the power of individual men to kill all forms of life including their own and has multiplied the numbers of the species and their occasions for collision. International trade has not provided an automatic and mutually acceptable device for winning and distributing the resources of the world. A new battle for resources has already begun, more bitter than those which have marked earlier stages in human history. And the agents in the drama, once tribes, then empires, are now 160 politico-fiscal units, most of which are too incoherent internally to act effectively as organized entities, except perhaps in war.

Most of these states have arisen from the dissolution in less than two hundred years of at least nine empires (Spain and Portugal in S. America; Austria-Hungary in Europe; Turkey in Europe and the Levant; Holland in Indonesia; Belgium in Africa; Britain and France in Africa and Asia; Germany in Africa) in addition to the creation of great nations by the colonization of areas so under-populated that their original populations could be ignored (North America, Australia, New Zealand). But the faith which powered these dissolutions has so far largely failed. This was the faith that individual freedom, then regarded as the highest good, would flourish and could only flourish in 'free' countries. But the violent conflicts of today, never so numerous before, are even more commonly within rather than between these largely new political entities, and are commonly sparked by collisions of collective consciousness, racial, cultural or religious as well as economic, often resulting from the inclusion in new political frontiers of older but still potent foci of loyalty.

Thus these collective conflicts are infinitely complex. But the contrast between collective conflict and individual violence remains, I think, valid and important. Nor is the concept of war as an aspect of collective relationship a purely European or a very modern creation. The history of China for all its physical isolation includes many wars both in the course of unifying the original kingdoms and in the perennial conflict between China and the Mongols. Genghiz Khan was a name of terror through the largest territorial empire ever yet established – at the estimated cost, according to Fisher,[1] of eighteen million lives. The recurrent wars between Egypt and the Mesopotamian empires fill centuries of history. The Ottoman empire rose and fell from a basically Asiatic base. Nor were wars confined to empire building. The founding of the state of Israel three thousand years ago was no more peaceful than its reestablishment in the twentieth century. Anthropologists can describe, as Professor Blacking and others have done, small contemporary tribes where war is either limited by conventions long lost in larger societies or eliminated by an imperial power to the general satisfaction of those who had previously regarded it as an inescapable fact of life. But it is noteworthy that in the case cited by him in the paper presented at this meeting peace was imposed by the intervention of an imperial and in that case a Western power. It is a significant historical fact, though not a surprising one, that throughout historical time peace between collectivities has usually been maintained by the exercise of superordinate power imposed by those very empires which we are so proud of having dismantled in the name of self-determination.

It does not follow that the world was mistaken to dismantle them. It follows only that it was naive to expect 'Balkanization' to increase the peaceful coexistence of the fragments thus liberated. When intrasystemic tensions become intersystemic conflicts the contrary is bound to occur, at least in some places and at least at first. But caution against generalization is to be found in the history of the Scandinavian nations, in the growth of the Swiss confederation, in the present happy state of disarmed but 'independent' Austria – all 'Western' powers.

Equally important and equally hard to interpret is the *Pax Sovietica*, as it existed before the invasion of Afghanistan – the only new form of imperial domination yet to emerge from the tide of imperial dissolution which has otherwise almost completed its historic course over the last two centuries. The Soviet empire has grown on a basically Asiatic base and is noteworthy partly because it includes so many important countries more 'Western' than itself and partly because it represents, with China though in partly contrasting form, the most conspicuous contemporary effort to engineer consensus on a more than national scale.

It remains to mention, if not adequately to examine three tendencies in the modern world which are new or which have grown to dimensions which have made them critical to a new degree and which are relative both to the present state and to the future prospect of war.

The first is the new ecological view. Ecologists today sometimes describe human societies at the hunting and food gathering stage as the first affluent societies, dining from a table spread by nature with little help from human hands. Even if this is too rosy a picture, the study of simple contemporary societies shows that groups could meet for purposes of ceremonial and could intermarry without constant battle for scarce resources. But the battle for resources to which I referred earlier has been sharpened during historic times partly by their depletion but chiefly by increasing numbers and rising expectations. The recent rise of agriculture and the much more recent rise of fuel-based industry have not been sequential phases of human development but cumulative ones. We still live in an agricultural age; photosynthesis still provides it 'free'. We still live in an industrial age and face deficits in the energy supply on which it has so far depended. The 'post-industrial' age, if the absurd term must be used, will be even more dependent on agriculture and industry. It will be an age of superabundant human beings in a state of widespread but ill-distributed scarcity, with immensely extended powers to send communications but little if any increase in their power to receive them, to act on them or even to understand them.

Consider the first of these propositions. In 1935 Fisher[2] estimated the population of the world at two billion and the destitute at 150 million. In 1974 the World Food Congress estimated the world population as not greatly increased but the destitute as having risen by a factor of three to 450-500 million. In 1980 the Brandt Report estimated population at three billion (the increase largely in the previous six years) due to rise to five billion by the year 2000 and the destitute at 800 million. But it gives these facts in an historical vacuum, with no indication of the trend of which they are only the latest expression. Later a recent analysis in *The Times* of London observed that the world's harvest of wheat and coarse grains would have fallen for three years running if this (1980-1981) season's estimates are confirmed; that Australia, North America and Western Europe have a monopoly of the exportable surpluses of these essential grains greater than OPECs monopoly of oil; and that the price of wheat has risen 30 per cent in the season.

Of course international maldistribution does not necessarily mean war. Millions – though not so many millions as today – have starved in the world's poverty belts in past decades and centuries without necessarily producing war or even awareness outside their own localities. But today the knowledge of these inequalities is world wide, if not the concern they produce. Moreover, the sense of inequality of enjoyment percolates every society, not least the richest. Professor Adolph Lowe[3] has persuasively argued that inflation is the inescapable substitute for agreed criteria of distribution, a tax which falls where it will because people cannot agree on principles which might be expressed constitutionally.

I see no reason to suppose, as the Brandt Report seems to do, that in such a world more technology and more credit will produce more consumer goods and more money with which to buy them, least of all where these are wanted. But there is one area in which the exponential growth of technology shows no present sign of abating its productivity. That is the area of weapon making, the second factor awaiting mention, and the resultant change in the intensity and in the distribution of its destructiveness. There can, I think, be no doubt that the change in cultural attitude towards war which has so notably marked the last fifty years in Europe and America, though perhaps not elsewhere, is largely caused by this factor. Even the most recent of past wars is no longer a guide to the course or later consequences of another waged on the same scale. Hence the effectiveness, such as it is, of deterrence. But wars are fought to preserve what are perceived as vital interests, at least as much as to improve an existing state; and vital interests are seen as not negotiable. This applies not only to the vital interests of states, societies and empires but with almost equal force to the vested interests of all those mutually exciting forces which President Eisenhower called the military-industrial complex. So the fact that war can no longer be expected to 'pay' even the victors is no guarantee against its repetition, especially in the field of what another of our papers describes as 'small wars', a description which deserves further analysis. Do we mean more than wars which do not involve 'great' powers on either side?

Finally, we have to take into account the cultural impact of the natural sciences. Even a hundred years ago the central topic of education was deemed to be the doings of men during recorded time and especially the achievements and reflections of those individuals who seemed most worthy of study and emulation. Few doubted that the biological evolution of mankind had released a new and radically different process of social evolution. None proclaimed this more passionately than that great protagonist of biological evolution, T. H. Huxley, who insisted that what he called the Ethical Process was a process different in kind from and even opposed to the Cosmic Process of biological evolution. It was the human task to create 'in opposition to the State of Nature, the State of Art of an organised polity capable of maintaining and constantly improving itself. . . .'[4] The State of Art which social, ethical, cultural men were required to make was as different from the State of Nature as a garden from the Amazon jungle. It was, he thought, a losing battle, though a noble one. In time the Cosmic Process would resume its sway. 'Evolution encourages no millennial expectations.'

Perhaps the Cosmic Process is already resuming its sway, more quickly than Huxley expected. But he would, I think, have been even more surprised at the disinterest shown by his successors in the Ethical, by contrast with the Cosmic process and more generally by their obsession with the natural sciences, rather than the human arts, especially the art of living together on an ever more crowded planet. Even where this is recognized as the major concern of twentieth century man, it is deformed by being formulated as a series of problems to be solved, often with no examination of the origin or validity of those standards of expectation which alone make deviance from them problematic.

These standards I believe to be historical and cultural. The most significant area of our ignorance in this context today is, in my view, the area of our greatest neglect – the study of human history and especially of the development of human cultures and the extent to which the world's human populations could influence for the better the future course of cultural evolution. The problem will be different for each of these populations. The so-called West, rapidly diminishing in relative numbers and importance, no longer monopolizes the high road into the future. When it did so a mere century ago, its claim to dominance was based not on its science and technology but on its belief that it had solved the age-old task of making power accountable and establishing ethical criteria of accountability. Impartial justice, representative government, a responsible executive and a humane ethic – these were the gifts which it prided itself on offering to the world; not lasers and atomic fission and genetic engineering.

These gifts are not generated by applying energy to matter. They are still largely problems to be solved within existing cultural boundaries, but each is so greatly affected by its neighbours, usually for the worse (as by sources of military threat) that a collective approach is needed no less than individual approaches. I have no idea whether either a common culture or a mosaic of compatible cultures is a possible goal for mankind or any part of it today, but I have no doubt that without one or other or some combination of the two there is no future for men – or at least for Western men – on earth.

Confrontation and trade-off are not enough.

## References

1. H. A. L. Fisher, *A History of Europe*, London, Edwin Arnold, 1936, p. 379.
2. H. A. L. Fisher, op. cit. p. 1219.
3. Adolph Lowe. Paper in publication.
4. T. H. Huxley, 'Evolution and Ethics', the Romanes lecture 1893. Published in *Evolution and Ethics and other Essays*, London, Macmillan, 1895.

# LEVEL II: SOCIETY

# Introduction

Much of Vickers' life was involved with national organizations, albeit such disparate ones as the Army and the National Coal Board. It is clear that he always saw himself as a Briton and a patriot and by the beginning of World War II he was increasingly interested in the affairs of the state. He was not, of course, a member of any government nor did he overestimate the ability of governments to manage the complex systems in their charge. Vickers was, however, concerned with the government of human systems and with political power; but as he stated in his last book, *Human Systems are Different*, for him, government meant, 'all aspects of the art of imposing on human affairs, whether in the public or the private sector, whatever kind and degree of order seems possible and desirable to those in seats of power', and by political power he meant 'all power which is exercised by anyone in so far as it affects anyone else, whether intentionally or not, whether knowingly or not. And let us describe as a responsible exercise of power any exercise which takes into account however partially or mistakenly the effect of that exercise of power on another, whether that other has any power to hold the other to account or not'.

In such a context Vickers wanted to make a contribution to the disen-tanglement of the issues faced by society – not just Britain. In these articles alone he shows concern for the provision of health care, the management of traffic, the death penalty, and land use planning. In *What Sets the Goals of Public Health?* he identifies very early in the life of the British national health service the in-built feedback loop whereby the availability of tech-niques actually changes people's expectations and hence influences the goals of the system. Now it may seem self-evident that the demand for health care provision would grow as more services became available, but in 1957 Vickers had to point out even in *The Lancet*: 'At one point it was widely, if half consciously, held that a health service was a self-limiting service. When the demands of health were fully met, there would be nothing more to do. Indeed better preventive services might in time reduce the total resources needed to provide optimum health for all. It is clear, I think, that health services are not self-limiting in this sense.'

This article, whilst addressing issues that are central to the provision of health care in Western culture, has much wider applicability in the whole of the public domain. *Community Medicine*, however, is at first sight a narrower paper which is included here for several reasons. Firstly, he contributed many articles to *The Lancet* and this is a significant aspect of his work. Secondly, in raising the concept of community medicine in 1967 he is very early in the field, and yet his framework and conception are still far from complete implementation and appear just as relevant today. Finally, of course, Vickers as always makes some general points, in this case his conclusion that 'technology and organization are not omnipotent; they cannot replace the personal and professional service on which com-munity medicine depends. They can only support it. . . .'

*Ecology, Planning, and the American Dream* is to some extent taking up a similar issue. Here in one of his most cited articles and at his most lyrical (of the ancient track he can see from his window) he says:

> Then comes the promise, and threat, of a far greater complexity. The track runs across the hill crests to Avebury; the rampart is rising; the men who are moving those millions of tons of earth with muscles and wicker baskets are being fed by the labours of other men who must feed themselves as well. What new forces, interacting in what new field, are setting here their strange, enduring signature?

Vickers is making the point that awareness of the physical characteristics of the world is not enough. The ecological issues of our time are issues of human ecology – the ecology of the inner world.

> Avebury *could* not have been built except by a society whose food-getting technology was good enough to free large numbers of its members for unproductive work, and whose social technology was good enough to permit elaborate division of labour. . . .
> Avebury *would* not have been built, even by such a society, unless the dreams of the decision-takers had taken that form and the total value system of the society had been sufficiently strong and stable to support the implications of that decision for decades. It was a strange dream for men who were little better equipped for digging than the foxes and badgers that shared their native hills. The lonely ring among the brooding hills reminds us that the quality of our dreams is neither masked nor redeemed by the quality of our technology.

Later in the article he is critical of claims made of objectivity ('The most objective observer looks out from an inner world and through an inner world which structures and gives meaning to what he sees.') and of science. (This point is exposed more fully in article 23.)

Finally he talks of an 'unshaken faith in the power and duty of the human mind to make judgement of value. . . .'; and in *Values, Norms and Policies* he explores the relationship between the three, thus reflecting some aspects of the public health article and leading us into more of the general considerations of the remaining papers in this section.

All of these remaining papers have major themes which are returned to in later articles and which recur in much of Vickers' work. Firstly, *Appreciative Behaviour* with its lengthy example of the Royal Commission on capital punishment 1949–1953 explains in some detail his concepts of appreciation and appreciative behaviour which in subsequent articles, particularly in Level IV: The Individual, are developed to include appreciative field and system. Appreciation appears again in *Values, Norms and Policies* which also spends some time developing the concept of the tacit norm which is a major subject in article 23 (*Rationality and Intuition*).

In a similar manner *Changing Patterns of Communication* can be paired with article 22, *Levels of Human Communication*, which was written at much the same time. The paper here maps out the changes taking place in six communication fields and later explores five levels of discourse – threat, bargaining, request, persuasion, and dialogue. Such discourse can play a major part in the development or resolution of conflict. In *The Management of Conflict* Vickers looks at sources, levels, and types of conflict and the contemporary models through which it was conventionally explained. By the end of the article, however, Vickers is considering the resolution of conflict at national level and touches on another familiar theme: 'The management of conflict is not the responsibility of authority alone. It is the responsibility of every member of every system in all their endemic conflicts.'

# 8

# What sets the goals of public health?*

## I

I ask what sets the goal of public health. I do not ask how we choose them, for manifestly our choice is only one element in a manifold process. When we open our eyes to the scene around us, we find goals already set. Policies are being implemented, institutions are in action with all the historical momentum of buildings and establishments. Men are in mid-career. Budgets, even budget headings, have acquired prescriptive rights. This dynamic configuration is resistant to sudden change. So the most obvious answer to my question springs to mind at once. History sets the goals of public health. We influence them no more and no less than we influence the course of history.

The process of interaction and mutual adaptation which we call history is an obscure, though familiar, mystery. Looking into the future, we see a widening vista of possibilities. Tomorrow is almost committed; but next year, ten, twenty years hence, what might not be possible? Yet looking into the past, the vista seems to narrow from past to present. We see a thin line of actualities detaching itself from all that might have been; and those who will some day look back over what is now the uncommitted future will see the same. Of all that competes for realisation, only a tiny fraction is realised, and in the process it excludes a host of alternatives. The eternal enigma of history is, 'Why from all these possibilities did these, rather than any of the others, come to birth?' Somewhere in the answer to that question lies, among many other things, the scope and meaning of human initiative.

Among the forces which make history, one of the most obvious is human need. Some would say that need sets the goals of public health. New needs emerge and evoke the measures which will satisfy them. At any moment, with a more or less significant time-lag, the goals of public health reflect the dominant needs of its time and place.

This statement is not so simple as it looks. The needs which evoke response are those which are recognised as needs, and this process of recognition has odd features. Our culture accepts some conditions of living which in other epochs would have moved slaves to rebel – such as going to work on a rush-hour subway; and on the other hand insists on others which

*From *The Lancet*, 22 March 1958. Also published in the *New England Journal of Medicine*, 20 March 1958. Originally an address given at the School of Public Health, Harvard University 26 November 1957.

other epochs never thought of – such as having its bread wrapped in 'Cellophane'. Why this particular selection of needs? Again, we cannot satisfy all the needs we recognise. Our age, with public health services more abundant and more active than in any before it, is probably more aware than any other of unsatisfied needs. How are they resolved, the conflicts between needs fighting for satisfaction? Are they resolved by human choice? And, if so, by what criteria?

In answering these two questions we discover how significant that time-lag may be. In 1946 the British Parliament, with the passing of the National Assistance Act, thought that it had destroyed the last vestiges of that 'New Poor Law' which the reformers of 1834 expected to abolish destitution. Yet every page of the new statute reflects attitudes which are not responses to the future but protests against the past. It is not only soldiers who start each war perfectly equipped to win the one before.

Previous ages had neither subways nor 'Cellophane', so they had no occasion to opt for or against them. The thought suggests another. To some extent at least techniques set the goals of public health. For techniques not only enlarge our responses; they mould our expectations.

Most obvious is the impact of therapeutic and preventive techniques. Pasteur set the goals of public health for many decades ahead. Every new technique, by opening a possibility, awakens a need – at least in our Western culture, where in matters of health we have a highly developed sense that whatever is possible for any should be available to all.

Therapeutic and preventive techniques depend on industrial techniques. Apart from the techniques of the pharmaceutical industry, on which all chemotherapy depends, the engineering industry is the main executant of sanitation. Equally important are administrative techniques. Large-scale public works are possible only in societies which are capable of administering them and of collecting and spending the money they involve, societies moreover which are tolerant of high taxation and of land requisition and which are accustomed to think in terms of social and geographical areas commensurate with the problems involved.

These factors also limit the goals of public health. As we, looking back a few decades, see our societies at a stage which not only did not attempt but could not have attempted much that we regard as a matter of course, so a not so distant future age may see us enmeshed in limitations of administrative vision which we cannot yet discern.

These limitations are manifold. Every executive authority concerned with public health is limited not only by money and technical skill but by the area of space and the span of time over which it is free to plan, and by its own past experience, which goes far to determine how it shall set about its new problems. And apart from these direct limitations, each authority is limited by its own current activity. For our powers of attention are limited, and the habit of placing something at the focus of our attention implies the habit of leaving other things in the periphery.

Techniques limit us in yet another way. A technological age expects to deal with its problems technologically. Consider the growing hazard of noise. To earlier ages the natural remedy would have seemed to be – to make less noise. That, I fear, would seem regressive and defeatist to us. So many alternatives are open.

We might take to wearing helmets which excluded all noise absolutely. Dual – or better, triple – microphones round the helmet could be so devised that they could distinguish and reject sounds, however loud, which came from remote sources, admitting only those which arose nearby. We could thus converse in comfort, while the roads roared with machinery and the air screamed with jets. The helmets would be bad for our hair; but we should not want hair if we were always to wear helmets. Medical technology would devise a painless and permanent method of depilating the scalp, and fashion stylists would have greater scope with our helmets than they could possibly have with our hair. Each incidental problem would offer a new opportunity for technology.

Furthermore, we should have achieved a moral advance in at least two directions. By getting rid of our hair, we should have abolished one of those tiresome, hereditary differentials which conflict with our ideas of equality. And we should have enlarged the area of human freedom, by giving us new powers of choice in deciding to what we should attend. Above all, we should have again eluded the regressive, defeatist solution of saying No. The engineers would no longer be threatened by the limitation of what our ears would stand. Progress would have burst another barrier.

To be exact, we should have avoided saying No in the one field where that word is unacceptable to us. Our impoverishment would fall only in areas of life which are – commercially – insignificant.

If this forecast of a brave new world sounds fanciful to you, does it seem any more fanciful than the thought of a technological age deliberately choosing to be less active in order to be less noisy?

So let us add another to our list of goal-setters. Ideology sets the goals of public health.

Needs, techniques, ideologies – these are names for aspects, dimly understood, of that mutually adaptive process which we call history. But among the interacting forces is one, unique and clearly identified – our individual human selves; no mere pointers recording the resolution of external forces but pointers dynamically charged, themselves contributing to the forces they record. We must determine our own role, if we are to complete our analysis of what sets the goals of public health.

## II

This is perhaps the moment to question whether public health has any goals. Is it not governed rather by avoiding threats? Let us not confuse ourselves by saying that a threat is only a negative goal. The psychologists have wrought havoc with lay thinking by popularising the term 'goal-seeking' as if it covered all purposive behaviour. It begins now to be widely recognised that threat-avoiding differs from goal-seeking in important ways. One of the most important is this. If I successfully seek a goal, I shall ultimately find it and then I shall discover whether I really like it. But if I successfully avoid a threat, I shall never experience it and so I shall never discover whether it was worth avoiding.

Threat-avoiding bulks large in our individual motivation; and I fancy that it plays an even larger part in the collective decisions of larger and less coherent bodies. In individual motivation the psychologists tell us how much of our behaviour is directed to avoiding what we recognise, often unconsciously and often wrongly, as a threat. The landmarks of political, economic, and social history are the moments when some condition passed from the category of the given into the category of the intolerable. The welfare legislation of Great Britain is based on a report which identified 'five giant evils' as goals for attack – disease, unemployment, ignorance, squalor, and want. I believe that the history of public health might well be written as a record of successive redefinings of the unacceptable.

It is safer, none the less, to assume that public health knows goals as well as threats; but it is not safe to assume that these are interchangeable – positive and negative ways of saying the same thing.

In any case, goals and threats are not ultimate governors of behaviour; on the contrary, they are the most superficial of all. Much of the confusion which surrounds the discussion of ends and means comes from the fact that a 'goal' or 'end', if it is attainable once for all, is never more than a 'means' to maintaining some relationship which must always be sought anew. My dinner is a 'goal', something I seek and either find or do not find; but it is only a means to maintaining that rate of metabolic exchange which must be maintained through time as long as I live. The specific goals we pursue – I will call them objectives – are always means to attain or preserve some relationship, internal or external, which we need or think we need. The specific threats we seek to escape are threats to some relationship, events which we think might strain the relationship perhaps beyond repair. These continuing relationships I will call norms. We seek to maintain them; when we deviate from them, we seek to return. But they have thresholds beyond which we may not – or think we may not – deviate without disaster, thresholds which in the clearest cases mark points of no return; and these I call limits.

Physiologically, our needs for food and drink and air fall readily under these descriptions. They are relationships with the environment; they have an optimal position and they have thresholds beyond which they cannot deviate without disaster. Our psychological and social needs, so far as we can discern them, seem to be of the same kind. 'To be secure,' 'to be successful,' 'to be happy' are relationships which no one expects to attain once for all.

Health is clearly a norm, not a goal, according to this terminology – a relationship not to be attained once for all but ever to be renewed. Disease is a deviation from this norm and includes a series of limits beyond which irreversible change takes place, the most dramatic being death.

This is not the normal meaning of health and disease. The constitution of the World Health Organisation does indeed define health as a state of complete physical, mental, and social wellbeing and not the mere absence of disease or infirmity. But who is to define for each individual that state of multiple excellence which under this definition would constitute health for him? It is easier to equate the norm with the normal and to count as disease only what falls below this assumed level of normality. Yet few, I think, would quarrel with the implication of the W.H.O. constitution that health is a form of individual excellence.

It is common today to describe human striving in terms of tension reduction, and this serves well enough to describe the norm-seeking and limit-avoiding which I regard as the basic governors of our activity. But it is not always remembered that our norms and limits are to some extent self-set. The architecture of our expectations determines the operative tensions, whether positive (between what is and what we think 'ought to be') or negative (between what is and what we think 'ought not to be'), and the process of adaptation consists no less in the redesigning of our own expectations than in the manipulation of our environment.

There is an intimate mutual relationship between these two processes. The development of the automobile did more than provide us with new means to satisfy our needs. It set new needs, new expectations, new norms of mobility, even new limits of unacceptable immobility. The essential character of industrial expansion and the root of its basic instability is precisely that it creates and continually changes the expectations to which it is supposed to minister. Commercial advertising is socially significant not as a medium for proposing and indirectly defining the specific objectives through which our expectations can be satisfied, but rather as a means of setting and constantly resetting the expectations themselves.

The process by which we set and revise our governing expectations is obscure, largely unconscious and immensely important. Consider in how short a time the United States has developed among a population so large and so diverse that wide conformity of expectation which is understood by the American Way of Life. I do not seek to explore that astonishing achievement here. It may serve to illustrate the fact that the character and coherence of a society or of an individual personality is largely a function of its governing expectations, the norms and limits which describe its setting as a dynamic system; and that the crucial task of adaptation is the adjustment of this inner architecture so as to maintain effective contact with the environment without losing that inner balance of forces whereby the individual or the society hangs together.

The process of history is a process of mutual adaptation. Every organism and every society is a dynamic system, an ever-shifting balance of forces, and it has continually to solve a double problem. It has to regulate the interaction of its inner forces whereby it hangs together; and it has to regulate the interaction between itself as a whole and its environment. Neither configuration is infinitely plastic; each can be changed only within limits and notably within limits of time. Thus the creature must learn to find the food it can digest or learn to digest the food it can find; and it survives only so long as it can find a viable compromise between its needs and its opportunities.

I invite you, then, to consider our behaviour in the field of public health as one aspect of that historical process in which we are engaged, a process of adaptation in which, consciously and unconsciously, we continually modify both our external environment and our inner system of expectations – behaviour which can be defined at any given moment in terms of the relationships which it is set to maintain and the limits which it is set to avoid, but which is as much and as properly concerned with redesigning its norms and limits as with modifying its external environment. It is within this process, still largely blind, that human initiative plays whatever may be its part and thus takes a hand in setting the goals of public health.

I hope I have made it clear that I regard the process by which these goals are set as largely beyond our control – largely but not wholly. Our conscious contribution, though limited, may be crucial. To explore its possibilities, I will consider the kind of situation in which it seems most operative – that is, in the taking of concrete decisions.

Suppose someone has to decide whether a particular child, at present neglected and ill-used, should be given institutional care or left in its ill-found home. The decision is taken within a framework of half-conscious value judgments as to the relative importance of children's rights and parental rights; the proper limits of official interference; the effect on children of separation from parents at different ages; the merits and demer-its of institutional as against familial care and so on. These judgments reflect the governing expectations of the deciding minds at the time, the norms and limits by which they are regulated, their 'setting', if you find it convenient to regard them as dynamic systems.

But within this framework of norms and limits there operates a set of practical considerations of a very different kind. Is there a place in a suitable institution? Will it be wanted for some other more urgent case? What is the quality of institutional care available here and now? The answer to the particular case may well be given by these practical considerations alone.

But the particular case is by no means all that is being decided. It serves to confront today's expectations with today's possibilities and thus to release into the stream of policy-making the consciousness of a disparity, a maladaptation. The institutions available now were built in response to the felt needs of an earlier decade. Today's revised intuitions of need will not be realised in terms of buildings, budgets, staff, training, and the rest for some decades to come. They are already muted by the past; for our inherited institutions have themselves contributed to our current ideas of what institutional care connotes; and our revised ideas, on the way to realisation, will have to fight for their lives against other equally valid intimations in totally different fields, which compete with them for resources, space, skill, and attention. Yet it seems to be through the deciding of concrete cases today that we crystallise the insights and the discontents which mould the standards and the institutions of tomorrow.

I have taken this cursory look at the historical process in the hope of discerning where human initiative comes in. So far the answer is far from clear. All decisions, it seems, are choices between a limited number of specific alternatives, all sometimes highly unwelcome. They challenge us first to distinguish these alternatives and to evaluate them. They challenge us further to inquire how those choices came to be posed and to consider through what inner and outer adjustment they may be answered more acceptably in future. The possibilities in this second field are, I think, the wider; and it is chiefly through them in my view that we have the power to take a hand in setting the goals of public health; and not the power alone but also a duty and a need of unusual intensity today.

## III

For public health in our Western culture would seem to be at a crossroads. For a hundred years it has been concerned mainly with the age-old threats which beset a species not too firmly established on the Earth – the threat of deficiency in our basic metabolic needs for enough food and rest; the threat of competition from the only other genus which still disputes with us for mastery of the planet, the bacteria. In its battle with deficiency and with infection public health achieved spectacular success. True, that success does not look so final today as it did twenty or thirty years ago. The world still contains many undernourished people and it is not clear that their numbers will be less a hundred years hence.

Bacteria and viruses become resistant to our present methods of attack and continually threaten us anew. The fact remains that Western societies are less preoccupied than ever before with the control of deficiency diseases and infectious diseases.

They are, however, no less concerned with disease. Metabolic disorders, mental disorders, disorders of excess rather than deficiency, have risen in importance as others have declined and with these we are at present less well equipped to deal. Our hazards from excess range from excessive nuclear radiation, through excessive smoking to the excessive consumption of ice-cream – products which have in common the fact that their superabundance is our own doing. Even the still obscure concept of 'stress' as a cause of mental ill health connotes excess – the impact of more challenge than the organism is able to bear.

A technological age was well equipped to partner public health in its attack on the deficiency diseases and the infectious diseases. Even where the new hazards were partly the creation of industrialisation, as in the growth of mammoth cities, industrialisation had the tools to remedy its own defects. It was as much at home providing a water-supply and a sewerage system as in building a hydroelectric power station or an arterial road. It was possible for Lewis Mumford in his *Technics and Civilisation* to describe the evils of industrialisation as merely features of an eotechnic age.

Today it is far from clear that a technological age is as well equipped to partner public health in the next stage of its journey. On the contrary, it is likely in my view that the requirements of public health will cut ever more sharply across the valuations of an industrial age. What matters most to human wellbeing in the coming decades may well be conditions which industry cannot provide and is in fact chiefly instrumental in denying.

These changes will affect every aspect of public health. Public health, as I see it, has three main concerns – with health services; with health conditions; and with the concept of health itself. In all three fields it faces important tasks of revaluation.

In Britain the introduction of a national health service has helped to clarify our thinking about health. At one point it was widely, if half-consciously, held that a health service was a self-limiting service. When the demands of health were fully met, there would be nothing more to do. Indeed, better preventive services might in time reduce the total resources needed to provide optimum health for all. It is clear, I think, that health services are not self-limiting in this sense. The amount of effort which can plausibly be devoted to the health of the individual and the community increases with every scientific development and will, I think, increase indefinitely. Thus the services which might be provided may well continue to exceed, perhaps by an ever-increasing margin, the services which can in fact be provided, since the total will be limited by the amount of resources available, having regard to conflicting demands. Consciously or unconsciously we shall still have to decide what is to be the total volume of resources devoted to public health and how it is to be distributed between different services, different needs, and different classes of beneficiary – for example, between the young and the old. These decisions will grow harder, not easier, with the passage of time.

Public health has always been especially concerned with preventive medicine; and here its function has been to establish the conditions of health primarily in the physical environment but also in the structure of society and of the individual personality. To change, for example, social attitudes towards mental illness or individual attitudes towards prenatal and postnatal care is to change the conditions of health, no less than to lay a water-main. Here it would seem that a much wider field is opening.

Current American culture is sometimes criticised by American social psychologists on the ground that it builds up and sanctions too many expectations which it does not allow to be satisfied and thus produces more frustration than most people can safely take. However this may be, it is clear that the culture and structure of society, including the many subcultures of which it is composed, set conditions which are potent for good and ill. These conditions are not under the control of public health but they are not beyond its influence and its criticism.

For public health has a unique opportunity, as well as a duty, to clarify our understanding of health and disease and hence our attitude towards it, and this field clamours to be further explored. Even the aetiology of those disorders which have hitherto been most prominent is far from fully understood; still more obscure is that of the diseases which claim priority today. The distribution of disease, even within the crude categories of our present statistics, is full of oddities. In Britain, though infant mortality has vastly declined over the past fifty years, the relative differential between the rates in different income-groups has not been reduced but has, if anything, increased. Why? Schizophrenia is known to have a genetically predisposing cause; yet its reported incidence in the lowest income-group is many times that in the highest. Why? Such challenging enigmas could be multiplied, I expect, among American statistics, as among British.

These thoughts arise only from the indices we at present use. But we have no reason to think that our present classifications of people are the most significant. We badly need a more adequate classification of human types – and perhaps of human situations also.

This again may give us a new idea of the conditions of health. We already know, though it is easy to forget, that a 'society' at any moment of time contains people of two sexes and all ages; and that the health of each of these is a condition to be preserved through the span of a lifetime. Add to this that these people consist not merely of an 'admired type', and varying degrees of deviation from it, but of a wide variety of types, each of which can claim the respect we accord to the normal. To do justice to all these diverse claims calls for a concept of the conditions of health more penetrating than any we use now.

So let me add another answer to the question which we are asking. I would like to think that in so far as the goals of public health are consciously set, they will be set increasingly by practitioners of public health and especially by physicians, epidemiologists, and social scientists working together, with the more abundant techniques and data now available to us, to disentangle more clearly the nature of that dynamic balance which we should recognise as health and the conditions which favour or threaten it.

IV

There are, I suggest, three contributions which public health can thus make to the setting of its own goals. It can evaluate health by the criteria which we currently use. It can criticise these criteria and thus help to deepen and refine them. And it can explore those processes of decision by which public-health policy is defined and implemented.

The first is a familiar function. Public health is at present measured largely by statistics of mortality and morbidity. Even these rough indices, as I have already mentioned, disclose differences between localities and categories of people and changes with time which we cannot explain and which challenge us to research. Moreover, this information, at least in Britain, is analysed today under categories which are almost certainly less adequate than they need be. This is serious; for the categories under which information is gathered are immensely important. They not only influence what we think about; they limit what we can think about.

There is thus much to be done in interpreting our simplest indices and in refining the tools and the methods whereby we work on them.

Next, there is much scope for refining those criteria of breakdown which we regard as indices of ill-health, individual or social. Already we use many beyond those basic figures of mortality and morbidity which not long ago would have seemed an adequate measure of public health. Alcoholism and drug addiction, crime and perversion, are readily used as indices of breakdown; but how to interpret them? Shall we seek the cause in the nature and history of the individual or in the structure of society? In reaction against the long centuries in which the criminal, the drunkard, the addict, the pervert were regarded as enemies of society, we tend today to assume that they are its victims. Fromm and Kardiner have used such statistics to impugn the health not of the individuals concerned but of the society which destroyed them.

Clearly, these indices and their interpretation are the concern of public health. Clearly, too, their interpretation is more complex than a decision whether they indict the individual or his society; for the interaction between the two is far too subtle and involved to permit any such simple alternative.

And here, I think, we are helped by another important change in our approach to health. It seems to me that Western medicine is at last getting around to the question which patients have always asked but which hitherto only witch-doctors have taken seriously. This is the question – 'Why me?'

Smitten by accident or disease, the savage, as I understand, asks – 'Why me? Granted that boughs fall and snakes bite, why should I be the victim, rather than another?' The question would have seemed trivial to the public health of only a few decades ago. Suffice it to eliminate, so far as may be, the risks from falling boughs and biting snakes or their equivalent in our day. What matter whether A or B is the unlucky one? It makes no difference to the statistics. Yet medicine has always known that immunity and vulnerability are in some measure characteristics of the individual. In its attack on the infectious and deficiency diseases, medicine is increasingly concerned to build up the inner immunity of the individual, rather than to eliminate the risk from the environment; and the study of individual variations in immunity is an increasing part of medicine's activities.

Vulnerability is the opposite side of the same penny. The study of psychosomatic disease leads medicine to view an increasing field of illness as highly individual behaviour, the response of a particular person to a situation to which he is vulnerable. Even having an accident is coming to be regarded as a form of such behaviour. The concept of accident-proneness plays an important part in industrial medicine and its exploration provides ever more material to answer the question – 'Why me?'

The concept of immunity and vulnerability as a characteristic of the individual applies no less to mental health and mental disorder and may find here its most important developments. We assume that here also there is need of a dual approach – on the one hand, to reduce the hazards of the environment; on the other, to increase the immunity of the individual. But we know much less about the meaning of either term. 'Stress', in the psychiatric as distinct from the physiological sense, is a very imprecise concept; and equally unsure is our understanding of the conditions which make the individual relatively vulnerable or immune to it. Even a small enlargement of our understanding here would alter our concept of health.

In the field of mental health it seems unlikely that we shall suffer in the near future from lack of hazards. It is the more important that we should get a better understanding of the nature of immunity. This, it would seem, is a function of the way in which the individual organises his experience on the one hand and his expectations on the other – if you will allow that word 'expectations' to stand for all those norms and limits which define the setting of his system. The two must be so related that the individual can remain internally coherent and externally effective – I would say 'adaptive', if that word had not acquired so one-sided a connotation.

Psychiatric literature is full of warnings against allowing our governing expectations to diverge too sharply from the realities of the world in which we live. Socially, it may be even more disastrous if they diverge too little, for it is precisely through our sense of this divergence that we exercise over events whatever initiative we can win. Every adaptive society must have its protestants, for protest is the mainspring of any adaptation that is not purely passive. And since the protester gets more than his share of stress, he needs more than his share of immunity.

We need, then, a concept of health which will take account both of the individual's ability to live in his society without breakdown and of his ability to resist its pressures. We are still so far from this that laymen at all events do not clearly distinguish the immune from the well-adapted or even from the conformist. Yet, if we had an adequate idea of what adaptation means, we should, I think, recognise the distinction as crucial. The agents of adaptation are not those who are commonly called well-adapted, still less are they the conformist; they are those who can carry within themselves without injury a more than usually large measure of tension – tension between the norms of individual and social experience, between the 'is' and the 'ought to be', between the present and the future; in a word, those who have a high degree of immunity to the pressures which threaten our mental health. I have no doubt that such a concept of health and its conditions would incidentally give a new clarity to our understanding both of individual freedom and of the process of democracy; for both freedom and democracy seem to me to be limited in extent and quality by this elusive factor.

Finally I suggested that it was within the field of public health to explore those processes of decision whereby the policy of public health is defined and implemented. These processes are important, because in them the process of adaptation breaks the surface of consciousness and becomes open to analysis at a new level. If we observed the behaviour of officials and politicians, of committees and pressure groups, in the making of some policy, might we not get some more precise insight into the way in which the disparate forces I have noticed combine to set the goals of public health?

Such a research, which would be difficult to design and to execute, would, I think, land us in successive areas of doubt, each more recalcitrant but also more fruitful than the one before.

First, we should find, I hope, that the decision which came out of the deciding minds bore some relation to the information which went in; and we should confront the problem how to make available to policy-makers, predominantly lay, the knowledge and attitudes of rapidly expanding sciences.

Secondly, we should find that the decision which emerged was a choice between a few specific alternatives; and we should be led to ask how these alternatives were selected and why others were ignored. We should encounter the enigma of attention.

Thirdly, we should observe that the alternatives between which the policy-makers chose were disparate. In that budgeting of resources which underlies all decisions, they have to weigh against each other short-term proposals and long-term proposals, preventive proposals and therapeutic proposals. At one level a paediatric project is competing with a geriatric one. At another level a whole public-health programme is fighting for a place in the national budget with something as disparate as a hydrogen bomb. How in the world do the policy-makers weigh against each other alternatives so different in character?

We should observe men in the process of answering that critical and ubiquitous question – 'what matters most now?' And we should thus observe valuation in action.

And here we should find that the alternatives which these men were comparing with each other were by no means so simple or so stable as they appeared. No issue ever is or ever ought to be decided 'on its merits', if that is taken to mean 'without reference to its repercussions on other issues which its decision will affect'. The views people take of an issue depend on how they 'see' it. It can be seen as part of many different questions; people will see it as part of those questions which most concern themselves. They cannot be proved wrong; they can all be proved right. So what? Does valuation dissolve in discrimination, and is discrimination simply a matter of what you fancy?

Perhaps research would throw some light on these questions. They are important and they are real. One thing I am sure it would tell us. The way we see the question depends very much on the kind of question we are accustomed to deal with. Our society is run by people who are accustomed and professionally trained to see and answer technological questions and financial questions and legal questions and administrative questions. Only very few people are accustomed and professionally trained to see and answer human questions about people as people. We may be thankful that their number is increasing, for this imbalance cannot fail to distort the goals of public health. But this alone is, I think, a very small part of the answer.

I have suggested a few of the many ways in which we can hope to deepen our knowledge of ourselves and of the processes of which we are part – of all fields of knowledge the most intractable and the most important. I believe that this knowledge will never equal the other sciences in giving us the power to predict, but that it can none the less promise something different and far more important – a greater power to understand. And it is this which in the end will determine how much and how wisely we can contribute to the seeking of our own health. Tyrants may shout orders, within us and without; but the voice we obey in the end speaks very quietly in the indicative mood.

# 9

# Ecology, planning, and the American dream*

## I

Here I sit in my rural, ecological niche, metabolizing a breakfast drawn from three continents, and quietly increasing the world's supply of carbon dioxide, which, as Dr Deevey explains, may be, but probably is not, helping to thaw the polar ice. Across the valley, through the tops of beeches, wych elms, poplars, well grown in a century, I see the crest of the chalk hill, which rose from shallow, warm lagoons some fifty million years ago and which has since mantled itself with humus – that tattered robe, inches deep, which life, dying, has laid over earth's barren nakedness and in which alone new life can root. No longer grazed by sheep or rabbits, it has lost also the fine flora which once found a congenial home in the close-cropped turf; and, being now protected from human 'development' by a public trust, it is swiftly reverting to the woodland from which it was cleared in medieval times. Between me and the hill, the Thames follows the course which it took when it broke through these hills after the last ice age; but it is hidden by the multitude of unfolding leaves which compose the slow dream of a single spring.

Along that hill runs a track where I often walk; an old track as human pathways go, for it has been trodden by men and beasts for four thousand years, perhaps far more. Over many miles of grass it leads to the great earth and stone circles of Avebury, where, early in the second millennium before Christ, my predecessors here – including, I may hope, a few linear ancestors – hewed with their antler picks, out of the solid chalk, a ditch twenty feet deep and a mile in circuit to guard their holy place; and piled up an artificial hill three hundred feet high. When they paused in that massive toil to look about them, they saw a landscape different from today's only in a few ways which I know or can guess. The bird voices, the hill contours, the shapes of leaf and tree which are familiar to me were no less familiar to them.

But from what *inner* world those men looked out, what the hill and rampart meant to them, what they saw as meaningful and what escaped their eyes for lack of foothold in their minds, all this I cannot even guess. If I could revisit them, I would expect to find much of their inner world alien or inaccessible. This, however, is equally true, though probably in lesser degree, of the visitor who will stay with me next week. And of them, as of

---

* From *The Urban Condition*, L. J. Duhl (ed), 1963.

him, I shall at least be sure that, though the objects of their hopes and fears may be beyond my comprehension, their hoping and their fearing will be to them as mine is to me. This conviction is itself odd, for it is unproved and unprovable; yet society in any form we know or value would dissolve if it were not universally held.

My inner world, I can safely say, would be far more strange to them. For at this moment, rooted here in a village community of man, beast, grass, grain, tree, I am equally absorbed in the community of minds which produced the papers in this book – men of other professions on the other side of the world, few of whom I have ever met; men engaged with problems of North American urban ecology, some of which have no counterpart here; yet men whose concerns I share and whose fellowship means much to me in two critical ways.

First, I share with them the excitement of a search for meaning, for understanding of one major aspect of mankind's current predicament: an interest sharpened both by the allure of intellectual challenge and by the need for action, no less here than there. (I live, maybe, in Arcady; but London is less than fifty miles away; and this village has its 'amenity association' of anxious citizens, trying to guide, if not to check, the tide of development which is submerging farm and garden and which will flood far more strongly when the projected motorway follows the neolithic track across the hills.)

Secondly, in my incommunicable inner world, I am upheld by the experience of this sharing, of making mine the thoughts of others, and of recognizing from their signals that my signals to them have been received. So, whether or no our activities have made any other contribution to mental health, they have certainly contributed to mine.

These thoughts epitomize the main conceptual framework which these papers have left in my mind.

'Out there' is a 'real' world, in which things happen. To be more exact, it is a world of happenings, of relations and interactions: for even a stone in the mud or a brick in the wall may be thought of as an event in time – internally, as a configuration of forces; externally, as one constituent in a set of dynamic relations with its surround. Such a world is, naturally, a world of change; but also a world of stabilities and regularities, reflecting the regularities of its underlying laws. Science offers us at least two ways of thinking about these happenings. If we want to know what science can tell us about the way plants grow, we ask the botanist. If, on the other hand, we want to know why this hill, which fifty years ago was covered with vegetation an inch high, bears rank grass today and will be woodland in a few decades, we ask the ecologist. He will describe the effect on each other of the life cycles of the various denizens of these slopes, from the sheep to the tiniest grasses, and the effect on all of withdrawing one. The sheep and the rabbits kept down whatever plant growth could not renew itself from buds at ground level. The fine herbage flourished under their grazing, whilst the saplings perished. Without sheep or rabbits, the balance was reversed.

If pressed to explain the disappearance of the sheep and the rabbits, he would have to widen his field from the hillside to the planet and to take note of a greater variety of interacting forces. His answer, if he tried to make it complete, would take us through the economics of British farming, the response of Australian farmers to a plague of rabbits and of half-urbanized Britons to 'urban sprawl', and much else besides – again, the interaction of disparate variables within a single field.

This is the point of view of the ecologist, and of these papers; and the scene before me serves to illustrate its growing complexity. Before life colonized these hills, the physical forces at play there had established their mutual relationships, sometimes self-stabilizing and sometimes not. The great cycle of evaporation and precipitation maintained the planet's water supply in roughly constant balance between the sea, the atmosphere, the land surface, the subsoil, and the deep reservoirs; and the water, in its unceasing circuit, slowly eroded the newly risen hills and carved ever more deeply each gully which it had begun to carve before. On so recent an outcrop, however, the colonizing forces of life would have been soon at work. The seeding plants and grasses were ready to occupy the bare slopes, checking the erosion, deepening the humus in which they rooted, and modifying even the rainfall on which they subsisted. Skip half a million centuries and we are in a familiar world, in which the conspicuous forces in the ecological balance are forces of life, a fully developed threefold hierarchy, through which solar energy and minerals pass into plant form, thence to form and sustain the herbivores, thence to the carnivores and back again, with countless elaborations and short circuits.

Already the ecological balance is being maintained by forms of inter-action which were unknown before the scene was animated. Each of these creatures, even the lowliest, can organize matter and energy into new and improbable patterns. Each can for a time preserve stable relations between its transient constituents by new methods of regulation; and each, equally, has new ways of regulating the relations between itself and its milieu, and hence new forms of interaction. In particular, most of these forms, even very lowly ones, can learn. There has been a progressive widening in the *field* of relevant interaction, in the *forces* operating within that field and in the *kinds of interaction* involved.

Then comes the promise, and threat, of a far greater complexity. The track runs across the hill crests to Avebury; the rampart is rising; the men who are moving those millions of tons of earth with muscles and wicker baskets are being fed by the labors of other men who must feed themselves as well. What new forces, interacting in what new field, are setting here their strange, enduring signature?

To understand Avebury, we should need to understand the social and technological organization of these neolithic men, which made possible this vast construction; and also their political and religious ideas, which caused it to take this form. To explain this development, we must admit the existence of a new field, unique within each head yet partly shared, an ill-defined but inescapable 'mental' field, which I have called their inner world: a world in which life can be not only lived but experienced and thought about, in which actual and hypothetical, past and future, can be equally present. The forces which operate in this new field, hope, fear, love, hate, ambition, loneliness, obligation, wonder, if not new, are raised to a new power and mediated by new forms of interaction – not only human speech, but all the arts of human intercourse, of mutual support, influence, coercion, manipulation.

This inner world, in which men inescapably live, develops in intimate relationship with the physical world, yet according to its own laws and its own time scale. Human history can be understood only as the interaction of the two worlds. The inner world has its own realities, its own dynamism – and its own ecology. Like the life forms of the physical world, the dreams of men spread and colonize their inner world, clash, excite, modify and destroy each other, or preserve their stability by making strange accommodations with their rivals. The meaning of Avebury, and the reasons why it was built, are to be found not in the ecology of the physical world but in the separate, though so closely related, ecology of the inner world – a world which was old when Avebury was built and which has developed since then far more strongly than the ecology of the surrounding hills.

This is even more true of all the institutions with which these papers[1] deal. Much of the paradox and perplexity which haunt them is due to this essential duality of the world in which we live. Consider in briefest outline the stages of ecological development which this glance has covered. When the first vegetation began to colonize that hill, it found no rivals. There was room, it seemed, for all. Similarly, when the first colonists settled in North America, there must equally have seemed room for all. Actually, in each case there was room not for all but only for the few, rare types which could strike root here and there in such a habitat. As the hillside became one settled home of vegetable and animal life – and equally, as North America became one settled home of human life – the variety of living forms increased; and so did the variety and power of the forces which they brought to bear upon each other, limiting, sometimes eliminating, what had earlier been 'successful' types. Increasingly, in both cases, these forces, whether mutually enabling or mutually limiting, were produced by the activities of similar kinds of life, coming, as they multiplied, into ever closer contact with each other. Even in a milieu without man, the result was an increasingly complex pattern of interaction which can be classified, without any teleological implications, as conflict, competition, or cooperation. Trees in a wood mutually stimulated their propensity to climb and mutually inhibited their propensity to spread. Sheep and rabbits maintained for the downland grasses and creeping plants a habitat as 'artificial' as the rich man's gardeners provide for his 'alpines'. With the emergence of man, these interactions of conflict, competition, and cooperation became elaborated in ways new in scale and character. Avebury *could* not have been built except by a society whose food-getting technology was good enough to free large numbers of its members for unproductive work, and whose social technology was good enough to permit elaborate division of labor. These were already achievements possible to human society alone.

Yet these alone do not explain the result. Avebury *would* not have been built, even by such a society, unless the dreams of the decision-takers had taken that form and the total value system of the society had been sufficiently strong and stable to support the implications of that decision for decades. It was a strange dream for men who were little better equipped for digging than the foxes and badgers that shared their native hills. The lonely ring among the brooding hills reminds us that the quality of our dreams is neither masked nor redeemed by the quality of our technology.

## II

The ecologist, in his complex analysis, develops some ideas which are of the greatest importance in assessing the significance of these papers.

He develops first the idea of *interdependence*. In a field of variables so closely and mutually interrelated, any change anywhere will in some degree affect the whole. As fields widen and variables multiply, this insight threatens to make the whole ecological approach too difficult to be useful. Happily, the ecologist finds that some groups of variables can be usefully studied *for some purposes* as if they were isolated. These groups may be local, be the locality as wide as the Amazonian rain forest or as small as the world under a paving stone. Alternatively, their members may be scattered over the planet, be their constituents as numerous as the members of the Roman Catholic Church or as few as the authors of these papers.[1] The developing importance of such non-local groups is a feature of human society, with its unique systems of communication for mediating mutual influence over physical and temporal distances. The individual constituent may be a member of many groups, local and non-local – as I feel myself to be. Whether local or non-local, what makes a group a valid and useful field of study is that the interactions which are the subject of the study are largely confined within the group field. The relevant forces which bear on the members of the group from outside (be they the tropical rains of the Amazon or the traffic problems of North American cities) may be regarded as conditions common to the group.

Next, the ecologist comes to recognize certain *recurring patterns* in his field of study. These are of four main kinds. Perhaps the most interesting, because the least obviously to be expected, is the steady state. In a world of flux, it is constancy, not change, that requires explanation; and the ecologist's world contains a number of patterns which preserve themselves over substantial periods of time with little apparent change. Populations, for example, like organisms, sometimes remain stable for long periods, by exchanging and renewing their transient constituents at a constant rate.

The ecologist also recognizes *change*, in the form of increase or decrease in the magnitude of one or more of the constituents of a field. Decrease is obviously self-limiting. Either the diminishing variable will disappear, as the thyme has disappeared from the scrub-covered hill and the Algonquin Indian from Manhattan island; or the diminution will itself be checked or reversed. Increase, however, is also found to be self-limiting. The period of increase is succeeded by a period of 'steady state'; or by a reversed trend, usually resulting in an oscillation; or by a 'crash,' in which the increase, often accelerating, is terminated by some sudden and radical alteration of the system. The first occurs when, for example, a local bird population is stabilized by a limitation of suitable nesting sites, or the number of lawyers in a small town by the number of their prospective clients. The second is exemplified by those linked oscillations in the numbers of prey and predators which have often caught the notice of ecologists; the lynx and the snowshoe hare in the Arctic tundra are a familiar example. Some forms of predation among humans show similar fluctuations. The third occurs when a tree growing on some steep slope outgrows the point at which its roots can support its weight and crashes down the hill – as once the last barrier crumbled to let the Thames flow through this gap and abandon its former bed. The self-exciting expansion of an arms race between nations, or of sedition and repression within one body politic, usually results in similarly explosive change.

Finally, the ecologist develops the concept of *regulation*. When he observes 'steady state', he concludes that the forces interacting in his field of study are so disposed that any departure from the steady state tends to change the balance of forces in such a way as to reverse the departure. When he observes 'oscillation', he knows that the span of oscillation defines either the degree of displacement needed to trigger the change which will reverse the process, or the temporal lag before the reversal can become effective. When he observes increase or decrease, he expects it to generate regulative forces which will prevent its continuance in one or other of the familiar ways. Engineers will model for him all the patterns which he can observe in nature and at least some of the devices involved in regulation; in particular, those whereby deviations are 'fed back' into the system to check – or sometimes to multiply – the incipient disturbance.

All these concepts are familiar to the social scientist. The anthropologist describes the self-regulating devices which, in 'primitive' societies, regulate the size of the population, the exchange of goods, the division of labor and the distribution of power; and he traces the disruptive effects, throughout such a society, of such changes as the introduction of firearms or gin or monogamy or a money economy, as the agricultural ecologist traces the repercussions through the whole rural milieu of chemical fertilizers or insecticides. The sociologist develops general concepts for understanding the dynamics of a social field. The stability of the subculture of West End, as Dr Ryan has described it, is ensured by the fact that every would-be leader within, every would-be helper from without, even every would-be deviant, is discouraged or neutralized or in the end extruded by built-in responses of the cultural ethic to the threats which the mere existence of such persons implies.

Ecology, as a science of interrelationships, has no use for the concepts of betterment, of value, or of choice. Men may release into the milieu a virus which destroys rabbits, and may develop a fertilizer industry which displaces sheep. No longer destroyed by sheep and rabbits, the coarse growth may displace the finer herbage. Woods may rise to overshadow their own seedbed so densely that only fungus will grow there. The self-destroyed wood may fall to let in the light and destroy the fungus. It is not for the ecologist to prefer beech trees to fungus or thyme to thistle. Equally valueless (at least in theory) to his impartial eye is the process whereby men build cities and cities attract men; cities breed plagues and plagues limit the size of cities; men curb plagues and cities expand into vast and formless aggregates, from which men try to escape. The automobile brings a means of escape for the few; the many follow and choke the roads. The roads multiply and let the traffic through; and roads and traffic carry with them the megalopolis from which they are flying. Ecology gives us a way of describing, not of valuing, the human process and its conscious and unconscious constituents.

Yet the human ecologist must take account, among the facts of his field, that men themselves are *valuers*. They seek and shun; and their seekings and shunnings are to be understood not in terms of the outer world, which the ecologist can observe, but in terms of the inner world which his subjects inhabit and which he may or may not share. In any field in which men function, the relevant facts and forces include not only what is happening but also what men think is going to happen; not only what they are doing to each other but also what they expect, hope, fear, from each other and from themselves. The inner world is fundamentally structured by human values.

It is thus a dynamic structure, a configuration of forces; and it behaves like other dynamic systems. Political beliefs, economic creeds, social attitudes, personal standards, change and develop partly in response to changes in the 'real' world and partly through their own dynamic interaction. As Professor Kenneth Boulding has observed, 'Such institutions as progressive taxation, inheritance taxes, ... countercyclical fiscal and monetary policy, and the like, are in part outcomes of the socialist criticism of a pure market economy and in part the result of feedback of experiences....'[2] Nor can the rate of such changes be understood without reference to the resistance of the established ethic to changes of a kind *or at a rate* which would undermine its own coherence. Equally, the dynamic of the inner world may accelerate change. The drive to solve the problems created in America by racial and national minorities, problems which constantly recur in these papers - indeed, even the problems themselves - cannot be described without reference to the development of political and ethical ideas, in particular to the felt need to give adequate and viable meaning to the faith in equality.

In this value-structured world live, inescapably, not only the objects of the ecologist's observations, but also the ecologist himself. The writers of these papers[1] are not only scientists. They are also as Dr Seeley has eloquently said, human agents, concerned with the 'quality' of the civilization in which they live and able to make – unable *not* to make – judgments about it of better and worse.

The most objective observer looks out from an inner world and through an inner world which structures and gives meaning to what he sees. This is as true of an astronomer as of an anthropologist; but the significance of the fact varies with the subject matter. It is worthwhile briefly to follow this variation along its course, which is punctuated with significant changes.

## III

From their earliest recorded days men have wondered about the heavenly bodies and have woven around them a great variety of meanings, religious, scientific, and cosmological. Today, a vast body of coherent theory links our solar system with the remotest nebulae and begets increasingly daring speculations, which in turn evoke new observations to confirm or disprove them. This speculative search is an activity of the human mind which seems to grow with exercise; and the body of theory to which it has given rise is a mental artifact, a notable constituent of our inner world. It does not, however, affect, directly or indirectly, the subject matter itself. Whatever may be the realities outside the astronomer's head to which his observations and speculations relate, they are not substantially affected either by his theories or by any action based on his theories – at all events, not yet. The celestial milieu remains an independent variable. For several centuries man's understanding of the solar system was blocked by his assumption that its motions *must* be circular, because circular motion was the most 'perfect'. The planets maintained orbits no less eliptical on this account; and when men belatedly discovered the fact, they had no means of bringing these orbits into line with their own aesthetic canons. Our inner view of the celestial milieu is a human artifact; but the universe itself certainly is not.

The terrestrial milieu is a different story. In the course of centuries of physical interaction, all intensively colonized land has become in some degree a human artifact. This valley where I sit was a swamp, until the river was controlled with locks and barrages. The depth and constitution of the soil is the product of a specific sequence of agricultural practices. Even the uncultivated spaces usually owe their shape and preservation to the feudal system of land tenure which declared them 'commons'. This interaction has contributed to and been affected by an inner view far richer and more complex in content than that which we have of the celestial milieu. The changing face of rural England reflected changes not only in agricultural science but also in men's ideas of land as a source of power, of prestige, of security, of aesthetic satisfaction, and much else besides; and itself contributed to these changes.

The physical city, 'urbs' – which Dr Deevey conveniently distinguishes from 'civitas', the city of rights and duties – is much more obviously and literally a human artifact. There is scarcely a physical object in it, from the skyscraper to the doormat, that was not born in a human mind and brought to being by human hands. It is also an artifact never finished, always in constant change; and it, too, is represented in our minds by a mental artifact, the body of our knowledge about and attitudes toward it. Between the physical and the mental artifact there exists the same elusive, mutual relation. Our ideas of it constantly change, both through our observations of it and through the development of our conceptions of what it might be and should be; and these changes in turn influence – perhaps very weakly, often mistakenly, and always with a critical time lag – what it will become.

What then of 'civitas', the city of rights and duties – not merely legal rights and duties, but all the mutual expectations which make citizens of those who dwell in 'urbs'? The mutual expectations which create the subcultures of West End and Harlem and Puerto Rico are there to be studied, as Ryan, Fried, Ellen Lurie, and Hollingshead and Rogler have studied them. They are 'facts'; but they are primarily facts of the inner world in which these citizens live, a world which the observer may or may not share. The West End is a slum to the planners, to the residents a home. Which is it *really*? It is both, and much more besides. For these words describe not facts of the physical world but judgments proceeding from the value-structured inner worlds of the observer and the participant.

Thus, as our attention ranges from stars, through the physical world, to men and their doings, the inner world becomes increasingly involved, not merely as the screen through which we look, but as an integral part of the material at which we are looking.

Of what does our inner world consist? Professor Boulding has described our inner view as 'the Image'[3] and he has most usefully stressed its importance and its dimensions; but to picture the inner world we must look behind the image and ask what causes an individual or a society to see and value and respond to its situation in ways which are characteristic and enduring, yet capable of growth and change. A national ideology, a professional ethic, an individual personality, resides not in a particular set of images but in a set of *readinesses* to see and value and respond to its situation in particular ways. I will call this an appreciative system.

We know something of the ways in which these readinesses are built up. Even our eyes tell us nothing until we have learned to recognize and classify objects in particular ways; and there is little doubt that our conceptual classifications are built up in the same way. So, equally, are our values and our patterns of action. Our appreciative system grows and changes with every exercise of image formation, a process normally gradual and unconscious; and like all systems, it is resistant to changes of a kind or at a rate which might endanger its own coherence.

These papers[1] are a series of exercises in image formation. Each includes its own individual *realization* of some aspect of the metropolitan environment as an on-going situation and its own *valuation* of what is thus realized. Their major value, as I believe, is to speed in us who read them the development of our own appreciative systems, sharpening and revising our readinesses not only to see but also to value and to respond to the situation in which each of us is involved, in thought and will as well as deed, as agent as well as observer. Such a revision is overdue; for the last two hundred years have left us with an appreciative system peculiarly ill-suited to our needs.

## IV

During the past two centuries, men gained knowledge and power, which vastly increased their ability to predict and control; and they used these powers to make a world increasingly unpredictable and uncontrollable. This paradoxical result flowed from the fact that the technologies to which science gave birth enabled man not only to predict but also to alter the course of events in his milieu. Consequently, the outer world began to change in content, form, and complexity at ever-increasing speed, far outstripping the growth rate of any corresponding power of control. Hitherto, learning had meant adapting to the given. Now the very idea of 'the given' became suspect and dim.

Nonetheless, the belief persisted that increased power to alter the environment brought increased control over it. This belief, still far from dead, is a manifest delusion. First, as every engineer knows, the difficulty of devising any physical control system lies not only – usually not chiefly – in generating enough power but also in generating enough information. Since the material world is a system, any change in the given is bound to have numberless, often unpredictable, repercussions throughout the system; so even if the effect of the intervention is to bring under control the variable which is directly affected, the total system is likely to be less predictable than before, while all learned skills based on the former 'given' are depreciated. Further, these interventions, and the further interventions to which their unpredicted results are bound to lead, are likely to be self-multiplying. The rate of change increases at an accelerating speed, without a corresponding acceleration in the rate at which further responses can be made; and this brings ever nearer the threshold beyond which control is lost.

Even the most liberal legitimate statement of the faith is that men can learn to do anything that can be done by applying energy to material things. But this itself is of depreciating value, far less useful in America today than in the days of the expanding frontier. For the course of human activity in the last two centuries has been not only to change the physical environment from a relatively stable datum to an increasingly unstable artifact but also, and even more importantly, to replace the physical by the social milieu as the most important field of human interaction. It is highly doubtful how far the social environment can be either changed or stabilized by applying energy to material things – even, as these papers show, when the energy is applied to remaking urbs or suburbs.

In consequence, the last two centuries have ushered in a period of instability such as the world has never seen; a period, moreover, in which every new instability was either welcomed as 'growth' or accepted as the price of growth. The ecological view was obscured, overlaid, lost, even denied, by the new ideology of 'progress', with its implicit faith in the possibility of linear change which would not prove self-limiting. Further-more, the idea of progress was itself confused by combining too uncritically the ideas of economic expansion and political betterment.

This identification was due at one extreme to mere naivete. 'Humanly speaking, the greatest happiness possible for us consists in the greatest possible abundance of objects suitable for our enjoyment and in the greatest liberty to profit by them.' So wrote the French economist Mercier de la Rivière in about 1760; and so says Madison Avenue today. At the other extreme, it was the expression of a new, passionate, and comprehensive faith. The wealth of nations was conceived as indefinitely expansible by the division of labor; and free competition was the means whereby the most efficient division of labor would be automatically achieved, internationally as well as nationally. This process would do far more than multiply 'objects suitable for our enjoyment'. It would eliminate national frontiers, abolish war, and unite the whole world in one great Commercial Republic.

'... we are living in a period of most wonderful transition, which tends rapidly to accomplish that great end to which all history points – the realization of the unity of mankind.' So said Prince Albert, when opening the Great Exhibition in London in 1851; and he was expressing a faith widely shared and more powerfully felt than any that had possessed the British since the days when the great cathedrals were built. Even Marx, who in the same city and at the same time was preparing his great attack on the very foundations of that faith, was sufficiently a child of his time to suppose that, once the victory of the proletariat had removed the cause for the exploitation of persons, history would thereafter become the uneventful administration of things.

There was, however, another and radically different view of political betterment. Society was perfectible because men were plastic; and human institutions were the means by which they could be moulded. This view was the heir of a long tradition. The earlier world expected betterment only from good laws; certainly not from blind or selfish interaction. Philosophers from Plato onward based their utopias on the wisdom of a lawgiver – though it was left to the age of hope to conceive of a *progressive* course of education and legislation, leading through ever better institutions to an ever improving polity.

So one way of classifying ideas about progress is to distinguish those which regard it as a form of social evolution from those which regard it as a form of social engineering. Here, to proclaim the first, is Joseph Priestley, prophesying at the end of the eighteenth century:

> ... nature ... will be more at our command, men will make their situation in this world abundantly more easy and comfortable ... and will grow daily more happy ... whatever was the beginning of the world, the end will be glorious and paradisiacal ... I think I could show [these views] to be fairly suggested by a true theory of human nature and to arise from the natural course of human affairs.

And here, to express the other view, is T. H. Huxley, writing in 1893:

> Social progress means the checking of the cosmic process at every step and the substitution for it of another which may be called the ethical process. ... That which lies before the human race is a constant struggle to maintain and improve, in opposition to the state of Nature, the state of Art of an organised polity; in which and by which men may develop a worthy civilization capable of maintaining and improving itself ...

To temper optimism, he added:

> ... until the evolution of our globe shall have entered so far upon its downward course that the cosmic process resumes its sway ... evolution encourages no millennial expectations.

The difference is radical. According to the first view, an acceptable, even a 'paradisiacal' future will arise 'from the natural course of human affairs', even though it lie the other side of a bloody revolution which we cannot bypass and do well to speed. According to the second view, such a future will arise only as it is conceived by the insight and imposed by the will of men on the recalcitrant material of 'the cosmic process'. Marx is nearer to the Prince Consort than is Huxley to Priestley or the 1890's to the 1790's.

Yet all these views lack an ecological orientation. Priestley never questions that the natural course of human affairs is linear. Marx seems to have assumed that the dialectical process would 'wither away' with the State. Huxley does not envisage that the ethical process will have constantly to wrestle not only with the cosmic process but also with the unexpected results of its own activities. None of them seems to envisage enduring debate about the meaning of betterment, the direction of improvement.

We stand today amid the wreckage of these nineteenth-century hopes and certainties. Though the debate between the two views just illustrated remains unresolved, the second view accords more nearly than the first with the insight and spirit of our age. 'A worthy civilisation capable of maintaining and improving itself' will not 'arise from the natural course of human affairs'. It will need a 'constant struggle to maintain and improve it'. It will be a state not of nature but of art, man's great, composite work of art; and it can be no more noble than his dreams. We know, however, better than Huxley's generation what is involved in that endless struggle and what are its limitations.

## V

The energy at our disposal has been multiplied and is now theoretically limitless. Our technology is sufficient to design and make far more than all the artifacts we are conscious of needing. Our means of communication are sufficient to transmit, store, and handle far more information than we can use. Increasing populations, increasingly urbanized, inhabit cities of increasing size, yet demand more space and more stuff per head with every year that passes. Man-made resources grow; natural resources shrink, especially the three most irreplaceable – clean air, clean water, and empty space. The ancient problem of equating populations with living space and food supply emerges on a planetary scale. The problems of our day are set in ecological terms more strident, more blatant, more urgent, than ever before. They are how to regulate the instabilities inherent in this dizzy expansion; how to keep rates of change within bearable compass; how to choose between so many mutually exclusive possibilities.

Yet neither our institutions nor our ideologies are apt for such problems. Both still bear the shape impressed on them by the epoch that has closed; both resist, as every dynamic system must, changes which threaten their own coherence.

One of the most pervasive products of the ecological view is that every choice has a cost: for every realization precludes a hundred others. We can spend time, attention, life, like money, in only one way at a time; and, unlike money, these precious commodities are not expansible.

The cost inherent in every choice is most obvious in the use of land, for even the most modern technology offers no hope of expanding the surface of the planet. Demand multiplies and scope narrows. North Americans, whose grandfathers were still pushing out the frontier between primal nature and agricultural man, meet a new frontier coming back, an ever-narrowing net woven by their own realized dreams. The cost of every new development rises, not only in money, but in the abandonment, often forever, of all alternatives. Land use illustrates with especial clarity the universal truth that betterment is not the accumulation of recognized 'goods' in an ever-increasing heap. It is the realization, within a dynamic system, of some *chosen* set of conditions to the exclusion of countless others.

How are such choices made? And what is the part of the planner in making them? Professor Webber gives a familiar Western answer. The planner helps by making 'explicit tracings of the repercussions and of the value implications associated with alternative courses of action'. The choice between them is not for the planner but for the agent whom he serves.

When the agent is the government of a large society, a state, or a city, comprising a diversity of 'interests', the choice is complex. The individuals concerned do not even know consciously all they want; even their individual wants may be mutually inconsistent; they cannot see ahead even as far as the planner, still less can they see as far as the executive's decision will commit them. How are they to arrive at a collective choice?

Professor Webber states a widespread view when he attributes any difficulties of collective valuation to the lack of a market. Where services are supplied through a market, the individual can express his own choice freely by buying or abstaining from buying; but where services are provided without direct charges, like education and roads and defense, the public must have some alternative means to express its opinion. How else can governments know 'what it is that customers prefer and hence what combination of services and facilities would benefit them and the community most'? In practice, governments must rely partly on the poor alternative of the pressure group, partly on their own 'value hypotheses' and those of their assistants who are 'able to make reasonably good judgments about the current preferences of some of the various publics'.

As an account of what actually happens, in America or elsewhere, in the making of collective choices, even through the market but far more in the political field, this account seems to me to miss an essential element. The men and women in England who abolished slavery, created the educational system, or gave women the vote were not acting on hypotheses of what the voters wanted. They were afire with faith in what people ought to want and in the end they persuaded their lethargic compatriots to give them enough support to warrant a change. American presidents, from Lincoln to Kennedy, do not speak with accents of inquirers seeking guidance about other people's preferences. Like most of the authors of these papers, they *criticize* contemporary values, urge *re*valuation, and appeal not to what people are thinking now but to what they ought to be thinking and would be thinking if they exposed themselves with sufficient sensitivity to the subject matter of the debate. A free society is one in which these initiatives spring up freely and in which men are free to espouse or resist them. It depends, like every other society, on the quality and abundance of these initiatives, as well as on the facilities for their debate, facilities which themselves depend partly on institutions and partly on the capacity of the current appreciative system to criticize itself.

Again, as a description of what actually happens, the foregoing account seems to me to underrate what the planner does and must do. A plan, whether it be an architect's plan for the physical rebuilding of a city center or an administrator's plan for a new mental health service, proposes a unique series of concrete, interrelated choices. It is a work of art, having already form but awaiting an executive decision to give it substance. It can be criticized, commended, compared with others; but the choice of the executive as such is limited to the plans before it. It may reject them all and tell the planners to think again; but in the end the planners will decide what alternatives shall be considered – and, by implication, will decide that all others shall be ignored. Only in the capacity of a planner can anyone propose a *new* answer.

'Government of the people, by the people, for the people.' How simple it sounds, until we explore the volume of meaning, different in each case, comprised in those words 'the people'. The responsibilities of 'government' are of many kinds and they fall differently on each one of us. We have all some responsibility for action, some area, however small, in which each of us and he alone can play the part of agent. There is a second field, wider and not congruent with the first, in which each of us can contribute to the making of policy. There is a third, wider still, in which each of us has power to give or withhold assent to the policy decisions of others. There is a fourth, yet wider, in which the only responsibility of each of us is the neglected but important responsibility of giving or withholding the trust which supports or inhibits our fellows in the exercise of their inalienable responsibilities, as their trust or distrust support or inhibits us.

There is, however, a fifth field, sometimes merged in the first or second but in public affairs increasingly separated from them: the responsibility for planning, the creative function which shapes the work thus and not otherwise, whether the work be a building or an institution, a nation's history or a human life. Here lies the possibility for the vision that is manifest, for good or ill, whenever a 'state of art' is imposed on a 'state of nature', but which is only vaguely missed when it is absent: the authentic signature of the human mind.

Planning thus conceived is viewed askance by Western culture, in measure increasing with its scale in space and time. Large-scale attempts consciously to impose a state of art on human affairs have often ended disastrously; men's most enduring and approved achievements, both in the outer and in the inner worlds, have usually been the fruit of long, unconscious growth, deriving from the unhampered creativity of individuals. To guarantee scope for individual creativity unhampered by limitations physical, historical, or institutional has always been an integral part of the American dream.

An ecological view helps us to understand what this ambition means in the conditions of today and what it will mean in the necessarily changed conditions of tomorrow; and how far these conditions might be controlled and at what cost. It does not encourage either arrogant hopes for social planning or easy optimism about the continuance of individual scope. The environment of the metropolis increasingly conditions us. Since it is man-made, we must acknowledge that through it we condition each other; yet, though it is a collective achievement, it does not represent a collective choice. Both its possibilities and its limitations are largely accidental; and it is a process in rapid change. How far could this process be directed? How far should it be directed – and in what direction? These papers supply no complete or coherent answers to these questions; but they contribute to our image of the process, and thus quicken and enlighten us for the debate from which answers may proceed. In particular, they help to pose those questions of value which are most easily masked.

For value questions do tend to be masked beneath the vast ramifications of our instrumental judgments, judgments of how best to achieve some already agreed end. We are so good at know-how, and so deeply immersed in it, that we scarcely admit, except in the relaxations of leisure, the value of the act done or the work produced for its own sake. Yet, obviously, no instrumental judgment can be final. If A is worth doing only because it leads to B, then why B? And C? Ultimately, this regress must be closed by the judgment that something is worth doing for its own sake. Dean Rostow is right; whether the City Beautiful is or is not likely to breed gracious citizens, it is something which even moderately gracious citizens will want to build, because they will 'enjoy' it – and this none the less if they differ passionately in their judgments of beauty.

Again, choices based on major judgments of value tend to be masked behind the frequent threats latent in the instability of our system. Too often, we can justify what we do by some manifest disaster that will otherwise overtake us. Watching a tyro on skates, staggering around in grotesque gyrations, each of which imposes the next, a spectator who asked, 'Why is he doing that?' might properly be answered, 'He is trying to keep his balance.' And indeed the pursuit of balance is enough to absorb the whole of the poor man's energy and attention. If, however, the spectator were to ask the same question about a master skater, weaving arabesques of bird-like elegance on the ice, it would be nonsense to make the same answer. True, the master, like the novice, must constantly seek a balance which must for ever be sought anew; for him, as for the novice, this is an iron law within which alone he can function. But the master has learned it so well that his obedience to it, unconscious for him and invisible to the spectators, is merged in the execution of what he is doing. He is *free* within the world of motion open to men on skates; and as a free man, his choice needs a different explanation.

Similarly a business, a city, a state, which bumps along from one crisis to another can explain and justify each response as the need to evade an imminent and lethal threat; but this is not the state in which human life, individual or collective, bears its most characteristic or its most gracious fruits. The stability of the *milieu intérieur* is only the *condition* of free and independent life. Its absence may explain a breakdown; its presence does not explain the achievement which it makes possible.

It seems to me that we sometimes elude the explicit value judgment also for a more fundamental reason. A hundred years have passed since Marx savagely denounced morality as the rationalized economic self-interest of the strong. Even his critics recognized that there was uncomfortable truth in this. That it was not the whole truth seemed probable, if only from the fact that his theories failed to account for his own moral fervor or for the success of his ideas within the world of ideas. What alternative could his critics offer? Physical scientists who, encapsulated in 'objectivity', made increasingly daring excursions into 'nature', reported on their return that they found no 'values' in the 'real world out there'. Anthropologists and psychologists, exploring the behavior of men and societies by methods as nearly scientific as might be, saw values as imposed by inner needs and outer circumstances through a determinism less crudely economic but not less rigid than Marx's age imposed on him. Neither physical nor social scientists could find a place for the creative originality of men *as agents* which their own activities so abundantly illustrated.

This was due, I suggest, to their unwillingness to accord even partial autonomy to that inner world which is structured and energized by human values. Happily, this difficulty which beset them as scientists seldom hampered their performance as human agents, for whom the making of responsible value judgments was an accepted major activity of life.

Human mental activity is indeed only part – a small and peripheral part – of the subject matter of science. It is, however, equally true that the whole of science is only a part – a smaller and more peripheral part than we always remember – of human mental activity. Confronted with these two Chinese boxes, each of which claims to contain the other, we may conclude that the human agent is more than he knows and probably more than he can ever know.

To me, at all events, the view implicit in these papers is consistent with, and seems even to require an unshaken faith in, the power and duty of the human mind to make judgments of value – judgments which can never be validated, though they may sometimes be falsified by appeal to any criterion other than another value judgment; faith qualified, nonetheless, by the knowledge that such judgments can never be final, that all dreams – even the American dream – must constantly be dreamed anew.

## References

1. Vickers refers here to *The Urban Condition*.
2. K. Boulding, *Conflict and Defense: A General Theory*, New York, Harper, 1961.
3. K. Boulding, *The Image: Knowledge in Life and Society*, Ann Arbor, University of Michigan Press, 1956.

# 10

# Appreciative behaviour*

## I

Information, communication and control are concepts of growing importance, which are being widely applied in psychology and the social sciences. They make it possible to form a model of what I will call appreciative behaviour – a model rough and speculative but better, I think, than no model at all.

Most current theories of motivation were conceived before it was possible to distinguish energy flow from information flow with the clarity possible today. In consequence, energy concepts were stretched to breaking point and beyond to cover situations where information concepts were needed. Confusion and unreal problems resulted. The apparent discrepancy between 'mental' and 'physical' work could be a problem, until it could be clearly seen as the disparity between the energy needed to work a control system and the energy which the working of that system might release – as, for example, between the energy needed to operate an automatic pilot and the energy released by its activity to turn the rudder of a great ship. The concept of tension reduction, apt enough to the physical relaxation of a creature which had just achieved the 'goal' of satisfying hunger or sex, was carried over in unconscious metaphor to describe the abatement of any mis-match signal. The concept of goal-seeking, apt enough as a model of behaviour in those situations in which effort leads through successful achievement to rest, was generalised as the standard model of human 'rational' behaviour, although most human regulative behaviour, as I shall try to show, is norm-seeking and, as such, cannot be resolved into goal-seeking, despite the common opinion to the contrary. Even the word motivation has an archaic ring, reminiscent of the days when minds seeking an explanation for a happening, were wont to seek first for a 'mover' and ultimately for a 'prime mover'. 'Drive', with which some writers seem to identify motive, has even stronger energetic connotations.

The language applied to man-made, self-controlled systems distinguishes sharply between the energetic and the informational components. There is an ongoing physical process, a ship at sea, a plant in operation or what you will, which is capable of changing its state in response to signals. There is an ongoing informational process (equally physical), generating

* From *Acta Psychologica*, Vol. 21, No. 3 1963. Also in *Value Systems and Social Process* 1968).

the signals to which the main system responds. The informational sub-system derives its signals essentially by comparing information about the state of the main system, including its relations with its surround (for example, the rate at which the ship is swinging or the rate at which the heat in a vat is rising) with standards or norms which have somehow been set as criteria for these variables. The disparity between the two generates a signal which triggers change in the main system, perhaps through the medium of a selective mechanism which chooses between a variety of possible changes.

This simple schema marks out three fields of enquiry, within which fall all the main questions to be asked by anyone trying either to design or to understand such a system. First, how does the control system derive its information about the state of the main system? Secondly, how does it derive the norms with which that state is to be compared? Thirdly, how does the signal thus generated cause the selection and initiation of change in the main system? These three areas are equally relevant as areas of enquiry into much of the activities of men and societies.

For, as energy systems, men, like other creatures, are active by defini-tion. Their biological nature requires them to discharge, as well as to generate energy at some rate within the range appropriate to their kind. Any question in the form, 'Why is he doing that?' is misleading unless both asker and answerer understand it in its proper form, 'Why is he doing that, *rather than something else?*' Psychologists and social scientists have to explain not behaving as such but the exceptional selectivity of human behaviour; and this is clearly due to the exceptional capacity of men for receiving, communicating, storing and, above all, processing information. As energy systems humans are sometimes and to some extent controlled, like the man-made systems of the engineer, by signals generated by a sub-system conveniently called the mind; and when they are so regarded, questions about the organisation of the sub-system can be asked in uncanny isolation from questions about the dynamics of the system as a whole.

The first and second fields of enquiry - the observation of the 'actual' and its comparison with the 'norm' - are indissolubly connected and important in their own right. This combined process I call appreciation. The third field - the choice of action - is separable and may be irrelevant. Appreciation may or may not call for - and if it does, it may or may not evoke - action which may or may not abate an observed discrepancy, action which I will call regulative action. There may be no observed discrepancy; match signals, no less than mis-match signals, are important and, as I shall seek to show, informative. There may be nothing to be done. The selective mechanism for action may act at random or may be systematically wrong. Appreciative behaviour is distinguishable from regulative behaviour and needs to be so distinguished if we are to make sense of some human activities, especially of those which are least illuminated by principles derived from the animal laboratory or the mental hospital. Statesmen, administrators, judges, executives, like ordinary citizens in their ordinary affairs, are often reminiscent of the rat in the maze and perhaps seldom free from symptoms known to psychiatry; but more sophisticated concepts are needed fully to explain their behaviour at its most effective – or the behaviour of the scientist, whose theories about them must be equally applicable to himself.

To clarify behaviour at this level need not invalidate other theories of motivation; for, as R. S. Peters has pointed out,[4] we have no reason to assume that any one theory of motivation will account for all human behaviour. On the contrary, there is abundant evidence that humans have developed new regulative capacities, in addition to those they share with other creatures and have great difficulty in reconciling the two. Indeed, there may well be not two but several types and levels of control fighting for power in a single individual in any given context.

Ever since psychology defined itself as the study of behaviour, the most characteristically human behaviour has presented peculiar difficulty; for it has manifestly depended for its explanation on 'unobservable' activities within the human head, which cannot be inferred either from observable input or from observable output. Some electors, for example, though by no means all, behave at election time in a way determined not merely by what has happened in the world since the last election but also by what has happened in their heads in the same time; and very little of the second can possibly be inferred from the first (input) because the total volume of the first is so vast and the selection therefrom which individual minds choose to notice is so limited and idiosyncratic. Still less can these 'unobservable' activities be inferred from the way the elector votes (output), because the range of behaviour open to him is so limited. He can vote for A or B – or possibly C – or spoil his voting paper or abstain – a choice almost as limited as that of a rat in a maze; and like the rat, even the moment when he must make his choice is decided for him. In so restricted a situation any choice might flow from any of a wide variety of appreciative judgments.

Our voter, in so far as he is behaving 'rationally' (and this is the strand in his behaviour with which I am concerned) will have made comparative appreciations of the parties which seek his support on a dual scale – his approval of their policies and his confidence in their abilities. Both will be derived from the past and projected into the future, in the highly selective context of his 'interests'. This complex operation (which I examine more fully in the next section with the aid of another example) can be analysed into judgments of fact about the 'state of the system', actual and hypothetical, past, present and future, which I will call reality judgments and judgments of the significance of these facts to him and his society, which I will call value judgments – reality judgments and value judgments being the inseparable constituents of appreciation. If we knew how our voter derives and represents these highly selective reality judgments and how he derives the standards by which to complete his appreciation, we should know all we need to know about his 'motives' at this level – whatever other motives may also be at work.

Most psychological research has concentrated on problems concerned with the selection of action; and for this purpose has held constant and made certain the relevant reality and value judgments. If we want to know how a rat solves a problem, we must know for certain what problem it is trying to solve; so we make it hungry enough to ensure that finding food is its dominant problem. But most of the problems which humans try to solve are set by their own appreciative judgments and cannot be guessed without making assumptions about how reality judgments and value judgments are formed.

There is a vast body of such assumptions. Even a behaviourist, when he writes a book, hopes that it will influence not the overt behaviour of his readers but the way they 'appreciate' the subject matter, and he addresses them as persuasively as he can in the light of half-conscious assumptions about the ways in which appreciative judgments grow, develop and change. He knows that the development of 'ideas' in the individual head has a history distinct from the history of 'event', though linked to it by close mutual bonds; and if he did not know this, he would be a poor scientist. For the history of science and the biographies of scientists are outstanding examples of the way in which the history of event and the history of ideas proceed in partial autonomy, though in intimate relationship, each conditioning the other yet each growing according to its own logic and its own time-scale.

The assumptions which we make about this ubiquitous and important matter of appreciative judgment seem to me to owe less than they might and should to such light as science could throw upon them. The concentration of study on behaviour which is observable in the sense in which stars and rats are observable, to the exclusion of such human behaviours as talking and thinking, is influenced by a supposed limitation of scientific method which, I suggest, is at least exaggerated. Talking, indeed, is receivable as a communication, rather than being simply 'observable'; and thinking is accessible only as the content of communication; but they are not on that account inaccessible to science or dispensable by it. Is it not a little illogical for a scientist to mistrust communication as evidence of what is going on in others and to rely on it – and expect others to rely on it – as evidence of what is going on in himself?

## II

The deliberations of a single mind are only accessible through reported introspection; but collective deliberations are more explicit. The agenda which accompany them are often accompanied by supporting papers, statistics, reports, forecasts and so on. Discussions and conclusions are recorded more or less fully in minutes. With the aid of tapes and ciné-cameras, the record could in theory be expanded to cover all the overt behaviour which accompanies collective deliberation. This activity is familiar and ubiquitous. It occupies much of the time of all those committees which occupy scientists, no less than other men, as of cabinets and law courts, boards of directors and university senates. Something, I suggest, can be learned from the study of these activities. Among this great diversity of bodies, one is of particular interest, because in it the appreciative function is isolated. This is typified by Royal Commissions and similar bodies in this and other countries, to which problems are referred not for action but for consideration and report. I will take as an example the Royal Commission on capital punishment 1949–1953, whose report in 505 pages is available for all to read, with its far more voluminous minutes of evidence. The proceedings of this commission illustrate as well as another the explicit processes of appreciative behaviour and have an additional interest from the psychological nature of the issue before it.

The Commission prefaces its report with a statement of what it has done, in words which should make a psychologist's imagination boggle. 'Our duty ... has been to look for means of confining the scope of (capital) punishment as narrowly as possible without impairing the efficacy attributed to it. We had ... to consider ... how far the scope of capital punishment ... is already restricted in practice and by what means; and whether those means are satisfactory as far as they go ... how far capital punishment has ... that special efficacy which it is commonly believed to have. We had ... to study the development of the law of murder and ... to consider whether certain forms of homicide should be taken out of that category and to what extent the liability ... might be restricted on account of ... youth or sex or ... provocation ... the extent to which insanity ... should ... negative or diminish criminal responsibility ... whether murder should be redefined ... whether any defects ... could be better remedied by giving either the judge or the jury a discretionary power....' and so on; leading to the conclusion, 'we thought it right to report at some length ... in the belief that, *irrespective of our recommendation*, (my italics) it would be useful ... to place on record a comprehensive and dispassionate picture of the whole subject....' The nature of appreciative judgment could not be better illustrated or defined.

By far the greater part of the report is devoted to describing all relevant aspects of the situation as it is and as it might be, by applying to a great variety of fact and opinion, partly conflicting, the selective, critical and integrating mental activity which I have called reality judgment. This is interspersed with comments expressing the commissioners' own approval or disapproval, their value judgments. Each section ends with recommendations for action, with regulative judgments.

The reality judgment is voluminous and complex. What homicides fall within the legal definition of murder? What kind and degree of insanity exclude the offence, what kind and degree of provocation reduces it to manslaughter? How varied are the motives and circumstances attending these crimes and the personalities of those who commit them? What is the purpose and what the effect of death or any punishment in such diverse cases? What are the respective roles of prosecutor, judge, jury and Home

Secretary in deciding which of those convicted shall hang? To these and many other questions answers are offered, definite or tentative, with whatever historical background is needed to make the present explicable.

The report has a double story to tell; the story of the relevant events and the story of the relevant ideas; and it moves easily, unconsciously between the two. The numbers and details of murders committed, of convictions, reprieves, executions belong to the world of event. The attitudes of men to murder and to the death penalty, the interaction of these two in giving murder a special status among crimes, these belong to the world of ideas, a world no less susceptible of factual report. Between the two worlds is an infinity of subtle, mutual connections which the commissioners must disentangle as best they may; for these interactions lie at the heart of the problems committed to them. What is, what should be the relation between criminal responsibility as a legal fact, defined by the common law; responsibility as a medical fact, defined, they are assured, by the criminal's neural organisation at the time and thus no less factual than the law but assessable only by the often divergent judgments of psychiatrists; and responsibility as a normative judgment passed by men on men, a standard of what *should be deemed to be* the scope and limits of their responsibility, yet a standard not without effect on the actual state of minds which know they are to be judged by it?

Based though it is on the present and the past, the reality judgment is concerned primarily with the future, which alone can be affected by any change now made. The death penalty could be limited by changing the definition of the offence or by subdividing it into 'degrees' or by admitting a discretion as to sentence. The reality judgment must arrive at an assessment of the probable effect of these alternatives, collecting what evidence seems relevant about the experience of other countries which have abolished, relaxed or reinstated the death penalty; and about the problems attending the long-term custody of prisoners convicted of crimes of violence.

Some of this evidence is significant in at least two ways. The commissioners, having collected the views of police officers on whether abatement of the death penalty will increase violent resistance to arrest, must evaluate these statements of opinion both as evidence of what is likely to happen in the world of event and as evidence of what is actually happening in the world of ideas. For the apprehensions of the police about the effect of a change in the law, whether well or ill founded, is both a fact and a force in the present situation and one which may indirectly alter the effect which such a change will actually have – for example, the willingness of police officers in Britain to continue to work unarmed.

The evidence on which the commissioners found their reality judgment varies vastly in certainty and in character. Statistics and estimates; opinions, often discordant, on matters both of fact and of value; the views of different authorities, past and present on the legitimate purposes of punishment; the views of psychiatrists on human responsibility and its impairment by mental illness; all this and more goes into the mill and out comes the reality judgment, balanced, coherent, urbane, a mental artifact which only familiarity robs of the wonder which is its due.

The report is also sprinkled with the commissioners' own value judgments - usually expressed as agreement with value judgments found as a fact to exist in the community but none the less their own. Insanity *should be* a defence to murder. The then existing rules defining insanity for this purpose were narrower than they *should be*. Among the sane who are convicted of murder, culpability varies so much that they *should not* all be sentenced to the uniform, extreme and irreversible penalty of death. The abatement of this penalty *should not* be left to so great an extent to the Home Secretary. It *should not* be left to the judge; or (for different reasons) to the jury. It *should* be expressed in the law itself. In these and a dozen other contexts, the commissioners, going beyond the recording of other people's value judgments, commit themselves to value judgments of their own. Whence came the norms which produced these value judgments?

The answer is simple but subtle. The commissioners used the norms which they brought with them to the conference table; but these norms were changed and developed by the very process of applying them; by the impact of the reality judgment which they focused; by the impact, attrition and stimulus of each commissioner on the others; and by the exercise of their own minds as they applied them in one way and another, on one hypothesis after another, in the search for a better 'fit'. As an illustration, consider their debate on the use of the Home Secretary's power of reprieve.

It was their value judgment that, among people convicted of murder, culpability varied so much that punishment should also be variable. This, they realised, could be achieved (within their terms of reference) only by elaborating the definition of the crime or by giving someone discretion to vary the penalty to suit the facts. The first alternative they found in practice to be immensely difficult. The second was already in operation, in that nearly half those convicted of murder were reprieved on the recommendation of the Home Secretary. Was it 'satisfactory' or even 'proper' that so large a discretion should be vested in the Home Secretary? Eminent witnesses were divided. To make the Home Secretary 'an additional court of appeal, sitting in private, judging on the record only and giving no reason for his decision' said some, 'does not fit into the constitutional framework of this country'. The Archbishop of Canterbury objected on different grounds. '... it is intolerable that this solemn and deeply significant procedure should be enacted again and again, when in almost half the cases the consequence will not follow ... a mere empty formula is a degradation of the law and dangerous to society.' Other distinguished witnesses found it not at all intolerable. Lord Samuel suggested that 'to maintain a degree of uncertainty as to what would happen in marginal cases may be very useful in retaining a deterrent effect on potential criminals'.

The commissioners' appreciative judgment was that the Home Secretary's discretion was 'undue'; but the only less objectionable alternative seemed to them still too repugnant to recommend. So their appreciative conclusions on the point were expressed without any recommendation for regulative action. Such recommendations as they did make, they admitted, 'would go very little way toward solving our general problem' (i.e. how to relieve the executive of this undue responsibility). They concluded that 'if capital punishment is to be retained and at the same time the defects of the existing law are to be eliminated ... the only practicable way of achieving this object is to give discretion to the jury to find extenuating circumstances requiring a lesser sentence to be substituted'.

This appreciation, though without a recommendation and indeed all the more on that account is perhaps the most important part of the report; for it amounts to a finding that there was no satisfactory halfway house between the existing state of affairs and the *abolition* of the death penalty. Their terms of reference precluded them from recommending or even considering abolition; yet a major contribution of their report to the appreciative judgment of their contemporaries was to support the movement for abolition which had in fact occasioned their appointment.

The report made some recommendations for action. Some were adopted in the Homicide Act 1957; some were ignored. Yet if all had been ignored, the major importance of the report as an appreciative judgment would have remained the same. The state of the commissioners' minds on the subject of capital punishment, after they had made their appreciation, was different from what it was when they began; and this change, communicated through the report, provoked change, similar or dissimilar, in greater or less degree, in all it reached, from serious students to casual readers of newspaper paragraphs; and thus released into the stream of event and into the stream of ideas an addition to the countless forces by which both are moulded.

Yet their terms of reference, on the face of them, required them only to recommend means to a given end.

### III

If words mean anything, the Commission's report attests a process which is as wide as history, yet endemic in each individual head. If we range over the doings of this island's inhabitants for the last millennium, we see the course of event and the course of ideas unrolling, each impelled by its own momentum yet each influencing and being influenced by the other – the 'entraînement des choses' which de Tocqueville found as a salient datum of history matched by an 'entraînement des idées' which is inseparable from it but which cannot be resolved into it. If we narrow our observation to the development of a few individual lives, say the members of the commission, we find the same duality. The attitudes of mind which they brought to the conference table were the fruit of this unending interaction of events and ideas in their individual lives; and the attitudes they took away were further changed, both by the event of the commission (and other relevant events which happened while it sat) and by the mammoth exercise and exchange of ideas which it involved. Psychology may leave the wider study to the historians but it cannot disown responsibility for the narrower one.

I am proposing that we should regard this mental activity as a specific form of behaviour, 'appreciative behaviour'; unobservable in the sense in which scientists observe the behaviour of stars and rats but attested by and studiable through the whole volume of human communication, not least the communications on which scientists invite us to rely when they formulate theories about stars and rats. This activity consists essentially in making what I have called reality judgments on selected aspects of their surround and evaluating these in terms of value, including 'interest', which I shall distinguish. A man's capacity for appreciative judgment can then be described as depending on (i) the quality of his relevant mental faculties, which seem to vary widely between individuals; (ii) the materials at his disposal, whether in memory or externally accessible or derivable from these by further mental process; and (iii) his current state of readiness to see and value things in one way rather than another, which I will call his appreciative setting. This setting is a product of past experiences in appreciation and will be confirmed or further changed, however slightly, by the next exercise. In the space remaining I will try to give these terms some more solid content.

Clearly we must credit our kind with the capacity to classify 'objects of experience' – what that covers I will examine later – according to categories, which give them meaning by relating them to each other. In the field of perception this capacity has been well explored. The child learns to see, building up by experience the schemata by which further experience may be classified; learning to recognise cows in all their variety by their correspondence to some generalised schema in which 'cowishness' has come to reside and by the same process amplifying, refining and sometimes revising the schema for future use. The same process attends the learning of an adult skill; the medical student cannot 'read' a pulmonary radiogram until experience of many has built up the interpretative schema. The learned character of such schemata is revealed most dramatically by the painful confusion of adults born blind who acquire sight first in later life.

Less work has been done on the development of concepts but a similar process is clearly involved. Indeed, concepts *are* schemata for classifying objects of attention of all kinds, perceptual schemata being one class among many. The growth of scientific theory is the best documented example of the development of conceptual schemata.

The self-determining process by which schemata grow by their own exercise is of particular importance. The child cannot recognise a cow until it has built up a 'cow-schema'; yet the schema can only arise from repeated experience of cows. G. H. Lewes well described this elusive process as long ago as 1879[2] '... the new object presented to sense, or the new idea presented to thought must be *soluble in old experience*, be recognised as like them, otherwise it will be unperceived, uncomprehended'.

The process is clearly seen in the growth of the common law. Negligence, for example, is a complex concept. It means such a lack of care as makes a man liable to those who suffer thereby; but this is a circular definition. How much lack of care brings an act within the category? The common law will not define this more precisely than by pointing to all those past cases in which negligence has been found to be present or absent. Every new decision leaves the existing schema reinforced or however slightly changed. It is by nature incomplete and incapable of being completed.

The mutual link between the use and the formulation of schemata – and equally between norm-setting and norm-seeking – is even clearer in an engaging legal abstraction called the reasonable man. How much care would a reasonable man take of his own property? In what circumstances would a reasonable man feel justified in defending himself with violence? The courts will tell you, never in general terms but in the specific circumstances of any particular case to which the standard is relevant. So the reasonable man remains perpetually young, changing his character from century to century, as custom and culture change and playing a potent part in directing, speeding or restraining the changes which he reflects. He came to the aid of the commissioners when they were debating what degree of provocation might abate a charge of murder.

It follows that the appreciative setting of an individual or a society must always be latent. It is not revealed even by the latest actual judgment; for the making of the judgment may have changed the setting of the system, as the commissioners changed their own settings and, in some measure, the setting of 'public opinion' by the judgments embodied in their report; and it will change further in the course of the next judgment which it guides. The dissolving of new experience in the accumulation of old experiences, to revert to Lewes' simile, does more than assimilate the new experience. It also modifies, however slightly, the 'solution' in which the next new experience must be dissolved.

It follows further that schemata, though readily developed, resist radical change. The medical student's teacher cannot help seeing in the radiogram what the student has not yet learned to see. This stability is bought at a price. Professor Selye has described[5] how, as a medical student under instruction in the different syndromes characteristic of various diseases, he was at first far more impressed by something which his teachers ignored – the striking *similarities* in the conditions of illness from whatever cause. This naive observation, suppressed at the time, recurred years later to be the prime mover in his studies of physiological stress. Every major development of scientific thought has been long resisted because of the disturbance which it brings to the coherence of existing ideas; and this resistance is well founded, for coherence is precious. The body of scientific thought, like an individual's understanding of his world, can ill afford periods of extended chaos. The revolutionary solution, whereby new schemata are developed in carefully contrived isolation from the past, though sometimes necessary, is difficult and expensive, whether in politics, science or the individual life.

Within this limitation, the schemata on which reality judgments are based are in constant development under three main pressures – the pressure of event; the pressure of other men's schemata; and the pressure of their own internal requirements. Events call constantly for new appreciations of the 'situation'. Other people's communications reveal schemata which confirm or challenge our own. And, apart from both these, the inner inconsistencies and incompleteness of our own schemata call us constantly to revise them. These are the occasions for appreciative behaviour – signals, whether of match or mis-match which confirm or question at the same time as they reveal the current appreciative setting of the system.

The subject matter comprised in our schemata is diverse. Only a very small part of it is given by sensory experience, even to the limited extent to which we now regard any sensory experience as 'given'. Most of it is the product of operations performed by our own minds and the minds of others. Such is a scientific theory – or for that matter an unscientific theory, like the Nazi theory of the Aryan race. The capacity of the mind to provide itself with artifacts on which it can perform further operations is one very good reason why the word 'mental' is needed; and would be needed, even if we fully understood the working of the brain and CNS. Professor MacKay has shown that the production of such artifacts can in theory be extended indefinitely.[3]

We can handle what seem to be very complex objects of attention. The commissioners found no difficulty in matching the activities of the Home Secretary and his advisers in the matter of reprieve for murder with 'the constitutional framework of this country' and finding that it 'does not fit'. In that case the relevant cues were relatively recognisable and few. The Home Secretary was intervening so often that he was behaving like an additional court of appeal. Once so classified, he was obviously a 'bad thing', for he was 'sitting in private, judging on the record only and giving no reason for his decision'; and a well-established norm ruled that this is not the way in which a court of appeal should behave. Moreover, he was a part of the executive; and another well-recognised norm ruled that a branch of the executive had no business to be playing the role of court of appeal. Yet if his interventions had been sufficiently infrequent to escape classification by the schema 'court of appeal', he would have remained an acceptable embodiment of the Crown's prerogative of mercy.

The animal ethologists have taught us how few and how simple may be the innate 'releasers' that trigger complex sequences of innate behaviour. It may be that our learned discriminations are basically simpler than we know. It should not be impossible to find out.

Clearly the objects of our attention include relations extended in time.

This we should expect; for organisms and organisations *are* relations extended in time. Their continuity depends on keeping the more essential of these relationships within critical limits. The need, for example, for a man or an organisation to preserve a balance between money in and money out is similar in character to the need to preserve a balance between energy in and energy out; and failure, beyond a critical threshold, produces no less self-exciting disturbances. The relations which a man, an organisation, a society is set to attain or preserve (and to escape and elude) are manifold, as the commission's report shows. They are for the most part a product, of the self-determining, appreciative process which we are examining. For the moment I am concerned only to point out that they are not goals to be attained once for all but ongoing relations, like a ship's course, which must be continuously maintained – relations which I call norms. It is usually assumed that such norms, from the agent's point of view, can none the less be resolved into goals, as the maintenance of a rat's metabolism, equally a norm, can be resolved into periodic quests for food. This, I suggest, is not so. The record of the commission – and of every deliberative body – shows it well able to represent to itself relations extended in time and to compare these with normative expectations, similarly extended; and the once-for-all connotations of goal-seeking make for confusion if they become attached to norm-holding. A man who wants to become Prime Minister may and probably does seek the satisfaction of being appointed to that office and he may properly regard the attainment of this as a goal; but it is to be hoped that he also looks forward to supporting the complex relations which attach to the role and which must be sustained as long as it is held.

I stress the importance of ongoing relations as objects of attention because they seem to be unduly ignored. The dominance of 'objects' over 'relations' in our conscious thinking has often been criticised but it still conceals the fact that we do not seek or shun objects but relations with objects. No one wants an apple; he wants to eat it, sell it, paint it, perhaps just to admire it, in any case to relate to it in some way or other. The relation may sometimes be taken for granted; people who avoid tigers need not be pressed to say why. None the less, at the level of mental behaviour which I am considering, the distinction is usually important.

We have no idea how these mental feats are accomplished but they seem less odd than once they did. To scan and classify according to schemata, even to build up better schemata by scanning are in their simpler forms not beyond the compass of existing machines. The coding of information admits of more development than we can foresee. Analogue computers provide curiously simple ways of comparing complex relations in ways which are familiar to us all in such simple forms as the map and the graph; it may be significant that relations in space and time are so much more easily grasped when presented in graphical or mathematical form than when expressed in words. Perhaps the dominance of objects in our conscious thinking is a by-product of the structure of our verbal language, which in turn reflects the dominance of vision among the senses.*

In any case, in thinking of appreciative behaviour, we need not suppose that the mental models which underlie appreciative judgment consist of words or images, though it is hard for those with visual imagination not to depict our judgment of reality as 'the image', as Professor Boulding has done in his classic assault on the problem.[1] We use, even consciously, more models than words and images can supply; and we have no reason to suppose that the mind is limited to those forms of representation of which we are conscious. Indeed, the contrary appears from the fact that some, if not all our activities in ordering experience and especially in grasping temporal and casual relations occur at least partly in states of abated consciousness, especially in sleep. The commissioners' judgment was formulated in a report which speaks from conscious mind to conscious mind but I have not enquired at what levels of consciousness the actual mental work was done and it is one of the merits of the approach which I am using that I need not do so. As Whyte has observed[7] '... the antithesis conscious/ unconscious may have exhausted its utility'. All I have assumed in this analysis is the absence of *pathology* attaching to either state.

There is a pathology of the unconscious, resulting from the mechanism of repression. There is also a pathology of the conscious, which still awaits its Freud – the pathology of those who, trapped in 'consciousness', become perpetual observers even of themselves as agents and who are thus cut off from essential conditions both of effectiveness and of joy. The man free from both these diseases functions none the less in a variety of states of consciousness, which subserve his performance in ways we do not understand; nor need we wait to do so before we try to model the overall process which they combine to mediate. It may well be that the conscious operations of the mind, though essential, are the least central to the process of appreciation. Such at least is the impression left on my mind by some experience of highly skilled 'appreciators'.


## IV


Appreciative behaviour involves making judgments of value, no less than judgments of reality; so a psychology of value is inseparable from a psychology of cognition. An adequate psychology of value, when it is formulated – and this, I believe, is a proper and feasible task for psychology – will cover far more ground than I am attempting now; but some of it may be illustrated from the deliberations of the commission.

---

* Not all languages are similarly handicapped. L. L. Whyte writes '... the Hopi and others appear to put the cognitive emphasis not on separable traces, representing isolable entities but on the actual process of experiencing'.[7] He also quotes Whorf as authority for the proposition that 'the Hopi ... view reality as "events" rather than as "matter" '.[6]

It is convenient first to separate judgments of 'importance–unimportance' from other kinds of value judgment. Objects of attention may be picked out as being important – or alternatively, parts of the field may be scanned with particular care as being likely to contain matters of importance – without making any qualitative assumptions as to what their importance may prove to be. The commissioners no doubt tried to approach their task with an 'open mind'; but this did not hamper them in deciding what evidence would be relevant. I will describe judgments of importance–unimportance as judgments of interest. Interest is the selector. It must precede reality judgment, even though other kinds of value judgment may follow later.

Next, I will distinguish two values which are inherent in the appreciative process itself. The first is certainty–uncertainty of expectation. Humans, it seems, have grafted on to an age-old capacity for 'action-now' a much more recently developed capacity to appreciate the future. Stress, as well as power comes from this enlargement of scope. Men maintain expectations of the future course of their manifold relations and constantly scan the unfolding present for confirmation or disproof. Confirmation, even of an unwelcome expectation, reassures the appreciator of the validity of his reality judgment and to this extent is positively valued. Disproof, on the other hand, erodes the structure of expectation and challenges the validity not only of the judgment but perhaps also of the processes by which the judgment was formed. Thus match, no less than mis-match signals are significant in the appreciative process.* This is true of the interaction of men with their non-human environment but far more true of their dealings with each other, in which confirmation of expectation is more needed and more prized; so it becomes more important as the social element becomes ever more dominant in the human milieu. It explains much in human intercourse which would otherwise be obscure. Communications which appear to add nothing to the recipient's stock of information are not meaningless if they confirm his expectation of the other party. Such, for example, are most small talk, greeting, and ritual.

Our expectations of the behaviour of the non-human world are largely based on 'laws', scientific or roughly empirical, which it is observed to obey; but our expectations of our fellow men are based on 'rules' which they are expected to observe and human intercourse is based on knowing, if not sharing the rules on which the other is acting. It is the argument of this paper that such rules govern appreciation as well as action; govern the way the situation is seen and valued, no less than the decision what action (if any) is called for. Thus the horizon of confident expectation entertained by men of each other depends on the extent to which they understand, even if they do not share each other's appreciative settings. The degree of this

---

* Some writers subsume 'match' under mis-match signals, but this usage seems to me to be open to objection almost as serious as the practice of subsuming 'threat-avoiding' under goal-seeking.

assurance is of value, irrespective of the contents of the rules themselves.

The second value inherent in the appreciative process is the value of 'coherence–incoherence' in the inner world of the appreciator. His schemata are interrelated; and though the schemata of everyday life may be less exactly articulated than the schemata of science, they too confirm each other by their coherence and proclaim inherent inconsistencies by nagging mis-match signals. The commissioners, seeking a repository for the discretion which they felt bound to lodge somewhere, found none where it could be placed without importing inconsistency into a complex, existing role.

It remains to consider those judgments of the commission which cannot obviously be reduced to judgments of coherence–incoherence. I will call these judgments of fitness–unfitness. As we have seen, the problems of the commission all stemmed from the fact that a change in the valuation of capital punishment as such had for some time been shouldering its way into the closely integrated system of values surrounding crime and punishment, producing new problems of 'coherence–incoherence' among the valuations which it disturbed. Whence came the change?

It came, I suggest, from a change either in the schemata used to classify reality or in the (not necessarily identical) schemata used for classifying value; or in both. To identify these changes is not, I think, an impossible task, though it is not to be attempted here. I will only add some comments on the relation between schemata of reality and schemata of value.

The simplest valuations are attitudes attached to schemata of reality. The kind of court appeal which the commissioners could approve was defined by objective criteria of reality. This is very common. In consequence many, perhaps most, changes of valuation come simply from changes in the corresponding schemata of reality. My duty to my neighbour shrinks and widens with my conception of who my neighbour is. My attitude to mental illness will change if I extend my schema of illness, with its value connotations, to include something which I had not previously recognised as illness.

Valuations, however, have also schemata of their own, not identifiable with schemata of reality, as the commission found to its cost when it tried to subdivide murder into definable categories of 'reality', corresponding to degrees of 'culpability'. A fair deal is different from a fair fight, because the rules applicable to the two situations are different; but fairness, as meaning the keeping of recognised rules, is a schema in its own right, applicable to both situations and to many more. (If the illustration seems too old-fashioned to be valid, it will serve further to illustrate the fact that schemata may lose their meaning through decay.) Value schemata develop, like reality schemata, by use through the subtle, self-determining process already described. The criteria of value, like the criteria of reality are always latent in the mind, waiting to guide and to be changed by the next exercise. The key to the problem of value lies in the further exploration of this self-determining, creative process.

There remains the key problem – how does the appreciative judgment settle conflicts of valuation? For such judgments usually involve choices between 'goods' and between 'evils'. Even this rough enquiry suggests that such conflicts are not settled by some predetermined 'rank-ordering' of norms or goals; for even where such priorities exist, the need to choose arises only in a concrete situation, as a choice between specific alternatives and cannot be separated from them. The commission's decision that it would be less unsatisfactory to extend the discretion of the jury than to continue to rely so largely on the discretion of the Home Secretary cannot be expressed, even in retrospect, as derived from a pre-existing 'rank-ordering' of norms or goals or principles, irrespective of the situation in which the judgment was actually made.

The example does not provide an adequate answer to this ancient question but it seems to me to make a useful contribution. The commission's judgment would alter the schemata of reality and value of the commissioners and of all who would be influenced by their report; and the commissioners, in considering it, were conscious that it would have this impact on the world of ideas, no less than in the world of event. They were responsible architects in both worlds; and in both they had to consider the impact of their action on the total situation. We are accustomed to think of judgment as a matter of 'weighing' alternatives, a dynamic metaphor, suggesting the comparison of forces. I have tried to show that it also involves a process of 'matching', an informational metaphor, suggesting the comparison of forms. We need this second concept if we are to understand and describe the commissioners' efforts to minimise incoherence and unfitness in the total situation. Here surely is a field of critical importance which information concepts can help to clarify.

# References

1. K. Boulding, *The Image*, Ann Arbor Paperbacks, 1956.
2. G. H. Lewes, *Problems of Life and Mind*, London, Trubner, 1879.
3. D. M. MacKay, 'Towards an Information Flow Model of Human Behaviour', *British Journal of Psychology*, 1956, Vol. 47, part I.
4. R. S. Peters, *The Concept of Motivation*, London, Routledge & Kegan Paul, 1957.
5. H. Selye, *The Stress of Life*, New York, McGraw-Hill Book Company Inc., 1956.
6. B. L. Whorf, 'Time, Space and Language', Thompson, L., *Culture in Crisis*, New York, Harper, 1954.
7. L. L. Whyte, *The Unconscious Before Freud*, London, Tavistock Publications, 1962.

# 11

# Community medicine*

I want to talk about something which in Britain today has no name; I shall call it community medicine, and I include in it all those resources which are devoted to managing illness within the community of the well. I distinguish community medicine from 'inpatient' medicine, by which I mean all the resources devoted to the care of the sick in hospital, and from environmental medicine, in which I include all resources devoted to reducing the hazards of the milieu. These distinctions do not correspond with the three administrative divisions of the National Health Service today, and they may do so even less tomorrow. Both hospitals and local authorities take a hand in community medicine; and this tends to blur its outline. I want to focus and define it as a distinct function, with its own expertise and its own standards of success. I believe that this distinction is as important for doctors as it is for laymen.

Think of all the communities where two people live and work, where food is bought and cooked, where children get to school and men and women to work, where the intricate, self-supporting pattern of human life goes on. It is the world of the well. Yet it contains most of the world's sickness. Here are children with measles, workers nursing broken bones, old and not-so-old people quietly dying of cancer and arteriosclerosis and others equally incapacitated with influenza; and here also among those at work, in factories, offices, and homes, are many who are ill. Almost all the sickness of the community, chronic or transient, grave or slight, disabling or only inconveniencing is here, in the world of the well.

## Inpatient and community medicine

About 1% of the population at any one time are not to be found in the world of the well. They have been withdrawn (or pushed out) into another world, the hospital world, where they are no longer agents but patients; a world where professionals do the work and cook the meals and look after them; a world of transient withdrawal, designed to contain that fraction of the sick which is selected for it.

How is this fraction selected? Its maximum number at any time is set by the hospital accommodation available. Within this limit, its constituents are selected by two different principles: some are there because they need

---

* From *The Lancet*, 29 April 1967. Based on a lecture given at the London School of Hygiene and Tropical Medicine in December 1966.

treatment or diagnosis which only a hospital can give or which can be better given there, and some are there simply because they cannot be contained within the world of the well.

The second principle is accepted unwillingly, and this unwillingness is likely to grow. With few exceptions, our hospitals today are designed not for care but for cure. If the occupant of a bed is not in a condition to use or respond to the increasingly expensive services which the accounts have charged out to it, the cry goes up, from doctors and laymen alike, that the bed is being used for 'social' rather than 'medical' purposes – an offence against the god of efficiency which should not be tolerated in a technological age. The founders of our great teaching hospitals would be surprised to learn that their descendants should have come to regard the care of the sick as an unsuitable use for their foundations; and we may be making avoidable trouble for ourselves by our relative neglect of institutions designed for care, rather than for cure. But in any case the contrast between inpatient medicine and community medicine will remain and grow more intense.

The purpose of inpatient medicine is to cure the patients sent to it from the world of the well and to return them to the world of the well as quickly as possible. The purpose of community medicine is far wider: it is responsible for managing, in the world of the well, the human estate of sickness and mortality. I include in this the management of the non-pathological crises of life, birth, growth, senescence – death also, unless we regard death as always pathological – and the management of all illnesses, whether curable or not. And in management I include more than therapy, even where therapy is possible. I include the relief of suffering, aid in living with disability, whether transient or permanent, limitation of disturbance in all the social systems which an illness disturbs, notably the household in which it is to be contained, and partnership with the layman or, more often, laywoman who is primarily charged with the care of the sick individual in the community and chiefly stressed by that responsibility.

This is what the layman expects of community medicine. He is right to expect it: it is what community medicine ought to expect of itself. It involves a set of expectations wider than those implicit in inpatient medicine. The standards of success and therefore the focus of attention of the two are subtly but critically different. Neither layman nor doctor need put one above the other; but both layman and doctor should reject the idea, the novel and mischievous idea, that 'inpatient' medicine is the only 'real' medicine.

My favourite definition of a doctor's function is the old French one which translates roughly: 'to cure sometimes; to relieve often; to support always'. That is where therapy used to stand in the concept of the doctor's function; and that is where I think it should still stand, if medicine is to be more than a technology. It is a concept to be realised more fully in community than in inpatient medicine; and, wide as it is, it does not do full justice to the last part of my description, which insists that the doctor-patient relationship is not the only one which concerns the community doctor.

The community of the well is a complex system of human relationships, organised in countless, interlocking subsystems. Every illness stresses one or more of these systems, notably the home where the sick person lives and the place where he works. These stresses may spread in widening circles of disturbance, no less than an infection. To control them, to mitigate and damp down their effects, is part of the function of community medicine. It is a function owed to the sick individual and to those not yet sick, whom his sickness puts at risk. It is owed also to the community, because the capacity of the community to carry its own sickness depends on its ability to contain the disturbance which such sickness creates. It is thus owed especially to the individual most affected by the disturbance and most important in containing it, who is normally not the patient but someone else – wife, husband, mother, father, or maybe some stranger whom accident has cast for the role of the doctor's partner. Doctors would not talk so much about the doctor-patient relationship and so little about the mutual rights and duties of doctor and lay partner, if doctors did not learn their medicine in hospitals, where, alone, this second relationship is always less obvious and usually less important.

Community medicine is growing in importance, relatively to hospital medicine, though the fact is obscured from us by a dissociation between declared public policy and actual allocation of public funds. The community is expected to carry more of the mentally ill, more of the elderly sick and the chronic sick, more of all sickness which does not compete for the growing technological resources of the hospital; it is expected to do more for the convalescent, whose frequent readmissions to hospital so often reflects difficulties on the path to rehabilitation which only community medicine can smooth. Economy finds an ally in psychology to show that therapeutic communities are more easily constructed in the world of the well and that admission to hospital is itself no small stress.

Community medicine must carry this increasing load with ever less traditional community support but ever higher community expectation. For the transient nuclear family and the fragmented family group are ill-adapted and ill-conditioned to support their own sick, as once they did, and at the same time have developed ever higher standards of what the sick are entitled to expect.

## General practice and public health

More than half of the doctors in Britain work in the world of the well. Most of these are general practitioners and they carry much of the load of community medicine, but by no means all. Sometimes, especially in mental illness, the hospital reaches out into the community to provide domiciliary care and to bridge the gap between community and hospital with new institutions, such as day and night hospitals. More widely, the hospital practises community medicine through outpatient services. Where it functions in these ways, it tends to dominate the partnership with the general practitioner. It is conceivable that, as our world becomes increasingly urban, this tendency may grow. Yet even if every general practitioner's surgery were absorbed into an extended system of out-patient clinics based on hospitals, the doctors who worked in those clinics would experience the same enlargement of responsibility, the same shift of interest and attention as general practitioners feel or should feel today. The difference between community medicine and inpatient medicine is not administrative, it is functional.

Thus as the hospital's function becomes more specialised and as our concept of health becomes more generalised, the concept of community medicine may be expected to disengage itself as a focus of interest and attention, increasingly separate and increasingly important in its own right.

Local authorities are also increasingly concerned with community medicine. Fifty years ago the general practitioner as a 'personal doctor' seemed far removed from the local health authority, administering policies of 'public health' which fell almost entirely in the field I have called environmental medicine. But the concept of public health has expanded. Besides reducing environmental hazard, it includes building up resistance and immunity, general and specific, and advising and supporting all who are exposed to or suffering from illness in the community and, especially, all who are exposed to special hazard or subjected by illness to special stress. In other words, it is extending its responsibility to include ever more community medicine.

This extension is slow, tentative, and patchy; but if we generalise from whatever is already exemplified, the picture is impressive. Somewhere in Britain services exist or are planned to cover most of the needs of almost every group in the community in the field of health: for infants, schoolchildren, and students; for men and women at work; for women during and after pregnancy and for perplexed married couples; for the physically handicapped, the sensorily deprived, and the mentally retarded; for new entrants and immigrants into the community and for re-entrants from hospital and prison; for the poor, the elderly, and the senile; and, not least, for those who are sick at home and for those stressed by the need to look after them. These services are organised in a great variety of ways – by local authorities, voluntary bodies, industry, and government departments. Some are autonomous medical services, notably the school medical service and the growing body of industrial medical services. Others are nonmedical. But all are engaged in community medicine; each helps to meet some need which doctors practising community medicine feel or should feel as they go about their job of managing illness in the community; and most of them, if not medical, need medical advice and supervision.

## Two future streams

In a society where this concept of community medicine was realised, the medical profession would divide into two main streams by an option which would usually be exercised early and which, though not irrevocable, would seldom be reversed. One stream would flow through inpatient medicine towards the familiar heights of consultancy: its main aspiration would be to cure and relieve illness in the patients sent to it from the other stream and its main research concern would be with the physical and biological sciences on which the working of the individual organism depends and on their clinical manipulation and control. The other stream would flow through community medicine towards what would be regarded as comparable, though different heights. Its main preoccupation would be to relieve and manage illness in the community. It would rely on the other stream for help in diagnosis and therapy, where this was needed; but its main aspiration would be to achieve more, within the community, both in the cure and relief of illness and in fortifying the primary group as a mutually supportive system. The focus of its attention would be the patient as a psychobiological and psychosocial system – more simply, as a responsible fellow member of the community. Its main research concern would be with the psychosocial sciences and with epidemiology and would extend into preventive medicine as it is and as it might become.

These differences in emphasis cannot easily be stated without seeming exaggerated. It is easy to insist that the hospital doctor must be no less aware of his patient as a person than is the general practitioner; that the general practitioner must be no less aware of disturbances in the fine structure of the organism. Yet the difference in viewpoint is of crucial importance and should not be blurred. For it seems to me that the doctor practising community medicine, if he is doing his proper job properly, must be spending much of his time on work different from that which would absorb him if he were in hospital, calling for somewhat different skills, interests, and experience and judged by somewhat different standards of success. It is of the greatest importance to laymen that the medical profession should be so organised that this necessary function shall be served.

## The development of community medicine

Several obstacles seem to impede the development of community medicine in which doctors and community services play the roles and support the mutual relations that I have described.

There are, first, logistical factors. There are not enough doctors to staff the general-practitioner service on a scale which would make generally possible this concept of its function; not enough health visitors, psychiatric social workers, and other service personnel to staff the community services; not enough money. These barriers could be breached in time if both doctors and laymen were united in their wish to breach them; but they are not to be ignored.

These are compounded by organisational difficulties. The threefold division of the National Health Service should not be assumed to be wrong merely because it creates arbitrary and inconvenient divisions. All organisational boundaries, facilitating one set of functions, are bound to impede another. Yet the price in this area is too high and must remain so at least until local-authority revenues are no less free to grow than the Exchequer revenues – or until they are subsidised from central funds far more liberally. For if community medicine is to grow, the three branches of the service must be free to contribute to its growth as need and convenience may require; and this they cannot do so long as they are not only separately organised but financed from different pockets of the public purse, each differently supplied.

For example, general practitioners need to have closely associated with them, amongst other services, health visitors; and these should be the servants of the local authority, rather than a separate team working in parallel. Yet any such association is bound to increase the load on health visitors, and on other community services, for the general practitioner should be more aware than any other agency of the homes where they are needed. Thus even where general practitioner and local authority are in close relation and accord, the one service can grow only at some cost in money to the other. The cost is in fact an index of the service being better used; but so long as local authorities are hampered in expanding their services by their archaic and restricted revenue base, they cannot always afford to welcome it.

Again, the load on hospitals could be reduced by increasing the resources of the community for carrying its own illness. But the hospitals service is usually not free to spend its funds in this way; and local authorities earn no corresponding financial relief by doing so. Where such barriers do not bar the way – as, for example, where mental hospitals relieve their inpatient load by providing domiciliary and accessible outpatient care for mental illness in the community – experiments occur, hospitals are relieved, and community medicine benefits.

History contributes its quota to the barrier. A 19th-century concept of public health had little in common with a 19th-century concept of personal doctoring. The 19th century ended quite a long time ago; even since the National Health Service came into being, the concepts of personal and social medicine have grown closer together. It is time the fact was acknowledged; but the rate of change of mental habits is reckoned in generations.

The breaching of barriers needs leadership; but the segregation of streams of experience tends to be self-perpetuating for it makes harder the emergence of those who command respect and carry influence in more than one of the fields concerned. In medical education, no less than in medical practice, the gulfs between hospital medicine and community medicine and between individual therapy and public health are still wider than they might be and should be; and so is the gulf between practitioners and teachers of community medicine.

## Training for community medicine

Even greater obstacles would seem to lie in the field of medical education. This is necessarily designed first to qualify the student as a clinician. Those who are to diagnose and treat disease, besides mastering much human biology, must learn to recognise, or at least to detect the possibility of, a host of diseases, from complex combinations of subtle cues. Such learning, like all skills in recognition, comes only from constant exposure to specific instances. It cannot be easy to keep alive, through the whole course of medical education, focal interest in the patient not only as an example of pathology but as a person social by nature, drawing support as well as stress from others of his kind, contributing support and stress to them and involved with them in weaving the social pattern within which all doctors in the community must work and in which they have a multiple part to play, educative, regulative, and supportive, besides therapeutic.

Every profession in some degree must solve the same problem of combining depth and breadth in its qualifying experience. The difficulties inherent in medical education seem greater than in others. How far they can be overcome no layman can guess. It is safe to assume that the interest and experiment now being devoted to the problem will broaden the profession's present educational base and bridge part of the gulf between hospital medicine and community medicine.

It is equally certain that in medicine, as in other professions, this base, however well designed, will have limits, which will circumscribe the specialisms which can conveniently be built on it. The chief of these limits must remain the time required for clinical training. The expanding field of environmental medicine needs people well versed in human biology but not clinically qualified. They will not be called doctors of medicine, for tradition will reject the idea of a doctor who is not qualified to recognise and treat individual cases of disease; but they will be better qualified than any profession today to chart emerging hazards to health in the physical and social milieu and to devise and administer policy to control it. I expect that at least one new profession will soon emerge in this field to relieve medicine of some of its burden.

There is room for the same cooperation in community medicine. An example of the present dichotomy is found today, at a different level, in the contrast between the normal training of a health visitor and a psychiatric social worker. The first is still normally a State-registered nurse and a midwife, though she has little occasion for nursing or for midwifery. On the other hand, she has no training in social work or any education in the psychosocial sciences. A psychiatric social worker, by contrast, has an extensive education in the psychosocial sciences and substantial training in social case-work but no nursing experience and no education in human biology. Yet the two jobs have a large common content. It is now possible, I understand, for a would-be health visitor to offer a qualification largely in social work but containing experience of nursing less than sufficient for a qualification but enough to guide cooperation. The innovation seems welcome.

Corresponding changes are greatly to be desired on the boundaries of all professions, even though all professions traditionally hate and resist them. For we are moving into a world in which professional people will function increasingly as members of a multiprofessional service, needing to rely on and extend to other occupations and professions an increasing measure of cooperation and mutual understanding.

This points to yet another difference beween hospital medicine and community medicine. Community medicine is less of a medical preserve than hospital medicine and correspondingly more of a multiprofessional service. The critical need which may prevent the community from carrying a particular case of sickness may not be a medical need but a housing need or a need for home help or equipment or transport or just human support. Community medicine merges without sharp boundaries into the manifold services of a Welfare State; and those who participate in it as doctors have to accept from and extend to other professions and occupations a degree of cooperation which has not higherto been in the tradition of medicine or any other profession.

It is equally important, I think, to preserve the distinction between community medicine and other community services, however closely linked. For the area which I have called community medicine is primarily one of *medical* responsibility, however important to the community doctor may be the non-medical services available in the community. And as a field of medical responsibility, it involves responsibility to persons and for persons. This responsibility can only be focused on the personal doctor to whom the layman has direct recourse and through whom there are accessible to him both the resources of the hospital and the resources of the community.

This, then, is the critical link in the organisation both of hospital medicine and of community medicine. It is essential to laymen that the role of the personal doctor commands, both within the medical profession and in the community, respect at least as high as any other medical role. It is also essential to medicine. For the status of a profession depends not only on its technical skill but on its success in solving the recurrent problems which determine the scope and nature of its social responsibility; and it is within the field of community medicine that these problems are most critically developing.

## Conclusion

Community medicine is perhaps the most striking example of a problem endemic to our time. The past twenty years have seen the growth of two great organisations – the hospital service and the community services. The first, depending more on technology, has typically been more favoured and has consequently grown the faster; but the second is not unimpressive. But technology and organisation are not omnipotent; they cannot replace the personal and professional service on which community medicine depends. They can only support it and even this they can do only to the extent that it too grows to the measure of its new responsibilities – grows in size, in authority, in ability, in prestige and in readiness to assume these responsibilities and to play its part in working out what they are and how they can be discharged.

We do not seem to have established yet the conditions for this growth. Let us at least achieve the first condition, which is to realise its importance.

# 12

# The management of conflict*

This paper analyses the ambiguous concept of conflict, its sources, levels and types and the (largely defective) models by which we represent it. Membership of many systems is found to be potent both to generate conflict and to resolve and contain it. The restraints and assurances which flow from membership of these systems are examined in both their objective and their subjective aspects. The importance of subjective aspects is stressed and the mutual relation between them and the higher levels of communication which they sustain. This leads to a summary of the ways in which conflict is resolved and contained and the conditions on which these depend; and thus to a definition of the threshold beyond which these means fail and conflict in a different sense erupts as unqualified struggle between those who deny all the restraints and assurances of any common membership.

## The ambiguity of conflict

Human societies survive only so long as they can resolve or contain the conflicts which they generate. This is especially important at a time when the level of conflict, both external and internal, is rising so rapidly as it is now, and when accepted means of resolving and containing it are showing such manifest signs of overstrain. So it is timely to explore these three concepts – *conflict* and its *resolution* and *containment*. They are important, imprecise and distorted by some inadequate ideas about them which history has bequeathed to us.

We use the word conflict in two very different senses. We use it of any situation in which the parties involved are constrained to decide between alternatives none of which is wholly acceptable to them all – or even when a single individual or collective decision-maker has to resolve a similar dilemma. We use it also of the hostilities which erupt when such conflicts can be neither resolved by 'acceptable' means nor contained within 'acceptable' limits. What constitutes acceptability remains to be explored.

During the last war, for example, the shortage of food created a conflictual situation, in that there was not enough to satisfy all demands. Yet people did not fight each other for food. The conflict was resolved and contained by a rationing system, centrally administered and popularly supported. There was not even a substantial black market in conflict with the rationing authority. In consequence the distribution of food caused

* From *Futures*, June 1972.

virtually no conflict in the second sense and was perhaps more equitable than it has ever been before or since. The example is worth exploring for the light it throws on 'acceptability'.

Before the war our society relied largely on market mechanisms to determine the volume and price of the food supply. Nearly everyone relied for their daily subsistence on the assumptions that they would have enough money to buy at least their minimum needs, and that there would be enough food in the shops to satisfy the total effective demand. Neither assumption was necessarily true. The first was imperfectly sustained by supplementing incomes in accordance with principles which had been badly shaken by the depression of the 1930s. The second collapsed with the limitation on imports by the submarine offensive and the needs of war. In a situation where rising prices could not elicit larger supplies of food, market distribution would have caused escalating prices and profits to suppliers and would have starved all but the rich. This would in time and in theory have immobilised the work force. In fact, of course, long before starvation could have had this effect, resentment at the inequity of distribution would have caused a change in policy or, failing that, attacks on food stores, food distributors and the most favoured classes of recipient, and these conflicts would have had quicker and more disruptive effects than the starvation which they would have anticipated.

The alternative solution introduced by rationing also rested on unspoken assumptions – that the State could mobilise enough competent and honest employees to administer the scheme; that the public would accept the need for it and co-operate sufficiently to make it work; and that the reduced food supply could be kept at a level which would be sufficient for all basic needs. If any of these conditions had failed, conflict in the second sense would in time have erupted between the worst pressed and the least pressed or between the worst pressed and the State or both.

Thus the point at which conflict degenerates into conflict-in-the-second-sense is a function of several factors both objective and subjective. Once a conflict passes this critical point, it becomes a threat to the system as such, not merely to its present state; and thereupon it changes both its nature and its parties, mobilising on one side all those who rally to the defence of the system, whatever their attitude to the particular dispute, and on the other, those who declare their indifference to the system in so far as it impedes their preferred solution or even their hostility to it because it does so. Those who become thus divided are almost bound to redefine each other as aliens or as enemies, at least so far as concerns their former common membership of that system. And the mutual relations within which they might have resolved or contained their differences will be disrupted by this change, perhaps irreversibly. International and civil wars are familiar examples of this crossing of a threshold. They have their counterparts in industrial relations, personal relations and perhaps even in the psycho-pathology which results when such conflicts can be neither resolved nor contained within a single head.

Such thresholds are a common feature of systems of all kinds. They mark the point, not always predictable, at which the system's capacity for sustaining itself is overwhelmed. The result may be that the system wholly disintegrates or that it re-forms in some more or less changed shape. How far, in the second event, its successor is to be regarded as a new system or as the old system changed depends on what aspects of the old system are regarded by the observer as most essential to its identity.

My purpose in this paper is to give a more definite meaning to this threshold in the context of political societies.

## The sources of conflict

The constraints which give rise to conflictual situations are of three kinds. Some I will call logistical constraints. There is a limit to what we can do, limits which can be only roughly estimated, within wide margins of risk and uncertainty. Moreover, resources are limited. Aspirations, even when not mutually inconsistent, compete for scarce resources. This scarcity cannot be remedied by increased abundance, partly because time and attention, most essential of resources, cannot be expanded, but also because scarcity is a *relation* between our resources and our aspirations. However rich we are, we can spend money, life, time only one way. So the more choices we have, the more we have to say no to.

So conflictual situations are increased, rather than reduced, by the growing powers of men to manipulate the physical world. And today these conflicts are further increased by a new factor. Multiplying populations, wasting resources and mounting pollution are making it evident that the greater our powers, the less we can afford either to use them or to restrain them without counting multiple and disparate costs. There could be no better illustration of a conflictual situation.

A much more dangerous source of conflict is the constraint necessarily imposed on us by the wishes and expectations, no less than the acts of other people. These constrain us in two ways, of which the most conspicuous today seems to be the constraints of 'authority'. Every society and organisation to which we belong has its expectations of us and can bring pressure to bear on us to comply with those expectations. It also has its own powers of collective choice, which commit us, whether we agree with the way they are used or not. These are the powers of *Authority*. In societies which become increasingly organised, and especially in pluralist societies which pride themselves on the multiplicity and independence of their institutions, authority is bound to be an ever increasing source of conflictual situations.

Individuals, societies and organisations of all kinds, in so far as they are *not* constrained by some common authority, constrain each other no less by the pressures they use to influence or restrain each other's initiatives and even by the mere fact of exercising their own. In an increasingly crowded and interdependent world, these mutual constraints also are bound to mount. Indeed, the need to resolve or contain them is one main reason for the extension of authority. Yet in so far as authority assumes more responsibility for resolving or containing such conflicts, it tends to raise correspondingly the level of tension between it and those who are subject to it.

Most Westerners today are more apprehensive of constraint by 'authority' than of constraints by each other. This balance could change – I think it will and should. But wherever it stands, constraint will flow both from all the authorities to which we are subject and from all the initiatives of our fellows which authority does not control. Both are mounting and must continue to mount.

The escalation of constraint is not of itself dehumanising. On the contrary, conflictual situations are the hall mark of human life. Their resolution and containment is the basic art of being human. It is what distinguishes a man from a bird on a bird table. Birds fly, feed, preen, mate, fight in sequences measured in seconds, each dominated by a single impulse. Every human choice, by contrast, whether it be deciding on a family holiday or settling a national budget, or even a wage claim, involves balancing through time a host of disparate criteria, not all of which – usually, not one of which – can be fully satisfied. The mark of a successful individual or a successful society is that it manages to sustain *through time* a host of different relationships, keeping each in accord with some standard of expectation, while containing all within the resources available; and developing all these standards in the process. These developments are easy to see when we look back over the history of any field of social policy. Progress in the human dimension depends on increasing skill in resolving and containing conflict.

So we should not be surprised by the need to increase this skill. We should not even be dismayed, unless it seems to make demands which cannot be met or which can be met only at what would seem to be some unacceptable cost. And this is of course the threat which dismays us today. For conflicts are best resolved and contained where the parties share strongly what I will call the constraints and assurances of membership; and this is precisely what is hard to generate on the scale and in the conditions of today, except at costs which we are accustomed to regard as unacceptable in the highest degree.

This brings us to the third area in which conflictual situations are generated and without which conflicts in other areas would be neither resolved nor contained – or even noticed. This is the organisation of our individual personality systems. We develop not only conflicting fears and aspirations but also more or less conflicting standards which define what we come to expect of ourselves in all our manifold contexts. These introduce conflict into our personal situations. The making of a reasonably coherent personality is a task which few accomplish in a lifetime. And even those who do so experience continual conflict between the demands of the various roles they play, as well as within each of their roles.

Moreover, the state of our individual personality system determines what conflict, if any, will be involved for us by the constraints of the natural world and of society and of the independent agents around us. We may recognise what others expect of us and deem it prudent to comply. But the degree of conflict in the situation depends on how far their expectations of us correspond with our expectations of ourselves.

Finally, the skills involved in the resolution and containment of conflict are in the last resort personal skills.

So the organisation of individual personalities is not only an independent source of conflictual situations but also the key factor in determining how all conflictual situations are perceived, resolved, contained – or not contained.

The three kinds of constraint which I have described are reflected in three familiar verbs. What we can and cannot do, must and must not do, ought and ought not to do are defined by the constraints imposed on us by circumstances, by other people and by ourselves. Each of these constraints can raise conflicts. Each conflicts with the others. And any or all of them may conflict with that simpler category, what we want and do not want to do. I will not pursue further here the permutations of this matrix of potential conflict or its psychological implications; but nothing less, I believe is adequate to represent the variety of potential conflict inherent in human relations at any level from the personal to the planetary.

## Levels of conflict

I need next to distinguish four levels at which conflictual situations may arise in a society. The first is the level, already distinguished, which does not involve authority. Individual citizens may bicker within the wide limits set by the law and social tolerance. Political parties and trade unions may feud with each other, and so within them may the members of each. Departments of businesses, no less than of governments and universities may engage in venomous infighting. I shall usually be little concerned with this level, because any such conflict must usually escalate to the level at which it involves 'authority' before it breeds one of those destructive exercises which rank as conflicts in the second sense.

In conflictual situations involving authority, we need to distinguish three further levels.

Every society has its own rules for settling conflicts, including rules which allot responsibility for decisions. The first level of conflict takes place within these rules.

But these rules themselves are open to change and are indeed in constant change, partly through the pressure of dissatisfaction generated by their earlier application. The second level of conflict is concerned with the changing of the rules by which the first level is contained. This is the level of most political activity. A century ago, for example, the right to pursue industrial disputes by strike action was just being established by changes in the criminal law of conspiracy. Today controversy about changing these rules concerns the need to ensure the contestants' public responsibility, rather than their private power.

But the power to change the rules is itself subject to restraints, legal, constitutional and conventional; and these form a third level of possible conflict and one which is especially important to my subject. It is the pride of democratic institutions that they provide constitutional means to change the rules and even to change a written constitution. But the histories of most democracies include periods when the pressure to change the rules used highly irregular procedures, from civil disobedience to armed revolution, from violent mass protest to personal communication through dramatic forms of murder and suicide.

Disputes at these three levels involve authority and its office-holders in different degrees and even in different ways. At the first level authority is neutral. The conflict does not challenge the existing order. At the second level the existing order is challenged, though not 'order' itself. The attempt at reordering is still 'orderly'; but it is more likely to engage representatives of the existing order on one side of the conflict. At the third level, authority is necessarily engaged as a principal in the dispute, since it has a primary duty to preserve the system's accepted means of growth and change and to resist attempts to impose or oppose change by other means.

## Types of conflict

It is useful also to distinguish conflictual situations according to what the conflict is about. Three types can be distinguished, though they are always found in combination.

The type least easy to recognise and hardest to resolve involves conflict about what the situation shall be deemed to be.

To a planning authority a decayed urban area is a threat to a number of sanitary and other standards which the authority has a duty to maintain. It is at the same time an opportunity to reshape part of the physical environment to meet more adequately the changed requirements anticipated ten years hence. The two requirements conflict. This conflict, however, is not visible to most of the residents in the area. To them 'the situation' is a variety of current shortcomings in dwellings and facilities, by no means the same as those which most worry the authority. The criteria which they apply to any proposal change are the benefits promised in terms of these shortcomings and the costs which these would involve in terms of current inconvenience and disturbance. Benefits expected ten years hence have little power to offset costs expected now – and no power at all to do so, unless the residents can learn to attach reality to that view of the situation which is natural to the authority.

An interested developer, on the other hand, has no difficulty in seeing the situation on the same time scale as the planning authority. Even if he sees only a site ripe for profitable development because of its currently depressed value, it may well be easier for him to understand the situation as seen by the authority and the wider criteria which they apply (even though he does not share these) than it is for those who live in the place.

Even on the authority there will be some councillors who see the situation primarily as the need and opportunity to improve the accommodation of specific ill-housed people, whilst others regard the expected increase in site values as a better criterion of the meeting of foreseen future needs. So differences about what the situation shall be deemed to be express and are affected by differences about the values to be attributed to different criteria of success. And even where agreement exists about the aspects to be included in the situation and about the criteria to apply, fierce differences may still arise about the best course to take. Of the alternative development plans submitted to the authority no logical deductive process can *prove* which is best even by the criteria agreed.

Disagreements about how the situation shall be seen and how it shall be valued are so intimately connected that I find it convenient to describe the two together as differences of appreciation. Conflicts about how to attain agreed ends, though they bulk so large in studies of decision making, are always subsidiary to appreciative problems and seldom, if ever, raise irresolvable conflicts between those who are at one in their appreciation of a situation.

All major conflicts involve differences in the values which different parties attach to different aspects of a situation common to them all, differences which often lead them to different definitions of the situation itself.

Some writers have tried to resolve this by distinguishing an in-built hierarchy of importance in the values which men and societies seek to realise. I view this distinction rather differently. It is true that some situations define a single criterion as being of overwhelming *urgency*; but when this happens, human initiative is at its nadir. Central and local governments, for example, like business enterprises, need to remain solvent; and when threatened with insolvency, they have to cut their expenditure to match their revenue before the course of events cuts it for them. In such emergencies cuts fall wherever they will be most immediately effective. A logistical constraint has become dominant. The system is threatened by the impending failure of one of its *conditions*, just as the performance of a statesman may be threatened by lack of food and sleep.

The example reminds us that social, like individual human systems, are partly hierarchic. Their higher functioning depends on sustaining the stability of lower levels. But these underlying stabilities are only *conditions* of higher-level success. They neither assure that the government or the individual whom they sustain will perform his regulative functions 'well' nor supply any criterion for determining between good and bad performance of that function.

Sometimes the situation attaches overriding importance to some function which is not apparently in such a basic relation to the hierarchy. An impending breakdown in traffic control or law and order may create an emergency in which the threatened relation has to be given top priority. But here again the explanation is the same. The impending breakdown would affect the functioning, even the survival of the system as a whole and claims priority on that ground alone. It reflects no priority inherently attached to the relationship as such.

It is important to distinguish this hierarchy of urgency, especially as it is so frequently manipulated by those who wish to increase the importance which others will attach to some particular relationship. But it seems to me to throw no light on the procedures by which we resolve or contain our endemic conflicts in those conditions where we have some scope for initiative.

Conflicts between rival criteria are sometimes distinguished from simple conflicts of interest. The distinction, I think, is fallacious. A conflict of interest is simply one in which differences about the definition of the situation and choice of relevant criteria derive more obviously than usual from the position of the parties. They merit attention none the less because they have been taken as typical in both recent and earlier models of conflict and its resolution.

## Models of conflict

Our understanding of human conflict has suffered from our readiness to think of it in terms drawn from much simpler areas of experience, such as mechanics or ethology or game playing. I have no space here to examine these models adequately but I need to define one limitation which is common to them all.

Our earliest models are mechanical. Rival demands or views are conceived as *forces* which, impinging at different angles with different strengths, produce not a result but a *resultant*; sometimes movement corresponding to a 'resolution' of these forces; sometimes the 'breaking' of the 'weaker' structure involved in the collision. These analogies ignore the fact that human beings, even in the crudest opposition, influence each of them primarily by communication, rather than by the transfer of energy. Even the bombs dropped at Hiroshima and Nagasaki were – and were intended to be – more effective as communications than as agents of destruction.

More recently the study of conflict in other species disclosed rituals for 'containing' conflict and led some ethologists to compare our species unfavourably with stags and wolves. When like is compared with like, it may be held that the human species' democratic methods of choosing leaders are more humane and more effective than trial by combat. But the real difference lies in the much higher level of communication involved, which renders the attraction of followers more important than the elimination of potential rivals.

More recently still the analysis of game playing and especially the scientific handling of risk and uncertainty has clarified strategic thinking and acknowledged the part played in human conflicts by the power of each party to build up for itself a representation of the other's strategy. But it is a characteristic of games that the rules and the criteria of success remain constant at least for the duration of the game, while in human life these are precisely what the major conflicts are about.

I would not belittle the contributions which these models have made to our thinking but none of them seems to me remotely adequate. Human conflict is an exercise in communication even when it is prosecuted with bombs and bullets. And it can have the chance of being adequate only if it can be prosecuted at a level very much higher than bombs and bullets.

The concept of 'levels' of communication is one to which communication theorists can now attach some specific meaning; in particular some of them are prepared to describe with precision the difference between 'dialogue' and those lower levels where each participant tries to manipulate the others, whilst remaining unchanged himself. Dialogue no doubt represents only a small fraction of the exchanges which constitute deliberate communication – itself only a small fraction of the total body of communication. To call the political process a dialogue is to flatter it.

None the less even a society the size of Britain does develop, within a single lifetime, views of itself and its situation more comprehensive, realistic and widely held; more exacting standards of what should be acceptable in internal and external relationships; more sensitive awareness of human variety and human need. And these changes are in part the product of mutual communication at a level much higher than that at which words are used as weapons. So we should not be surprised to find similarity, even identity, between the conditions which favour dialogue and those which favour the resolution and containment of conflict.

## The restraints and assurances of membership

Persons in conflict, whatever divides them, are usually also related through common membership of one or more systems; and this may impose on them some restraints and give them some assurances which they would not otherwise feel. This factor is of very great importance both to the resolution and to the containment of conflict. I refer to it as the constraints and assurances of membership, or for brevity, as the membership factor. It deserves to be examined in detail.

The constraints of membership stem from those three sources which are also the source of our conflicts. They may arise from an objective appreciation of a common situation. Men at sea, for example, even when in open mutiny, may remain aware of their common dependence on the ship and, in extreme danger, may abate their conflicts sufficiently to co-operate in keeping it afloat. Examples no less cogent are implicit in the situation of Britain, dependent for half its food on imports from abroad and even in the total dependence of the human race on the resources of a small and misused planet.

The constraints of membership may also arise from an objective assessment of the expectations sustained by others and by authority and of the results of disappointing them. A ship's crew is subject to ship's discipline and a seaman's knowledge of the sea and of the conditions which it imposes may make acceptable a discipline which would not be acceptable ashore.

Finally, the constraints of membership may stem from what we have learned to expect *of ourselves* in response to the situations in which we find ourselves as members, in so far as these reinforce the constraints imposed on us by the situation, by other members and by authority.

The assurances of membership spring from the same sources. The sailor is assured that other seamen will read the same message from the ship's predicament and will know, as he himself does, the expectations held of him by his fellows and by authority and the cost of disappointing them. And he can sometimes assume that they expect *of themselves* what he expects of himself.

But constraints based on *self*-expectations and assurances based on trust in the *self*-expectations of others differ from the other constraints and assurances that I have described in ways of the utmost importance, which are often overlooked. They and they alone create those bonds of responsibility, loyalty and mutual trust without which human societies neither function nor cohere in face of any serious challenge to their integrity. A mutinous ship's company might conceivably co-operate to save the ship, even though bound to each other by nothing but obvious present danger; but their co-operation would not outlast more than the most acute phase of the emergency. Much more striking is the extent to which men *disregard* their most obvious common interests when they lack the common loyalty and mutual trust *corresponding to those interests*.

As I write, the miners of Great Britain on official strike have withdrawn nearly all safety and maintenance labour from the pits which are their livelihood and are allowing the pressures of the earth to destroy their workplaces, perhaps irrevocably. These are men conspicuously noted for loyalty, responsibility and mutual trust; and the enterprise on which they are now engaged makes great demands on both and has made even greater demands over the long past in which those loyalties were forged. But this enterprise is not the getting of coal. It is the prosecution of an ancient dispute against parties who have changed and multiplied through the long century of that endemic conflict. The system which claims their allegiance at this time isolates them from the other systems of which they also inescapably form part – the country, the industry, even their own pits.

Hence the enormous importance which attaches to this distinction between the subjective membership factor of loyalty, responsibility and mutual trust, and the constraints and assurances to be derived from an objective assessment of the situation and its demands. The subjective membership factor determines which of the multiple claims of membership we shall accept and powers our revolt against those which we do not accept, however inescapably we may be involved in them.

We all belong to many systems; far more than have ever claimed the allegiance of men before our day. Some are hierarchic. Political states, federal and even unitary, comprise many foci of loyalty of smaller scale and often with longer history and greater power; and they are themselves systemically related to each other, however lacking their common loyalty and mutual trust, through common dependence on spaceship earth. Other large organisations, notably industrial and occupational, present a similar hierarchic structure. Community of race, religion, education, profession and economic interest cut across these hierarchies and establish between their members systemic relations often of great supportive power.

All these memberships make partly conflicting claims on us. It is not surprising that the structure of our loyalties, even among the most mature and informed of us, should not measure up to this pattern of demand. It is none the less the greatest danger of our time. For all our means of resolving conflict and nearly all our means of containing it depend on preserving among the disputants a pattern of loyalty and mutual trust roughly comparable with the structure of the multiple memberships involved in the dispute.

## Force and violence

In so far as conflicts are not contained by the constraints and assurances of membership, they can only be contained by impotence or by coercion, by which I mean the *threat* of injury. Not all forms of threat, whether mutual or unilateral, are banned by the rules of most societies but most are so banned, because threats between fellow members are in themselves inimical to the constraints and assurances of membership and are likely to escalate into more extreme threats or into attempts to put the threat into action. But authority, banning coercion among its members, assumes the responsibility of enforcing its own ban and thus saddles itself with the difficulties which attend all exercises in coercion.

A century ago it was widely supposed that political authority rested largely on the coercive force of sanctions. Later, a more sociological view recognised the extent to which both law observance and law enforcement depend on public acceptance of law and of the legitimacy of the lawgiver. Both views are valid and both can be illustrated in any society. But they correspond to two largely incompatible attitudes to authority. The members of most societies are sharply divided between those who feel themselves to be consenting members and those who feel themselves to be alien, if coerced non-members.

This divide is expressed in every society by the startlingly different attitudes to force and violence, two words which though similar, have come to have deeply different connotations.

Political authority has always commanded force, to which some dissident individuals have always responded with violence. To the system member, force, however disliked in principle, is redeemed by being at the service of responsible power, whilst violence is the epitome of that anarchy which authority exists to suppress. To the dissident, violence is the expression of individual freedom against enslaving authority, whilst force is violence debased by being institutionalised. Violence as distinct from force has played and still plays an important part in revolutionary theory and in the revolutionary mystique. Force, on the other hand, has become a more equivocal concept in politics partly through failure of the sublime self-assurance which once justified its use, partly in reaction against exaggerated notions of what it can do and partly through a new appreciation that force exercises its greatest and least predictable effects as communication, rather than as act.

These irreconcilable views of force and violence are rooted in two different views of political history. One sees the State as the entrenched preserve of a ruling class and a fount of injustice against which lovers of freedom and equality have always a right, if not a duty to rebel. The other sees it as the embodiment of the ordering process by which the weak are enabled to coexist on relatively equal terms with the strong. Both views are true and the tension between them is probably inescapable. But the more seriously democracy takes itself and the better it succeeds, the greater is the support which it is likely to generate for the second view and the more anachronistic seem the attitudes and slogans of the first.

Anachronistic though they be, our inherited tendencies to suspect force and condone violence when opposed to force are deep rooted. 'God forbid' cried Thomas Jefferson 'we should ever be 20 years without such a rebellion ... what country can preserve its liberties if its rulers are not warned from time to time that this people preserve the spirit of resistance? Let them take arms ... The tree of liberty must be refreshed from time to time with the blood of patriots and tyrants.' The implication that the users of force must be tyrants, whilst the users of violence are probably patriots rings out loudly after two centuries presumably devoted to disproving it. More disturbingly, it is audible in Britain today.

In fact the credentials of force are at least better than the credentials of violence and the weak have today, I think, far less to fear from it. But though authority usually commands more force than the potentiality of violence opposed to it, it works under a handicap which exponents of violence are quick to exploit. Force is of very limited use *for the purposes for which authority exists* and is hard to use even within its limited scope without impairing authority's remaining armoury; while for the negative and simplistic purposes of revolution or even mere protest violence is apt and adequate.

In brief, the regulation and containment of conflict depend today on a level of communication so high as to be doubtfully attainable even in a society which knew its importance and was dedicated to its achievement. To block such communication by violence is easy. To preserve it by force is difficult in the extreme. Yet the essential role of force is to preserve the conditions within which such communication may be possible.

THE MANAGEMENT OF CONFLICT


# The resolution and containment of conflict

I can now attempt a brief account of the ways in which conflict is resolved and contained.

The main social mechanisms for resolving and containing conflict are rule and role. Rules, from formal laws to the subtlest conventions of courtesy, provide ready-made answers for a host of conflictual situations; sometimes directly (as with the rule of the road and the convention of queueing); sometimes indirectly, by allocating responsibility for decision in controversial matters, executive, legislative and judicial. Roles define what is to be expected of the holders of defined positions by others and by themselves, notably including those positions which carry responsibility for such decisions. They thus express and help to generate those self- and mutual expectations which I have described as the main agents for resolving and containing conflict. They are partly the product of the process which they regulate, partly because of the element of discretion which they always contain; and they are thus a principal agency of change.

Roles long antedate the existence of any authority capable of enforcing them. Cornish tin miners in neolithic times could not have traded with sea-borne visitors, unless both they and the strangers had been able to distinguish with some assurance the roles of trader and raider. None the less, the web of mutual confidence could not have attained even its present tenuous consistency, especially in a society in rapid change, but for two inventions, one of which is political authority on the scale of today. The other, less remarked but not less remarkable, is what I will call the contractual role.

In traditional societies positions and their roles, political, social and even occupational, were relatively fixed and their tenure depended far less than in contemporary societies on contract terminable by either party. Our current freedom to devise new organisations, and new positions, even new organisations with new roles and to appoint and dismiss their holders is a social invention of great importance. One of its merits is that conflict between such role holders can often be resolved by changing a role holder. He can resign; he can be dismissed. Conflict is always far more intransigent between parties who cannot escape from their mutual relationship. This is, of course, a conspicuous feature of political societies, which can neither choose nor rid themselves of even their most disruptive members. Indeed, they can do so even less today than in earlier days. And similarly, as frontiers close, even their most dissident members can less easily change their political allegiance or simply go elsewhere. All these rigidities are growing and are likely to grow.

So the load mounts on that mediating factor which I have called the constraints and assurances of membership and especially on its subjective element, which is the main source of responsibility, loyalty and mutual trust. This, the membership factor, operates with very varying degrees of potency in human systems of different types and sizes and even in the same system at different periods in its history. It is normally far more potent in small systems united by a common objective (such as a team of explorers or even a professional partnership) than in a diffuse political society or even a large business corporation. However strong or weak, it improves the system's capacity to resolve and contain conflict in at least three ways. In so far as it makes the operation of rule and role acceptable, it *mutes* potential conflict so that it scarcely arises. At the other extreme it helps to *contain* even the fiercest conflict by reinforcing whatever sanctions authority commands. For dissenters cannot rebel against any specific decision without challenging the system as a whole and awakening the opposition of all who feel protected by it. Moreover, the would-be rebel cannot pursue his rebellion without putting himself out of membership of his society, redefining his former fellow members as aliens or enemies and correspondingly redefining himself and the whole system of his self- and mutual expectations. The stronger his sense of membership, the more reluctant will he be to restructure himself so radically. Thus the system of self- and mutual expectations from which these constraints and assurances proceed is powerful to sustain itself and therewith the social system that depends on it.

Between these two extremes of muting and containing conflict, the membership factor greatly enlarges the possibilities of *resolving* conflict.

Even a bargain is useless if neither party can be trusted to keep it. But the resolution of conflict does not depend merely on compromise or bargain within the limits of a given dispute, but on changing the parties' perception of the dispute itself. This is a function of mutual persuasion, a process which has received little attention from psychologists but one on which we should not spend so much time if we did not think it important.

## Mutual persuasion

Negotiators often go on talking even when there is apparently nothing to discuss, because they know from experience that communication sometimes produces changes which are important, even though they are hard to specify. These changes are in the constraints and assurances of membership.

In any conflictual situation debate serves first to articulate the parties' views of the logistical constraints under which they are acting and the possibilities and costs of changing them. This helps to produce a more widely shared view of what the situation should be deemed to be and what can be done about it. And this may well include a more adequate view of the parties' own interrelationship, in other contexts as well as in the context of the dispute.

It also changes or reinforces the way each party *values* the situation. Every debate on a conflictual situation appeals to criteria of value, as well as to threats and counter-threats; and these appeals, unless wholly disbelieved, affect the way in which each party pictures to itself the way the other party appreciates the situation. They may do more; they may affect – as they are intended to do – the criteria which each party accepts as relevant and the weight to be attached to it. There may thus result an appreciation more adequate and more widely held.

This is reinforced by articulating what the parties expect of each other and what pressures they are prepared to bring to bear on each other. This brings to consciousness the second of the constraints already described; and this has some effect both on the willingness of potential coercers to coerce and of the others to be coerced. But it also makes clear and so confirms or varies how each party views and values its relation with the other, the restraints acknowledged by it and by the others and the assurances on which each can still rely.

Thus debate brings to consciousness and inevitably changes or confirms the self-expectations of the parties. Not only does each have to decide how far to acquiesce, how far and by what means to press its view, what action to take on the final decision. Even more importantly, it has to decide how its relation with the other party is to stand thereafter.

Thus all debates on conflictual issues are conducted at two levels. They are concerned not only with the matter at issue but also with the future relation of the parties as fellow members in that context and perhaps in many others. This second level of debate tends to grow more important as the debate proceeds and often ends by overshadowing the original issue. The constraints and assurances of membership may or may not contain the conflict over the specific issue. And if they do, the constraints and assurances of membership may be stronger or weaker in consequence. The second is usually by far the more important result.

## The threshold

This analysis seems to me to provide material for a better understanding of conflict and its management and particularly of that elusive threshold which is its particular subject. The argument so far can be summarised as follows:

> Conflict is endemic in human affairs and its management is the most characteristically human function and skill.

> The management of conflict includes and depends on containing it within the threshold beyond which it will become self-exciting and destructive of *the resources for resolving and containing conflict.*

> This threshold is largely set by the constraints and assurances which the contestants feel as implicit in their common memberships.

> These memberships are multiplying, as the systems in which people are organised (political, economic, social and other) become more numerous, more unstable and more interrelated.

> All conflicts, whatever effect they may have on the conflictual situation, affect the relations of the parties in that and other contexts, notably by weakening or strengthening the constraints and assurances which

they feel as implicit in their common memberships. So the management of conflict needs to be even more concerned with preserving these relationships than with the actual conflict.

This involves articulating a common appreciation of the multiple objective relations which these subjective relations are required to support; but it is not achieved or maintained by that alone.

All human conflicts are both prosecuted and contained by communication at varying levels, from force and violence, through calculated falsification upwards to levels dependent on the highest levels of common appreciation and mutual trust. Bad communication, like bad currency, drives out the good; so the management of conflict is properly concerned with banning lower levels of communication so far as may be.

Coercion and deterrence, though legitimate and effective in limited fields, are low levels of communication, because they are inimical to the subjective constraints and assurances of membership, which are also the conditions for higher levels of communication and because threats are peculiarly liable to engender escalating conflict.

No authority is entitled to monopolise the loyalties of its members and no individual has the duty or the right to accord exclusive loyalty to any one of the systems to which he belongs. But equally no individual has the right to deny responsibility to his fellow members of *any* system to which he in fact belongs or to its common authority. The resultant conflict of loyalties is the most familiar example of that conflict which I have described as the essence of the human condition.

Total failure to meet this challenge results in the polarisation of conflict. At its extreme this results in the parties' loyalties becoming exclusively attached to one or other of two conflicting systems. When this occurs, the only duties felt to be owed or expected are owed to or expected from fellow members of a single system. All other persons, even the same persons in the context of a different membership, become alien, and probably enemy. For to be mutually dependent on those whom one does not trust and towards whom one feels no duty is an intolerable burden. So once the subjective constraints and assurances fail, the objective ones are potent to generate an overwhelming desire to cut loose from or destroy the entangling, threatening other. Hence the peculiar virulence of civil war, wars of secession and all such struggles.

This analysis prompts three personal reflections:

The management of conflict is not the responsibility of authority alone. It is the responsibility of every member of every system in all their endemic conflicts. The present tendency to regard authority as a precipitant, rather than a manager of conflict seems to me to be due partly to the fact that when conflict reaches what I described as its third level, authority does indeed become a protagonist, as the residuary legatees of society's failure to resolve the conflict at an earlier stage. Even more it seems to me the pathological projection by individuals onto political authority of their own failure or refusal to face reality at the level at which they need to appreciate it, or to accept their own responsibility for containing it.

Political authority is of course not free from the tendency of all authorities to claim for its own system more autonomy than it can or should have; and it consequently needs to be constrained by other authorities, speaking for other systems, wider, narrower and overlapping. None the less political authorities, having general responsibility for regulating all relevant relations within their system, have usually a wider view than any functional authority and all but the most informed and mature individuals. Their officials, in my experience, appreciate conflictual situations more comprehensively, tolerate frustration more patiently and serve the common interest more devotedly than do most of their non-institutional critics. They thus give an example of a human approach to the management of conflict which those without such wide responsibilities might well follow and admire.

It would be vain to expect them all to do so; for a system so large and loosely integrated as a political state should not be regarded as composed of indistinguishable units. There will surely be some predators; some would-be destroyers; a variety of protesters, suffering varying degrees of alienation but with messages entitled to attention; and a body of assenting members, who will vary greatly in their capacity to attach reality to the wider implications of their memberships; in the strength of their sense of responsibility, loyalty and trust; and in the relative dominance of the systems which elicit these attitudes. It is the need and duty of every such society, despite these internal differences and weaknesses, to preserve the conditions in which the political dialogue can continue by neutralising its enemies; and to do so it needs to use both organised authority and its own diffuse controls.

It seems to me impossible to hope for so subtle an exercise of power to preserve the conditions of freedom unless the relations of individuals and their other organisations to their organs of political authority become far more mutually responsive than they are now. The common factor in all the major revolutions of our time, from Ataturk to Castro, from Mussolini to Tito, from Lenin to Mao Tse-Tung has been the need to make the individual more politically responsible than he has been in the past. Most of them have been more obviously successful at institutionalising the individual than at humanising their institutions. In any case solutions to political problems are not easily transferred from one culture to another. Answers are individual – but questions tend to be universal, none more so than the question how to manage conflict. One step towards answering it would be to accept the fact that institutionalised persons are at least as much needed as humanised institutions. By an institutionalised person I mean one who accepts the constraints and assurances of membership in *all* the systems of which he forms part and therewith the responsibility for managing his share of the conflicts which they involve.

# 13

# Values, norms and policies*

## Abstract

Norms are defined as specific but tacit standards of what is socially and individually acceptable; values as explicit but general statements of principle, of which the content is continually changing through changing norms, changing circumstances, changing policies and the accompanying ethical debate. The relation of norms, values and policies is shown by a historical example. The inherent conflict within both norms and values is discussed and the role of the policymaker is defined, both as an artist in conceiving and devising one among many possible but always partial realizations of contemporary norms and values, and as a partially conscious agent in reshaping the norms and values of his time. The psychological implications of this are briefly indicated.

## 1. A definition of norms

In his book *Technological Planning and Social Futures* Dr Erich Jantsch[1] provides a diagram showing the sequence of mental operations which lead from policymaking through planning and decisionmaking to rational creative action. Policies precede strategies; strategies precede tactics. But policies occupy not the top level but the third level of his diagram. Above the policy level come two levels labelled 'Values' and 'Norms', with mutual interactions shown between values, norms and policies. Unlike some writers in this field, Dr Jantsch does not take 'goals' for granted. Values and norms bombard the policymaker with multiple disparities between the course of events as it is and is likely to be and its course as he would wish it to be. These signals often mutually conflict and their demands always far exceed what he can achieve. It is his job to choose and realize one among the many possible partial solutions of this intrinsically insoluble problem. And if he understands his function as well as he should, he knows that his solution can and should be only temporary, since its successes as well as its failures will set new problems for his successors. On the other hand, his solution must last long enough to realize its own promise and pave the way for what will follow.

Though many – not all – writers on policymaking would agree in general with this statement, few if any have addressed themselves primarily

*From *Policy Sciences*, Vol. 4, 1973.

to elucidating the relations between values, norms, and policies or even the meanings of these terms. The reasons are obvious but the result is none the less disastrous. Values and norms, as I shall seek to show, are terms of unusable vagueness today not because they cannot be usefully defined, but because they have not yet been sufficiently analyzed, although an abundant store of accessible fact is available for the purpose. This paper is a contribution towards filling this gap.

Although policymaking is common to public and business affairs, and indeed to the management of all human affairs, it is liable to be oversimplified in the study of business decisions in a way which is impossible in the public sector. So it is convenient to choose an example from the field of social policy.

A century ago most homes in Britain had a well in the garden, a privy in the garden, and a tank to catch the rain water. Much of the washing was done with rain water, being soft and (then) clean. The well supplied the rest, including the drinking water. The slops and the excrement went on to the garden, either directly or through the compost heap. The generation, use and disposal of water was contained in an area no larger than the site of a cottage. Human waste was disposed of by a separate system, equally small and self-contained.

Today the universal use of water to dispose of sewage has linked the two systems and each combined system covers an area which in Britain is at least as large as the largest river's catchment area and will soon be much larger. The factual interdependence of people in the matter of water and sewage has hugely proliferated. So have their expectations of the system, of each other and of themselves. It is today regarded as 'unacceptable' that even an isolated home should lack indoor sanitation and an indoor water supply. In the debate on social policy and its priorities 'bad housing' bulks large: and among its constituents the standards of water supply and sanitation have an important place. Other criteria, such as the ratio of persons to rooms, have similar levels which define the unacceptable. Houses which fail to satisfy current standards of the acceptable are 'substandard'. Even policymakers who do not respond to pressure to bring houses up to standard seldom venture to deny that such standards exist and are valid today, even though they were different or even absent a century ago.

Standards of this kind provide the structure of social policy; countless other examples suggest themselves. They illustrate a very common form of mental operation. Some state of affairs, actual or hypothetical, is compared with a standard of what ought to be and is found not to 'fit'. In cybernetic terms a mismatch signal is generated. The agent who makes this judgment may for the moment be unable to do anything to remedy the disparity or he may be unwilling to do what he might because some other mismatch is claiming his resources and his attention. None the less the signal has been generated and will in time have its effect on policy.

Standards of this kind are what I think should be meant by norms. They are concrete, specific and tacit. They reveal themselves only by the signals of match or mismatch which they generate when they are evoked by specific cases. They may indeed be made explicit in formal rules and regulations. But these also are only effective when applied to specific cases; and, once formalized, they are liable to diverge increasingly from the developing tacit norm which they try to express.

Tacit norms are common. We tend to overlook them, because we are conditioned to ignore the tacit aspects of our thinking, unless they appear to be pathological. Christopher Alexander[2] in a book primarily devoted to physical design, says in effect that the designer's task is to 'eliminate misfit', rather than to create form, which is a tacit standard knowable only through the agreeable abatement of mismatch signals which mark the designer's approach to it. And in support of his argument that norms are necessarily tacit, he cites the difficulty of doctors in defining health and of psychiatrists in defining psychological normality.

Clearly nothing is more important to mankind than the process by which these tacit norms develop. This process, though complex, is familiar and is more easily studied in a social than in an individual context. To return to the example already given, the standards of the single dwelling self-contained for water and sewage had long been changing in towns through simple pressures of density. In England in the mid-nineteenth century the inconvenience of density was amplified by increased consciousness of the attendant health hazard. Cities have always been prone to epidemics and plagues; but by the mid-nineteenth century dawning understanding of the possibility of *controlling* disease began to generate standards of acceptability regarding those factors which were recognized as contributing to health. Amongst these were the supply of pure water and the disposal of human excrement.

A host of diverse factors sped the change. The promise of a market for pipes of all sizes encouraged the production of the necessary hardware. The convenience of indoor water and sanitation attracted the rich and made the bathroom a status symbol. Soon its absence became a negative status symbol, which began to offend sensitive consciences. Widening political suffrage made the poor more influential. Growing concern for equality and social justice made those who felt it readier to measure the deficiencies of the poor against standards once peculiar to the rich. Both of the two influences last mentioned helped to determine who stood for election in local government, what they proposed and to what standards they appealed.

In this familiar mixture of motives and pressures two critically important trends can be discerned. One is the transition of some state of affairs from the status of 'act of God' to the status of 'act of man.' Toil, inconvenience, sickness and death have always been part of the human condition. But in the past century in the West, far more than at any other place or time, aspects of this condition have been distinguished as something which could and should be controlled by men.

Once this happens, the burden and its distribution becomes a matter of public policy about which it is relevant to argue that it *ought to be* other than it is. It is judged by the sort of expectation that we entertain not of the natural world but of the human world – to use a distinction which Herbert Simon[3] recently drew between what is as it is, independent of man's design and what owes its form partly to human artifice. What men might shape otherwise allows and invites *ethical* criteria.

The other trend is the continual readjustment of the standard thus set by all the influences illustrated by my example. The standard may be more or less agreed. It may go down rather than up. But only a political cataclysm is likely to relegate it again to the field of the uncontrollable.

## 2. Norms and values

Among the many factors contantly at work to change the setting of these tacit norms, one is explicit mutual persuasion. Textbooks of psychology have very little to say about the process by which concerned people persuade others to share their concerns merely by talking to them. But it is a matter of common experience that they do so; and we should hardly devote so much time to the process if we did not think it important. For example, although many factors prepared the way for the elimination of slavery in the nineteenth century, few people would be satisfied with an account that did not mention Wilberforce.

The debate on social policy is full of appeals to concepts such as equality, justice and liberty. These are abstract words of great ambiguity and imprecision. Therein lies their power and their value. Freedom, for example, deserves and needs to be discussed in every generation precisely because every generation needs to redefine its content. This it could not do if the word were not open-ended, a classification constantly growing and changing with use.

Another reason why these abstract qualitative words deserve endless debate is that they come in complementary and partly inconsistent pairs, such as freedom and order, independence and interdependence, equality and self-development, justice and mercy. Each member of a pair is a compendious label for a number of 'values' more or less inconsistent with those implied by the other, as well as being the contradiction of its own opposite. They thus supply an indispensable means to discuss the always conflicting and disparate costs and benefits which can be anticipated as likely to flow from any deliberate human intervention in the course of affairs.

These explicit abstract terms refer to what I think should be regarded as values. They contrast strikingly with norms in several ways. Values are general and explicit. Norms are specific and tacit. Yet each affects the other and both change in the course of the process already illustrated.

That values affect norms is the faith behind all attempts at mutual persuasion and the experience which sustains them. But norms equally affect and even generate the values to which they appeal. Wilberforce could attack slavery in the name of freedom, justice and equality and these appeals helped to change in more lethargic or insensitive minds the tacit standards of what they should find unacceptable in the actual laws and practices of their day and age. But these tacit standards had been and would still be the sources from which the abstract values gained their emotive power.

Freedom had been a potent word for centuries in earlier ages, which accepted slavery as a human condition. But its content had been different. The anti-slavery campaign enlarged it in ways which would not easily be undone. Similarly reformers today, urging higher priority for providing every one with a home of 'acceptable' standard, appeal to the same explicit general values. But the standards of what is acceptable have risen, giving a new content to those generalities. And the new content will play a part in changing still further the current tacit standards. This is precisely the object of the reformers' explicit persuasion.

The meanings which I have given to norms and values, though still imprecise, seem to me a useful step towards distinguishing them and understanding their mutual relationships. It also makes clear the inconsistencies inherent in each.

I have already described those inherent in 'paired' values. Our tacit norms equally lack inherent consistency. The mismatch generated by unacceptable housing invites action which will mitigate it; but any possible action, when examined, may well generate equally intense mismatch signals by comparison with some other norm and may be rejected at first, for long or even indefinitely, on appeal to the same or other values. And the signal itself must compete for attention with many other mismatch signals, equally valid, all competing for limited resources, often also competing with each other in that any action to abate one will intensify another.

Thus neither our tacit norms nor our explicit values is a stable system. Perhaps it never should be. Certainly neither was ever so unstable as now for two reasons already given. Increasing human power over the natural environment focuses human expectations on what man should do rather than on what nature will do and thus hugely expands the ethical dimension. And the response of authority to these expectations speeds the rate at which they grow.

This then is the situation in which the policymaker works. It is for him to choose some attainable mix of the disparate benefits and costs with which the current babel of 'mismatch' requires him to deal. He *must* reject some of these requirements. What he rejects, no less than what he accepts, will influence the future setting of the norms and values of his society. And his actions will influence them no less through their successes than through their failures.

The Beveridge Report and its resultant legislation in Britain is a good example of this threefold interaction. The report identified five 'giant evils' – unemployment, sickness, ignorance, squalor and want. The dramatic language is significant. Giants, in folklore, are not only strong and bad but also vulnerable. A hero comes who does not accept them as part of the natural order. He kills them. The report invited its readers to regard these age-old human conditions as equally defeasible. All were already under some attack but the legislation based on the Beveridge report expressed a new sense of what was unacceptable and a new determination to alter it.

Twenty-five years later, the situation is different. So are the levels of the tacit norms and the contents of the explicit values. A new Beveridge report might identify some new giants. Among the agencies which have changed the situation, the norms and the values, a major one has been the report itself and the stream of policymaking which it has stimulated and influenced.

## 3. Policies and policymakers

This then is what I conceive to be the distinction between norms and values, the relations between them and the mutual relation between them and the policies which give them partial expression. What does all this tell us about the role of the policymaker and the abilities which we implicitly attribute to him?

The policymaker is subject to constraints, which limit what he can do – or what he thinks he can do. The distinction is important. If he attempts what he cannot achieve, events will constrain him. If, on the other hand, he does not attempt something because he estimates that it is impossible or too costly or too risky, he is constrained by his own appreciation of the situation. Since it is usually disastrous to go blindly on until we are powerless to go further, the second is or ought to be the more normal form of constraint. None the less, those who accept such constraints can never *prove*, even after the event, that if they had ignored them, they would in fact have suffered the disasters which they anticipated.

Such constraints may derive from an appreciation of circumstances wholly beyond the policymakers' control. More often, they are beyond his control only because his own decisions have made them so. Where they derive from lack of resources, this could often be made good, if he were willing to divert resources earmarked for other purposes. Where they derive from resistance or lack of support among those whose assent or support would be needed, these attitudes could often be changed, quickly or slowly, by bargain, threat or persuasion. Only in the limiting case, usually rare, are these constraints wholly independent of his own action and his own judgment.

These constraints can usefully be classified in another way. Some are imposed by his expectation of the course of event. Some are imposed by his expectations of other people, and especially by his knowledge of what they expect of him. Yet others are imposed by what he has come to expect of himself. The distinction between these three is important and often overlooked.

Human beings often tell each other what they want each other to do.

The wish may be expressed as a command or as a request or as a piece of information which has obvious implications for action. It may or may not elicit the desired response. But whether it does so or not, it is a communication different in kind from those which we derive from observing the natural world. And whether the recipient complies or not, his response has an effect on the human sender which has no counterpart in our relations with the natural world.

Moreover, such express communications supplement and depend on a much larger set of assumptions about the tacit norms and explicit values of those with whom we are in communication. This tissue of mutual expectations is what structures the human world and makes human communication possible.

The policymaker, surveying the constraints which other people's expectations place upon his freedom of decision and action, is estimating the way they will judge and respond to the various actions and ways of action which are open to him. But he need not accept these as independent variables, as he would accept the laws of the natural world. They may be abated or intensified by what he does, even by the way he does it, because they are responsive to human communication; and between human beings all acts are also communications. The domain in which people persuade, bargain or even coerce each other has its own distinctive laws, the laws of communication, which operate at many levels. Even the bomb at Hiroshima was, and was intended to be, more effective as a communication than as an agent of destruction. Much higher levels than bombs are possible and necessary in making and implementing policy.

Apart from constraints, the policymaker is also conscious of pressures, identical in origin with the corresponding constraints. Some are inherent in the logic of events. Dominant among these is the need to preserve the stability of the system which it is his function to regulate, a condition, though by no means an adequate criterion of his success as a policymaker. Some come from pressure groups of his constituents, and others who are concerned with his policies and able to bring some influence upon him. These pressures always conflict with each other and often conflict with what would otherwise be the course of his policy or even with what seems to him the logic of events.

It is sometimes supposed that the policymaker is no more than a broker among these conflicting pressures, concerned only to find a viable compromise between them within the overall limitations imposed by his constraints. Even if policymaking were no more than this, it would put a premium on high levels of rare skills. The policymaker would need to be adept at working out the logical implications of alternative possible actions, and ingenious in devising novel courses which would better combine diverse benefits and minimize unacceptable costs. I will call these logical skills and heuristic skills. He would also need persuasive skills, to get others to share his insights. Few people combine these skills in an outstanding degree, so good policymakers, even at this level, are likely to be rare.

Yet although much policymaking is no more than brokerage between competing constraints and pressures, none worth calling a policymaker will confine himself to this role. He has his own norms and values, never quite the same in character or level as those which move the pressurizers and the containers. He has the right and the duty to advocate them. And his advocacy will surely make a difference, dissolving resistance, polarizing resistance or both.

So the policymaker, whatever the level at which he operates, is also an artist in the creation of coherent and viable form in human behavior; and like any other artist, he must believe in the goodness, as well as the coherence and viability of the design which he is trying to realize. And even beyond this, he is an artist in shaping the norms and values from which his policy is made. For he affects these both directly by advocating his policies and indirectly through his policies when they are in operation.

He thus has scope for initiation and for creation. So have we all. It is what we should expect in a human communication system in which every factor is a function of all the others. But the policymaker's role magnifies this scope and makes him more than usually potent for good and ill.

## 4. Some implications

This analysis may seem to imply a view of human motivation more complex than is currently fashionable. It is not, however, more complex than we all use in common speech. The distinctions which I have drawn are reflected in four common verbs. What we want and do not want to do is limited and often transformed not only by what we can and cannot do, but also by what we must and must not do, where those words are used of social obligation in the widest sense, and also by what we ought and ought not to do, where those words cover at least those expectations which we have developed of ourselves. Thus in the example already given, the last century has seen a change in what people want in the matter of sewage and water supply; a change in what they can have and in what they actually enjoy; and changes in what they expect of their institutions, of each other and of themselves. It would be strange if the verbs which distinguish these changes did not correspond with some psychological realities. If these need detailed justification, they require an exposition more elaborate than could be added to this paper. But it may help to make the argument clearer if I summarize the levels of control of human behavior which are here implied.

It is abundantly clear that animal behavior is subject to a hierarchy of controls which often conflict, and that human behavior derives its greater coherence from higher levels of organization, which have their own costs and ultimately their own limits in the greater conflicts which they engender. (This contrast will become apparent to anyone who compares his own behavior, in his more human moments, with that of a bird on a bird table.) I find it useful to distinguish five main levels.

The lowest is the level of innate response. I will call it the level of *control by releaser*, since the study of it has shown that response is a function of the state of the organism, as well as of the environment. This level is constantly qualified by the second level, which is the level of conditioned response, and which has also been exhaustively studied. Conditioned responses frequently conflict with each other, as well as with the level below. I will call this level *control by rule*, since its formula is – 'in these circumstances, do this,' where the 'circumstances' may range from a simple signal to any complex of events sufficiently characterized to be recognizable.

When the agent develops any capacity for recognizing causal relations and for modelling the future course of events on various hypotheses, simpler controls are further modified. The expected *result* of the intended activity, becomes potent to evoke or inhibit action. I will call this level *control by purpose*. The new logical and heuristic powers on which it depends are just visible at levels below the human; but both attain in man levels so outstanding that purposeful behavior has become the paradigm of rational action. Whilst these logical and heuristic powers increase the range of possible coherent action, they equally increase its inherent motivational conflict. For control by purpose not only conflicts constantly with control by rule (still very strong in all of us) but also breeds endless internal conflicts of its own, as it uncovers ever more inconsistent and disparate costs and benefits, flowing from an ever wider repertory of conceivable actions.

But these three levels do not encompass the whole of what men manifestly do. No ingenuity of logical or heuristic process can of itself explain why the agent chooses one course rather than another. For this we must postulate criteria and make assumptions about their origin, development and relevant strength and cogency. In doing so we credit the agent with power to respond to a new and more refined sort of signal, though one no longer unfamiliar, since it is a common feature of all man-made control mechanisms. These are signals internally generated by comparing the course of event, actual or hypothetical, with standards present in his mind and acting on the signals of match or mismatch which the comparison generates. Such signals, as I have argued elsewhere,[4] are different from those which operate control by rule and are a necessary supplement to those which operate control by purpose. Now that science has legitimized such signals, we can allow ourselves to see them throughout the human scene. It is no longer necessary to stretch the concept of tension reduction to breaking point and beyond to account for the human tendency to preserve match and abate mismatch signals. It is not even necessary to postulate a 'drive' to account for this familiar behavior. The concept of motivation itself, with its outmoded implication that form depends on energy, gives way at this level to the more comprehensive and appropriate concept of control by standard or norm.

Once again, the potential increase in coherence is bought at the price of increasing conflict. For standards conflict with each other and obedience to them frequently frustrates specific purposes. These stresses, however, are likely to find acceptable solutions, so long as the standards remain relatively constant. Even so, their slow change with time, visible in the course of history, invites the question how they develop and how those who obey them can also be those who change them. This problem was an unsolved intellectual scandal within living memory even in the field in which it is most visible and has been most studied, namely the growth of the common law. But as the rate of other changes quickens, whilst the rate at which the generations change becomes, if anything, slower, the need to change the standards we live by even while we use them becomes ever more important and ever more threatening. The function of resetting norms and values becomes a conscious one. And with it we can discern a new level of control, a level of collective self-control or self-determination which casts special responsibility on the policymaker.

These five levels of control are summarized in the appendix. They are a crude and oversimplified approach to a familiar story of development. I hope that further study will soon refine them out of all recognition. I feel only one confident assurance about them. They will not be 'reduced' by one of those 'nothing but' hypotheses, so dear to some scientists when they approach the human realm. The fourth and fifth levels will not be dissolved into the second and third – unless, of course, human life itself is so dissolved.

In that case we shall no longer study the more important aspects of policymaking.

## Appendix

### A summary of five levels of control

Level 1 Control by releaser – the realm of innate response qualified by

Level 2 Control by rule – the realm of conditioned response, amplified as logical and heuristic powers develop, to create the often conflicting level of

Level 3 Control by purpose – the realm of know-how, generating a volume and variety of choice which is unmanageable without

Level 4 Control by norm – i.e. by match and mismatch signals generated by comparing hypothetical as well as actual courses of events with tacit standards which define their acceptability. This level breaks down so soon as norms cease to be relatively stable and universally held unless it is supported by

Level 5 Control by self-determination – a process both individual and social which depends essentially on ethical debate and reflection about changing values and on the policymaking which both ex-presses and generates that debate. It is neither more nor less 'rational' than the process already described which has fixed the current standard of an acceptable British house.

# References

1. Erich Jantsch, *Technological Planning and Social Futures*, London, Associated Business Programmes Ltd, Cassell 1972, p. 16.
2. Christopher Alexander, *Notes on the Synthesis of Form*, Harvard University Press, 1967.
3. Herbert Simon, *The Sciences of the Artificial*, MIT Press, 1969.
4. G. Vickers, 'Motivation Theory – a Cybernetic Contribution', *Behavioural Science*, Vol. 18, No. 3, July 1973.

# 14
# Changing patterns of communication*

## Six fields of change in communication patterns

My title implies that communication can be considered in terms of pattern as well as substance; that there are more than one such pattern; and that all are changing. I will distinguish six fields in which such changes are taking place.

The first of these is the technological field, most obvious but important chiefly because of its effect on the others. The second I will call the distributive field, the complex of variables which determines who can communicate what to whom. The third I will call the educative field. It is focussed by the question: Who can receive what communications? The fourth I will call the interpretative or better the appreciative field. What meaning do people attribute to the communications they receive? My fifth field is the field of constraint. What may not be communicated? Under what constraints do communicators work? Under what constraints should they work? And how are these inhibitions enforced? My sixth field is the field of trust. Who trusts what communications? Who trusts whom as communicators?

I will say what I can in the space available about changes in these six fields and draw some conclusions.

## The technological field

Technology is affecting communication in two major ways which need to be distinguished. It is hugely increasing both our means of sending signals and our means of 'processing information'. This last expression holds different promises for different people and I will return to it.

Consider first the explosive extension of our power to send signals. Within my lifetime we have moved from the megaphone to the microphone; from the earliest silent film to satellite-mediated TV; from the howitzer shell to the hydrogen bomb. Let us not forget to include these last. Although threats are a low form of communication, they are an ancient and an increasingly important one. The bomb at Hiroshima was designed primarily not as an act to destroy a city but as a communication to secure the

---

*From the proceedings of an International Symposium in Spokane, Washington, in October 1974.

capitulation of an empire. All our acts are also communications; and they are often more important as communications then as acts.

This increase in our power to send signals has not increased our power to receive them. Although transmitters may multiply in all dimensions our equipment for receiving signals, our senses, brain and central nervous system remain very much as they were in Cro-Magnon days. Thus, the limitations on communication have passed from the sending end to the receiving end. There has resulted an enormous overload, which I will consider when I come to the distributive field.

The other technological revolution is the power to process information. Information today can not only be transmitted but stored, retrieved and subjected in theory, if not yet in practice, to any logical process which can be fully specified. The invention which makes this possible is the computer, a term which we should understand as including both digital and analogue computers, whether now existing or clearly within the bounds of what is practically achievable. The body of knowledge and skill which is expanding their use I will call the computer sciences. These together constitute an immensely powerful tool, providing an extension to our brains, perhaps more important than all the extensions which the tools of energy technology have brought to human muscles.

This tool is not neutral; tools never are. It is ambivalent. It is bringing and will bring costs at least as dangerous and benefits at least as great as the mechanical tools of the past. The mechanical inventions of the last two centuries have left their mark on the way we organise work and the way we think about work and thus on the way we organise our societies, the way we think about them and what we expect of each other and ourselves. Even our most important personal services are organised and 'delivered' in accordance with a pattern impressed on industry by the tools it uses. The computer is shaping our organisations and our lives in the same way but perhaps more radically since it is a tool of thought.

The benefits are great and obvious. We already depend on the computer for routines essential to our present way of life; telephone services, banking services, the collation of statistics and so on. We do not yet use it for more than a fraction of the services which it can already render. It is capable to some extent of offsetting the overload on our receiving capacities created by the abundance of available information. The corresponding dangers are that it will lead us to depreciate and ignore whatever it cannot handle.

Both costs and benefits are seen by some on an apocalyptic scale. For some the benefits predominate. 'More informed and logical' means 'more rational' means 'better'. At its extreme, this view produces one or both of two Messianic visions. One revives a dream – and I think an error – which is at least as old as the French revolution. Give us abundant information freely available to all and unfettered individual freedom to act on it, and we shall have all we need to live together in freedom and amity. For these believers, the computer promises a new populism, free from bureaucracy and even technocracy.

The other Messianic vision is even more radical. Its exponents nourish the hope that we have in the computer an analogue, even potentially a homologue of the human brain. Patient development will make explicit all those mental processes of judgment, design and creativity. The computer and its sciences will give us more than a tool for our use. They will give us a model for our self-understanding.

These dreams have their corresponding nightmares. Some, sharing the first view that knowledge is power, are fearful of the concentrations of power likely to result from these organised bodies of knowledge, which, even if they are in theory accessible to all, will be useful only to those with the skill and resources to use them. And they are equally fearful of the undetectable errors which may be built into the assumptions underlying the huge structures built on them.

The second dream is equally a nightmare to those who believe that mental process is a partnership between explicit elements and elements which are necessarily tacit or which *need to remain* tacit if they are to be reliable. For these it seems highly unscientific, as well as critically dangerous to assume that all mental processes can either be made explicit or ignored. And since our ideas of ourselves are potent to shape what we in fact become, the proponents of artificial intelligence are seen not as discoverers but as ideological architects in the most crucial dimension of humanity.

All these hopes and fears are real and all have some justification. They mark out what is in my view the most crucial ideological battleground of our day, as well as a crucial field in which patterns of communication are changing.

## The distributive field

The abundance of communication and its attendant overload affects the distributive pattern of communication in opposite ways, creating costs and benefits which cannot be compared with demonstrable certainty. Radio, TV and the proliferation of the printed word increase the volume of one-way communication which reaches the many from the few. It also makes possible more mutual intercourse. It may do so even more insofar as technology makes possible joint discussion between people who are physically far apart.

These trends make hugely important the ways in which the new channels of information are controlled. Statesmen and revolutionaries alike can talk to hundreds of millions but only if they can get access to a microphone coupled to a suitable network. Such networks are necessarily limited in number and are controlled by a limited number of organisations. In theory their number could be multiplied and their control freed from political and commercial constraints; and in some instances, as in various 'public' systems of radio and TV service, this has been largely achieved. But *some* criteria must be used to apportion what must be scarce and expensive resources among a host of disparate would-be users.

The exponential growth of books, journals and articles raises obscure and important questions about the current distributive pattern. What gets written? What gets printed? What gets read? Does this abundance increase our freedom of choice, even though it thereby necessarily increases our difficulty in choosing what to read and what to leave unread? Often it seems rather to restrict our choice. For everyone who is today in a seat of power and influence, whether as politician, administrator, academic, businessman, or trade union leader, there is an increasing mass of paper which he must read. When this exceeds his capacity and available time, his trap closes. He is lucky if it is only half shut.

And yet, in the countries and in the fields where I have any experience the resultant mess is less and the resultant benefit more than I see any reason to expect. One might expect that specialists would become even more ignorant of everything outside their specialism, whether in academia, business or politics. In fact, in my experience, the reverse is true. Scholars do find their way to each other through the jungle of words. Professions do draw on wider fields of knowledge and define their fields in wider ways. Businessmen and politicians do try harder and more successfully to think what they are doing in terms wider than their immediate objective. Facts are more widely diffused than they were and the more outrageous myths do get closer scrutiny. Although the increased volume of signals sent does not produce anything like a corresponding increase in volume of communication, it does produce and increment, which in itself, is welcome.

Taking together the first two fields in which I have described changing patterns of communication, I have constructed even in this summary survey a bewilderingly complex balance sheet of disparate costs and benefits. Only one clear conclusion seems to me to emerge from it. The outcome depends far more on the skill, capacity and judgment of the receivers than on any present or possible change in technological or other patterns of distribution. The remaining four fields are largely concerned with limitations and possibilities at the receiving end, though always bearing in mind the promise and threat offered to receivers by the technological possibilities of 'information processing'.

## The educative and appreciative fields

The pattern of receivers has changed through changes in their ability to receive. I will call this the *educational* pattern. Far more people have learned to read. Moreover, radio and television have enormously widened the accessibility of people whether literate or not. In shanty towns around Rio, for example, places without water, drains or electricity, impoverished crowds cluster endlessly round color television sets. And this exposure to communication must be in some sense educative.

But what do the receivers receive? Senders may send signals; but communication occurs only when these make some difference to some receiver. This difference, which is their meaning, may be far from what the sender thought he was sending. The meaning and extent of communication depends on the way receivers interpret the signals they receive. Every sender knows (though we often forget) that what he sends must be designed to fit the state of the receiver's mind, as a key must be designed to fit a lock.

Yet this simile is too simple. For much communication, including all formal education, is designed to enlarge or change the receiver's powers of interpretation. Words are to some extent skeleton keys; and our minds are skeleton locks, capable of learning to respond to keys which at first make no difference to them.

So there is also an interpretative or 'appreciative' pattern of communication. Indeed there are many and they battle continually over which shall prevail, and all are changed by their struggles. These rival patterns of interpretation are also among the changing patterns of communication.

Suppose that an ecologist, a real estate developer, a chain store operator and a cab driver are discussing problems arising from the rapid growth of the town where they all live. They have divergent interests, sometimes conflicting even within their own life-situations. The cab driver suffers from the congestion which also increases the demand for his services. They are also all citizens of the same town. Abundant experience shows that they can usually agree on common policies if they can learn to entertain each other's 'appreciations' of the situation as views complementary to their own.

Experience shows also how difficult this is. The developer and the chain store operator are accustomed to assume that economic growth is necessary, desirable and inevitable. To question such basic assumptions is threatening as well as difficult. The cab driver will not easily examine the costs and benefits of a city center relieved of congestion and pollution by excluding (amongst other things) cabs. The ecologist will not easily attach reality to the costs, especially the costs to others, of the ecological benefits which so deeply engage him.

This is not due to stupidity or to total economic determinism. It is inherent in the way we learn. Stereotypes are classifications necessary to ordering our perceptions and our conceptions; and we have a valid interest in maintaining a shared world in which we can confidently move and about which we can talk with confidence that we shall be understood.

But this shared world is not simply a discovered world. It is a social artifact which each of us can in some degree confirm or change. Our educative system today is, I believe, gravely deficient in two respects. It fails to instil, from an early age, a sense of the relatedness of things, a systemic view such as is currently exemplified by the accepted need for more ecological thinking. (These ideas, I believe, are not inherently difficult to understand.) It fails also to instil in us from an early age a sense of our power and responsibility as architects of the conceptual world in which we live.

This world is essentially normative and we need to understand from an early age the nature of its normative character. Piaget, in an early work on moral development in children, shows how in the course of four years his subjects changed their concept of the rules of a game. At first these were 'givens', of unknown origin and unchangeable but they were often broken, in order to 'win'. Four years later they were seen as conventions, which could by agreement be changed but which in the meantime could not be broken without changing the game itself including its definition of success.

Our appreciative assumptions do not usually grow more flexible with age. Long ago, as a boy between school and college, I spent several weeks in Germany in the home of a professor. He patiently explained to me the way of life in pre-first-war Rhineland. If this moved me to describe differences between this and English habits, his invariable comment was: 'Wie komisch!' (How queer!) This, therefore, was one of the earliest German phrases I learned, and I took my first opportunity to use it when he next described some feature of German life which was unfamiliar to me. He replied indignantly, 'Das ist nicht komisch! Das ist natürlich!'

I am not making fun of him. I, too, assume as 'natural' what is familiar to me. We all do so. We need to do so. But we need to *know that* we are doing so; that this so natural form is not a natural datum but a human artifact, alterable but only with difficulty and at costs which are hard to assess in advance. Who knows what other changes may not be involved by a single innocent-looking change in our appreciative systems?

These differences between cultures are uncomfortably clear to an English visitor in America. After every visit I leave with a new area of ignorance charted, with additions to my list of words which I cannot use with confidence that they will be understood as I understand them. Early entries on that list are 'money' and 'authority'. The latest is 'social democracy'. This phrase has a widely accepted meaning in Western Europe and can hardly be avoided by a European trying to explain current tensions between two political viewpoints currently labelled 'social democratic' and 'Marxist'. Yet, it has no reliable meaning in the USA, although it is understood in Canada. This is a reminder of the many cultural differences which distinguish the two great nations divided by your northern frontier.

And what of that greatest of stereotypes, the word 'Marxist'? In the last seventy years a billion people, about half the word's exploding population, have come under political regimes which are called or claim to be 'Marxist'. How varied are the connotations attached to that word and how much they have changed in the last century. Even greater perhaps are the connotations attached to that familiar phrase – 'the West'.

The task of receiving communication has become infinitely difficult. This is what demands the greatest development of our communicative skills. We need discrimination far more sensitive than that primitive distinction between what is 'natural' and what is 'queer'. We need a structured reality strong enough to uphold us but not so rigid as to entomb us. This need makes great demand on our intelligence. It also attaches huge importance to the remaining two fields of my analysis, constraint and trust.

## Constraint and trust

Every culture inhibits some kinds and even some topics of communication. The inhibition may be enforced by visible laws, procedures, and sanctions, including censorship or by less visible but not necessarily less efficacious systems of reward and penalty socially applied. The more reliable the latter, the less need for the former. Confident and coherent cultures sometimes permit an illusory degree of freedom. Orthodoxy is too well established and heterodoxy too weak to threaten the established order. Uncertain cultures, especially those seeking to establish new order after revolutionary change, are characteristically more prone to assure themselves both by teaching orthodoxy and by inhibiting deviance. The institutions developed for these purposes will certainly outlive their usefulness, certainly try to extend their empires long after history requires them to contract, certainly themselves require constraint, even in the end destruction. It is, nonetheless, inevitable that the degree of constraint should bear some relation to the need for constraint and that this should be a function of the historical situation.

It is natural also that the degree of accepted constraint should be a function of the confidence and coherence of the culture. When institutions lose confidence in themselves and cease to inspire confidence in others, a vicious circle is likely to develop. The lack of spontaneous inner coherence demands a greater imposition of restraint but at the same time powers greater resistance to it. This is a situation familiar in 'the West' today.

Yet, there is a close connection between constraint and the field of trust which has yet to be considered. For our trust in other people consists very largely in the confidence with which we expect them to be constrained by the duties and requirements attached to their positions and not least by constraints in what they might otherwise say and do to us.

Communication has a threefold effect. It tells us something about the subject matter and something about the sender. When we are the sender, it tells us something about ourselves: for it is part of an inner dialogue which often affects us even more than those to whom it is addressed. Thus, in appraising a communication our attitude to the sender is crucial. Our interpretation and our response depend enormously on our assessment of his honesty and his competence. In greater or less degree it depends on our trust in him, as ours depends on the trust which we inspire in others.

The 'other' thus involved may be a personally identified other. It may be the anonymous holder of an office. It may be an institution. It may be that complex of roles and institutions which we call the system. There have been times and places when the only other who could be trusted was an individual personally known to be trustworthy. But complex societies cannot cohere on such a basis. We are, in fact, accustomed to extend to unknown others an immense network of confident expectations based on the positions they hold and the roles they play, largely in organisations. Our complex world depends absolutely on the widespread assumption that people transiently occupying positions assigned to them, usually by contracts of employment, will do what their positions require and will thus maintain our economic and political institutions. This is probably the greatest social invention of Western man. When we complain of its impersonality and its fragmentation, we are identifying costs closely, if not necessarily, associated with benefits which we have come to take for granted, though they are rare both in history and even in the world today.

Trustworthy officials do not necessarily warrant trust in the organisations which they staff. Those who believe that our military or political or economic institutions are set to pursue goals which we reject will not be solaced by reflecting that the officials who serve those institutions are honest and competent, even dedicated. It is, nonetheless, necessary to create a world of trustworthy role-players as a condition precedent to making a world of trustworthy institutions. Similarly, although trustworthy institutions will not necessarily make a trustworthy total system, untrustworthy institutions certainly will not. Thus, a trustworthy system can be seen as a hierarchy of reliable expectations. These reflections are uncomfortably relevant today to the situation in most parts of 'the West' which was so self-confident until so recently. 'The System', particular institutions and particular role-players, have generated their own specific areas of mistrust; and these have reinforced each other.

The extent to which trust is needed varies also with the relationship of the communicating parties, but it can seldom be ignored. When it is shaken, a vicious circle easily develops; for trust is both the fruit of good communication and its necessary pre-condition.

## Five levels of communication

Bearing this in mind, I find it useful to arrange types of communication in five levels. Each is distinguished from the lower ones in demanding from each party to the communication a more complex and reliable model of the other or more trust in the other or, usually, both.

At the lowest level, I put communication by threat. I put it at the bottom because it requires from each party the minimal understanding of the other and the minimal trust in the other. The sender need know or think he knows only what, among his possible actions, the receiver will hate and fear. He need not anticipate the effect of his threat on the receiver except to induce, or deter some action and to establish an attitude of submission, however, unwilling. The receiver need only believe in the reality of the threat.

Note that despite these limitations, a threat is still a communication. It is not coercion in the sense in which the mildest physical restraint is coercion, because it depends on imparting information, not on using energy directly to affect or prevent physical change.

An act is nonetheless needed, though it may not be a verbal act. But its significance as a communication is separate from its effect as an act, sometimes contradictory and often far more important.

At the next level of communication I put bargaining in its strict sense, where one or both parties offer something to secure something from the other. In the situation implied by this strict sense of bargaining neither party *need* agree. Each makes and adjusts a conditional offer or invites the other to change what he has offered. Trafficking such as this can take place between people with no common language. Phoenician merchant adventurers were trading with Bretons and Cornishmen four thousand years ago. Yet subtle communication takes place as each tries to conceal the extent of his interest and to divine the extent of the other's.

Neither need know more of the other than that he may desire what the offerer has to offer. Nonetheless, bargaining involves a body of shared assumptions. At least it involves recognition by each that the relation is a bargaining one and trust that the other will treat it as such. Bretons and Cornishmen, when they came down to the beach to parley with a boatload of Phoenicians, needed to be reasonably sure that the relation about to develop was one of trading, not raiding.

In its full modern development trading depends on a very high level of mutual trust that each will abide by the rules of the game. 'Credit' means trust. Merchant bankers get very rich by filling what would otherwise be gaps in the structure of trust on which international and national trade proceeds. Thus, the communication which I class under bargaining, though it involves only a simple representation of the other's situation, may call for an assurance of mutual expectations which is very high in degree though limited in scope.

The next level I will describe as the level of request. A asks B for something; perhaps for information, perhaps for practical help, perhaps for sympathy. Why should B respond? What are the minimum assumptions that each must make about the other to generate both the request and the desired response?

A must be able to elicit in B's mind a representation of A's situation and of A's need. He must also be able either to rely on B to meet this need merely because B has become aware of it or he must awaken this willingness in B. The second may involve persuasion which is the next level in my hierarchy. I will defer such cases. Even without them there is a wide gamut of situations in which A can confidently call on B for help without considering even the possibility of refusal or deceit or exploitation.

This assurance comes partly from the astonishing wealth and variety of roles which Western societies have learned to create within institutions designed and changed to suit changing circumstances and to which I have already referred as the most striking invention of Western culture. These institutions are staffed by a transient body of people, recruited by contract, free to leave and usually subject to dismissal. Yet, without any personal knowledge of them we rely on them confidently for all kinds of help and information, simply because their role requires it of them, be they doctors, postmen, teachers or whatever.

The level of request extends upwards from this lowly level to elusive heights. The asker is aware how far the service he is seeking will be seen by the other as within or beyond the range of what the other is normally expected or expects himself to provide. The asker expresses his request accordingly. He may appeal simply to the common humanity of asker and receiver. Different societies, even different sub-cultures within a single society, define differently what each of its members should expect of others and of himself towards others in this regard. A money economy may erode this level of communication but does not destroy it. A well-known study compares the effectiveness of two systems of blood-banks, one based on donation of blood by volunteers, the other on its purchase. The first was found the better, qualitatively, as well as economically.

Response to requests, whether by individuals or institutions, may be regulated by role or routine or collective ethos; but where this does not suffice, it requires in the respondent a closer identification with the asker than is required at any of the levels previously described. It may require a much more complex representation of the other and of his situation as the other sees and feels it. It also requires a wish to help the other to amend his situation, so that to do so brings a sense of satisfaction.

Consider next the level of persuasion. A is trying to persuade B to see a situation as he A sees it or to join with A in doing what A thinks should be done. B, when the scenario opens, is either uninterested or already committed to a view or a course of action different from the one advocated by A. A's concern may be for a community action program or a charity or a political campaign or the redress of something which he regards as a wrong. Whatever it be, it differs from the earlier levels of communication in the demands it makes on both parties.

A does not intend to threaten B and is not offering to buy B's support. And although success for A will take the form of an accession to a request, the changes involved for B will be greater. B must restructure his view of some situation or his sense of its importance or his sense of the need and possibility to do something about it – or perhaps all of these. And often 'just talking' does indeed have all these effects.

This is remarkable and ill-understood. It is tiresome, confusing, even dangerous to alter the way we perceive familiar situations, the importance we attach to them and our commitment to action about them. When someone tries to make us change in such ways, we may feel threatened and seek to avert the threat. Equally we may be challenged to change the other's appreciation or action to a form more consonant with our own. In this situation mutual persuasion may become a kind of battle. Each party tries to preserve his own position and weaken his opponent's.

Even this requires of each a fuller understanding of the other than any of the previous levels. We need to understand both the mental stance of the other, which we are trying to change, and our own, which we are trying to defend. At intervals, even in such a situation, the parties may abandon for a time the stance of adversaries in order to clear up some manifest misunderstanding of expression or some disputed matter of fact. This cooperative aspect may be more or less dominant.

Insofar as the cooperative aspect becomes dominant, the level of persuasion approaches the next and highest level which I will call the *level of dialogue*. Each party is still alert to expose logical fallacies in the other's argument – but also, if they exist, in his own. Each still needs to understand the other's mental stance, not as something he need accept but equally not just as a target for better attack. Each must be willing to accept the other's help in doing so and to reconsider his own, equally with the aid of the other. Each must go through this painful work with suspended judgment, possessed by the desire not simply to understand an adversary or even to understand himself, but to engage with a partner in a joint effort to reach a common appreciation of a situation, even where this includes an understanding of differences in the parties' appreciations.

The process of mutual persuasion, whatever its level, will probably change both A and B. Even at the level of conflict each, in making explicit and defending his appreciations and his commitments to action, may expand them or at least confirm them or even come to question them. The nearer the exchange approaches to the level of dialogue, the greater such changes are likely to be and the more likely they are to facilitate further exchange at that level, rather than to harden attitudes, polarize conflict and debase the level of discourse.

I have described five levels of discourse. I have called them threat, bargain, request, persuasion and dialogue. Negotiation may be no more than the first or the first two but at its best it rises to include the third and fourth and occasionally even the fifth. I believe that these levels serve equally to describe the communication within and between corporate entities of all kinds and between them and individuals, all of which are equally conducted by persons playing the roles attached to their positions. Such communications are subject to special constraints but also to special enablements. A role greatly clarifies and confirms the expectations which others have of the role-holder and he of them.

These levels of communication are distinguished from each other in two ways. Each ascending level requires each party both to understand the other better and to trust the other more.

Both understanding and trust may be mistaken and a secondary function of all communication is to watch for signs of such errors and to correct them. When misunderstanding frustrates communication, this secondary function becomes primary and the parties have to stop talking about the subject matter while they clear up unidentified differences in the ways in which they are interpreting what is said, differences in their understanding of each other's appreciation and doubts about each other's trustworthiness.

Trust is even more fundamental. Each level of communication depends on each party assuming that the other is abiding by the rules which govern that level of discourse. When these assumptions are shaken, communication at that level ceases to be possible. The higher the level, the more complex and far reaching the level of mutual trust required.

Trust is a fruit of experience, slow to grow, quickly destroyed. It is destroyed not only by discovering deliberate deceit. It may also be eroded by discovering that the other is prone to deceive himself or simply by doubt about the rules to which the other is committed. Mistake and deceit are subtly related. But one sense of trust is of preeminent importance. The parties must trust each other to desire and seek to preserve or restore whatever degree of trust is needed by the level of their communication.

## Conclusions

From this summary survey of an enormous field a few conclusions seem to me to be specially clear and important.

1. The world we live in demands and depends on skill in communication and in knowledge relevant to communication to an extent far beyond anything previously known. The essential skills are those skills in appreciation which I have briefly described. The essential knowledge includes knowledge not only of the subject matter but also of the other communicating parties and of the process of which all are part. These skills, even more than the knowledge on which they are based, can and should be taught to a degree far exceeding what is now conceived by any educational system known to me.

2. Communication depends also on trust, as I have described it, and imposes on communicators a duty to sustain the level of communication, not only by their skill and knowledge but by being trustworthy communicators.

3. This is the more important because there is a 'law' of communication similar to 'Gresham's law' in economics. Bad communication drives out good communication. A small minority with a few bombs and a lot of self-righteousness can soon reduce the level of communication in a whole society to the basic level of mutual threat.

4. Thus the duty I have described assumes an importance, as well as a difficulty which can hardly be exaggerated. It seems to me a transcultural human duty to sustain the level of communication, to resist its debasement and to cooperate in raising it.

5. The direction in which this duty points seems to me to be the direction of the more human, rather than the less human, a vector which we can recognise as trans-cultural and which claims the allegiance of the whole species. It may be the only dimension in which any kind of progress is possible. It is surely a precondition for progress of any other kind.

# LEVEL III: ORGANIZATIONS

# Introduction

Vickers was writing about organizations and management at a time of increased specialist management training, a time when technical support for managers – from computerized forecasting to operations research – was growing in scope and importance, and the nonquantifiable aspects of management were often downgraded in importance. Vickers' concerns largely cut across these prevailing developments. He was interested in the cognitive processes of managers and focused on what was general about the activity of managing – its parallel with other activities – rather than what was distinctive and specific to management. Psychologists and managers, for instance, ought to maintain a mutually fruitful dialogue. He argued in *The Role of Expectation in Economic Systems* that psychologists could learn much from business about the workings of the individual mind; and managers for their part had much to learn from psychologists. The activity of managers, he argued in *Judgment*, had much in common with that of statesmen, artists, connoisseurs of art, and doctors. What they had in common was the exercise of judgement, the weighing of moral issues, the creation of form. He criticized the large claims then being made for what he called the 'mechanical and mathematical models of decision-making' which emphasized action judgements, to the neglect of reality and value judgements.

The importance of cross-fertilized learning across conventional boundaries – a characteristic emphasis of Vickers – is again apparent in *Industry, Human Relations, and Mental Health*. Here he related his experience of industry and management to the concerns of a very different audience – the World Federation of Mental Health. He explored the effect on individual mental health both of participating in the human relations which industrial organizations involved, and of being excluded from them. He appreciated with exceptional foresight in 1965 the as yet little understood threat posed by the impending loss of industrial jobs:

> ... there is every reason to think that industry as now organized will progressively cease to be an acceptable producer or distributor of *jobs*, as distinct from goods. The problem of the displaced person is the greatest growing problem of our industrialized societies, and it is a problem of mental health.

Another issue which much concerned Vickers in the 1960s and 1970s was the level of acceptance and support for institutions. Young people were, he believed, increasingly rejecting the constraints of institutional life as dehumanizing or impoverishing. This trend alarmed Vickers: he was convinced that increasing interdependence meant inescapably that society would need organizations on an even larger scale, making even bigger demands on their members. There was, he urged, no reason to retreat from institutional role-playing. The resolution and containment of conflict, which was what role-playing was all about, was humanizing and enhancing to individuals. The challenge of playing an institutional role and coping with the conflict of different roles were among the most important tensions involved in the making of a personality. We should accept conflict management as a creative activity. 'Men without role conflicts would be men without roles: and men without roles would not be men.'

Vickers stressed the importance of the qualitative aspects of management partly because he was keenly aware of the prevailing influence of technology. In *The Changing Nature of the Professions* he argued that the professional – including the professional manager – is more than a technologist. Elaborate techniques, in medicine as elsewhere, threatened the eclipse of the traditional professional qualities. Technological skills were essentially operational skills: what all the professions demanded, on the other hand, was a developed capacity to discover form and to distinguish order from disorder, usually at more than one level. The professional needed above all the advanced skills necessary for understanding existing systems and creating new ones.

Technology was of greatest significance for its impact on ways of thinking. Both the major benefits and the major disbenefits of technology were conceptual. The distinction between hardware and software, for instance, now widely understood as a result of the development of computers, enabled people to grasp the hitherto elusive distinction between brain and mind. But advanced technology tempted the present generation to beat their problems into a shape that computers could handle and further encouraged 'the delusion that scientific and technological problems are typical of human problems'.

At the organizational level, as at the others, Vickers is recurrently concerned with epistemology and how we can learn to develop ways of thinking to address the current issues which confront us.

# 15

# The role of expectation in economic systems*

## Business as a hierarchy of systems

I invite you to regard as the prototype of an economic system one of those biological communities which ecologists like to study; a community within an area in which a characteristic set of conditions is sharply isolated, such as a rain forest or pond. Such a community is entitled to be called a system because of its capacity for self-regulation. And we can call it an economic system, because the aspects of it which we study relate to the way in which the creatures composing it maintain themselves and multiply. We can regard it as a complex of biochemical factories, continuously engaged in meeting their own and each other's needs.

Within such a system is a hierarchy of sub-systems. We can distinguish groups of organisms, each linked by so close a net of mutual relationships that it can usefully be regarded as a system. These vary in degree, from the roughly systematic relations between a population of predators and its prey to the almost organic interaction of a colony of social insects. And within these subordinate systems, each individual organism is a system in its own right. All these systems are open systems, maintaining themselves by exchanging matter with their environments at a rate dictated by their metabolic needs and in ways resulting from the manifold interaction of their individual capacities for behaviour. And each of them, like every open system, continues only so long as it can maintain within acceptable limits the external relationships by which it lives and the internal relationships by which it hangs together. Thus an animal must learn to digest the food it can find or must learn to find the food it can digest; and it survives only so long as, by one means or the other or both, it can find a viable compromise between its needs and its opportunities. Every open system is the expression of a double dynamic balance, internal and external, these being two adjacent levels in the hierarchy of relatedness.

When we raise our eyes from the rain forest and the pond to observe the sterling area or I.C.I. or the individuals debouching from the 8.45 at Liverpool Street, we find a scene basically familiar but changed in important respects. One notable change is the immense proliferation of intermediate systems, deliberately organised. The individual business undertaking is a system. Externally, it must exchange with its environment goods and

* From *Occupational Psychology*, Vol. 32, No. 3, July 1958. Originally presented at the Annual Conference of the British Psychological Society in April 1958.

services, money and men on such terms as at least to make good its losses. Internally, it must maintain such relationships between its members as will secure their effective co-operation. But here, as in the rain forest and the pond, the dynamism is supplied by the seekings and shunnings of individual creatures; and the economist, like the ecologist, as he studies the regularities, the oscillations, the correlations of systems above the level of the organism, is always reaching frontiers beyond which he cannot pass without asking, 'What regulates the behaviour of the individual?'. And this is a psychological question.

I am to discuss one of these regulators, the regulator called expectation. It plays a conspicuous part in the regulation of economic systems but it is not, of course, peculiar to them. On the contrary, it is a basic regulator of human behaviour and therefore of psychological interest in its own right, more particularly because, as it seems to me, psychological theory has not yet paid it sufficient attention. To some extent it also governs the behaviour of non-human organisms; but at the human level it seems to assume a peculiar measure of importance.

## Expectation as a control mechanism

The direction and control of a business at the conscious level is based on maintaining and continually comparing two running representations of what is going to happen next. One is a representation of the actual, the other of the intended. Thus the building contractor plots on charts against time the intended course of many interdependent operations; and, as work proceeds, he plots against these the results which are actually being realised and projects these also into the future so far as he can. Any divergence of the actual from the intended is a signal, first for enquiry and then for action designed to bring the actual into line with the intended; or, if this proves impossible, to alter the plan so as to produce an attainable governing course. There is a continual two-way interchange between the two expectations, as those in charge mould the future course of events to match their intentions or modify their intentions to take account of the future course of events. Sometimes one is dominant and sometimes the other.

Such controls may be positive or negative. A positive control is signalled by the divergence of the actual from some norm, such as a shortfall in planned production. Negative control is signalled by the approach of the actual to some limit which we regard as unacceptable – such as the limit of our overdraft facilities. There are, incidentally, important differences between the operation of positive and negative control and I believe that negative control is the more common, not least in business. I suggest, therefore, that psychology has done a disservice to lay thought – perhaps even to its own – by talking of goal seeking as if it is comprised all purposive behaviour; and that economists forget how often men in business are motivated by fear rather than by greed.

In any case, neither positive nor negative control would give adequate guidance, unless both the actual and the intended (or the feared) could be projected into the future.

Such controls, positive and negative, also govern those internal activities of a firm which are directed to securing through time enough of the right men of the right level - activities which include its policies of selection, recruitment, training, education, promotion and staff development. The firm knows what it wants and what it must avoid and against these standards it continually compares its actual and unfolding achievement - sometimes unconsciously and in general but often explicitly and in detail. Its adaptive behaviour is geared to the resulting mis-match signals.

When I speak of comparing the actual with the intended - or with the feared - I simplify the process in what may be a dangerous way. What we actually compare are two representations similarly coded, be it in words or figures or graphically - how else could we compare them? The actual cannot be more than a representation of some aspects of what we think is in course of occurring. It is selective; it is hypothetical; it has an inescapable time dimension and in representing change-with-time it is as much at home in the future as in the past. And finally it is represented in a symbolism which limits and distorts it in many ways which we can recognise. Thus the 'actual' and the 'intended' are constructs of the same kind. These considerations, I suggest, apply with equal force to the mental processes by which the individual mind compares the actual with the intended. For it, also, the actual, no less than the intended, is selective, hypothetical, extended in time and rendered in a symbolism which may limit and distort it in ways still unknown. But I will defer the consideration of these psychological implications until the end of the paper.

I want first to focus the familiar fact that the conscious representation of the expected plays an important part in the conduct of business - that is, in the way in which systems of the kind we are considering today maintain both their inner coherence and their relation with the environment. Policy making and executive decision and the continuous process of control within which these decisions are taken depend on the power to build hypothetical models of future events and to respond to these models. Collectively and individually, we constantly maintain and continually revise our inner representation of the environment and of our relation with it - or rather those aspects of it to which we think it worth while to attend - and our responses are governed not directly by what is happening 'out there' but by changes in these inner representations.

The part played by expectation in the regulation of our behaviour, in business as elsewhere, is, of course, much more ubiquitous and less conscious than this. Our conscious expectations are built on assumptions on which we have come unconsciously to rely but which are no less expectations. That our customers will pay their bills, our suppliers will keep their contracts, are expectations which form part of our basic set of assumptions. We can sometimes attach to them degrees of probability of considerable refinement but we cannot do business unless the degree of probability is fairly high. Some of these assumptions are essential to the working of the system – for example, the assumption that banks will remain solvent. This is an 'on or off' phenomenon; any position other than complete trust brings to an end all business which depends on the bank or banks concerned. By contrast, our expectations regarding inflation approach a threshold more gradually. Business can continue in the expectation of a continuing moderate rate of inflation, though this introduces elements of instability; for example, it leads to overstocking, which in turn leads to an unreal expansion of activity, which in turn contributes to the inflationary spiral. But in time a point is reached when the system breaks down, either because the rate of change in the value of money is too rapid to be accommodated within the time scale of business operations or because sheer uncertainty removes the basis for action. No business system can long survive the inflationary conditions in the Germany of 1924.

These expectations affect the situations to which they relate. Whether the current American trade recession gets worse or better depends very much on whether people expect it to get worse or better. Even the efficacy of some steps which may be taken to reverse it, such as a reduction of taxation, depends to an important extent on whether people expect them to succeed.

Implicit and unconscious assumptions are no less basic to the internal relations on which the stability of a system usually depends. The division of labour, within an organisation, no less than between it and others, depends on a network of mutual expectations, of which the most important are unconscious.

Let me at this point distinguish between three related ideas, expectation, confidence and co-operation. By expectation I mean simply the power to make representations of the future, itself a derivative of our power to represent the hypothetical. It does not imply any particular degree of certainty; and the idea of certainty is itself a little uncertain. At a roulette table I am certain that the result will be dictated by chance and this certainty, whilst it rules out short-term prediction, enables me to make some long-term ones with a high degree of precision.

Most business decisions involve attaching degrees of probability to various hypotheses; and with refinements in mathematical and electronic techniques we may become able to handle probabilities in the future with much greater precision. Expectation does not imply certainty.

But for purposes of action it is useful to be able to attach to some expectations such a degree of assurance that we can act on the assumption that they will occur. I think it convenient to keep the word 'confidences' for our attitude towards expectations of this kind, expectations which, though they are hypothetical, do not require us to apply probability factors or to work out alternatives on the supposition that they will not be realised.

Unhappily, the word 'confidence', when applied to the mutual relations of men, has acquired an overtone, linking it to co-operation. I want to exclude this overtone from our discussion. I am confident that my business colleague will do all he can to make my work easy and effective; but I am equally conscious that my competitor will try to outsell me. In war I am confident that my enemy will destroy me if he can. And all three confidences are guides to action, giving me far more guidance than I should have, if I did not know whether my opposite number was friend, competitor or enemy. I regard co-operation, competition and conflict as three distinct and characteristic forms of human interaction; and expectation, including those assured expectations in which we can feel confidence, regulates all three forms, though in co-operation they have greater extension and refinement for reasons which I mention later.

## The build-up of expectation

Expectations arise through experience but we must accord a special place to that peculiar kind of human experience which consists in receiving verbal communications. Thus I may go to market in the expectation that I shall be able to buy some tomatoes, merely because in the past I have always found them there. But equally my expectations may derive from the fact that I have ordered them and that the merchant promised to have some. At first sight it would seem that a single promise has cut out the need for a long process of experience but this, of course, is not so. My confidence in the promise reflects a long experience of promises; and not merely of promises but of promises being kept. The information conveyed by language depends not merely on the semantic capacity of the language but on the confidence with which it is received. Thus communication both depends on and contributes to those structures of expectation on which economic systems, like other human systems, depend so much for the regulation of their inner and outer relations.

The deliberate building and moulding of these structures of expectation form a large part of business activity. Externally, the goodwill of a business is the sum of the expectations entertained in regard to it by customers, suppliers, employees, investors and the general public. Advertising is directed to building up in the minds of potential customers expectations which clamour to be satisfied. In the field of internal relations the building of stable systems of expectation is a growing activity of management. An organisation is a structure of roles, to which functions are attached. If these are known and are suitably related to each other, the organisation will remain coherent and effective, though men come and go; for newcomers will find themselves guided and supported by the structure of expectations which has become attached to their roles, defining what the holder can expect of others and what they expect of him; and each will act on the basis of these expectations, unless and until they are destroyed by further experience. This stability is a pre-condition of effective, collective action over long spans of time.

It also imports what may be a dangerous rigidity. Any change in organisation which re-distributes roles, and especially one which splits the functions previously associated with one role only is likely to create confusion proportionate to the degree to which the previous structure of expectations was well-established. Much attention has lately been given to the problem of minimising such disturbances. Everyone knows from experience that it is not enough to issue a new directive, however clear; and much has been learned about the conditions in which men will adapt themselves most quickly to such changes.

One of these is the presence of confidence in that special sense to which I referred earlier. This has two constituents. It includes the assurance that the other will perform the functions which attach to his role competently, including those discretionary functions which are its most important element. It includes also the negative assurance that the other will not use his position in a way inconsistent with another set of expectations, the set which define the ethics of the situation – that, for example, he will not use his position to pay off private scores or to steal credit for other people's work or to do any of the other things which in the particular circumstances of time and place he is expected not to do.

The reason why confidence in this sense is so important to co-operation is that in any large organisation people are constantly being embarrassed by the decisions of their colleagues and seldom have the opportunity to form their own view whether the decision was right. They have to take nearly everything on trust. I happen to have served in two organisations which sprang into existence from a blue-print, rather than by a natural process of growth and in which consequently these assumptions were at first weak or lacking, so I have had occasion to observe how utterly this condition limits what can be done and increases the strain of doing what little is possible.

There is an inherent difference between the growth of mutual expectations between men and the growth of other expectations. Since, when men are in interaction, each is able to build hypothetical models not merely of his own expectations of the other but also of the other's expectations in regard to him and to his still hypothetical behaviour, there arise possibilities of understanding and of misunderstanding, of co-operation and of deceit, such as is not otherwise possible. Vicious circles and gracious circles, those ubiquitous phenomena, attain their most extreme elaboration in human relations; and they do so through the human capacity for expectation.

## Psychological implications

I have been talking about one of the governors of human behaviour, part of our familiar control mechanisms, which we know not only from introspection but from observation. So far as I know, we lack at present a conceptual model adequate to relate these controls, which I have described at the business level, to the rest of our knowledge about human and non-human behaviour. Psychologists could greatly help economists and business men by providing such a model. Hitherto they may have been deterred by the teleological overtones which attach to such words as 'intention' and 'expectation'. Today I hope the enterprise may be attempted without hazard to scientific respectability, since we are developing a language apt to describe the self-control of open systems of all kinds. I will venture some suggestions for filling this gap or at least for defining more clearly the gap to be filled.

First, we need a better model of the cognitive process by which the brain abstracts regularities from the stream of experience and uses these abstractions to classify future experience, a circular process which progressively determines what further experience it can assimilate and in what form. Creatures much simpler than we structure their perceptual experience in this way, by comparing abstracted features with pre-existing patterns innate or learned. The process involves matching and it is of some complexity, even in its simplest form. The herring gull chick responds not directly to the red patch on the feeding bill but to the similarity between an observed red patch, itself an abstraction, and a pattern which has been built in; a similarity not absolute but falling within limits of tolerance which are themselves built in.

Learned cues may be far more elaborate; they may include patterns in time as well as space and can thus represent change with time – how else could swifts feed on the wing?

Clearly the cognitive capacity of the brain in man has been notably developed. We can classify experience in a greater variety of overlapping categories. We can build hypothetical representations of experience as it is and as it might be, both on a time base; and we can include therein representations of our hypothetical selves. This has vastly extended the controls which we can derive from comparing the two sets of representation. But the basic faculty or at least the basic principle seems common to nervous systems much simpler than our own. All cognition is re-cognition.

I suggest that the processes by which business controls its operations through the explicit building and projection of estimates and standards parallel and illuminate the less conscious processes of the individual mind. I have little doubt that a clearer model of this process would help to make more precise the mechanisms of adaptation at the human level and the ways in which these mechanisms break down.

Consider two familiar ways. A long-term and ambitious policy requires us to live for a long time with a stream of imperious mis-match signals which no immediate action can abate. The disparity between the 'is' and the 'ought to be' is sharp and can be corrected only over years. The tension is correspondingly great and is none the less for the fact that the disparity has been created by the policy decision.

Again, a well-balanced policy requires us to live with many streams of mis-match signals, prompting us to inconsistent action. Short-term profit, long-term stability, internal coherence, public relations – all these are names for standards with which the obdurate course of events has to be brought into line. Stress in the board room may be well defined in terms of the number, the loudness and the inconsistency of the streams of mis-match signals which fight for attention. It may be that the concept of stress in the individual mind might be made somewhat less imprecise by the use of the same conceptual model.

For any survey of the role of expectation in business must point the fact that expectation multiplies and makes explicit the awareness of conflict; and this is its most useful, as well as its most painful feature. Every action is a link not merely in the sequence of action in which it arises but in many others also; and in some of these other contexts it is bound to be unwelcome. For A the proposed development of a housing estate is a way to get people housed. For B it is an addition to the rateable value of the area and to the demands on the rates. For C it is a threat to a Green Belt; for D an increase in traffic load on a road; for E an attempt by F at empire building; for G a threat to the coherence of his administrative team. All these disparates are relevant; but how are they weighed against each other? Or is weighing an inept analogy?

There is here, I suggest, a further gap to be filled in the conceptual model. For it is clear that such decisions involve both weighing and matching and that the two are separate but related. If, as I am suggesting, our responses are linked to the way we classify the situation, they will be determined cognitively, by matching rather than by weighing; but the classification will be affected by anticipation of the action to which it will lead. Most revaluations are only re-classifications. I once participated, as a lawyer, in a decision which took fourteen months of agonised and tedious debate. These were made tolerable for me by watching the one board member who realised in the first five minutes that one solution was bound to triumph in the end, if only decision could be deferred until his colleagues had brought themselves to revise their initial classification of the situation, so as to admit of an adaptive response. The reappraisal, when it came, was a cognitive act, a decision to regard the situation as being primarily of type A rather than type B – it being clearly both; but this decision would not have been made but for its dynamic implications.

In this paper I have used the word 'control' in a sense much wider than 'keeping constant'. Deviation from a norm or approach to a limit may be used to signal the need for corrective action, whether the standard so used is constant or not. Often in business the standard set is a constantly expanding one; it may none the less prove an effective governor.

The language which I have been using is still associated too closely with the idea of homeostasis. True, the homeostatic devices with which physiology has made us familiar, such as temperature control, hold constant the 'milieu interieur'; but at the same time the body as a whole is conforming in an equally controlled way to the expanding pattern of growth and maturation. Homeostasis is only a special case of control, within a context of much wider scope. Professor Waddington[1] has suggested the word 'homeorhesis' to fill this linguistic gap.

Our biological governors are built in, though even these can achieve more complex patterns than holding constant. Our psychological governors are more plastic; they pursue an unpredictable course of change and development within the experience of a single lifetime.

In the setting of these positive and negative governors, far more than in the devising of new responses, lies the scope for human adaptation. When we better understand how these governors are set, we may find that some of the processes which are made conscious and explicit in the control of business are closely analogous to the workings of the individual mind.

## Reference

1. C. H. Waddington, *The Strategy of the Gene*, London, Allen & Unwin, 1957.

# 16

# Judgment*

I am honoured to have been asked to give the sixth in this series of lectures, founded to perpetuate the memory of Edward Tregaskiss Elbourne, to whom, as founder of the Institute of Industrial Administration, the British Institute of Management owes a special, as well as a general, debt of gratitude. My five predecessors have painted comprehensive pictures, worthy of the wide-ranging interests and unifying concepts of the man we are here to honour. My approach is more selective. I ask you to consider one only of the qualities which are needed for management: the quality of good judgment. But my short title will invite us to a longer journey than we shall compass in the period of the lecture.

I choose this subject because it fascinates me, but I have more respectable reasons for my choice. Judgment is an important quality in a manager; perhaps more eagerly sought and more highly paid than any. It is also an elusive quality, easier to recognize than to define, easier to define than to teach. To some it has an aura of mystery, suggesting unidentified, intuitive powers behind the inexplicably accurate hunch. Others believe that its deepest secrets are already familiar to those who programme computers. Our language and our thought on the subject are alike imprecise. If I can contribute to their better ordering, I feel that I shall be doing something worthy, at least in intention, of an Elbourne lecturer.

We use the word judgment in many contexts. Applying it to business executives, we have in mind, I think, the power of reaching 'right' decisions (whatever that may mean) when the apparent criteria are so complex, inadequate, doubtful or conflicting as to defeat the ordinary man. Even in this sense judgment is, of course, not confined to business executives for it is required equally by statesmen, generals and princes of the Church; and even in this sense we may be unsure where it begins and ends. When our Government in 1940 shipped tanks to Egypt, through precarious seas, away from a country still in danger, to take part in operations still unplanned, Sir Winston Churchill took responsibility for a decision, apparently rash, which was justified by results. Shall we call this 'good judgment'? What of the decision of Bolivar, when, in the swampy delta of the Orinoco, he announced to a few ragged followers that he had that day founded the Republic of Gran Columbia and had fixed its capital at Bogota, a thousand miles away across the Andes? He too was justified by results. Are these

---

*From *The Manager*, January 1961. Originally the 6th Elbourne Memorial Lecture given to the British Institute of Management in November 1960.

exercises of the same faculty which led Mr Henry Ford to create Model T40?

Judges of the Supreme Court exercise judgment; yet politicians and civil servants, who take what they call administrative decisions, have generally maintained, in a controversy now thirty years old, that the rightness of their judgments is not a matter which courts of law can competently review. The opposite view is now gaining ground. What is the difference between the judgment of judges and the judgment of administrators?

What of the scientists? Vesalius rejected the view, accepted in his day, that the dividing wall of the heart is pierced by invisible passages. He proved to be right, and he is rightly remembered as a hero of scientific scepticism. Harvey assumed the existence of invisible passages connecting the arteries with the veins, an assumption then new and commended only by the fact that it was required by his theory of the circulation of the blood. He proved to be right too; and he is rightly remembered as a hero of – scientific intuition. Did these two men show 'good judgment' in the same sense?

What of the doctor making a diagnosis? What of the artist painting out a tone or a form which, in his judgment, disturbs the balance of his picture? What of the connoisseur who chooses that artist's work from among a hundred others, because he judges it to be of higher and more enduring merit? What of the man in a moral dilemma who judges one personal claim on him to be more weighty than another; and of his neighbours, who judge his decision as right or wrong? All these are exercising judgment; and though their fields are remote from that of the business executive, their activities are not. For the business executive also has occasion to act judicially, to make diagnoses, to weigh moral issues, to judge as connoisseur, even, perhaps, to compose in his own medium as an artist. It seems that we shall have to decide whether the word 'judgment' in all these contexts stands for one mental activity or many.

## Three types of judgment

I shall distinguish three broad types of judgment. Harvey and Vesalius made judgments about the state of affairs 'out there'. They revised the currently accepted view of external reality. I will call such judgments 'reality judgments'.

Churchill, Bolivar and Ford also made reality judgments; but they went further. They made judgments of what to do about it; and they committed themselves to action on the basis of these judgments. I will call such judgments 'action judgments'. In my examples, what strikes us most about their action judgment is that it 'came off'. In each case it achieved the desired result.

There is, however, a third element in these judgments – the judgment of what result was most to be desired. This I will call a value judgment. Churchill, Bolivar and Ford would not be remembered in these contexts unless they had been convinced of the value of victory in the Middle East, of creating independent republics of the Spanish–American colonies, of building a popular car; and these were not the only judgments of value which underlay their decisions.

In each case the value judgment is separate from the action judgment: it can be separately criticized. That the action succeeded does not prove that it was well conceived. Some strategists criticized the British emphasis on the Middle Eastern theatre of war. San Martin thought that the new states of South America should have been set up as constitutional monarchies. Even Henry Ford's 'tin Lizzie' was criticized – on aesthetic grounds. Hindsight often leads us to wish that our well-laid plans had failed.

I shall return in a moment to consider the part played by these three kinds of judgment – value judgment, reality judgment, action judgment – in the making of business decisions. First, I want to inquire how we recognize these judgments as good. The answer is curious and somewhat disturbing.

## The credentials of judgment

The capillaries which were invisible to Harvey can now be demonstrated by improved microscopy. His judgment has been confirmed by observation. Yet even the so-called facts of observation need judgment to give them meaning, a judgment often difficult and hazardous. Moreover, few reality judgments can be confirmed by observation, even after the event; for many relevant facts of a situation – the state of someone's mind for example – are not observable and change constantly and unpredictably, not least through the effects of judgments made about them. In the ultimate analysis, all reality judgments are matters of inference and can be confirmed or challenged only by new judgments, based on further inferences.

With action judgments we feel on firmer ground; we can check them against their results. Yet this is at best a rough and ready test, especially at the level of my examples. Who can say whether the courses which were not tried would not have worked out better than the one which was chosen? Moreover, every choice involves weighing probabilities. The course rightly chosen as of least risk may none the less prove lethal; the course of most risk may still come off. Results no doubt confirm judgments with some assurance when similar choices are repeated in controlled conditions often enough for the laws of probability to speak with authority; but it is hard to see how such an objective test can be applied to the judgments of the statesman or the top executive. It would seem that the validation of action judgments also is a matter of judgment.

When we consider value judgments we find the same situation in a much more extreme form. The validation of a value judgment is necessarily a value judgment. Churchill, Bolivar and Ford told themselves what they meant by success. Those who disagreed with them could do so only by appealing to different standards, representing value judgments of their own. There would seem to be no means whereby the adjudicating mind can escape responsibility for the standards of value to which it commits itself.

I have distinguished three kinds of judgment, often present together – value judgment, reality judgment and action judgment – and I have reached the conclusion that the higher the level of judgment involved, the less possible it is to find an objective test by which to prove that the judgment is good. The appraisal of judgment is itself an act of judgment. In particular, value judgments are logically incapable of being validated by any objective test. They cannot be proved true or false. They can only be approved as right or condemned as wrong by the exercise of another value judgment.

Does this condemn us to pure subjectivism? In my view definitely not. The status of judgments which are neither objective nor subjective has been analysed on a grand scale, with special regard to scientific judgments, by Professor Michael Polanyi,[1] himself an outstanding physical scientist – and I find myself broadly in agreement with his views, as far as I understand them – but to pursue the philosophic issue involved would take me far beyond the limits of this lecture. Nor need I do so, for the concept of responsible choice – that is, of decision which is personal yet made with a sense of obligation to discover the 'rules of rightness'[2] applicable to the particular situation – is a familiar concept in business, which we trust and use many times a day, even though neither philosophers nor psychologists can explain it.

## Judgment and decision

We sometimes use the word 'judgment' as if it meant the same as 'decision', but this is too narrow an interpretation. A good judge of men, for example, *reveals* his good judgment by the appointments and changes he makes, but the judgment which guides those decisions is something which he exercises continually as he observes and appraises the people around him. I will ask you to consider an example of this sort in some detail.

One morning, Mr Redletter, the managing director of The Weathercock Company (all the characters in my illustrations are imaginary) reached the conclusion that the company's chief supplies officer, Mr A, was not up to his job; that somehow he must be removed from his post and replaced by Mr B. What precipitated this decision I will inquire later. For the moment I ask you to accept it as a fact and to follow it backwards and forwards in time.

To reach this conclusion Mr Redletter must have had in his head an idea of where the Weathercock Company was going and of where he wanted it to go; of the part which the supplies department was playing in the company's effectiveness and the part which it should be playing; of Mr A's performance as its head and of what its head's performance should be; and of the probable performance of Mr B. All these ideas were the cumulative result of several years' experience of the company and its staff. They were not mere observations, they were judgments. These judgments go in pairs; a judgment of the situation as it is, is compared with a judgment of the situation as it might be. It is the disparity between the two which has moved Mr Redletter to his decision. These are the two types of judgment which I have already distinguished as reality judgment and value judgment. They are closely connected.

Mr Redletter's idea of Mr A is not a mere catalogue of Mr A's past performances. It is an hypothesis sufficiently comprehensive to explain all he knows about Mr A, and from which he can assess Mr A's probable performance in various roles: his potentialities and power of learning: his current trend of development or deterioration: his probable response to promotion or transfer. Even so, it is not complete. It is selective and the selection reflects the nature of his interest in Mr A, which is that of a manager in a functional subordinate. Mr A's doctor or wife or colleague on the local borough council would each have a different picture of Mr A – different not merely because of their differing gifts and opportunities for forming a judgment, but also because of their differing interests in Mr A. Someone who had no interest at all in Mr A could have no picture of him.

Thus the nature of Mr Redletter's interest in Mr A defines what aspects of Mr A he shall select for attention and valuation. The same is true of his interest in the supplies department. So when Mr Redletter asked himself, 'Can we wear Mr A any longer as Chief Supplies Officer?', he found the materials for an answer already in his head. Nor were these merely 'raw' materials. They were an accumulation of judgments, leading to ever more complete hypotheses about Mr A and the supplies department. On the other hand, what he found in his head was not *the* answer. This question redefined his interest and called for a revaluation of the problem, leaving his ideas of Mr A and the supplies department however slightly changed.

The result we know. For the first time, on this particular morning, Mr Redletter, comparing his value judgment with his reality judgment, reached the answer 'no'.

Let us now follow that silent decision forwards. What is to be done? This I have called the action judgment. It takes the form of a dialogue between Mr Redletter, the man of judgment, and an invaluable but irritating boffin in his head who makes uncritical but sometimes brilliant suggestions.

'*Move him to another job?*'
'He'd be worse elsewhere.'

'*Retire him early under the pension scheme?*'
'We can't – he's below the minimum age.'

'*Give him his notice and let him go?*'
'We couldn't do that with old A in all the circumstances, it wouldn't be fair.'

'*Make him an* ex gratia *allowance?*'

'Anything big enough to mitigate hardship would be a most awkward precedent.'

'*Must you really do it now?*'

'Yes.'

Silence: then –

'*Well, you could divide the department, leave A in charge of the bit he knows, put B in charge of the rest, let them both report to C for the time being; then, in two years when C retires ...*'

'M'yes. We *might ...*'

You will notice that all these tentative action judgments except the last one are rejected because they are either impracticable or inconsistent with Mr Redletter's idea of the sort of employer the company wished to be: in other words, by a reality judgment or a value judgment.

I have now squeezed all I want from this example. I summarize the results.

1. Judgment is a fundamental, continuous process, integral with our thinking.

2. It has three aspects – for simplicity, three kinds of judgment – value judgment, reality judgment, action judgment. The first two are the more fundamental and important. Action judgment is only called for by the interaction of value judgment and reality judgment, and is only selected by further use of the same criteria.

3. The aspects of the situation which are appreciated (reality judgment) and evaluated (value judgment) are determined by the interest of the judging mind.

All these forms of judgment are mental skills. It remains to ask in what they consist; and how they may be trained. Before I turn to these questions I will take up one which I have left unanswered. Why did Mr Redletter reach his conclusions just then? This inquiry will lead me to explore the meaning of initiative and the relation between initiative and judgment.

## Judgment and initiative

What precipitated Mr Redletter's action judgment? Had Mr A just dropped an enormous 'clanger', costing the company most of a year's profit? Or had Mr Redletter so radically revised his ideas of what a supplies department should be that Mr A's interpretation of his role, though unchanged and accepted for many years, suddenly became intolerable?

These are remote points on a continuous scale. The disparity between reality judgment and value judgment may widen, because of a change either in the situation as we see it (our reality judgment) or in the standards of value which we apply to it (our value judgment). This scale is important and I will illustrate it by two other episodes in the earlier history of the

Weathercock Company. The decision involved in both is collective. What I have said applies equally, as I believe, to collective and to individual decisions. In collective decisions, however, varying views on reality, value and action are expressed by different voices and are more easily distinguished than when their clashes and accommodations take place within a single head.

The first episode presents the directors of the Weathercock Company in an emergency meeting one Thursday. The bank has refused to extend the overdraft sufficiently to provide the pay packets on the following day except upon unwelcome and onerous terms. After long debate, the directors accept the bank's terms, telling each other that they have no choice. Strictly speaking they had a choice; they might have said 'no' or failed to say 'yes', which would have been the same thing. To choose this alternative, however, would be to choose the immediate and irreversible dissolution of the undertaking and of their own authority, and that in the most untidy fashion. The bank's terms raised no objections which could make such a course preferable.

I will now introduce you to the board of the Weathercock Company some years later. The situation has been transformed. Output is maximal, orders and cash are alike embarrassing in their abundance. The only troubles are troubles of growth, and the worst of these is that the company has no longer any physical room to grow.

They are agreed that something must be done but embarrassed by the variety of possible courses and divided on the merits of the few which are seriously considered. Mr Redletter wants to build a new factory and a new site in a new town 20 miles away; and in it he wants an impressive slice of space to develop a new business in moulded plastics, which, with the reluctant consent of his board, he had set up in some precious floor space of the present works a year or two before.

None of his colleagues supports the managing director; the arguments against his plan are impressive. The firm will lose most of its present employees and face others with hard choices. It will break its connections with its home town and its home site. The economies claimed for the move are offset by an $x$ representing the unknown variables which will be set loose by so radical a change. And why moulded plastics, when the traditional business is doing so well?

The final decision was in no one's mind when the debate began but was unanimously adopted in the end and pleased everyone. The undertaking would stay where it was, make better use of existing space, and would swallow the coveted area begrudged to plastics. It would also buy a large site in the place favoured by Mr Redletter and build there a small factory – for the moulded plastic business only. Mr Redletter was well content; his pet venture could expand all the better in this relative isolation; the rest could still move out, maybe, one day later on. The others were content also. They got what they wanted, escaped all threats – and kept the managing director happy. You will note that the managing director, though in a minority of one, got his way in what most mattered to him, because all his colleagues felt it was essential to any settlement that they should keep him, and keep him happy. These two situations illustrate what I will call the gradient of initiative.

## The gradient of initiative

The first is an extreme case. The company is on the verge of insolvency. An instability – the imbalance between money in and money out – which has been progressively affecting its performance for some time, is about to cross a critical threshold, beyond which its effects will overflow in all directions and bring the system to disorganization and dissolution.

The effect of instability on a system is usually of this form. The most clear-cut example is physical death. A living organism is an organization, maintained by the delicately balanced intake and outflow of air, food and water, and equipped with admirable devices for keeping these balances – and many others – within critical limits. The maintenance of this system is a necessary, though not of course a sufficient, condition for the highest achievement of human intellect and feeling; and among the humble but necessary skills of living we recognize the skill of keeping alive and healthy – normally as a condition of all we want to do with life, occasionally, as when we are escaping from a fire or a furious bull, as an end in itself.

Similarly, for businesses, solvency is not an end, but it is a pre-condition of successful existence and when threatened it may become an end in itself.

Political organizations such as nation states are similarly liable to changes of this step-function form. There is, however, a difference in the degree of irreversible change illustrated by these examples. The dead organism dissolves; all its constituents rearrange themselves in new and less improbable configurations. The bankrupt business, after liquidation, may reappear more or less changed. Someone will probably carry on much the same business in the same building with some of the old plant. Some of the former employees may be re-engaged. Only the accounts will show a complete break. Alternatively, if technical liquidation is avoided the only continuity may be the old losses, carefully preserved for the benefit of the newcomer's future income tax.

Wars and political revolutions raise even more difficult questions as to the identity of the future system with that of the past. These difficulties are due largely to our habits of language and thought, which invest their objects with an unreal degree of wholeness and independence. I refer to them only to establish two ideas which are important to my argument.

I wish to distinguish first between the conditions which establish a given measure of freedom and the reasons which explain how that freedom is actually used. In my case-history, the establishment of the company's liquidity was one of the conditions which enabled it to grow and ultimately to go in for moulding plastics; but it throws no light at all on why the company chose to go in for moulding plastics. For this we must explore the past history of the managing director.

This may seem obvious; but it is often by no means easy to be sure whether a given explanation explains why something happened or merely explains how its happening was possible. The theory of evolution has been supposed for the last century to explain why life on this planet has developed as it has; but serious and respected thinkers today contend that the theory merely explains how that development, among others, became possible.[3]

Arising out of this distinction, I wish to establish the idea that an organization, like an organism, can conveniently be regarded as a hierarchy of systems, each dependent on, but not explained by, those below. The variables which determine the solvency of a business could be described and discussed without any reference to the nature of the undertaking's product, the interests of its staff, the ambitions of its directors or a host of other things which fill the agenda at its meetings. In the first situation, solvency was in such peril that the field of choice was minimal. As with the man escaping from the bull, the preservation of basic conditions had become itself a dominating goal of policy. In the second situation, the basic conditions of existence were sufficiently secure to enable the directors to realize a variety of possible values, even some which they had not contemplated before. The future depended not on the adroitness of their actions but on the quality of their dreams. The gradient of initiative leads from the familiar track, where events are in control, to the uncharted spaces where dreams, whether 'right' dreams or 'wrong' dreams, can and must take charge and where that man is lost who cannot dream at all.

Thus skill in value judgment is increasingly demanded as human initiative widens. It is to be expected that some leaders who show the greatest resource in conditions of extreme difficulty will be less successful when they must seek guidance, not from without, but from within themselves.

## The action judgment

I will now revert to the question left unanswered at the end of an earlier section. What are the mental processes underlying the three aspects of judgment?

The judgment which has been most carefully studied is what I have called the 'pure' action judgment. This is typified in Köhler's classic learning experiments with apes. The motivation (value judgment) is standardized; the animal wants a bunch of bananas which is out of reach. The situation is standardized; the materials for a solution are all in sight. Only one solution is possible, so no choice between solutions is involved. The means to be used – a hooked stick, a few boxes – are not, as far as can be avoided, charged with an affective meaning of their own. The issue is simply whether the creature can see how to use these neutral objects as means to an end.

The process by which one ape does, while another ape does not, succeed

- suddenly, but after prolonged incubation – in 'seeing' the boxes as a potential increase in height, the stick as a potential increase in reach, remains a fascinating psychological puzzle.

Now consider a human example. As a very inexperienced subaltern in the old war, my company commander once said to me, 'Vickers, the company will bathe this afternoon. Arrange.' In the Flemish hamlet where we were billeted the only bath of any kind was in the local nunnery. The nuns were charity itself but I could not ask them to bathe a hundred men. I reviewed other fluid-containing objects – cattle drinking troughs, empty beer barrels – and found practical or ethical objections to them all; and at that point I had the misfortune to meet my company commander again and was forced to admit that I had not yet found the answer. He was annoyed. 'Whatever have you been doing all this time?', he said, and then, turning his own mind to the problem, as it seemed for the first time, he added, 'Take the company limbers off their wheels, put the tilts inside, four baths each four feet square, four men to a bath, do the job in an hour, why don't you use your brains?'

Simple indeed; but his solution involved two steps which my mind had not taken – the apprehension that a vehicle is a collection of bits and pieces, of which, for some purposes, the wheels may be irrelevant; and the apprehension that a tilt tailored to cover a protruding load and keep rainwater out, would fit and serve equally well, pushed into the empty waggon, to keep bathwater in.

My company commander – unlike myself – showed a mental ability like that of Köhler's more successful apes, though higher in degree; a facility for uncoupling the elements of a familiar idea and recombining them in a new way – for seeing a limber as two potential baths on irrelevant wheels, without forgetting that it is primarily and must again become a vehicle. This is a faculty useful in the research and development department and equally in the board room. Let us call it ingenuity.

## The meaning of ingenuity

Yet it must involve more than we usually associate with ingenuity. The mere multiplication of alternative means to an end might only make the choice harder, unless it were accompanied by some gift which guides the problem-solver in the general direction of the still undiscovered solution. The literature of problem solving, no less than common experience, attests our capacity for searching with a lively sense of 'warm ... warmer ... *warmer* ...', when we do not know what we are looking for.

It would seem then that even the pure action judgment involves mental faculties which are still highly obscure. Yet the pure action judgment is too simple a process to be seen outside the laboratory. Even my efforts to improvise bathing facilities were hedged about with reality judgments and value judgments of great complexity; reality judgments about what our Flemish hosts would stand with equanimity from their British billetees, and value judgments defining the kind of solution which would be acceptable to me, having regard to its impact on the troops, the inhabitants, my company commander and myself.

The action judgment is involved in answering any question of the form, 'What shall I do about it?' when 'it' has been defined by judgments of reality and value. In implementing a decision, this question may have to be asked several times. 'What shall we do about the supplies department?' 'We will change the head.' 'What shall we do about changing the head?' 'We will divide the department and ...' 'What shall we do about this decision to divide ...?' 'First we will tell A and then B and then ...'

Thus each decision sets a more precise problem for the next exercise of action judgment; and at each stage there is assumed a set of criteria for determining between different solutions. These criteria are supplied by further judgments of reality and value. 'That would not be legal.' 'That would not be fair.' 'That would not be possible.' And so on.

This process has many interesting aspects which I have no time to pursue. I will refer to two only.

First, what solutions are considered and in what order? Professor Simon[4] has pointed out that the solutions which are weighed are usually far fewer than the totality of possible solutions which exist. Often the totality is too large to be reviewed, however briefly, in the time available. Random selection seldom if ever occurs. Some mental process narrows the field rapidly to a short list of alternatives, which alone are carefully compared.

Some elements of this selective process are apparent. A man seeking a solution to a problem will usually review first the solutions which are approved by custom or his own experience for dealing with problems which seem similar; or he may try first the responses which are most accessible to him or which he most enjoys. Occasionally, however, explanations fail us and we have to credit the problem-solver with an intuitive feeling for the approach which is likely to prove fruitful, though we can see no clue by which it is recognized. This is the heuristic element in ingenuity, to which I have already referred.

Professor Simon assumes that the fully rational course is to examine every possible solution and to choose the 'best'. It seems clear to me that this is not the way the brain works. The criterion, I suggest, is not the best but the 'good enough'. The human brain scans possible solutions in an order which is itself determined by the complex and obscure factors to which I have referred; and it stops as soon as a solution is not rejected by criteria of reality or value.

If all solutions are rejected and no new ones can be devised, the standard of the acceptable has to be lowered and the process is then repeated. The unsuccessful series of rehearsals is not wasted, for it prepares the mind for the change of standard.

## The reality judgment

I turn now to the reality judgment. This, too, involves analysis and synthesis, often repeated. It requires the ready handling, dissociating, reassociating of the elements in our thought which I have called ideas or concepts. It, too, has scope for ingenuity. Yet it seems to me to require somewhat different qualities of mind.

The problem-solver has his problem to guide him. The reality judgment, on the other hand, leads us as far afield as we let it; for the aspect of the situation with which it is concerned is as wide as our interest, and we can follow it in time until imagination fails us. One of the gifts needed by those who make reality judgments is to know where to stop: to sense the point beyond which the best estimate of trends is not worth making.

The maker of reality judgments is for the time being an observer; not like the maker of action judgments, an agent. He needs detachment, objectivity, balance, a clear head to follow the complex permutations of the possible and the practicable; a stout heart, to give as much reality to the unwelcome as to the welcome. Where the maker of action judgments must above all be ingenious, persistent and bold, the maker of reality judgments must be honest, clear-sighted and brave. Above all, perhaps, he needs a ready sense for those aspects of the situation which are most relevant. And here, too, the man of outstanding judgment shows such an unerring sense for those facts which will be found to matter most that it is safer to give his unexplained facility a special name and call it also an heuristic gift.

## The value judgment

The value judgment raises problems far more obscure. Clearly it is fundamental; if we were not concerned with values which we wanted to realize and preserve we should have no interest in the situation and no incentive to action. The basic difficulty in all complex decisions is to reconcile the conflicting values involved – in my first example, the supply needs of the undertaking, the deserts of Mr A, the board's reputation as an employer, the preservation of tacit rules governing promotion and discharge and so on.

All these values are standards of what the undertaking should seek and expect of itself and others. I will call them norms. They are not settled in abstract terms but they are implicit in every major decision. Executives absorb them from these decisions and still more from the experience of participating in the making of decisions, and by the same process they contribute to the setting of these standards and to their constant revision. Thus the maker of value judgments is not an observer but an agent. He needs not so much detachment as commitment, for his judgment commits him to implications far wider than he can know.

In approaching their decisions, executives usually find the appropriate standards of value ready to hand. They cannot depart abruptly either from their own past standard or from those current in their industry. In deciding how to treat Mr A, for example, the possible range of decision was closely limited. Thus executives, in making value judgments, are seldom conscious of doing more than apply a rule.

Yet, viewed over time, it is obvious that these standards are constantly changed by the very process of applying them, just as the common law is developed and even changed by accumulating precedents. The ghost of the economic man should not persuade us to ignore the fact that business undertakings today are governed by most complex value systems. Those who direct them must somehow provide themselves with standards of what the undertaking expects of itself – standards sufficiently coherent to be usable, yet sufficiently comprehensive to define its divergent responsibilities to employees, shareholders, consumers, suppliers, locality, industry, government and community. In every one of these fields the standards of industry today are markedly different from what they were a few decades ago; and the standards of individual undertakings differ from one to an- other and also change with time.

Thus in every value judgment there is latent a creative process; a resetting of the norms which are being applied.

We can as yet give no satisfactory account of the process by which we resolve problems of conflicting value. We only beg the question when we talk of maximizing satisfactions, for the satisfactions we maximize are set by ourselves; and there is no evidence that we reduce those disparate imponderables to a common measure, so that they can be added and weighed. There is indeed much evidence that we do not.

I have already expressed the belief that in the ultimate analysis, the validity of our norm-setting cannot be validated or falsified by results. It can be approved or condemned only by reference to a sense of rightness for which the adjudicating mind must take responsibility. This is obviously true of the artist and the connoisseur of art and conduct. That it is equally true of the scientist is the theme of Professor Polanyi's book. I believe it to be equally true of the business executive.

This survey of the processes involved in judgment may well leave us in doubt how far the mechanical and mathematical models of decision-mak- ing – now so popular – as distinct from mechanical and mathematical aids to decision-making are of any relevance. On this important and contro- versial question I have time for only one comment. In so far as these models are concerned only with what I have called pure action judgment they would seem to have no bearing on any of the main issues which I have raised; for the pure action judgment is unknown in real life. In so far as they assert or suggest that the pure action judgment is the typical decision-making situation, they do a vast disservice both to the inquiry and to the undoubtedly great contribution which, with a more modest approach, they could make to it.

## Innate capacities for judgment

The extent to which we can develop judgment in ourselves and others is limited by our, and their, inherent capacity for the many mental activities involved. In these it seems clear that human beings differ widely. Minds differ greatly in their capacity for handling, arranging and combining the symbols with which we think. They differ in their ability to recognize causal and other relationships within actual or imagined sequences of events. We can say with confidence of some problems that they are too difficult for A to solve: of some situations that they are too complex for B to comprehend.

It may be that men differ in the faculties they use. Dr Grey Walter[5] has suggested that those who are unusually gifted with visual imagination reach some decisions in ways quite different from the ways used by others, not less intelligent, who are unusually devoid of this gift. He claims further that the electro-encephalogram distinguishes the two types, each of which contains, he suggests, about a tenth of the population.

Men differ further in the moral qualities involved in judgment. C could comprehend the situation, he could solve the problem: but has he the guts to go on trying until he succeeds? Will the mere stress of having to try impair his capacity for success? (Examinations rightly test this moral quality, no less than the intellectual ones which they are designed to explore.) This difference is so important that we rate executives for decisiveness, as well as for good judgment, reserving the highest rewards for those who excel in both, but recognizing that the ability to decide at all is a prior requisite, and in some cases a major one. Lord Wavell, in some famous lectures on generalship, said that stupidity in generals should never excite surprise. For generals are chosen from that small, pre-selected class of men who are tough enough to be generals at all. From such heavy-duty animals, refinements of intellect and sensibility should not be expected.

Lord Wavell's dictum, to which he was so notable an exception, is of general application. No one can exercise good judgment unless he can support both the stress of the office in which the judgment is to be exercised, and the stress of the judgment itself. Not all high offices are in themselves as stressful as that of a general in the field; but the stress inherent in judgment itself is inescapable. Between value judgment and reality judgment there is tension, characteristic of all human life. It may lead to the kind of breakdown which psychiatrists meet in patients who have lost touch with reality, or who torment themselves with an impossible level of aspiration. Distortions of judgment due to the same cause are common enough in board rooms, as for instance, when a board is faced with a problem of redundancy too large to be handled within the rules of what it has come to regard as fair. The opposite error of those who protect themselves by failing to aspire enough is more common, and much more wasteful, but more easily overlooked.

Again, the sheer difficulty of keeping the judgment of value and reality from running away into irresolvable complexity is itself a source of stress, and accounts for the familiar distinction between men of action and men of thought. The simplicity which characterizes the thought processes of men of action has often seemed to me excessive; but it is nevertheless essential to individual good judgment that a man's capacity for judgments of value and reality shall be related to his own capacity for action judgment. One of the merits of business organization is that these different human capacities can be combined.

Finally, clear judgment of value and reality only makes more frustrating the common human state of helplessness, when no effective action can be taken; and this is as common in business life as in life at large.

Courage and endurance are not the only moral qualities associated with good judgment. D has guts in plenty but he is conceited, full of personal prejudice, takes offence easily; in brief, is not sufficiently selfless or sufficiently disciplined to achieve that combination of detachment and commitment which good judgment demands.

Finally, apart from these moral qualities, I have expressed the belief that judgment needs that sensitivity to form, which, in various guises, distinguishes the connoisseur of art or conduct, the scientist and the judge, and which is equally required in the business executive.

## The training of management

Have I given the impression that good judgment is to be expected only from those who combine the qualities of philosopher, hero and saint to a degree rarely found even among top people? I hope not. In so far as it involves peculiarly human qualities of intellect, sensibility, character and will, it does indeed give scope for every kind of excellence, yet equally, just because it is so human a quality, it is not likely to be lacking in anyone we recognize as fully human.

It is indeed ubiquitous; for it is involved in some degree in every exercise of discretion. Among the debts of gratitude which business people owe to Dr Elliott Jaques, I give a high place to his finding[6] that, among all the jobs, from highest to lowest, in the undertaking which he has studied so carefully, not one fails to involve some element of discretion, some duty, essential to its performance, which is not and cannot be specified in the instructions given to the holder. We are not paid, says Dr Elliott Jaques, for doing what we are told to do, but for doing rightly that part of our job which is left to our discretion; and we rate our own and our fellows' jobs on our estimate of the weight of the discretionary element.

If Dr Jaques is right, judgment is the most universal requirement not only of managerial work but of all work. The distribution of roles on an organization chart may thus be seen, not merely as an allocation of duties but as an allocation of discretions, increasing up the hierarchy in the quality of the judgment they demand.

This picture helps us to answer the question, 'How is judgment developed?' The whole structure of industry is or should be a school of judgment, in the course of which individuals may develop, by practice and example, both the general qualities of mind, heart and will, which all judgment demands, and their own particular aptitudes which determine the kind of judgment in which they can become most proficient.

In such a school everyone is both learner and teacher. The teaching function is both positive and negative. It is positive in that it requires every member of the organization, in his daily work, to set an example in the exercise of judgment, and to supervise its exercise by those for whom he is responsible. It is negative in that it requires everyone to respect the field of discretion of his subordinates, as he expects his superiors to respect his own – especially when he himself is more expert than they in the very same field.

## Conclusion

As I feared, my short title, like a conjuror's hat has produced more curious objects than I have had time to examine to your satisfaction or my own. The material is far from tidy; the hat is far from empty; and my time is overspent. Apart from displaying what I believe to be the main dimensions of the problem and setting question marks in appropriate places, I have tried to do no more than to couple the higher executive – in the exercise of this, his most precious and highly-paid endowment – on the one hand with those excellent minds in other fields, whose function he must so often copy unawares; on the other hand, to link him with the humblest servants in his own undertaking, on whose judgment he must rely, as they on his, and from among whom it should be his delight, as it is his duty, to develop minds capable of better judgment than his own.

## References

1. Michael Polyani, *Personal Knowledge*, London, Routledge & Kegan Paul, 1958.
2. The expression is Polyani's, op. cit.
3. See, for example, M. Grene, *British Journal for Philosophy of Science*, 1958, IX, 34 and 35.
4. H. A. Simon, *Administrative Behaviour* (2nd edn), New York, Macmillan, 1959.
5. Dr Grey Walter, *The Living Brain*, London, Duckworth, 1953, p. 152.
6. Elliott Jaques, *Measures of Responsibility*, London, Tavistock Publications, 1956.

# 17

# Industry, human relations, and mental health*

I think the best way to explore the very general subject which has been given me is to try to answer three questions. First, what do we mean by 'human relations in industry'? Secondly, in what ways do these relations differ from human relations in other social contexts – for instance, in the family or the national society? Thirdly, to what extent is it useful to appraise these relations by criteria of mental health, rather than by the more usual criteria of individual prosperity or industrial efficiency or economic growth? None of the answers is obvious or uncontroversial.

## The place of human relations in industry

An observer from another planet, endowed with power to see all our economic activities displayed before him in space and time, would get an impression of immensely complex but not random activity. He would notice countless centres to which people flocked daily and through which flowed, in varying volumes, streams of material, money, and information. He would, for example, be fascinated to watch Antarctic whale oil and tropical ground nuts converging and mingling to become margarine in European larders. When he had taken in the whole picture, he would realize that the greater part of the whole product was consumed, as food or fuel, in providing the energy needed to keep the process going, while the rest replaced and on balance enlarged the total stock of human artifacts on the planet. He would sense a subtle net of coordination which regulated these flows but he would have no means of guessing what it was. If he asked us, the most complete answer we could give in two words would be 'human relations'; for we could not explain the workings of the commodity markets or the stock market, let alone the self-maintaining activity of an individual undertaking, without reference to a vast underlying system of mutual human expectations, embodied in complementary human roles.

If this planetary visitor focused his attention on a single factory, he would see the same process in miniature. He would notice material of many kinds flowing from many sources towards the centre, where part, the fuel, for example, would be consumed; part would be absorbed into the productive equipment; and part would pass through the fabricating process and flow out again as finished products or as scrap.

---

* Originally presented to the 17th Annual Meeting of the World Federation for Mental Health in 1964.

He would notice that this stream of materials was made up of constituents flowing at different rates. Materials might be processed in a few weeks, machines would last for a few years, buildings for some decades; but ultimately even the channels through which the material flows would be revealed as themselves transient, processes rather than structures, destined in time to be replaced by others. The entire assembly would appear in its true light as a process not unlike a candle flame but more complex; for the 'steady state' representing the balance between inflow and outflow may wax and wane without imbalance and is composed of constituents flowing at different rates.

Parallel with this flow but opposite in direction, would be observed the flow of money, inwards from consumers and outwards to suppliers, employees, and providers of capital; and this flow also would fluctuate in volume. Even the human beings whose activities keep all these tides flowing would be seen to obey the same law. Any individual watched for long would disappear from his accustomed place, to reappear elsewhere or not at all; and his place would be taken by another. Viewed as an organization of people, the enterprise would appear as a stream of men and women, flowing into, through, and out of the undertaking through invisible but enduring channels.

At this point the planetary visitor might well turn to us, perhaps with embarrassing expressions of admiration and respect and ask – 'How does it work? What ensures that these flows shall be maintained at their appropriate relative rates, overall and in detail, notwithstanding these frequent changes of personnel?' Our first answer might be to produce the organization chart. These people, we might say, are organized in a hierarchy of sub-systems. Each department is responsible for maintaining some aspect of this dynamic balance; for processing, for marketing, for recruitment and promotion of staff, for financial control, and so on. Within each department, each place, from the director to the cleaner, has its allotted role, consisting of duties and discretions which are expected of the holder and rights which he is entitled to expect from the holders of other roles. This pattern of complementary roles distributes responsibility for action, establishes channels of communication, and makes it possible for large numbers of people to combine in complicated and enduring operations, even though few of them have even a summary notion of what is being done.

We should have explained only a fraction of this extraordinary business. The visitor has seen the factory from the viewpoint of the manager but he has not seen what the manager sees; still less has he felt what the manager feels. For the manager is not only the centre of the regulative system which governs the internal and external relations of the undertaking. He is also an individual agent, to whom the undertaking is the means of support for himself and his family; one source, perhaps the greatest, of his status and success, in the eyes of himself and others; the principal outlet for his energies; his principal social milieu; and the focus of his professional interests as an engineer and a manager. This is equally true of every individual agent in the system. Each man, be he on the assembly belt, in the drawing office, behind the controls of a crane, or in the manager's chair, is a separate, unique world, maintaining and depending on an unique set of relations with his milieu, including the social milieu provided by his fellows, and finds in it and in them his stresses and his supports. Only some of these relations are implicit in his role and even these have for him a significance different from their meaning for the undertaking. The social unit which the sociologist observes is never visible to any of the agents who compose it, except perhaps by an intellectual effort which none can maintain for long; nor is their vision accessible to him, except by an intuitive sharing of experience which is open to him not because he is a sociologist, still less because he is a scientist, but simply because he is human.

Let us simplify this inquiry by concentrating on three main aspects of the industrial agent's role. He has relations with his working group, including his immediate superior and his subordinates, if he has any. He has relationships with his employer, as the source of his income and the controller of his future employment, his promotion, and the conditions of his work. He also has relations with his trade union or professional or occupational group. This triple subdivision holds good for nearly all in industry, whatever their role, though those whose roles are primarily regulative are associated in the working group in a manner different from that of the operatives.

In all these relations I will distinguish personal relations, such as exist between a man and those of whom he is conscious as individuals, from other human relations such as those which he has with more remote persons and organizations, relations which, though human, are not personal. Remote directors may be wholly impersonal to an employee whose livelihood their decisions affect but the employee knows well enough that they are human, open to the pressures and persuasions which distinguish human interaction. So he may refuse to accept some fruits of human decision that he would accept without question if they were the result of natural forces. We can bear blind fate better than a blind boss. On the other hand, human relations may be highly supportive, even when they are non-personal. It is the merit of a role structure that it can support human expectations across the gulf which would otherwise be created by changing personalities.

So I would answer my first question as follows. By human relations in industry I mean all those relations between people which are implicit in industrial roles, whether between worker and worker, worker and supervisor, worker and employer, or any others related hierarchically or laterally in the organization; and I include both inter-personal relations and those larger-scale relations which are impersonal but still human. An extreme example of these is reached in negotiations between an organized industry on the one hand and a national organization of workers on the other, negotiations which may be intensely personal between the negotiators but which involve and are limited by their relations with perhaps millions of others, to whom the negotiators on both sides are an impersonal but highly human 'they'.

## The peculiarities of human relations in industry

Human relations in industry are sharply distinguishable from human relations in any other social system in our Western culture, for reasons that are partly inherent and partly an unhappy legacy of history.

Industry involves more extensive division of labour, more deliberate co-ordination of policy, and more rapid and radical changes in the volume and direction of effort than any other human activity of our time, except war. It must therefore require to an exceptional degree among its participants acceptance of role, exchange of information, and mutual trust, especially perhaps the last. For in industry, even more than in politics, the normal feedback cycle, whereby experience and anticipation alert us to the need for change, is fragmented. Trends visible from the board room may need action on the factory floor – and consequently disruption of familiar behaviour patterns and perhaps serious disturbance to individuals – years before the need for them becomes apparent to those who must give effect to them and to those who will suffer by them. Conversely, troubles on the factory floor may be obvious and clamant to those on the spot years before they can be dealt with by an echelon high enough to make the changes that they demand. In industry, then, above nearly all other social systems, people have to vary their action, often to their own inconvenience or even detriment, in reliance on the judgement of others; others often above them but sometimes below them in the hierarchy. Yet in this complex but flexible organization all the roles are deliberately designed; they are allotted and changed by the holders of roles above them in the hierarchy; and they are occupied transiently by successive holders, each associated formally only by a contract of employment. The right of the employer to design and change the size and shape of his role structure and to choose and change successive role-holders is as jealously guarded as the right of the employee to choose and change his job. To combine flexibility and coordination on such a scale, the most obvious way is to make industrial roles easy to learn and easy to inspect and to reduce in each of them the content of discretion and the amount of information and mutual trust that the holder needs to do his job.

In earlier days these goals were pursued by industry to a degree which proved self-defeating; today industry is busy reversing these earlier mistakes; seeking to build into its workers' roles enough discretion, enough use of information, and enough cooperation to provide an acceptable occupation for a human being. Yet even if industry were free from the traditions of the past, it would still be bound by these inherent limitations. It is useless to design an industrial role requiring of its holder skills, habits, or attitudes that cannot be found ready made or quickly learned by those who will successively fill it.

One way in which roles can be simplified and made less dependent on the ability of their transient holders is to stress the authoritarian nature of the hierarchy and to rely increasingly on direction from above. Here again industry in the past carried the principle to a self-defeating point and is now busy correcting the mistake; yet here again authority can be dispensed with only to a limited extent. It is inescapable in a type of organization such as I have described that relations up and down the hierarchy should play a larger part than in social systems less concerned to achieve coordinated yet flexible action on a large scale.

These, then, I suggest, are the inherent peculiarities of industrial organizations and hence of the human relations of which they are composed. Roles are less socially sanctioned than those of most other social systems; they are allotted by contract, rather than by custom; and they contain a more than usually large proportion of relations involving subordination or superordination to the holders of other roles in a hierarchy. Even newly developing countries, which are happily at liberty to evolve a system of industrial roles free from the legacy under which Western societies labour, will be forced, I think, to accept these facts and the limitations they involve.

In Western countries, these difficulties are magnified by the legacy of a past which implicitly denied much of what we now believe to be true and important in the field of human relations. This may apply especially to my own country, which, being early in the field, absorbed into its industrial system an especially large element of nineteenth-century concepts and values; but I understand that these handicaps are not unknown elsewhere. I will distinguish three. First, proud of an age which was replacing status by contract, our ancestors did not realize that aggregates of human beings, assembled like aggregates of machinery or of capital through 'the market', would none the less insist on becoming, for good or ill, social systems; must indeed become social systems if they were to function adequately; and that, though contract might be a welcome passport to status, it could never be a substitute. Secondly, their minds were dominated by mechanical analogies of a kind which seem infinitely crude to the technology of today; so they conceived of human organizations as operated by 'pushes and pulls' and devised a 'kick and carrot' psychology of corresponding crudity. Thirdly, by equating labour with other commodities and creating a 'free market' through which to distribute it, they built into the vertical relations in the business hierarchy a relationship inherently incompatible with that which the working of the system would require.

Since then the business world has changed past recognition. Its still nominally 'private' institutions have become the focus of complex public responsibilities; they are expected and even expect themselves to sustain external relationships, as employers, suppliers of services, earners of foreign exchange, land users, and so on, in accordance with norms of behaviour undreamed of a few decades ago. They are even more concerned to humanize their internal relations, partly in response to public expectation but partly also in response to the need to become social systems sufficiently effective and responsive to survive. Even their machines are increasingly controlled by signals, rather than by pushes and pulls, that is to say by the passing of information, rather than by the transmission of energy; and this is helping to make acceptable more true and sophisticated ideas about the control and self-control of men.

But the inertia of the past, our safeguard in adversity, is a drag on the wheel when we would reverse our mistakes. The ghosts of the past walk so freely through our minds that we can hardly tell them from our friends. One example must suffice. A free market meant to our grandfathers a market containing so many buyers and so many sellers that no one of them could affect it. It provided an independent criterion of value in the market price only because this expressed the result of numberless individual choices. In this sense the free market has virtually ceased to exist in any field and especially in the so-called labour market. Yet in national wage negotiations in my country and in others too a single buyer and a single seller, partners in what is in fact an indissoluble partnership, still sit down to what is described as 'collective bargaining'; and if they fail to agree, an arbitrator, applying no known law yet going through the forms of judicial inquiry, produces an award, after hearing arguments in which the medieval idea of 'the just price' figures far more prominently than the supposedly governing idea of the market price. In taking part in such 'negotiations' I have sometimes felt as if I were assisting at some late form of medieval tourney, in which, under the ritual forms of combat, some new procedure was quietly taking shape.

Let me summarize my answer to my second question. Human relations in industry are not different in kind from human relations in any other social context but they are different in degree; partly because industrial activity necessarily requires an organization more hierarchic and more authoritarian than most other social activities and thus depends to an unusual extent on acceptance of role, ability to handle information, and, especially, on mutual trust; and partly because the legacy of history makes these conditions especially hard to create.

## Mental health as a criterion of human relations in industry

It remains for me to answer my third question. What are the significant aspects of this complex of human relations that we call industry, when we regard it not as a means of providing goods or distributing incomes but from the viewpoint of mental health?

We are not here as industrialists asking what has mental health to do with industry. We are asking what has industry to do with mental health. I need therefore spend no time describing industry's need for men and women free from mental illness and possessing the skills and the stability of personality which are commonly identified with mental health. Nor need I recount the shocking estimates of man-hours lost through mental illness, let alone the less measurable, but probably greater, losses which come from attitudes that can be called psychopathological.

Nor have I been asked to explore the effect on mental health of the industrialization which is transforming our world at an accelerating rate, though these are for mental health far the most significant changes of our time. They produce far denser and more rapidly growing populations, far more rapid changes in the physical and hence in the cultural milieu than have ever before been known or dreamed of; and, in doing so, they cramp our living space, frustrate our expectations, depreciate our skills, make nonsense of our experience as a basis for prediction, condemn our institutions to perpetual obsolescence, if not ineptitude, and destroy the cultural assurances by which we live. This accelerating spin into chaos will not be mitigated by any change, however welcome, in relations *within* industry; and it could be controlled, if at all, only by changes in the organization and culture of our Western societies which could be barely compassed in the time available to us, even if the only powers that could achieve them were not committed to resist them.

All this constitutes, in my view, a threat to mental health so huge as to dwarf any other; but, happily perhaps, it is not within my subject. I am concerned not with the impact of industrialization, as now organized and controlled, on Western society, but with the effect on individual mental health of participating in the human relations which that organization now involves. Even this is a vast subject. I will consider briefly the three areas of relationship that I distinguished earlier. Consider first relations within the working group. The psychological hazards commonly recognized here are too much dictation from outside and from above and hence too little opportunity for self-direction; too much fragmentation of work function and hence too little satisfaction in creative achievement, whether individual or collective and too little support and enjoyment through human cooperation. Never, it might be said, did so many men cooperate so closely to produce such marvellous artifacts; and never did they get less satisfaction either from the experience of cooperation or from the experience of creation.

This, though far from wholly true, has more truth than it need have or should have in our Western societies today. It is in part due to the attempt to make industrial roles 'foolproof', easily assimilable by a succession of holders with no high degree of skill or motivation. As I have already pointed out, the obvious way to do this is to minimize the dependence of each role on experience, information, and mutual trust, to set the tempo through the machine and to supply the coordination from above. This trend has produced types of organization that industry already recognizes as inefficient. Fascinating studies in the British coal industry, for example,[1] have shown the danger of associating men in technical interdependence which does not permit the growth of a corresponding sense of social interdependence; as when coal-getting is organized in a 24-hour cycle of three shifts which never meet.

This danger may perhaps be less with more advanced technology. Changes in the organization of coal-getting, made possible, and indeed necessary, by the full mechanization of the process, not only permit but require more socially integrated teams, responsible for less fragmented work. There is still a large field in which even our present knowledge of the psychological needs of men at work can point the way both to greater efficiency and to conditions more favourable to mental health. The conditions of mental health, however, cannot be left solely to the enlightened pursuit of efficiency, any more than can the conditions of physical health. I hope that the pursuit of them for their own sake will not be based on too limited a view of the variety and adaptability of men. There is room for team jobs and solitary jobs, regular jobs and jobs irregular in their hours and their demands, exacting jobs and jobs of the simplest routine.

I turn to the second field, the relations of men in industry with their employer. This field is shadowed by the insecurity of industrial work, derived from the uncertainty of employment and sharpened by the fact that continued employment depends on the unfettered discretion of some other role-holder. We should not underestimate this insecurity. The number of unemployed is no clear index of the fear of unemployment; nor is this fear limited to some lower echelons of the pyramid, especially in the older age groups, where adequate provision for retirement is still exceptional, if 'adequacy' is taken to mean what may secure a reasonable man from anxiety. I know of no evidence to show that uncertainty is of itself inimical to mental health; wartime experience suggests that the reverse may sometimes be true. Yet memories of the thirties should leave us in no doubt of the dangers that result (both to individuals and to society) when individuals are displaced from society through unemployment which no personal initiative of theirs can avert. The unemployed of those days foreshadowed the problem of the displaced person, a problem made more challenging by the fact that they were displaced within their own community. We have not yet shown, nor have we reason to hope, that we can banish unemployment in the automated future or that we can distribute it as leisure in any form compatible with our present ideas of status and success. Indeed, there is every reason to think that industry as now organized will progressively cease to be an acceptable producer or distributor of *jobs*, as distinct from goods. The problem of the displaced person is the greatest growing problem of our industrialized societies; and it is a problem of mental health. In this alienated and atomized world we are all more or less displaced persons.

It is the employer, whether public or private, who distributes, enhances, or withdraws this privilege of working and with it the most essential status our society has to offer; and he does so in the course of regulating a system primarily governed by other and unrelated requirements. The existence of this power, whether used or not, is bound to charge with stress the whole relationship between those who can exercise it and those who are subject to it; and this stress is bound to increase as the implicit threat becomes, for whatever reason, more serious. It is further amplified by all the resonances with which it has been charged by a century of industrial strife. The political and legal rights to which we are born, precious as they are, are psychologically less protective and supportive than are the social rights, inherent in many cultures, including our own at an earlier date, which are our birthright no more.

I turn to the third area, the field of relations subsisting between a man and his occupational or professional group. These have always had, and have today, strong supportive significance for their members; it is one of their major objectives. The organizations which subserve them have always served, among other things, to protect the group against attack or attrition from without and to support its status against other competing groups. In our modern industrial world this function has grown in relative importance. Many trade unions exist for no other purpose and are structurally inept for any other purpose.

For the historical reasons I have mentioned this field includes large areas of institutionalized combat. These include relations not only between organized employers and organized employees but also between rival organizations of the employed. These bellicose attitudes are too crude for the needs of societies in such peril as I have described. Industrialists, politicians, ordinary citizens, even some trade unionists view them with justified alarm. They are open to criticism in many ways. Whether they are bad for mental health is, I think, less clear. A fight is a refreshingly simple and supportive situation; in few other circumstances do we have so many comrades and so few doubts. If our industrial societies relapse into patterns of increasingly unqualified conflict, as their problems become ever less amenable to more integrative solutions, it will be a symptom of large-scale disaster; but from an individual viewpoint it may none the less be the least bad psychological defence available. Let us not make mental health the scapegoat, if we fail to grapple with the problems we have generated.

And yet – this is a field in which mental health is equally relevant; for whether we are speaking of mental health or of general public health – of which, I hold, mental health is an inseparable part – we should not describe conditions of health only in terms of freedom from hazard.

Health, physical or mental, is a function of three variables – the hazards of the milieu, the support of the milieu, and the immunity (or resistance) of the individual. The relation between the three can be clearly seen in the attack on infectious disease, that prototype of public health activity. Its earliest efforts were towards the reduction of hazard – clean water, efficient drainage, antisepsis – but it has won its successes at least as much by building up immunity, both specifically, by increasing resistance to particular diseases, and generally, by improved diet and living conditions. It started from two biologically given facts, the variable vulnerability of the human constitution to infective organisms and the increase of these organisms in the conditions of urban living; and its task has been to find a *cultural* solution which would so match man and his milieu as to hold infectious illnesses at an acceptable level.

This task is wider than the commonly accepted field of public health. Today, in our search for what in my country is called social security, sickness of all kinds is only one of 'five giant evils', identified as major enemies of human well-being. Again the solution sought is a cultural one, in which the age-old threats of sickness, ignorance, unemployment, squalor, and want may be held at an acceptable level, partly by reducing their incidence and partly by increasing the personal and social resources of those who must cope with them. The second of these approaches is proving just as essential and much more elusive than the first.

Mental health is an inseparable constituent of public health; and industry is an inseparable part of our culture. We know relatively little in this field about the nature of the three variables, hazard, protection, and immunity; and even less about how to control them. They are all the more essential as landmarks, marking out three fields of inquiry, none of which can be ignored or resolved into the others, though none can usefully be studied in isolation.

Industry will always present some hazard to health, including mental health, as will all the activities of life. It is the responsibility of our culture, including the industrial sub-culture that forms part of it, not only to minimize these hazards and to increase the supports that can avert or mitigate the breakdowns of the vulnerable, but also to foster in the individual the power to preserve that internal stability which, as Claude Bernard observed long ago, is the condition of free and independent life. When Bernard spoke of '*la stabilité du milieu intérieur*' he was not thinking of psychological maturity; yet if we were to adopt his famous phrase as a partial definition of mental health, we should make clear to every manager what mental health has to do with that singular net of human relations which we call industry.

## Reference

1. E. L. Trist, G. W. Higgin, H. Murray and A. B. Pollock, *Organizational Choice: Capabilities of Groups at the Coal Face under Changing Technologies*. London; Tavistock Publications, 1963.

# 18

# Institutional and personal roles*

Increasing numbers of people in this and other Western countries are losing faith in all their institutions, and especially in their institutions of political government. They mistrust their competence and, more radically, they mistrust their goals. They express this positively by demanding more participation, more accountability and more responsiveness to the needs of ordinary people here and now. They express it negatively by withdrawing their tacit acceptance of authority which is the source of its legitimacy and most of its power.

On the other hand, the increasing interrelation of multiplying people on a shrinking planet calls for organizations on an even larger scale of space and time, with even wider authority to settle even sharper internal differences. There seems to me no hope at all of meeting those international demands, when we cannot even sustain the institutional relationships we have now.

So it seems to me appropriate, in a series of lectures concerned with world planning, to talk about our relations as persons with the institutions on which we have come to depend so completely. It seems obvious to me that however radically we change them, we shall have to go on living in a world of institutions and that they will go on making demands on us, in proportion to the increasing demands we make on them.

We recognize that the institutions of government and business in this and other Western countries have become so closely interwoven that we may regard them as a system. The system is run by men, but by men playing institutional roles. Their criteria of judgment and their standards of success seem to us to be those of the institutions which they serve. So when the system produces threats which alarm us or wrongs which outrage us, we may conclude that the system's ideas of success are quite different from our own. Some people feel so about the Vietnam war. Apart from external relations, many people are equally offended at the way the system distributes incomes, wealth and power.

Apart from criticisms of what it is trying to achieve, we may also become anxious at the system's failure to do even what it is trying to do. We are sometimes told that the greatest cities are becoming ungovernable. And when we hear of great enterprises threatened with bankruptcy we may question whether they have become unmanageable. Like men at sea, we

* From *Human Relations*, Vol. 24, No 5, 1971. Based on a lecture given at the University of California, Berkeley, in April 1971.

may become anxious either about the course the ship is taking or about its ability to keep afloat or both. Either is sufficiently alarming.

The managers of every kind of institution are equally familiar with both anxieties. They are expected to keep the institution in being and at the same time to realize the most acceptable mix of all the various things they are trying to do. The goals of balancing and optimizing (or 'satisficing') always conflict; yet the same set of decisions must serve both.

Our present institutions can be criticized both on grounds of responsiveness and on grounds of efficiency. They may need radical change. But unhappily we cannot assume that all our troubles are due to these defects. There are problems which attach to human governance as such and they are mounting. They would be making greater demands on our institutions and on us, whatever our institutions. We have no reason to be surprised at the mounting instability of the system.

The first of these general factors is the enormous expansion of the ethical dimension. The question, Who gets what? becomes an ethical question whenever the answer depends or is thought to depend even in part on human decisions. As our environment becomes increasingly human, so an increasing proportion of our threats and blessings seem to stem from the decisions of other men and so fall into the class about which we can argue that they ought to be different and which we can change, if at all, by the techniques which influence men, rather than by those which manipulate the physical world.

The present storm of ethical protests is largely due, I believe, to the huge expansion of issues which are rightly deemed to be ethical. The wilderness does not owe us a living. Even the market does not owe us a living. But between us and those impersonal worlds is spread an institutional world on which we subsist, all of us as members, most of us also as employees. And all our individual rights as members, even as employees, have an ethical dimension. We can meaningfully argue about what they ought to be.

A second factor is the ambiguity which surrounds the concepts of forecasting and planning when we apply them to human affairs. Nothing human is predictable in the sense in which the movements of the moon are predictable; and no operations on them are plannable in the sense in which moon landings are plannable. Some years back an English study showed that the population of S.E. England would increase by five million in the next 20–30 years. Plans were proposed for new towns, new highways and so on. But the already overcrowded people in S.E. England refused to accept this figure as a prediction. If the towns were not built, the population would not expand. Of course this view, like the other, was only partly true; demographic changes are not wholly obedient to a planner's will. But equally they are not unaffected by a planner's plans or even a forecaster's forecasts.

A third factor is the growing disparity in scale between problems, agencies and beneficiaries. In 1961 a British minister of transport commissioned a report on urban traffic congestion. The committee observed that this congestion was not a problem but a symptom of the problem that modern cities generate more activity than they can contain. The smallest system worth studying was the city, not just its roads. Cities could indeed be redesigned to contain more activity than they do now. But any such redesigning would have to take account not just of accessibility by vehicle but of access on foot, safety, parking, amenity and so on; of which disparate and conflicting goods, different partial satisfactions were to be had at varying prices.

The problem involved a whole physio-social system. But the agency which commissioned the study was a functional department responsible only for transport. And the people for whose benefit the exercise was being done were concerned with even smaller fragments, differing radically with their position. Those with cars were frustrated by the restricting houses. Those who lived in the restricting houses were frustrated by the encroaching cars.

The example brings out a fourth factor-conflict between the divergent interests of the beneficiaries, bred by this disparity of scale. These conflicts must grow greater as larger scale problems impose larger scale solutions.

So apart from any defects of our present institutions, any future institutions are going to make greater demands on their beneficiaries, who in some capacities must also be their victims – greater demands on their intelligence; greater demands on their breadth of interests; greater demands on their confidence; and greater demands on their ability to reconcile conflicts, including conflicts of role; greater demands in fact on their humanity. As human beings we should not object to that.

But it sets us thinking about the nature and the limitations of these nets of mutual dependence in which we are enmeshed and so about the expectations on which they depend. And this brings us to the ubiquitous concept of role; because role systems are precisely nets of self- and mutual expectation.

I spent 20 years as a lawyer, and experienced the relation of professional and personal roles. I spent in all another 20 years as an official in a variety of institutions and I know something about the relation of institutional and personal roles. I spent another 16 years as a student, trying to make sense of the previous 40.

This has left me with some unfashionable conclusions of which I will warn you.

First, I attach a wider meaning to the concept of role playing than some of you may find familiar. What I have come to expect of myself and of others and to regard as legitimate expectations of them from me seems to describe a good deal of what I am and what others trust me to be. So I do not hesitate to talk of personal roles, which some of you may regard as a contradiction in terms.

Next, I think of role playing as a creative, sometimes revolutionary, activity and of role holders as agents of change. This is partly because I have been lucky in playing many roles in new and fluid organizations, apart from the role of being myself, which was once more new and fluid than any.

Thirdly, I attach great importance to the element of conflict which is present in all role playing. There is conflict between institutional and personal roles. There is conflict between institutional roles and within each individual role, whether institutional or personal. But this does not frustrate them or make them unplayable. The resolution and containment of conflict is what role-playing is all about.

Finally, I have learned from personal experience, as well as from observation, that the capacity for resolving and containing the conflicts inherent in roles varies with the role player, no less than with the role. I am thankful that there should be men and women willing and able to play, even badly, all the roles I cannot play at all.

I should add that I have lived a long life in a country where the level of internal conflict has been lower and the level of trust, especially trust in officials, has been higher than it commonly is in the U.S.A. So I assume as possible and even normal some ways of resolving and containing conflict which some of you may have come to regard as impossible or even undesirable. The contrast may serve to remind both you and me that the limitations of social and political life are functions of the state at the time of specific, historic societies. The limitations might be even narrower and the possibilities are surely greater than anything any of us has yet experienced.

I am also impressed by the extent to which my country, in the last 70 years, has been not merely adaptive but creative in the field of human values. Its operative standards of what human relations are acceptable and unacceptable have greatly grown and changed; and on the whole I approve those changes. The span has had its moments of abysmal stupidity and dishonour; but so, in retrospect, has mine. It is at the moment in a trough of some confusion and disillusion, faced with regulative challenges that it cannot meet and with intellectual and moral problems that it cannot solve. So am I. There is nothing in that to alienate me from my institutions. I think no worse of my country's development than of my own. Those who are not constrained by so humble a view must make allowances for me.

## Some conceptual innovations

For two millennia Western philosophers have been debating the relations of the individual and society or of the individual and the state. The problem is an artifact of our culture. In traditional societies the social dimension comprises both the political and the personal. As the development of our societies bred, on the one hand, gigantic political and economic organizations and, on the other hand, atomized individuals, so the gulf which this fission created demanded an explanation. It is no less a problem for being a cultural artifact.

In the last century or so, psychologists, sociologists and cultural anthropologists have joined the debate, to refine or confuse the underlying assumptions about human nature, human thinking and human values. I have neither the time nor the competence to link all I have to say with that huge volume of conflicting authority. But it may be useful to mention some conceptual changes which have marked the last 30 years and which have influenced my resumed education.

About 30 years ago scientists began formally to distinguish information from energy. This was a major conceptual revolution. For nearly three centuries the physical sciences had been almost wholly absorbed in disentangling energy from matter, with which at the end of the 17th century, it was still utterly confused. Thereby they had answered some important 17th-century questions, such as the nature of heat and light; and they had established the continuity of organic and inorganic processes and of human life with other forms of life. But they had hardly begun to explain the *differences* between men and other animals, because they had hardly begun to explain organization in terms of information, still less, in terms of shared individual response to information, which is the essence of human social life. To distinguish information from energy as a means of inducing change, still more as a means of preserving form, set scientific minds free from the shackles of their most recent success, though it did not thereby break the habits of many lifetimes.

Ethologists, comparing the human with other species, established some useful similarities. It is useful, for example, to remember that men are biologically social but not biologically political animals. The largest societies which have supported them through all but the last 2 per cent of their existence as a species have been loose associations of families. Men have depended on men since men were men; that is how they became men. But human societies have not depended on each other until a few centuries ago. The reminder is useful but it tells us nothing about human possibilities. Our peculiar gifts for creating, through communication, a common conceptual world have enabled us to create societies different from those of other creatures. Whatever be the limitations on making a planetary society, they are likely to be no less specific to our kind.

In view of the course which scientific thought had taken, it is perhaps inevitable – though I think it is unfortunate – that the greatest stimulus to new thinking about the difference between men and other creatures should have come neither from the biological nor even from the psycho-social sciences but from physicists, mathematicians and communication engineers, designing neo-mechanical systems. The common factor in these is that they are designed to hold some set of relations constant or to a prescribed course – first, thermostats and automatic pilots; then self-directing anti-aircraft guns; then automatic factories, homing missiles and space probes. These stimulated a lot of theoretic, especially mathematical thinking. They also generalized in common usage new words and concepts, such as feedback, which were to prove conceptually important. Our ways of thinking are always much affected by the machines we use.

One idea which was to prove curiously liberating, though it seems so obvious, is the idea of the mis-match signal. A pilot, whether human or mechanical, responds not to the changing compass bearing but to the comparison of that bearing with a given course. The same compass reading will have a different meaning for him, if the course is changed, because the effective signal is generated internally, by comparing the incoming information with an internal standard.

This shows that information is an incomplete concept. It implies a receiver capable of being informed. Its meaning, if any, depends on the organization of the receiving end – for the automatic pilot, on the course. This, however obvious it may seem to non-scientists, is a more sophisticated idea of a signal than many psychologists had allowed themselves for 50 years. It does not mean that all the work on conditioned responses was wasted labour, or even that all the current work on exciting the so-called pleasure centres – or are they addiction centres? – is wasted labour. But it does insist on the obvious fact, so constantly ignored, that human beings are systems regulated at different levels, by different regulators which often conflict. And it stresses the importance, when dealing with the more human aspects of personal and social – and equally of institutional – behaviour, of identifying the internal standards which give meaning to information, and the ways in which these standards grow and change.

The design of man-made control systems has been made possible by the computer, and this new tool has also had conceptual side-effects for good and ill. On the credit side, it has made visible a category difference between a computer and a programme which no longer frightens communication scientists; so I hope it will in time encourage the more timid psychologists to draw a category distinction not less wide between mind and brain. On the debit side, it tempts us to beat our problems into a shape that our computers can handle and thus further encourages the delusion that scientific and technological problems are typical of human problems, which they are not.

Has it ever occurred to you that to design a bungalow is a problem different in kind from designing the first atomic bomb and basically much more complex? The difference is that for the Manhattan project the criteria of success were simple and compatible, whilst for even the smallest bungalow they are multiple and conflicting. Scientific questions are 'why?' questions. Technological questions are questions of 'How?' or 'How best?', where the criteria of 'best' are given. But the simplest policy question is a question of what *is* best, where the criteria of 'best' are multiple and conflicting and their relative weight is just what has to be decided.

These questions have given new authority and direction to the study of systems of all kinds and especially of social and political systems. System concepts have long been familiar in other fields, notably in biology. Early last century Claude Bernard, impressed by the advantage gained by those creatures which had developed means to keep their blood heat constant, coined his famous statement that 'the stability of the internal milieu is the condition of free and independent life', a statement which has extraordinarily wide applications.

From the 1940s onwards people have been becoming ever more conscious of other fields in which systemic relations are important to them. One of the earliest to be noticed was in the ecological field, at first in the local phenomena of soil erosion and consequent dust bowls. Today mounting pollution, wasting or committed resources and multiplying populations combine to form an obviously unstable system of enormous size which cannot continue for long as it is going now, and so invites regulation to achieve some pattern even slightly less repugnant to our human values than that which it will otherwise take. The example helps to make clear what the regulative function of government really is.

Again, the economic system is increasingly seen as part of a sociotechnical system which not only links men as consumers with men as producers but also conditions men as members of society. So we increasingly accept that it needs and admits of regulation in accordance with multiple conflicting standards, within the limits of stability.

For there is a difference between the biological norms studied by Claude Bernard, built-in, stable and changeless over many generations and the norms that regulate personal and social and political systems. These are multiple and conflicting. They operate to achieve and preserve not just stability but the most acceptable combination of relations that can be reconciled with stability. They often jeopardize stability in the process.

When I compare the intellectual world in which I have lived for the last 30 years with the world in which I grew up, the changes are remarkable. Matter has ceased to be material and machines have ceased to be mechanical, as those words were used at the turn of the century. Stability, not change, demands explanation; and the explanations we look for are in terms of communication rather than of energy transfer. Communication is limited not by the means to send messages but by the organization at the receiving end; and this consists of historically generated standards by which incoming information is interpreted and without which it would not even be noticed. Energy, mankind's most ancient limitation, is for the moment superabundant, and so are the means for sending messages. But the means for interpreting messages are in total confusion; and in consequence all the relations on which human life depends, at every level from the planetary to the personal, in every aspect from the economic to the ethical, are in danger of dissolution, because the regulative standards on which they depend have become confused or polarized in conflict.

So the major threat at every level is the lack of what I have called an appreciative system sufficiently widely shared to mediate communication, sufficiently apt to guide action and sufficiently acceptable to make personal experience bearable. The major need of collective existence at the moment is to generate such a system. The aspect of that system with which I am concerned today is the net of self- and mutual expectations which mediates our mutual relations.

## Self- and mutual expectations

None, I think, will question that, whatever else we learn, we learn what to expect; and that men differ from other animals partly in the variety and assurance of the expectations that they learn to build. I want to distinguish between our expectations of other people and our expectations of the rest of the natural world; and also between our expectations of each other and our expectations of ourselves.

We are born into a world of people. We develop expectations of them which we confirm or revise in the light of experience; but we also do all we can to make them behave in the way we would like to expect. They do the same to us. The staggering success of the result is hidden from us only because we take these expectations for granted, until they are shaken.

We also develop expectations of ourselves, partly but not wholly by acknowledging the legitimacy of other people's expectations of us. It is these which make our behaviour more predictable than that of a bird on a bird table. They develop a personality on which other people can rely. These self-expectations may be more or less what others expect of us and it is useful sometimes to distinguish between what we do because we think it well to comply with what others expect of us and what we do because we expect it of ourselves. Both give us the experience of self-regulation.

If we did not have these self-expectations, we could not have the same sort of expectations of other people. We assume that they are regulated in the same way; and in varying degrees, we assume that we know what their self-expectations are. With a close friend, the assumptions we make may be wide, detailed and confident. With strangers they become more attenuated. Members of a close but functional body, like a ship's company, are usually linked by a net of self- and mutual expectations which is exceptionally firm and detailed but in an exceptionally narrow context. With those remote from us in language, culture, or experience the net of assumption is weaker. But it is seldom wholly absent. I find it curious and encouraging that it should transcend cultural differences even so much as it does.

I stress the importance of this net of self- and mutual expectations because I wish to distinguish it from those more general expectations on which our other external relations are based. The brain and CNS can recognize and abstract regularities in experience and use them for prediction at levels far simpler than the human. Thunder presages rain. Night follows day. Human prediction based on regularities such as these is familiar and impressive. From the measurement of the year which made agriculture possible to the measurements which guided the last Apollo landing on the moon, the human mind has systemized its experience of the natural order so as to guide its expectations with impressive scope and accuracy.

This, however, is in the field of natural science which Herbert Simon recently and most usefully distinguished from what he called the sciences of the artificial.[1] Natural science is knowledge of what would be as it is if men were not here to know it. And though what men can know of it must bear the imprint and limitations of the human mind, our knowledge of it is different from our knowledge of other human beings, because we have personal experience of being human.

The sciences of the artificial are wider than the psycho-social sciences. A steam engine is a human artifact, explicable only in terms of human purposes. Polyani has been insisting for some years now that, though we can explain a broken crankshaft in terms of metal fatigue, we cannot explain the crankshaft itself except in terms of the human purposes for which it was designed.[2] But I am not concerned to pursue the sciences of the artificial in that direction; I want to focus on the fact that all dealings of men with men are made possible and conditioned by a network of expectations which each has of the others and of themselves and by assumptions of each participant about the self- and mutual expectations of the others. Next, I want to enquire what part this net plays when human relations transcend the personal and become institutionalized.

Human societies survive and grow only in so far as they can resolve or contain the conflicts which they engender. The principal mechanisms by which they do so are rule and role. Rules, from formal laws to the subtlest conventions of courtesy, provide agreed solutions for common situations of potential conflict. Think how much conflict is prevented from even arising by the habit of queueing and the rule of the road. Within the system of rules, a more flexible and comprehensive system of roles distributes responsibility for decision and action and makes the distribution acceptable by supporting the role holder within his role and constraining him from stepping outside it.

Unlike a rule, the criterion for a role cannot be fully and explicitly defined. The role player has a discretion and a duty to exercise his discretion within his role. In an effective organization, each member trusts the others to do so and to extend the same trust to him. To take a very simple example, in all the English versions of the game of football, a player often has to choose between whether to pass the ball or to try to make progress himself.[3] If he sticks to the ball and fails, his fellow players are quick to judge whether he was in breach of his role or only unsuccessful in achieving a legitimate intention. There is no room in a team for a player who is either too selfish to play his role honestly or too unskilful to play it acceptably; but the two judgments are quite different. A breach of role is likely to be more unanimously spotted and more violently condemned than an act of incompetence, in a business organization or a government department, no less than on a football field.

The example is simple but its importance is general. Members of organizations are expected to exercise discretion within limits precise enough to allow others to exercise their discretion but not so precise as to exclude adaptation, learning and experiment. They are traditionally be-devilled by two types – the buck-passer, who leaves his discretion unexercised; and the insubordinate, who commits other people's discretions and sabo-tages their decisions if he does not like them. Our current ethos prefers the second. Before we accept this view, we should reflect on its history.

Traditionally, in all civilizations, men have used official seats of power to enrich themselves, advance their friends and torment their enemies – in other words, as enhanced opportunities for playing personal roles. In Britain, it was not until the latter half of the 19th century that no public office could be bought and that none offered substantial opportunities for predation. Not all societies can say as much even today. The harnessing of private men to public roles is a social and civilizing achievement of the greatest importance. And its present extension is perhaps the greatest achievement of our culture.

For the modern world which Maine described as the transition from status to contract was in fact the transition from a world of inherited status to one in which positions, with their attendant status and roles, could be transferred by contract; and not only transferred but designed and created. Our facility for creating organizations of such variety for any purpose, for designing the most complex distributions of power, vested in positions whose holders can be selected and changed at will, this is a novelty. It is this which has accustomed us to the skills and restraints of institutional role playing and which has made possible the huge institutions on which we depend.

And it is this which has produced in our day a revulsion against official role playing quite different in emphasis from that which marked previous ages. We are no longer afraid of the man who uses his official position to feather his private nest. We are afraid of the dehumanized institution, made even more inhuman by the devotion of its officials. The symbol of the bad official is no longer the Roman tax farmer, that immemorial symbol of oppression. It is – Eichmann.

If we do not believe in the justice of our laws, we shall not be proud that they are enforced without fear or favour. If we think that our defence institutions are endangering and dishonouring us, we shall not be com-forted to reflect that their officials are playing their roles honestly. If we think that profit-making institutions have a built-in interest inconsistent with that of the consumers they serve and the workers they employ, we shall not be reassured by the reflection that their officials are serving that interest successfully. If we think that trade unions have a built-in need to escalate the inflation that threatens their members, derived from a built-in duty to protect them against it, we shall not be sustained by knowing that they are doing that duty devotedly.

Similar beliefs can be honestly if not always validly entertained about universities and even about student organizations.

In such situations the first need is to examine the communication networks, internal and external, which serve the policy-making machinery of the criticized institution, and consider whether and how this can be made sufficiently responsive to the needs and wishes of those whom it affects – *all* those whom it affects, not only its critics. We may conclude that it cannot be made so responsive, either because it is locked into an exclusive relationship with one or more special interests or even because it has become independent of all the interests it is supposed to serve and serves only its own self-generated purposes, possibly only its own survival and growth.

At this point we may be tempted to generalize and assert that *all* institutions develop standards of success which are alien to the persons whom they should serve, and that *all* officials of institutions are depersonalized by the mere fact of playing an institutional role and are thereby disabled from exercising any criticism of their institution's policy. Eichmann will then indeed become the symbol of officialdom. Official roles will appear as the antithesis of authentic selfhood and we shall have to choose between withdrawal and endless war on all institutions.

The last step in this familiar sequence is always, I believe, a slide from the challenging through the defeatist into the absurd. To make and keep institutions responsive and responsible may indeed sometimes need radical and abrupt change, sometimes necessarily from without as well as from within. But the art of institutional role playing will be needed to work the new institutions no less than the old; and it is in fact the main innovative and creative agency of peaceful change.

## Changing the institutional system

The conflict between personal and institutional roles varies with the situation. I was dramatically reminded of this at the end of the first World War. On the morning after the armistice, the commander of the division with which I was serving pointed out to his battalion commanders that the object of the exercise had changed overnight. The war being won, their role was to ensure that the potential civilians under their command passed their time until their demobilization as usefully and pleasantly as might be. They should therefore form soviets, as the Russians had recently done and invite them to think out and organize their activities. (The word was new; the Russian revolution was less than a year old.) They should remember that discipline, relaxed in some directions, would be more demanding in others, notably in relations with the French civilian population on whom we were billeted and who no longer needed in their midst these huge concentrations of foreign armed men. I have always remembered with respect the sensitivity of that regular soldier to the effect which a change of situation would have on institutional and personal roles conditioned by four years of war. It worked like a charm and saved a lot of trouble. It would not have worked a week earlier.

Changes of situation seldom solve our problems in that way. They usually demand the pursuit of goals even further from the natural implications of personal roles than those of their individual constituents; and sometimes the change from without of institutional structures too rigid to change themselves. An English banker in Shanghai, when the communists first took over, observed with admiration that their soldiers no longer pillaged the civilian population and that their judges were no longer venal. That change was brought about by a revolution. I would suppose that for the most part new men, with new conceptions of their roles, were holding the old positions. But these reforming roles were more, not less institutional. As soldiers, as judges, as revolutionaries, the new men had developed self- and mutual expectations which could subdue the variety of their personal standards. An immense institutional conditioning produced that cultural change.

I had personal experience of an institutional change which, though legally effected, was revolutionary in character, in that an intervention from outside replaced one system by a different one at short notice. The Act which nationalized the British coal industry created a new public board, to be managed by nine men, and transferred to it the assets, the contracts and the employees (numbering three-quarters of a million) of more than 600 private companies. The Board was told to get the coal, organize the industry and satisfy the consumer; duties never before expressly laid on anyone. It was to cover its costs from its proceeds; but this requirement of financial stability was a condition, not a criterion of success. Success was to be measured by comparing its achievements with what informed opinion thought it might have achieved in the dimensions of its public responsibilities.

In principle there is nothing new in this. It is, for example, the way we measure the success of a City government in traffic regulation, sewage disposal and all the other diverse and conflicting fields which it is required to regulate. It makes clear but does not create the conflicts which exist – and which ought to exist – between the various goals of every organization. There is some necessary conflict between the interest of producers and consumers; between the technical task of coal getting and the equally technical task of conserving the surface; even between the interest of different classes of user of a single type of coal, produced in different places at necessarily different cost. The interest of the exercise lay in the process of generating a new role system in an organization new both in structure and in express purpose, yet consisting almost entirely of individuals trained in the previous system. The opportunity was created by legislative intervention but the changes were produced by the mutual communication of men holding new or changed positions, inventing and discovering, learning and teaching each other new roles. This was partly a conscious process, speeded by deliberate techniques which I have no time to describe.

The newest element in the system was the requirement, imposed by statute, to consult with all the employees on all matters of policy. This involved role relationships which were most unfamiliar to most of the personnel in the industry and indeed elsewhere. Its possibilities and limitations remained to be discovered. Its potentialities for good and ill were very great. Its actuality, I believe, was great and almost wholly good. It was a heartening experience of the creative possibilities of role playing in a sufficiently unstructured situation.

Now consider a third example, where the initial impulse towards institutional change came from within. In 1951, a social worker in a London teaching hospital (she was formerly a nurse but had been invalided out of that profession) reached a climax of discontent with her role. Hospitals, she felt, had become so obsessed with cure that they were neglecting care, especially the care of terminal illness. This surely was a betrayal of their founders' intentions and of the proper role of medicine, which is the management, not just the cure of illness. It also impeded rather than helped the dying to make dying a significant experience. But what could one woman do, practising her profession in an institution designed to frustrate its proper exercise?

The answer depends partly on the woman. This one gave up her job and her profession – she was then aged 33 – and qualified as a doctor. Then she got a grant for research in the control of intractable pain and made a reputation in that specialty as a physician in a cancer hospital. Then she took enough time off clinical and research work to raise half a million pounds and build a 70-bed hospital to her own design; and became its director. By that time she was 49. The hospital has been running now for four years.[4] It will soon have 100 beds, which is as large as she wishes it to be. But in cooperation with the local general practitioners, it is already treating in domiciliary care as many patients as it has in its beds. It is building a teaching unit; and last year it handled 1,400 visitors. So many different sorts of people came to see and learn.

Her main role conflicts now are between therapy, administration and teaching. But at least she has solved for herself the conflict that drove her out of hospital into a medical school 20 years ago. She has solved it also for all who work in her hospital. She has articulated the problem and one solution on such a scale that it is heard and considered at the policy making levels of our national health service and in other countries.

And in the course of all this she has done her own thing, which was concerned neither with nursing nor with doctoring as such but with the significance of dying.

That is one way of reconciling a personal with an institutional role.

There will not be many who have as much of what it takes as Dr S. Those of us who have less must do the best we can. She might have practised her ideas as a social worker outside a hospital. She might have escaped the personal conflict by getting out of the field altogether, into a dress shop or a travel agency or a market garden. She might even have stayed put and stilled the nagging mis-match signals by learning to be a passable organization woman – not a good one, because a role player who cannot both innovate and criticize without being false to his (or her) role is less than good at the job. Any of these courses might even have been the best for her – if it had been the best she could do. Most of us may have to put up with such compromises. But let us not suppose that the best we can do is necessarily the best anyone could do.

## Bearing the institutional system

What we cannot change, we have to bear, as lesser people than Dr S. have borne the conflict that she resolved. But bearing is a far from passive affair. It can make a difference.

Though Dr S.'s dilemma was one which only an exceptional woman could solve so well, it was relatively mild by the fearful standards which this century has set. The most evil and yet most strongly self-supportive system of this century was, I believe, the system which possessed Germany from 1935–45. It is there, if anywhere, that we may expect to find examples of individuals imprisoned in institutional roles that denied them humanity. So we do; and the denial affected also all of us who became engaged in trying to destroy that system. But even in the darkest corners of that dark system, there were surprising gleams of light.

The German occupation of Holland caused mass starvation. Years after, an old Dutch woman, rich, if riches had meant anything at the time, told me that by the end she was subsisting largely on boiled tulip bulbs. A fortnight before the war ended, the British high command received through Switzerland an invitation from the German chief of medical services in Holland. He was involved in the problems of nation-wide famine. When the war was lost, this would devolve abruptly on the incoming allies. Four British doctors should be sent to Holland at once – to prepare to take over. Instructions were added for getting them in. Four British doctors joined German headquarters in Holland, while the battle was still raging; and the shambles of transition later was a little less in consequence. The German who took that weirdly risky initiative partially resolved a role conflict in a way which would not have seemed feasible, if he had not shown that it was.

There were even more rigid institutional traps – for the commandants of Jewish labour and death camps. Victor Frankl, an Austrian doctor and psychiatrist who spent most of the war as a prisoner in Auschwitz and Dachau, ended it in a smaller camp to which he had volunteered to transfer to deal with an epidemic of typhus.[5] When the camp was liberated, three Hungarian jews seized the commandant and hid him in the woods. Then they sought the commander of the liberating American division and offered to give him up on one condition – the general's personal assurance that no harm should come to him. The puzzled general agreed; the commandant was given a job in organizing relief; and when time permitted, facts were found that justified the prisoners' odd response. The only medical supplies the camp had had for months had been bought by the commandant in the nearby town with his own money, through intermediaries sworn to secrecy. The rapport between him and his prisoners had developed unerringly through a tacit communication network most dangerous to both.

I have arranged these examples on a descending scale – descending towards the point at which a bad institution extinguishes the possibility of good personal initiative. There is one lower rung on this dismal and frightening ladder. What of the prisoners, enmeshed for years in a system designed to dehumanize them?

Frankl expresses his conclusions with alarming simplicity. There is, he says, only one question worth asking about the meaning of life. It is addressed not by men to life but by life to men. The question is – 'What does this situation require of you?' To this question, says Frankl, there is for every respondent always one and never more than one right answer, which is accessible to anyone willing to do the work needed to find it. Correspondingly, there are always alternative answers which for that re-spondent would be wrong. Human initiative is never exhausted.

I would not venture to express so stark a faith; but I respect Frankl's and I take some comfort from it. Life has not yet questioned me so sharply as it questioned him.

## The personal role

I wish to challenge the escapist, defeatist and irrational illusion, so sedu-lously cultivated today, that integrity, even 'personality', can only be ex-pected to flourish in those who can elude the challenge of institutional roles, whilst they depend unavoidably on our institutional world. These challenges cannot be avoided; even the role of beneficiary (or victim) is an institutional role, containing a discretion of critical importance to the institution and the individual. They should not be avoided, because they are among the more important of the tensions involved in the making of a personality.

I am not alarmed at regarding the making of a personality as the creation of a role. It offers wide discretion in the making; but as it develops it is as demanding as any other role. Is not a *persona* a person? If we say to someone – 'What you have done was not like *you*', are we not appealing to a set of expectations which he, by his past actions, has invited us to have of him and which we, in consequence, expect him to have of himself?[6]

A personality is a personal creation, controlled like any other work of art, by its own developing logic. It generates its own rules, possibilities and limitations. The supposed antithesis between the determinate and the ar-bitrary is, I believe, a fallacy, generated by carrying the concept of linear causation into human life, to frustrate at every level our understanding of the process we call self-determination. The dynamism and the direction of this process is provided by the constant need to resolve those conflicts which are endemic in all our systems of self- and mutual expectation.

Among those conflicts, we are today especially conscious of those between institutional and personal roles. Institutional roles can indeed be dehumanizing. So can anti-institutional roles, notably the role of the revo-lutionary. And so can those personal roles which evade the challenge of the institutional world by opting out of conflict with it to a greater extent than their own limitations require.

But any world which generations younger than mine may create or preserve on the other side of the dark decades ahead will include an institutional dimension and will make the same demands on us as players both of institutional and of personal roles. It will generate the same tensions and will require at least as much mutual trust as ours today. No organizational panacea will relieve any of us of the duty to sustain those tensions or to generate that trust. Institutional roles may impoverish or enrich us; and so, as they develop, may the personal roles which are so much a part of our personalities. But, equally, both are our opportunities for making ourselves and our societies. Men without role conflicts would be men without roles; and men without roles would not be men.

## References

1. Herbert A. Simon, *The Sciences of the Artificial*, Massachusetts Institute of Technology, 1969.
2. Michael Polyani, *Personal Knowledge*, Routledge & Kegan Paul, 1958; and many later writings.
3. I do not know the American game well enough to know how far this is true of it, also. Those familiar with the English versions notice with surprise that the American game admits of tactics explicitly formulated during the course of the game.
4. St. Christopher's Hospice, 51–53 Laurie Park Road, London SE26
5. The incident is recorded in Victor Frankl, *Man's Search for Meaning*, New York, Washington Press, 1962.
6. I have developed this idea further in *Freedom in a Rocking Boat*, London, Allen Lane, The Penguin Press, 1970; and New York, Basic Books, especially Ch. 6. 'Men Without Roles'.

# 19

# The changing nature of the professions*

Walking in the West of England long ago, I met a stranger who said with passion that a man's most important doings were what he built and what he begot. Since we are not more than half responsible for what we breed, he might have stated his case even more strongly. The most enduring signature that a man can inscribe on the world is a building.

## Architecture and planning

As a lawyer, I thought he overcalled his hand, remembering that the law codes of Hammurabi and Justinian had long outlived those Emperors' palaces. But now I begin to feel that there is some truth in what that stranger said. We live and work in buildings; they enable and constrain us in countless ways; and so do the buildings in which other people live and work. Visual impact, functional conveniences and inconvenience, facility and impediment of movement all depend on buildings. The whole physical milieu is increasingly a human artifact; and this artifact is a commitment ever more permanent and ever more potent for multiple good and ill.

Some of my architect friends, overwhelmed by this responsibility, seek passionately for ways to avoid it. Cannot buildings be made more expendable, expansive, portable, adaptable to the unpredictable whims of their unknown future occupants? Such humility has its obvious value both in mitigating the arrogance native to all professions and in conditioning the architects' imagination to take account of change-with-time. But it seems to me to be also an echo of that escapism which today affects all those whose roles commit them to choose for others, including the unborn. These responsibilities are indeed fearful, but they have to be faced and carried. I think it is better to bequeath to the future a world shaped by our best insight than a world shaped by accident or entropy or mindless power.

My nameless acquaintance made another point which is relevant to my theme. He asked me indignantly why William the Norman, moving the capital of England from Winchester, took it to London rather than Southampton. And he painted a glowing picture of what England would be like today if its capital had been on Southampton water.

The decision where to place a country's capital seems to be a political and administrative rather than an architectural decision. It involves considering where political power and the threats to power are placed, how

* From *American Behavioral Scientist*, Vol. 18, No 2, November/December 1974.

trade flows, the location of resources and population, the natural courses of transport and so on; and all these will in turn be affected by where the capital is placed. And yet the decision is also a decision about how to use physical space. So is the siting of a third airport or the making of a Channel tunnel. And these decisions in the field of physiosocial planning are decisions into which architects tend to be drawn, because they profess to have highly developed spatial imaginations, facility in understanding spatial relationships, and a sense of physical form and its relation to human needs.

So, to me, an outsider, the profession of architecture seems to cover an immense spectrum, with significant changes of emphasis. At one extreme I would place the stations on Montreal's new subway. Each station was given, I understand, to a different architect with instructions not merely to make it less like a public lavatory than the type we know in London, but to make it so full of character and if possible of character so related to the unseen district which it serves, that passengers would know where they were without reading the name. From that extreme example, a continuous spectrum extends through small buildings, large buildings, and complexes of buildings to new towns, and so to even wider decisions of land use like a major airport or a road system or a water grid.

My concern in this paper is to trace what the professions have in common, what makes a professional commitment, what is the relation between the professional man and his client and the public and how far, if at all, this has been changed by the transition of all the professions from dependence on a world dominated by private property to dependence on a world dominated by institutional power. I shall draw most of my illustrations from professions other than architecture, but architecture is especially important because we are at a moment of history when we cannot avoid decisions which will commit us, often irrevocably, to one rather than another of the alternatives now open in shaping our physical home. It is no less important because the decisions involved in physical planning and design reveal in a way anyone can understand the conflicts between multiple, disparate costs and benefits which are inescapable in all policy decisions. So their educative value extends far beyond the bounds of architecture and physicosocial planning.

## The characteristics of the professions

The professions in England multiplied at the end of the nineteenth and the beginning of the twentieth centuries. Some developed to meet the requirements of more widespread private wealth – for example, the solicitors who made the Forsytes' marriage settlements and the architects who designed their country houses. Others developed to serve growing governmental power – the armed services, notably the Navy and the new professionalised Civil Service, as well as the professional staffs of the new local government authorities. Yet others developed in response to the explosion of knowledge and of respect for new knowledge. These staffed the world of learning and scholarship and included the expanding profession of teaching. Others again developed in response to the expanding demands of industry, where all sorts of technical skills were growing into technological professions.

Painting, music, and literature also responded to new sources of patronage; and their exponents, if sufficiently 'successful', ranked as professionals and were supported sometimes lavishly by the Establishment. The Victorians made Dickens rich for reproaching them with the sorrows of the poor. And I have still to mention the ancient professions of medicine and the Church, each at home in a world separate from the world of property and power; doctors familiar with our biological infrastructure, priests with our spiritual stratosphere; each a power in its own domain, and each confined to its own domain by subtle constraints which were no less professional than social.

All these professional activities were ancillary either to private wealth or to institutional power. The professional needs a client to make him effective (or at least a public) and sometimes both. He may himself become a man of property or the controller of institutional power – even a prime minister or the chairman of a company – but only by a transition in which he lays down what I shall describe as his professional role – namely, a particular relationship with a client or clients, who use and pay for his service and live with or die of the result. On the other hand, the professional is no mere instrument of his client, even where that client is his employer. He is also a partner and an educator. If we look at the history of any profession, both of its internal relations and of its relations with the lay world, we find it a history of activity and innovation. This is obviously true in the fine arts, such as painting and music. It seems to me equally true of others. The law produced law reformers, even revolutionaries. Those who stormed the walls of medical prejudice were usually doctors. Theologians pioneered the innovations of the higher criticism which issued from Tübingen. Architect innovators showed the laity as well as their professional colleagues previously unconceived alternatives which were available for the asking and educated them to ask for what was offered. The professions, for all their conservative reputation, have in fact been founts of innovation.

What distinguishes the professional from the mixed class of client-employer on the one hand and from the rest of the self-supporting populace on the other? I shall distinguish six elements.

He has special skill in *understanding* some types of situations; doctors, for example, in understanding biological order and disorder, lawyers in understanding patterns of legal right and obligation. These skills are often comprehended today under the name of systems analysis.

He also has special skill in *designing* new situations within the limits set by these conditiong laws of the system. Doctors do not yet design new types of human beings, though there is some hope or fear that they may become genetic engineers. But architects have a wide scope for choice in the structures they design, within the limitations imposed by site, materials, the laws of physical stability. So do lawyers when they use the media of contractual and corporation law to devise new forms of organization. This element includes all we mean or should mean by systems design.

The professional's skills in understanding and designing give him value and authority as an adviser. But his skill in *advising* depends on more than the knowledge needed for understanding and designing, so I will distinguish this as a third element in his professional skill.

The professional also has special skills in *operating* on his media within the scope of the situations which he claims to understand, and he has standards of excellence by which he expects his work to be judged. The doctor must master a host of techniques for intervening in the biological systems which are his concern, largely by drugs and surgery, and equally for ascertaining their present state and monitoring change, whether induced by him or not. The lawyer, the architect, the planner also need to master operating techniques. In some professions, technology has so amplified these techniques for *doing* as to obscure the skills of *understanding, designing*, and *advising* which I put first. I shall call these *operating* skills technological, and I shall distinguish them from the other three which I regard as more distinctively professional.

As *understander*, as *designer*, and as *operator*, the professional needs special *knowledge*. Very often the same body of knowledge serves all three purposes (though by itself is not enough to make him a good *adviser*). Sometimes what he needs to know simply as an operator is so bulky, so difficult, and so remote from lay knowledge that both he and laymen are tempted to regard his technical knowledge as the mark of his professionalism. I think this is to be avoided. This knowledge is his fifth characteristic.

Finally the professional has special *responsibilities* to the lay client to whom he makes available this mixed body of expertise and sometimes other responsibilities, perhaps conflicting ones, to the lay public who are affected by it. He invites a more than usual degree of trust, so he has a more than usual responsibility to exercise his function rightly. The obligation is both positive and negative. Positively, it is the obligation to use his skills with due care for the client's purposes, not his own. Negatively, it includes the obligation not to use the influence flowing from his professional relation for any purpose beyond that justified by his professional position; and also the obligation not to use his professional skills for any purpose barred by his professional ethic, even if his client wants him to do so. All professions develop codes, of varying extent and cogency, to guide their members in defining the limits of professional conduct. These old-fashioned obligations and constraints are by no means outmoded and can still generate important conflicts, especially since professional men become increasingly the employees of their clients.

Understanding, designing, advising, and operating with their partly common background of theoretical knowledge and practical experience are the basic abilities of the professional. But in exercising them, he needs to be able to judge the professional requirements of his role in relation to his client, the public, and his fellow professionals. This capacity for *judgment* is his sixth professional ability.

These six functions attach in principle to all roles, but they are more important and more visible in the professions. I will examine them in more detail and in a different order.

The professional is a skilled operator and shares with the artisan standards of excellence in work done. A painter working on the external woodwork of my house once said to me, 'My instructions are to rub this down and paint it over. But it *ought by rights* to be burnt off.' I recognised also his tacit appeal to me to get his instructions as an employee altered so as not to conflict with his standards as a craftsman.

The professional regarded as a skilled doer needs theoretic knowledge far beyond that of the artisan and, insofar as he does so, he may regard this as the badge of his professionalism. I think this is mistaken, so I distinguish this as the dimension along which an artisan or a technician becomes a technologist.

The professional is also a skilled 'understander' of some type of system. The importance of this role is especially clear in medicine, because the doctor of medicine, until quite recent times, had little power of therapy, let alone design. What distinguished him were his powers of diagnosis, prognosis, and advice. He knew more than the laity about human biological systems, their disorders, the probable courses of these disorders, and the conditions most favourable to survival and recovery. And this made him invaluable as an adviser even when he had no more power to cure disease than to create a new level of biological health.

Some doctors have become so technologically minded as to question the value of diagnosis and prognosis, apart from therapy. I think they thereby debase the concept of a doctor in the minds of both doctor and layman. Consider this example. One Friday afternoon I went to my doctor and said, 'For some days I have had a small sensitive swelling under my right eyebrow. A similar swelling appeared this morning in my neck. I feel perfectly well and trouble you only because I am due to fly to Philadelphia tomorrow for a week's hard work and this small symptom is new to me.' My doctor replied, 'I would not go to Philadelphia tomorrow if I were you. You will have shingles by Monday. You will not be fit for work next week. You will embarrass and possibly infect your hosts. And by the end of it you will be such a visible mess that no airline will want to fly you home.' His medication, using discoveries made within a decade, shortened the length of my illness and eased its passage, and this was welcome, but nothing like so welcome or so important as his diagnosis, his prognosis, and his advice.

You will notice that my doctor's competence as an adviser depended on something more than his diagnostic skill. Viewing me first as a biological system, he recognised the swellings as inflamed nerve endings served by a single nerve trunk and from these and other indices formed a view of what was disturbing the biological system. Then returning to the human level, he advised me what effect this was likely to have on the quite different system of activities which included my commitments in America. His value to me consisted in his ability to link his biological understanding to the situation which I was trying to order and thus to become also an effective adviser.

There are analogies in other professions. The lawyer is both an analyst and an architect of structures of legal rights and obligation. But he needs also to understand the state of the social system on which he is working and the temporal and other limits of its capacity for change, if he is to be a useful adviser. So, to anticipate a later example, did the Buchanan Committee, exploring those unstable urban systems which produce, among other things, traffic jams.

All the professions in some degree seem to me to demand a developed capacity to discover, create, recognise, and appreciate form, to distinguish order from disorder, to impose order on disorder, usually in more than one level. And the professional needs to distinguish the levels in which he is expert from those which mainly concern the client. The doctor must be human enough to help his patient use his biological conclusions. This requires of him some professional knowledge of psychological order and a professional expertise in understanding the individual worlds which his diverse patients inhabit. The same is true of all professions.

Unlike the doctor, most professionals also have professional scope as designers. The mediaeval master builder was expected to understand, intuitively if not explicitly, the statics and dynamics of stone-built structures, systems of self-supporting physical stresses subject to laws as rigorous as those of biology. But he was free, as the doctor is not, to create a variety of form within those limitations. Stability was only a condition, not a criterion of his success. His cathedral was also to be an aesthetically satisfying form, a spiritually appropriate symbol, and an enclosure functionally suitable for crowds engaged in the manifold activities of Christian worship. His success was to be measured in more than one dimension. Five centuries later, the designer of the 'Chapel' at the Massachusetts Institute of Technology had a similar task, symbolically far more subtle, since he had to design a building devoid of all specific religious symbolism yet intensely apt for worship or meditation by people of any religion or none. And for me his technical inventiveness and his symbolic sensitivity blend in a sense of multiple yet unified success.

These illustrations may help to explain why I reserve the word 'technological' for advanced skills in *operating*, whether in ascertaining the state of some existing system (from blood analysis to opinion polls) or in changing the state of a system (from damming a river to stopping a riot) or building a new system (from casting a turbine casing to drafting a nationalisation statute). I keep the word 'professional' for advanced skills in *understanding* existing systems and *designing* new systems and new states to which existing systems might be moved, and for making the two available to a client by the process I call *advising*. In practice, understanding and designing are inextricably mixed, but I find the distinction useful because the functions of understanding the old and designing the new combine in ways so varied as to cover an enormous spectrum. At one extreme, doctors have infinite scope for understanding but virtually none for designing biological systems. At the other extreme, painters appear to start with an empty canvas (though what appears will in fact be part of an ongoing effort with its own constraints). But architects, like lawyers and administrative planners, may be required to range over the whole gamut, from reconditioning a neighbourhood to creating a city in green fields. However dominant the existing system, there is room for innovation. However clear the field, there is somewhere a constraining existing system with which the new must be related. One end of the spectrum is dominated by what doctors call diagnosis and prognosis and what in the new sciences of planning, management and government are called analysis and forecasting. The other end is dominated by innovative design. But the function is integral, and it deserves a separate name, even if you do not accept my appropriation to it of the word professional, whenever it is exercised in the advisory context inherent in the relation of professional and client.

The distinction between technological and professional functions is important for two very different reasons. Some so-called professionals have so much scope for technology and so little for professional judgment that they are hard to distinguish from super-artisans, while others, with which I am specially concerned, have developed a field of professional judgment so wide that it is hard to distinguish them from those they advise. The planner and the policy maker are the classic example of this extreme.

## Professionals and laymen

The relation of the professional to his client and to the public is clearly complex and important in defining the professional role. So is his relation with other members of his profession.

Because their professional and their technological skills are so refined, professionals of all kinds expect their competence to be judged by their fellow professionals. They sometimes treat the judgment of the laymen who pay for their services with what seems undue disdain. But these laymen, though they may be galled by such treatment, accept its basic validity to some extent, in that they leave it largely to each profession to train its new aspirants, to certify their qualifications and, where necessary, to pass judgment on their performance and behaviour and even on their fitness to retain their professional status.

This last is important because increasing areas of activity are marked out as the preserves of particular professions. No one lacking the professional qualification may practice the activity. They are closed shops, and closed shops are suspect to all outside the shop. Though it is natural for practitioners of any activity to make it a closed shop if they can, society would not accord the claim so readily to professions if it felt capable of judging professional performance by lay standards.

We give everyone a voice in choosing and dismissing our highest political leaders. But only practising dentists can decide whether an aspirant to their profession is fit to stop a tooth. This is not so odd as it seems. We choose our dentists, no less than our prime ministers – indeed, we have a far wider, more direct and personal choice. But we chose them from a field limited by professional certification, a position not yet reached in government or even management. The layman's freedom of choice, however, is valuable only insofar as he can trust his own standards of judgment. In medicine he can at least assume that he and his doctor have the same standard of success. But most laymen are as reluctant to defer to an architect on the acceptable form of a building as they are to defer to a teacher on the acceptable content of a syllabus. Nuffield College, Oxford, as it exists today is remote indeed from its original plans. These were so far from the traditional Cotswold-domestic style of older colleges that Lord Nuffield was explosively unwilling that they should perpetuate his memory. I shared his view, and, even if I had not, I would have accorded his right, as a citizen of Oxford, to a view on what accorded with its character, no less than his right as a donor to a view on what he would wish to bear his name. Yet if an architect I respected had assured me that the rejection of that steel-framed red rectangle wasted a unique opportunity to strike a new, uplifting chord in an old grey city, I would have allowed that he might well be right.

In this partnership of laymen and professional, the layman is not merely a constraint. I do not suppose that William Owen or the Cadburys spent much time at the drawing board. Yet we think of New Harmony and Bournville as expressions of them, rather than their architects. I do not doubt that the Emperor Akhbar himself, not his architect, gave central meaning to the mile-square architectural extravagance of his burial place by so arranging the tomb itself that its upper surface – unsculpted and uninscribed – is precisely on the level of the dust.

The professional uses his skill for the purposes and at the expense of another. This requires of him the capacity to see the situation through his client's eyes as well as his own. He may enlarge or even radically change what he thus sees, by the advice he gives, just as his own first views may be changed by fuller understanding of his client's concepts, purposes, and constraints. But the relation is a partnership which may breed increasing mutual confidence, understanding, and receptivity, or alternatively, may breed too much conflict for either party to bear. I will explore a little further the skills required of the professional in his advisory role and the avenues of escape open to him if conflict becomes unbearable.

The skills are the skills of human understanding and empathy, whether the professional be a nurse or a planner. And they are enjoined and controlled by the two complementary ethics which I have already mentioned. One is the professional's obligation to serve the client's purposes, not his own, so far as he properly can. The other is the obligation not to do so where professional ethic resists.

The present Nuffield College was designed by the same architect whose original design was rejected. A style which he would not have chosen was imposed on him. But it was a style which he might legitimately have chosen; and within that style he had the usual professional freedom. He might have refused the second commission, simply because he did not wish his name as architect to be associated with such a selection, just as his client did not wish the earlier design to perpuate the client's memory. What the architect could not do was to retreat into a purely technological stance, to 'do what he was told' without accepting any responsibility for the result.

Professional life is much easier when the professional can say, 'This is within the field of my expertise; you must leave it to me. That lies outside my field; it is no responsibility of mine.' But the extent to which he can do so is much more limited than at first appears; and it is more limited in some professions than in others. It is least limited where the professional's role is purely technological and where his professional standards of success are most clearly separable from those applied by the client to the enterprise as a whole. Along this spectrum we might place the engineer, the doctor, the teacher, and, at its extreme, the planner, still distinguished from his client, the policy maker, by the fact that the policy maker must carry the responsibility for decision, but nonetheless more identified than any other professional with the whole range of his client's criteria.

Because of this delicate relationship, the professions attach importance to their independent status. This is most simply expressed by the right of the independent practitioner in most of them simply to withdraw or decline to act.

Consider this bizarre and extreme example. A press lord rang his solicitors and called not for the partner who dealt with his newspapers' affairs but for the partner's clerk, who was equally familiar with them – a man who was also a qualified solicitor but an employee of the law firm, lacking the authority of a partner. Calling this man to his office, the great executive proposed a startling project and asked, 'Would that be legal?' The clerk reflected and replied gently, 'I don't think, sir, that we should advise you to do that.' The great man showed – or feigned – irritation, brought all his coercive power to bear, and said, 'I'm not asking your advice whether to do it. I'm asking you as a lawyer whether it would be legal.' The clerk replied with the greatest deference, 'I don't think sir, that we should advise you to do it. So the question whether it would be legal does not arise.'

The great man closed the interview abruptly, rang the partner, told him the story with enormous gusto and amusement, and concluded, 'Your Mr A. is a winner.'

Professional rectitude does not always pay off so handsomely. But the story is an extreme example of the independence of the professional, dependent on the good will of no single client, however large, and setting his own definition of the way in which his skills should be used. Perhaps such firms have some reason to call those who consult them not patrons but clients.

The professional has also some responsibility to 'the public'. Where he depends wholly on a 'public' as writers largely do, that public can at least ignore him. But increasingly the client chooses a public which must enjoy or endure the results. I was recently on a new university campus. The friend who took me there warned me, 'The style of this campus is described as Aztec-Fascist.' I had not realised that concrete could be so threatening. Windows which could not be opened or even broken enclosed a climate regulated solely by 'them'. Neon lights throughout the night banished all trace of darkness and hid the stars. External doors opened one way only, usually outward – perhaps in the interests of defence. Some cost-benefit analysis must have persuaded the client that these features were good. The imprisoned inmates would have been as hard to persuade as I. But they had not been consulted; they could not have been consulted, because they could not exist until the place had been built. Participation is a fine principle, but how often those with most claim to participate are necessarily not available – usually because they are not yet born.

## Recent changes in the professions

Five great changes have transformed the professional world in England and, I expect, elsewhere in the past seventy years. First, in many professions, the members are now wholly or mainly functionaries, whole-time officials in governmental or business organizations. This reflects the huge enlargement of these sectors, by comparison with the sector of private property.

Second, most professionals are also technologists. Their skills include the mastery of elaborate techniques. This also was always partly true, but the change in degree has transformed many professions. The law is perhaps unique in having almost escaped this impact. In medicine by contrast, the techniques of monitoring the state of the patient's biological system and the techniques of intervening in it (largely drugs and surgery) have expanded so hugely as to breed a score of specialties – and incidentally, in my view, to degrade the concept of medical care, as distinct from cure.

Third, the general level of education has risen so much as to mute the distinction which once gave prestige to the 'learned' professions as such. Even in medicine, where the professionals' knowledge still exceeds the general cultural standard more than in most other professions, the layman's basic knowledge of biology and psychology is generally sufficient to make him expect, demand, and understand explanation as well as advice, and claim a role as participant, rather than merely as patient in his own treatment.

Fourth, the area of professionalism has hugely widened, in at least four directions. The applied physical sciences, from electronics to biochemistry, have produced one crop. The applied social sciences have produced another, from probation officers to personnel managers. The information sciences have produced a third, from computer programming to system designing. The fourth, and the one I want to pursue (which draws freely on the other three), is the professionalisation of business management (and to a lesser extent of government) and the associated professionalisation of the planning function.

Finally, the professionalisation of our activities especially in the field of management and government, have produced what I can only call the multiprofessional profession. In all professions until recently, a single corpus of knowledge and qualification has been dominant. Although the health service, for example, employs many professions beside doctors, it would still be heresy to suggest that it is not and should not be dominated by doctors. In the same way and for the same reason, mining is still largely dominated by the mining engineer, although mechanical and electrical engineering play an even greater part in it. But in the professionalised activity of what I have distinguished as the fourth field, it becomes increasingly difficult to define a single professional qualification which should always distinguish the leader of the professional team. This, I shall suggest, presents its most acute but not insoluble problem in the multiprofession of planning.

The professions have been profoundly affected by these changes. Most of them have been fragmented, each fragment dependent on a field of expertise more specialised and smaller, though often more esoteric than before. The word specialised has developed a derogatory flavor, implying a lack of interest or competence in fields of general experience. This, coupled with the rising level of general education, has reduced such claim as the professional formerly had to authority derived simply from higher education. Yet, in sharp contrast to this trend, the professions dealing with management and government and the ancillary function of planning have a field of reference wider than has ever before been associated with professional activity.

When applied to management and government, this extension has two further linked effects of great importance. It extends the concept of professional competence to roles which are not advisory but central in a decision-making process. It thus calls in question, perhaps usefully, what has been an accepted distinction between two methods of control, especially in the public sector.

In Britain, it was customary until recent times to distinguish sharply between democratically responsible policy makers and their appointed administrative staff. It is recognised today as untrue that the former alone make policy while the latter merely give effect to it. Even the idea that it was ever true is particularly British and relatively recent. But though misleading as a description of what actually happens, it is useful as a means of combining continuity of administration with the discontinuity of democratic politics. If administrators are to function as the competent and trustworthy servants of successive political governments, they need to be protected from much, if not all, of the responsibility for the actual policies which they administer, however much they may have helped to devise them. The British system protects them more than most; it may be held that it protects them too much. But the alternatives all have costs. I do not propose to argue these here, but only to point out that as policy makers become more professional, the skills expected of them come to resemble ever more closely the skills expected of their closest professional advisers. These are their senior administrators (whose main function is precisely analysis, synthesis, and advice) and still more those who bear explicit responsibility as planners.

## Management, government and planning

The first school of business management in England was started after World War II, despite much doubt about the extent to which management could have become a profession. Business schools have proliferated. But despite the fact that some of them – fewer I think in Britain than abroad – claim to be concerned with the public as well as the private sector, government has moved toward professionalisation much more slowly. There are good (as well as bad) reasons why management should have been a slow and government an even slower starter along this road.

What concerns me is that the main class of today's clients are themselves becoming 'professionalised'. It is timely to ask whether this will affect the traditional relationship of professional adviser and lay client. My confident answer is that in itself it will make no difference in principle and should be a considerable help in practice. The client will understand and use his adviser better if he is himself professionalised, but their relation will remain the same because of the inherent difference in their roles. This becomes clear if we analyse the profession which comes nearest of all to the comprehensive function of the policy maker, the newly emergent profession of planning.

The principles of planning were lucidly explicated in the Buchanan Report. This working party was set up in 1961 by a Minister of Transport to study problems of vehicular congestion in towns. But its report begins by pointing out that urban vehicular congestion is not a problem but a symptom of the wider problem that towns today generate more vehicular activity than their present layout can contain. The smallest selection of facts relevant to this problem and hence to its symptoms is the physical shape of the town, including its roads, on the one hand, and its traffic-generating activities, on the other. Both can be modified, at varying costs. The town can be redesigned in three dimensions – in four dimensions, if we include, as we should, the possibility of restricting particular uses to particular times. The activities also can be modified by excluding or finding new ways to meet those that make the heaviest demands – for example, by new forms of commuter transport. In different ways and at different prices, the symptom can be in varying degrees abated.

But anything done to abate vehicular traffic congestion will affect other valued aspects of urban life – access on foot, safety, parking, amenity, even an aesthetic negative value which the committee called visual squalor. These cannot be ignored, just because the symptom which evoked the working party was the traffic jam. There is a minimum number of interrelated values in terms of which we must assess the costs and benefits of any solution, just as there is a minimum number of factual aspects so interrelated that none can be ignored in assessing the situation.

The Buchanan Report is illustrated by three alternative plans for a particular area, but it is not itself a plan for an area. It is an admirable exposition of the planning function and shows precisely where that process falls short of policy making. It illustrates the planner's analytic function, the exercise of professional understanding. Whatever threat or aspiration first led him to action, his definition of 'the situation', though as simple as it can logically be, will be more complex than was at first perceived; and his definition of 'the issue' will include costs and benefits more varied than seemed at first to be involved. The result may be embarrassing; the Buchanan Report, for example, showed that a problem examined because of a 'transport' symptom was far wider than the authority of a minister of transport.

It also illustrates his synthesising function, his professional skill both as designer and as adviser. The report bombards the minds of potential clients, mostly local authorities, and of the public with new ways of combining what seem incompatible benefits; not only new professional ways of doing, like those now familiar techniques which prevent access roads from becoming thoroughfares, but new professional ways of seeing familiar situations. Why still accept the multipurpose street of mediaeval times, though we learned long since to subdivide the mediaeval great hall? Why leave roof space unoccupied, while hunt for parking space at and below ground level? Such suggestions are aimed at enlarging the imaginations of the laity rather than the planners and, thus, relieving one of planning's main constraints. The report is an educational document and is clearly designed to be so. I think it should be used as a textbook in secondary schools.

In the making of an actual plan, the analytic, the synthetic, and the educative functions proceed together, and each influences the other. A novel way to overcome one constraint makes relevant new costs and benefits and may change both the situation and the issue.

In this dialectic process, the policy maker and the planner are indissolubly linked. The policy maker cannot make his often agonising choice between alternative plans until he knows what mixes of value he can realise with the resources available. The planner cannot engage in his effort to synthesise what seem incompatible values without at least distinguishing those that matter most to his client. And even these may change in relative value as the search proceeds.

But however far-reaching the analysis and however ingenious the alternative syntheses, the planning process will not provide one best answer. The Buchanan Committee ventured to guess at those values (other than free-moving traffic) which no government could afford to ignore. It offered an ingenious way to measure how much of each would be realised by alternative plans. But its procedures could not reduce disparate costs and benefits to a single measure, could not show, for example, that so much more safety was worth so much less convenience. This was for the policy maker to decide.

This ultimate responsibility for decision is what distinguishes the client. And in his decision is implicit his judgment - not the planner's - of what matters most.

Nonetheless, I do not think that a planner can engage in this arduous exercise without some deep commitment of his own to the values which seem to him to matter most. It is not surprising, then, that most memorable planners have themselves supplied the vision which their clients come to adopt. A value-free planner is even more of a contradiction in terms than a value-free administrator. The possibility of a clash is always latent. So it is not surprising that most of the planners who have made history have been men of some independence of position as well as of mind. William Beveridge was an academic, who produced his plan during one year as unpaid, part-time chairman of what was supposed to be a minor inter-departmental committee. Professor Buchanan was not dependent on the whole-time whole-life career of a civil servant. The recent blueprint for Britain's future water supply was produced by a Water Resources Board deliberately created as an independent, nonexecutive advisory body.

And where shall we place Ebenezer Howard, a man who never held public office and who had no private wealth, but whose profession as a shorthand writer provided him throughout his life with an independence modest but sufficient to enable him to create two new towns, influence countless others, and start a world movement which still has power today?

## Scenarios of threat and promise

We have, nonetheless, to face the fact that more than ever before professionals are functionaries in the employment of institutional clients and that many of them have no other potential employer on comparable terms. This fact involves three very different threats, each of which has been dramatised by real events in recent history, in the West, if not in Britain.

The first threatening scenario depicts the professional doing a good job in the service of a bad policy which he cannot change and may not fully know but in which his activities gradually involve him. At what point does his professional ethic rebel? An uneasy path leads from atomic scientists of Los Alamos and biologists at Porton - whither - whither? Far down the road stands the unheroic but not untragic figure of Eichmann, the organi-sation man.

The second scenario is sequel to the first. The professional functionary, caught in a dilemma from which it is too late to withdraw, leaks to the press the secrets he has sworn to keep, rather than becoming a party to the hated policy. The theme is as old as Sophocles' *Antigone* and as recent as the Ellsberg trial.

The third scenario is the opposite of the other two. Professional functionaries, screened by the anonymity of service, manipulate the elected puppets whom the people vainly hold responsible. In Britain, this, rather than the others is, I think, the most common anxiety; and the professional villain par excellence is the planner, indifferent alike to sociology, common sense, and the views of the man on the spot, on whom he imposes his own professional standards as the criteria of successful planning.

All three threats are real. All have been illustrated by real events in recent years. They raise real issues, which all professions need to debate and may have to answer. These are not confined to the sector of defence. I do not want to belittle them. But what most often happens, in my experience, is the reverse of all three scenarios. The professional is fruitfully disciplined by having to cooperate with other professionals in work of public importance; and the public service also is fruitfully disciplined and made more sensitive by depending on multiprofessional teams, each acknowledging the ethic of a profession as well as an employment.

The life of a professional functionary is not, in my experience so comfortable as that of the self-employed professional – but does anyone deserve the elysium of being self-employed for a whole lifetime? Can anyone survive such pampering? Think what feedback is denied to one so placed that he needs not to talk to anyone who is not willing to pay for the privilege!

Some things can best be done from outside an institution. I wish the professions to preserve their professional identities. But on the whole I do not regret the functionalising of professions, still less the professionalising of functions. The examples that come to my mind are not cautionary tales but comforting ones; comforting at least to the common man, the governed, the planned-for – and in nearly every context we are all common men, governed, planned for, our greatest responsibility being to know when to give or withhold trust.

I once heard a treasury official explain to his department over a long-distance telephone why the plan he advocated was far better than any other, was indeed the only plan which could realise an acceptable mix of the things he had been sent to attain. The answer was, 'But that's politically impossible.' He tried again, his case was unanswerable, but the answer was the same, 'Sorry, old man, I'm sure you're right but it's just not on.' He dropped his plan and spent weeks patiently salvaging the least bad alternative from the resultant mess. It was the first time I realised that a political fact may be as obdurate as a physical or a financial fact. I admired his patience and I did not criticise his acquiescence in limitations defined in effect by the client – the minister who would be responsible for what the official arranged. Although there are situations which the professional and even the technologist should not accept, I did not question the judgment that this was not one of them.

I recall an official in the Office of the Custodian of Enemy Property just after the war. A German Jewish banker had come to England before the war, bestowed his property in an English company, and gone to live in

France, where he soon found himself under the Vichy Government and German occupation. He concealed his affairs from both by a smokescreen so effective that it was hard to dissipate after the war; but his right to have his property returned depended on his persuading the Custodian to disbelieve much of what he had thus said and done. A compromise agreement was suggested; but first the official interviewed the banker. He then said to me, 'Your client has told us all a lot of lies and made us all a lot of trouble; but [with suppressed passion and a blow on his desk] this Act isn't to catch liars. It's to catch enemies. The fact that the Custodian holds all his property gives my department no bargaining power, now I am satisfied that your client is entitled to have it back. I'll make an order releasing it this afternoon.'

My client was impressed; the law was not so professionally administered in Vichy France or in Nazi Germany. I too was impressed, remembering a rather different attitude to the power of possession in another case in the same office. Professionals, have, of course, no monopoly on honesty, but responsibility becomes more important when it monitors great power not easily controlled from without. I sensed from the gesture and the tone of that official's voice that he was fighting some battle unknown to me in the name of an ethic which his professional commitment had raised to an unusual power.

One further example claims a place among many which clamour to be included.

Round a huge table in the Reichsbank in Berlin sit 31 bankers representing the banks of 14 countries, and opposite them 3 German bankers. The date is 1935. They are renegotiating an agreement by which the volume of bank credits available to finance international trade in and through Germany was maintained through the years of the depression. It had been suggested that some of these might be used for another purpose which would in effect allow them to be reduced. The German delegation has just expressed its agreement but coupled it with a plan for giving effect to the proposal – a plan which seemed to every creditor banker so plainly unworkable that not one of them doubted it had been devised to frustrate the scheme. The atmosphere of the meeting changed suddenly to intense hostility and mistrust.

The Germans observed that it was not their plan but the Reichbank's. It was for the Reichbank to defend it. The creditors should express their views to Dr Fuchs.

And so they did, abrasively, to the small tired man who arrived, after an icy, silent pause, to hear what the creditors thought of his plan.

The meeting then adjourned for lunch. When it resumed, Dr Fuchs looked smaller than ever. Looking round the hostile faces, he said 'Gentlemen, you do not like my plan. Many of my colleagues do not like my plan either. They all think I am wrong. So perhaps I am wrong.

But I have thought all over again. And I still think I am right.

So I hope you will now accept my plan – because I am responsible for the mark, and you are not.'

The Chairman looked round the circle of faces, from each of which every trace of anger and suspicion had passed away.

'Well, gentlemen, you have heard Dr Fuchs. After all it's his responsibility. If that's the way he wants to work it.'

There was no discussion. Dr Fuchs got up wearily. 'Thank you gentlemen.' He walked out – floated out, rather, on a wave of confidence and sympathy from 31 fellow professionals, each thanking God he had not got Dr Fuchs' job to go back to.

Their change of heart was dramatic, but it was perfectly rational. They had seen enough to satisfy themselves that the decision which had so affronted them was a professional one. And they had been reminded that it had been taken against a background of enormous risk and uncertainty. If it was unduly cautious and restrictive, it was so by a professional judgment which they themselves might have made if they had been Dr Fuchs. It may have been overcautious and overcomplicated, but it was meant to work and it worked.

## Professional commitment

The only discernible common feature in the examples I have quoted and a host of others which I might have quoted is commitment to a role which is in substance professional in the sense which I have attached to that word. Every role, however high or humble, involves discretion as well as duties and a commitment to exercise the discretion, as well as to do the duties, in the way which the holder thinks most appropriate to one in that position. We can distinguish professional roles only generally by excepting them on the one hand from roles which are substantially instrumental, however much technology they may involve; and on the other hand from roles which carry total responsibility for the decisions which the role player helps to make. This distinction involves treating roles as complex; even the most obvious professional is not playing a professional role, according to this definition, in all he does. The architect or lawyer, if self-employed, is also an employer of others. In any case, he may often act as a manager, an operator and in other capacities common to nonprofessional roles. The most characteristic feature that I can attribute to him is the relative importance of his function in contributing his special skills in understanding and designing to the making of policy in a field wider than his own. This involves a type of judgment which can be called professional because it can be trusted neither to shirk proper responsibilities nor to arrogate improper ones.

It is manifest enough when it is absent. Every profession has its own set of *déformations professionelles*. The professional thus limited sees situations *only* as defined by his professional field, and defines success *only* by the criteria of his field. Every profession breeds sick jokes like 'The operation was successful but the patient died.' They emphasise only the importance and the difficulty of judging what is the full proper professional contribution to the wider context in which it is sought and contributing neither more nor less than that.

This is an ethical obligation as well as an intellectual challenge. It is far more extensive and subtle than what nonprofessionals understand by a professional ethic, but it is clear enough to all who have felt it. It was manifested by the bankers around the conference table no less than by Dr Fuchs – perhaps even more, since his professional responsibility was clear and cogent enough. (Only twelve years before, in a few frightening weeks, the German currency had eerily disappeared, leaving notes, coins and money symbols with no meaning – until some of them regained a different meaning in terms of a new currency based not on gold but on rye.) These other bankers were engaged in a political enterprise remote from the experience of any of them, on which the future of Western and world economies depended no less than of their own banks and themselves. Their responses distinguished clearly enough the professionals (by this definition) from those who were only technologists.

What then of professional managers or even governors? These executives surely need many new professionalised skills which few sufficiently possess. Equally surely in my view – influential voices would dissent – they will not reduce their task to a technology in which 'correct' analysis of the situation will produce one best answer. But they are in dialogue with their advisers no less than their advisers with them. Although the apportionment of responsibility is in my view more important than is generally allowed, it does not affect the essentially dialectic character of the policy-making process. Central to this dialogue, as I believe, is this essential element which I have described as professional judgment. So long as it remains central to the concept of a profession, the spread of professionalism can be warmly welcomed. But if the opposite tendency prevails, if professionals and clients alike become obsessed and limited by their technological functions, then the outlook will be as bleak for public polity as it will be for the professions.

# LEVEL IV:
# THE INDIVIDUAL

# Introduction

Whilst it is clear that a hierarchical framework from planetary through societal and organizational levels to the individual can provide one grouping of articles such as these, there will necessarily be interactions and cross-references. In the case of Sir Geoffrey Vickers, papers about the individual interact with the other three levels even more because it is always *human* systems with which he is concerned. The role of the individual and his/her relationship with the world, society, or organization, are constant themes in his work, and in our previous three sections. In this last selection of articles, therefore, we have concentrated on his contributions to our understanding of human behaviour and thought processes at a more technical level.

Despite the foregoing, it is typical of Vickers that in addressing the professional psychologists and psychiatrists he not only seeks to present fresh ideas and suggest areas for their future work but he also draws upon parallels in organizational life. Thus in *The Concept of Stress in Relation to the Disorganization of Human Behavior*, he commends the work of an early exponent of cybernetics, Ross Ashby, and others, picks up their idea of 'matching with a pattern' and applies it. 'It seems clear that the raw material of experience is not the whole of the "blooming buzzing confusion" which beats on us but a selection of the regularities which we can detect; and that these in turn provide the categories for the classification of future experience. Conditioning – and perhaps more beside – depends on recognizing regular relations between recurrent events in the categories thus distinguished. Judgments of value ... are linked to situations recognized by their correspondence to some pattern, however complex.' Vickers then goes on to point out the importance of expectation and pursues at length the analogy between the individual thought processes and the decision making processes in the field of business and administration.

In *The Psychology of Policy Making and Social Change* Vickers spends some time explaining to a similar audience his ideas of *appreciative settings*, *fields*, and *systems* and pointing out the shortcomings of contemporary psychology before detailing ways in which contributions by psychologists would be valuable. Many of the concepts in this article will be familiar to those who have read the last two sections of this book, but in this article Vickers throws considerable more light on his thinking about the appreciative process. Here he defines an appreciative system as a set of readinesses to distinguish some aspects of a situation rather than others, and goes on to make pleas for it to be 'taken seriously' as a system; neither a pale reflection nor a pathological distortion of the 'real world out there', but a semi-autonomous system in its own right. It is here also that he points out that 'any appreciative system has an upper limit to its possible rate of change, which cannot be passed without disaster'.

In passing, Vickers states that there is a general tendency 'to underestimate the extent to which we live in and are confined to a communicated and communicable world'. In *Levels of Human Communication* he explores human verbal communication more fully in its own right as well as its relationship to his ideas on expectation and appreciation. 'The natural world, the human world, and the personal world are built of expectations formed, nourished and monitored largely by verbal communication. Communication has built and constantly renews the appreciative system which is both its product and its interpreter.' Interestingly, the appreciative system he talks about here is the 'state of affairs in our heads which is the fruit of past communication and which is both the target and the interpreter of present communication. . . . (It) accounts for nearly everything which we and others do – and, more important, are. . . . Nearly all our communication is directed to changing its state in others or in ourselves.'

On much the same lines, Vickers says, in *Rationality and Intuition*, that the appreciative world 'is structured by readinesses to conceive things and relations in particular ways, readinesses which are developed in our brains by experience, including experience received through human communication.' However, appreciative systems and a detailed explanation of Vickers' ideas of a tacit norm are secondary to the major argument that 'the human mind has available to it at least two different modes of knowing and that it uses both in appropriate and inappropriate combinations in its endless efforts to understand the world in which it finds itself, including its fellow human beings and itself. One of these modes is more dependent on analysis, logical reasoning, calculations, and explicit description. The other is more dependent on synthesis and the recognition of pattern, context and the multiple possible relations of figure and ground.' The article is one of the few in which Vickers publicly hints at the dangers of 'scientific thinking' and its potential for damage. In private he was much more explicit. He wrote to Guy Adams (10 April 1980):

> The culture of the natural sciences continues to erode and debunk all human insights, especially ethical ones which lie at the heart of culture. Social Darwinism rides higher than it did a hundred years ago, with all its initial fallacies uncorrected . . . I hate to talk with natural scientists now, especially biologists. They remind me of minds trapped in the culture of the mediaeval church, determined to deny or ignore anything however obvious which might question their orthodoxy as scientists – far more important to them than their humanity as men.

The final article in this section completes the circle for the section and in some ways for the book. For in *Will and Free Will* Vickers is again talking about the detailed workings of the human brain including the relationship between neuro-physiology and psychology. The ability to exercise free will is at the heart of much of Vickers' analysis in the Level I articles in this collection. Moreover, this article, like the very first (*A Classification of Systems*), is more conventionally academic in its development of an argument and pursuit of a thesis.

# 20

## The concept of stress in relation to the disorganization of human behavior*

It seems clear that at present the phenomena which the psychiatrist studies are more readily comparable with those which concern the student of animal behavior than those which concern the physiologist. The animal experimenter, like the psychiatrist, starts from an observed correlation between a 'situation' and a 'disorganization of behavior'. The disorganization may take many forms. The unbearably frustrated man may break down into rage or tears or lethargy; he may begin to act at random or he may begin some apparently irrelevant behavior or he may cease to act at all. And so, within its compass, may the unbearably frustrated rat. Differences in the form of breakdown are interesting as pointers to differences in temperament but they are irrelevant as indices of disorganization.

How then are we to recognize this characteristic disorganization? Shall we take as our index the fact that the behavior under review has become 'non-adaptive' – inept to the situation which has evoked it? The judgment may be only superficially true. Neurosis may be protective in man, perhaps also in other animals. In any case, is it really 'adaptive' for the man in the bewitched cockpit or the rat in the bewitched maze to go on for ever ringing the changes on a repertory of responses which have clearly become irrelevant? I recall the comment of a psychiatrist when a colleague had described some particularly devilish design of animal frustration. He asked – 'What would be a non-neurotic response to a situation like that?' and I do not recall that he received any convincing reply.

It would seem that what appears as disorganization may in fact be defensive reorganization. Some kinds of psychological stress response appear to have a protective value. Yet this protection is bought at a cost. Field Marshal Lord Wavell, in some famous lectures in the last war, pointed out that stupidity in generals should never excite surprise, since they are chosen from the exceedingly small class of human beings who are tough enough to be generals at all. Their essential qualification is that they should continue to function, even if not very well, in conditions of stress which would cause less stable organisms to break down. His point seems equally well made whether by 'breakdown' he meant 'disorganization' or 'protective reorganization'.

---

* From *General Systems*, IV 1959. Originally in *Stress and Psychiatric Disorder*, J. M. Tanner (ed) 1959.

I remain in doubt about the criteria for determining disorganization. They seem to imply the passing of some threshold beyond which external relations can no longer be handled at the previous level, either because internal coherence has been lost or because it has only been preserved at the price of some withdrawal. For the purposes of this discussion, however, it is sufficient to raise the question of their definition and significance.

If pressed next to define the situations which provoke such disorganization, both the psychiatrist and the student of animal behavior would be driven to some tentative formulations. The animal experimentalists in particular could not refuse to formulate the assumptions which govern the design of their experiments. Pavlov,[1] I understand, used four main types: one, a progressive increase in the intensity of the signal to which the animal was conditioned; a second, a progressive increase in the delay between the giving of the signal and the arrival of the satisfaction to which it was attached; a third, confusion, by the introduction of anomalies in the signals themselves; and a fourth, interference with the animal's physical condition. Leaving the fourth aside for the moment, it seems useful to subdivide the third, in the light of other experimental work, into at least three subclasses – doubt, where the signals are ambiguous; conflict, where they are mutually inconsistent; and frustration, where response to a clear signal does not produce its accustomed result. Professor Liddell's[2] paper names several other situations, including loneliness, monotony and self-imposed restraint, which may need categories of their own.

It is interesting that the factors common to these animal experiments can be most readily described by words drawn from the subjective vocabulary of humankind – apprehension, suspense, doubt, conflict, frustration. Psychiatrists, I think, would agree that these categories also cover the situations which they recognize as provocative of disorganization in man. This suggests that these states, which we know by introspection, reflect conditions of neural excitement which are not confined to conscious states or to nervous systems so complex as our own.

Furthermore, many of these states involve the concept of expectation, whether it be the hateful expectation which can be neither accepted nor escaped, the pleasurable expectation which is intolerably deferred, the conflict of expectation which evokes conflicting responses or the sheer confusion of expectation which destroys the basis for action. The frequent presence in experimental situations of something which we can only describe in terms of expectation suggests that this also is something we need to be able to describe in terms of neural activity not necessarily related to conscious human states.

At this point the psychiatrist and the student of animal behavior may legitimately seek the help of the physiologist. The organism is not functioning as it was. What is this change in its manner of functioning? How and why has the change occurred? Proper questions, surely, to put to a specialist in organic function.

Until recently the physiologist would have had little to say. He could supply an impressive model of the internal relations of the organism. He could describe the homeostatic mechanisms which neutralize the impact of external variables, such as heat and cold and the course of their defensive activity, as they are overcome by forces too strong for them – forces which, following Dr Selye's[3] classic formulation, he knows as stressors. He could describe the adaptive changes which enable the organism to hold its own for a while against such forces – the changes by which, for example, a man chased by a bull mobilizes for a few minutes an abnormal amount of energy. But why should the approaching bull function as a stressor, no less than a fall in temperature? Why, stranger still, should the hope of winning an Olympic mile function as a stressor, no less than an approaching bull? These were questions physiology was not prepared to answer. Nor is it clear that the collapse of the runner after he has leapt the gate or burst the tape has anything in common with the breakdowns studied by the psychiatrist and the student of animal behavior.

Clearly the stressful situation which concerns the psychiatrist is given not by events but by the organism's interpretation of events in relation to itself. This in turn is a function of the way in which the individual personality is organized; and any model of this must include the organization of experience.

We have several conceptual models of organization. We have the physiological model; but this until recently had little to say about the organization of experience. We have the body of psychological concepts dealing with perception and learning theory. We have the multi-dimensional models implicit in psychodynamic theory. All these models deal with systems constructed by abstracting different sets of variables from the bewildering, observable entity, man. Their better integration is an urgent need.

Some recent developments already make for better integration. The anatomist finds in the nervous system paths by which past experience may modify the sensory input even before it reaches the associative areas. Observations with the electroencephalograph may provide a physiological measure of some aspects of personality and personal integration, and have suggested to Dr Grey Walter a physiological theory of learning. Both psychiatrists and animal experimentalists are adding to the correlations, hitherto curiously rare, which relate physiological and biochemical to psychological changes at the threshold of breakdown: and pharmacologists are placing at their disposal an increasing repertory of drugs of known composition which have predictable effects on mental state. A genetic difference has been shown by animal breeding to underlie variations in vulnerability to stress. And animal ethologists like Mr Tinbergen[4] have provided us with language and concepts which everyone from the physiologists to the psychoanalysts seems to find acceptable.

A further important factor making for integration is the current development of language and concepts apt for describing open systems generally. The concept of stability, for instance, which Dr Ross Ashby[5,6] has done so much to generalize seems equally applicable to the systems studied by the physiologist, the psychiatrist and the sociologist. The same concept is applicable to the much more numerous cases in which the governing controls of the system are not fixed but change with time, such as the pattern of growth and maturation, or a changing cultural norm. Homeostasis is a special case of the much wider process which Professor Waddington[7] has called homeorhesis.

One idea, which recurs in all these fields, may be of central importance in the study of stress. It is the idea of matching with a pattern.

It seems clear that the raw material of experience is not the whole of the 'blooming, buzzing confusion' which beats on us but a selection of the regularities which we can detect; and that these in turn provide the categories for the classification of further experience. Conditioning – and perhaps more beside – depends on recognizing regular relations between recurrent events in the categories thus distinguished. Judgments of value – most refined of tropisms – are linked to situations recognized by their correspondence to some pattern, however complex. Thus if I say that A has given me a fair deal, I must first have selected for attention a particular group of features of my relations with A; I must have judged these to be a deal, rather than, say a fight; and applying the standards of fair deal, rather than fair fight, I find them to match. The evaluative judgment 'fair' no less than the cognitive judgment 'deal' is an act of classification, of matching with a pattern. Thus pattern governs throughout. The mind may boggle at the thought of a black box no bigger than our heads which can group, regroup and handle shifting configurations of symbols so complex, so plastic and yet so enduring; but we boggle rather at the complexity than at the principle.

It is not surprising that expectation should figure so largely in the organization and the disorganization of personality; for what we know consciously as expectation is only the exposed part of an iceberg that floats very low in the water. In pursuing, maintaining and eluding the external relations by which we live and die, we are guided by symbolic representations of what is happening and what ought to be happening. We need a model of this process to understand the nature and noxious operation of stress; and contrariwise, in seeking to understand the working of stress, we may well contribute to our understanding of controlled behavior. Organization and disorganization are opposite sides of the same penny.

Meaning derives from relationship to the familiar. When experience does not provide us with a templet, we have to invent one. This is exemplified at the conscious level by another model, with which I happen to be familiar; and I will venture to describe it briefly, because it presents a clear and simplified picture of control by expectation.

In the practical affairs of life we assume that conduct is controlled to an important degree by structures of expectation; and the implications of this have been worked out both in theory and practice with a high degree of refinement in the field of administration. No one today would try to run a business without maintaining and continually comparing two running representations, both projected into the future. One of these is a representation of what is happening and what is likely to happen next. The other is a representation of the course of events which we want to bring about or prevent. I will refer to these as the 'actual' and the 'standard' or, sometimes, as the 'is' and the 'ought to be'. The comparison of the two representations yields a stream of mis-match signals on which we act.

Thus the building contractor plots on charts against time the planned course of many interdependent operations; and, as work proceeds, he plots against these what is actually being achieved and projects these trends also into the future. Divergence of the two is a signal for action to bring the actual into line with the standard; or, if this proves impossible, to revise the plan, so as to provide a realistic and hence an effective control.

This homely illustration has features which are equally relevant to individual organization.

The controls used in business are representations of relationships which we seek to maintain, to alter or to escape. Some are relationships between the organization and its environment, such as the rate of intake and the outflow of money, materials and men; we might call these metabolic relationships. Some are relationships within the organization itself. In either case the control may be negative or positive; it may be directed to bringing the relationship continually back to some optimal position or to preventing it from straying beyond some critical threshold. And it must represent in the same code both the actual and the standard; it becomes meaningless if either term is absent.

Thus what I have called the actual is a highly artificial construct. It is hypothetical; for our information about what is happening is never complete or exact or direct. It is selective; for we can attend only to a few aspects of it at a time. It is represented in a code, be it in writing or figures or graphically, which limits and distorts what can be represented; and this is necessarily the same code in which we represent the standard – how else could we compare the two? Finally, it has an inescapable time base. In all this, I suggest, it closely parallels the working of the individual mind.

The controls used in business, like those of the individual mind, do not always give clear or correct or adequate guidance. First, they apply only to those aspects of experience to which we have chosen to attend. We may have chosen the wrong variables for attention. Again, the signals may be ambiguous; or, being clear experience may supply no apt response; or, responses proven apt in the past may let us down. But their most inescapable embarrassment is their conflict. It is a feature of practical life that any projected action is relevant not merely to the purposive sequence in which it arises but to many others also; and it cannot be equally congenial to all. If apt for some, it will be inept for others. Whatever doors it opens, others it will shut. In business, short term profit, long term stability, internal coherence, public relations – each of these disparate standards, when compared with an appropriate selection from the actual, maintains its own stream of warning and advice; and these are no more consistent in business than in private life.

Moreover, their inconsistency is inescapable. The highly organized business, like the highly organized personality, necessarily generates more inconsistency in its governing expectations than one less highly organized. This curious fact, which deserves closer analysis than I can give it now, may account for the fact that the stress of war produces relatively so little civilian neurosis. Life in wartime may be harder but it is also simpler.

Apart from the inadequacies already described, the controls of business are themselves partial and intermittent; for either the actual or the intended may be inaccessible. Like the fog-bound navigator, we may know where we ought to be but not know where we are; or, like the climber following an unfamiliar route, we may know where we are but have no assurance that it is where we ought to be. And experience cannot be guaranteed to remedy either case; for the results of our actions may return for judgment after so long an interval and with so large an admixture of other variables, that they provide neither validation for the past nor guidance for the future.

In the board room, then, stress is associated with doubt and conflict of clearly definable kinds. We may have to live for years with deafening streams of mis-match signals, either because we can devise no suitable response or because the action they invite, if taken, would elicit even more violent protests in another context. Alternatively, we may have to live in an eerie silence, because either the actual or the standard is not registering in the appropriate code. And either of these states may lead to disorganization (or protective reorganization) suggestive of the forms familiar to the psychiatrist and the animal experimentalist.

Far flung analogies deserve to be considered with suspicion; yet this one seems to me to be useful in three ways.

First, controls of the sort which I have been describing seem to be closely related to controls at simpler levels. The pecking response of the herring gull chick is pre-set to be released by information sent in a particular code. The chick responds to the red patch on the feeding beak – which is itself an abstraction – because it corresponds to the pre-set signal, a correspondence not absolute but falling within limits of tolerance which are themselves built in. Learned responses can, of course, become attached to much more elaborate cues, controlled by patterns distilled from past experience. It would seem then that the process of matching with a pattern is inherent in the control of behavior from the simplest cue-governed response to the most sophisticated act of cognition, for all cognition is recognition. Moreover, the patterns which our brain can record are patterns in time as well as in space. An instrument which can symbolize change with time can presumably represent the future as easily as the past.

Then, secondly, the model seems useful to me in its representation of conflict as endemic and necessarily increasing with more complex organization. By more complex organization I mean not increase in size or increase in the power and variety of responses available or even increase in sub-division of function. I mean increase in the number and diversity of objectives to be sought and thresholds to be avoided, of those positive and negative standards by which behavior is regulated; in other words, in the norms which the system is set simultaneously to seek and the limits which it is set simultaneously to avoid. This is the dimension in which, as I see it, organisms and organizations tend to develop and in which they tend to fall back whenever they set themselves a task of reconciliation which proves in face of events to be too much for their powers.

Thus, thirdly, the example is useful in stressing a new dimension in which the higher organisms, no less than organizations, are adaptable. Most biological work treats as given the acceptable and unacceptable states which act as governors, positive and negative, of a system's behavior; and in so far as this is so, the only scope for adaptation within the individual life span is the development of responses and skills to serve these needs. But at higher levels and conspicuously at the level of human life, the individual's wants and needs, no less than his responses and skills grow and multiply within his life span. Many different but mutually exclusive possibilities compete for realization within the framework of the biologically given. We win increasing – and embarrassing – scope in the setting of our own systems.

So the psychologist needs a model of organization more complex than would meet the needs of the physiologist. The biologist, at grips with the code built into the structure of the gene, is seeking the key to a program. But the psychologist needs a model not only of the organism's program from birth to death but also of its self-programming capacity and its self-programming propensity; a model which will represent our goal-setting as well as our goal-seeking. For though these two activities are so closely related that they cannot be considered separately, they are also, as I believe, so distinct that they cannot usefully be simplified by resolving one into the other.

Finally, I remind myself that a model of conflict does not necessarily tell us anything about pathologic stress; for we cannot assume that conflict in itself is noxious. Conflict-solving is the normal activity of our brains. And if the threshold is quantitative, it is also relative. We need to understand both the noxious nature of a given stress in relation to the organization of a particular individual and the vulnerability of a given individual to a particular situation.

You may feel that a model of conflict in such conscious and cognitive terms as I have used has little bearing on our subject matter. In fact, of the governors of corporate behavior, some of the most powerful of them seldom register in the board room and it is a major task of administration to bring them to the central consciousness – often despite the censorship of powerful repressing mechanisms. But I will not pursue the analogy any further. If it seems an unduly cognitive approach to a problem essentially dynamic, it is at least in tune with the times. When men's basic conceptual models were mechanical, people seeking the explanation of some happening looked first for the force which made it happen. In these servo-mechanical days we seek first not the force but the program, not the source of energy but the source of information. The world is full of energy, waiting to be borrowed; the weakest signal may release force to move a mountain. So naturally interest centers on the signalling system. And it is here, it seems, that the development of our mental powers has endowed us with so alarming a capacity for organization – and disorganization.

## References

1. I. P. Pavlov, See W. Sargant, *Battle for the Mind*, London, William Heinemann, 1957, p. 9.
2. H. S. Liddell, *Stress and Psychiatric Disorder*, J. M. Tanner (ed), Oxford, Blackwell Scientific Publications, 1960.
3. H. Selye, *The Physiology and Pathology of Exposure to Stress*, Montreal, Acta Endocrinologica, 1950, p. 27.
4. N. Tinbergen, *The Study of Instinct*, Oxford, Clarendon Press, 1951.
5. W. Ross Ashby, *Design for a Brain*, London, Chapman & Hall, 1952.
6. W. Ross Ashby, *An Introduction to Cybernetics*, London, Chapman & Hall, 1956.
7. C. H. Waddington, *The Strategy of the Genes*, London, Allen & Unwin, 1957.

# 21

# The psychology of policy making and social change*

I am grateful to those who have included me in the honourable company of Maudsley Lecturers. When you invite a speaker from outside psychiatry, I think you hope to find one who will speak from his own central interest and experience in a way which will illuminate your own. After some inner debate, I decided that I would try to justify that expectation, even though my experience may seem remote from yours. I hope none the less that what I have to say may have some relevance to some of the sciences on which you rely, perhaps even to your profession.

I have spent my life in practising the law and helping to administer public and private affairs. I have thus had the chance to observe and even to take part in the making of policy; and since I retired from these activities sufficiently to reflect on them, I have tried to understand them – so far with very limited success. The more I think about the process, the stranger it seems. And yet it is obviously important, not only because we all suffer or benefit from the decisions of those who control our destinies but also because we all do it. The behaviour of boards of directors, cabinets and courts of law displays in a conveniently explicit form some of the commonest workings of the individual mind. I will begin by explaining what seem to me to be the central enigmas. Then I will ask you to follow some examples which will, I hope, make them clearer. Then I will speculate on the growing points of psychological knowledge, which may in time make these riddles less puzzling than they seem to me now.

## Appreciation and regulation

I can best begin by examining the concept of regulation. By regulation I understand keeping some relation in line with a standard. The relation may be quantitative, like the rate of recruitment of nurses to fill vacancies in a hospital or the rate of money intake to balance spending from a bank account. Or it may be qualitative, like the standard of service given by the hospital or the value for money achieved by the spending. There are many types of situation which involve regulation in this sense. They all have in common that what is to be regulated is a relationship extended in time; not

*From British Journal of Psychiatry, Vol. 110, 1964. Originally the 38th Maudsley Lecture delivered before the Royal Medico-Psychological Association in November 1963.

something which can be attained once for all, but something, like a mariner's course, which must constantly be sought anew. There must therefore always be some governing relation by reference to which the actual course of affairs may be judged. I will call such governing relations 'norms'.

These norms may be no more than those expectations which we regard and accept as 'normal' or they may set levels of aspiration far beyond the expected. It is a feature of modern societies that their 'norms' diverge from their 'normals' in a way which traditional societies would find dangerously disturbing – as perhaps it is.

I thus distinguish regulation in the sense of norm-holding both from goal-seeking and from rule-following. I believe that psychology has done a disservice to the study of higher mental function by making goal-seeking the paradigm of rational behaviour. I do not accept the view that all norm-holding can be reduced to the pursuit of an endless succession of goals. Rats, it is true, maintain their metabolic balance – a norm – by a series of excursions after food, each of which can be regarded as goal-seeking. Some humans similarly maintain their solvency by periodic excursions after money. But this is not a sophisticated form of financial control, precisely because it shows a failure to appreciate relations in time; and an enhanced capacity to appreciate relations in time is clearly one of the distinguishing marks of our species. Anyone familiar with the papers presented to any governing body will realize how much trouble is taken to present the major variables as flows in the dimension of time.

It seems odd to me that while this is familiar to administrators and engineers, psychologists should still present 'goal-seeking' as the normal if not the only type of rational behaviour; for to explain a 'doing' solely by reference to its intended results would seem to raise insoluble pseudo-conflicts between 'ends and means', rules and purposes, while it leaves the ongoing activities of norm-holding with their inherent, ongoing satisfactions hanging in the air as a psychological anomaly called 'action done for its own sake'. Even to drive a car is *always* an exercise in the maintenance of a complex set of spatial and temporal relations, though it is often also resorted to as a means of getting from A to B. To practise a profession, to live a life, is even more obviously, as it seems to me, a norm-holding activity, in which goal-seeking plays an occasional and subordinate part. I sometimes wonder whether the absorption with goal-seeking reflects the limitations of research method or even the diseases of an acquisitive society, rather than the structure of the human mind.

As Professor Peters[1] has observed, we have no reason to suppose that any one formula will suffice to explain all human motivation; but on the contrary, we have every reason to believe that biological and social evolution have added new and disparate regulators to those we share with our fellow creatures and that we are often confused by their inconsistent promptings. I am concerned to follow the regulator which I have called control by norm.

This process has been modelled by communication engineers more effectively than by psychologists. The engineers have surrounded us with self-controlling devices, from the simple thermostat to the complexities of rocket control, all of which exemplify control by norm and all of which involve a circular process, falling into two main segments. In the first segment, the actual course of affairs is compared with the norm and the comparison generates a signal. In the second segment, the signal sets going processes which select and trigger some action. In due course the effect of this action, along with all the other changes that have happened in the meantime, is 'fed back' to the first segment through later observation of the 'actual course of affairs' and so plays its part in further regulative action. This greatly over-simplified picture describes a process which is illustrated no less by a human helmsman than by an automatic pilot, no less by a government controlling its international balance of payments than by an automatic regulator controlling a chemical plant.

The second pair of these examples introduces a complication. Controlling the balance of payments is for a government only part of its total task, a task which involves pursuing also a vast variety of other norms not wholly consistent with each other and greatly exceeding in their total demands the aggregate resources available. The whole task can be neither completely specified nor completely performed. No one would willingly design a robot chemical plant controller to cope with such a situation and it is not clear to me that anyone could.

Where the norm can be taken as given, much important work has been done both by psychologists and by system engineers in exploring the mechanisms of problem solving and learning; in discovering and imitating the mechanisms by which organisms solve problems, devise alternative means and choose between them and improve their performance by practice. All this has greatly illuminated the second segment of the regulative cycle.

I, on the other hand, am concerned with problems of choice arising in the first segment; with the setting of the norms to be followed and hence of the problems to be solved. The norms which men pursue, and hence the problems which they try to solve, are, I suggest, largely self-set by a partly conscious process which merits and is susceptible of more study than it has yet received; and it can conveniently be studied in the overt processes of public life, where it is more than usually explicit.

It has been my experience that the debate which occupies hours, days, even months between the posing of some problem and its disposal serves not so much to produce a series of possible new solutions as to alter what those concerned regard as the relevant facts and the way in which these are classified and valued. I recall an occasion when an important governing body debated for a year what should be done in a situation which seemed to require some radical solution. They finally decided that there was nothing to be done. No action followed – yet nothing was ever the same again. The mental activity which reached this negative conclusion radically changed their view and their valuation of their situation. In particular, it changed their idea of what can be put up with, a most important threshold in the regulative cycle.

Men, institutions and societies learn what to want as well as how to get, what to be as well as what to do; and the two forms of adaptation are closely connected. Since our ideas of regulation were formed in relation to norms which are deemed to be given, they need to be reconsidered in relation to norms which change with the effort made to pursue them.

So I shall concentrate on the processes involved in the first segment, and I need a word to describe them. Since I cannot find one in the literature, I will call them collectively 'appreciation'. I will credit the appreciating agent with a set of readinesses to distinguish some aspects of its situation rather than others and to classify and value these in this way rather than that, and constantly to revise these readinesses; and I will describe these readinesses as an appreciative system. I call them a system, because they seem to be organized as a whole in ways to which I will return, being so interrelated that a change in one part of the system is likely to be affected by and dependent on changes in others. I will use the term 'appreciative setting' to describe the governing relations (norms) to which such a system is for the time being set to respond; and I will describe these settings as an appreciative field when I am concerned with the way in which they interact with each other. These terms, I hope, will gather meaning as I proceed.

## The appreciative process

Let me give some examples to make the point more precise.

The classic example of appreciation and regulation is, of course, the helmsman, whether human or automatic. He must read continuously from the compass card not only the current direction of the ship's head relative to its course, but also the direction and rate at which it is swinging and the rate at which that rate of swing is itself increasing or diminishing. These rates must be compared with his learned knowledge of what they ought to be to steady the ship on her course; and it is this comparison which does or does not generate a signal to the powered gear which controls the rudder. The sending of no signal is as much the result of this matching process as is the sending of a signal, and either may or may not occur when the ship is momentarily on course.

Thus even with so simple an appreciative mechanism as the automatic pilot, appreciation is a fairly complex, continuous process. It is not, however, obscure, because the course is given. The relevant facts may indeed be enlarged to almost any degree of refinement, but the process itself is specifiable, comprehensible and exact.

It thus contrasts with even the simplest parallel from daily life. The closest parallel which occurs to me is the function of keeping stocks of material in an industrial plant at some predetermined level. The buyer must watch the rate at which, say, steel is flowing out of store, and adjust his orders with due regard to the delays in delivery to be expected from his suppliers; and he must be alert to changes both in the rate of consumption and in the speed of delivery.

Thus the buyer, like the helmsman, must regulate rates of flow in accordance with learned norms. This, however, does not exhaust his job or define his success. He must get good value for money, yet keep good relations with his suppliers. He must be alert to new sources of supply, to variations in the reliability of his suppliers and to varying nuances in the needs of those who will use what he buys, and in other even less specifiable ways he must be an acceptable member of a team. What constitutes good or bad performance in these dimensions is not a norm which can be defined, as stock levels can be defined; it could not be modelled, as the maintenance of stock levels could be modelled, with a tank and a few pipes. Yet it is a norm which is in constant use, for it is used by the manager to assess the buyer.

It is a changing norm. It may change with the growth of the business. Standards which are good enough in a small concern, where the occasional shortfall can be easily made good and relatively large surpluses do not matter much, may become unacceptable to the manager when the business has grown or has come to operate in a more competitive market. Equally, the manager may change his standards, unprompted by any change in the observed actual. He reads an article or goes to a conference or talks to a friend; and thereafter, looking at the buyer plying his accustomed task, he judges the familiar performance for the first time unacceptable, because he has revised his appraisal of the role. Or again, the buyer may himself re-define his role and invite the manager to reset his expectations.

The norms embodied in a role are for the most part unspecifiable, like the skills analysed by Polanyi;[2] yet an important industrial study by a psychiatrist[3] finds in the extent of these unspecifiable, discretionary duties the true differential between one job and another.

Thus the buyer's job is different from that of the helmsman. He must maintain several not wholly compatible relationships within limitations which are either inherent in the situation (such as the amount of his available time and energy) or imposed from without (like the stock limits set by the manager). His performance is in its way a work of art, *one* answer to a continuing challenge which no two men will answer in the same way. And the challenge itself, what is expected of him by himself and others, grows, shrinks and changes partly through extraneous forces and partly through his own activity.

These aspects of policy making become more marked as we climb the hierarchy of an organization. The stock levels, which were a datum for the buyer, were for the manager who set them the fruit of an exercise of appreciative judgment. He wanted to lock up in idle stocks as little capital as he thought would guard against the risk of stopping the plant for lack of some essential material. These governing relations were in turn only two among many conflicting norms governing the use of the capital available to him, which in their turn were linked with other norms involving the rate of development of new products, relations with creditors and a host of other disparates.

It is often supposed that all such norms can be ordered in a hierarchy in which all but one are ultimately subordinate. This I believe to be untrue even of profit-making enterprises. Are businesses supposed to be as human as is consistent with efficiency or as efficient as is consistent with humanity? Neither simplification holds water. They are regulated by a complex of expectations, political, economic, legal, social and personal, none of which has a prescriptive right to precedence. These norms have, of course, what we might call a 'pecking order', but the order is open to be re-disputed whenever occasion arises. Every feed, so to speak, results not only in the consumption of corn but also in the revision of the pecking order; and the second effort is often more important than the first.

The point is, perhaps, more clearly evident, if we consider policy making in a local authority. The authority, like the business enterprise, must maintain its existence as a dynamic system by keeping men, money and materials flowing through its organization, as a cow must maintain its intake of grass, air and water. In this respect they are comparable dynamic systems. In addition, usually as another aspect of the same activities, it must provide a variety of services, each of which consists in maintaining through time a complex of relations quantitative and qualitative – for example, both school accommodation and the education which goes on there. Each of these services is judged more or less acceptable by the current and diverse standards of those concerned; and each is competing with all the others for further realization within the overall limitations of the authority's resources and powers. The whole set-up is a dynamic system of precarious stability. Its balance may be disturbed in either of two ways; in practice it is constantly being disturbed in both ways. Total resources may shrink or grow relative to current demand, making overall restriction necessary or expansion possible somewhere; and policy must decide where the restriction shall fall or the growth occur. Alternatively, the norms by which these services are judged may change, increasing or reducing the claim of any one relative to the others and demanding a redistribution of energy and attention over the whole field; and policy must decide what redistribution shall be made.

In any case, any major change will reverberate through the whole system, affecting and affected by even such apparently remote variables as the personal ambitions of officers and the nostalgic memories of councillors. What some see as a housing issue, others will see as a problem of road development or sewage disposal or even as a matter of personal relations; and all these views are valid. There is no one answer to such protean problems. Whatever the solution, it will leave the appreciative setting changed and the appreciative field still unstable.

In observing such situations, I think we can usefully distinguish two strategies, which alternate with changes in the situation. When for whatever reason achievement is falling in relation to current norms, thresholds of acceptability have to be dropped; and a hierarchy of values develops, which appears more obvious as things get worse. The system in jeopardy sheds first the relations least essential to its survival. An organism in danger of death from cold restricts its surface blood vessels and risks peripheral frostbite to preserve its working temperature at more vital levels within; businesses facing bankruptcy and nations facing invasion experience a similar clarification of values. But an understanding of this *protective* strategy will not suffice to explain what will happen when achievement is expanding in relation to current norms. What new, more exacting norms will structure the new possibilities? *Expanding* strategy needs its own explanation. An executive who is outstanding at salving undertakings in danger of dissolution is not necessarily so successful in exploiting success; certainly his course in an expanding strategy is not predictable from his performance in a protective one. In the same way, I suppose, theories of ego development cannot be inferred from any study of ego defences.

Whether in conditions of protective or expansive strategy, the policy makers in any local authority must resolve conflicts which we tend to describe as pressures, suggestive of the pressures of a barometric map; but these pressures operate in a field which is structured by the way in which it is regarded; and this selection of what shall be noticed and how it shall be classified is often decisive of the way in which it will be valued. A local authority is unlikely even to notice issues to which it is not organized to attend; and since its departments are designed for action, its appreciative capacity may be grossly limited or distorted by its organization. The current debate about the best way to assign ministerial responsibility for higher education and research attests an awareness common to all the disputants of the importance of organization in deciding what issues shall be distinguished for regulation; and the distorting effect on appreciation of an organization which is purely action-oriented is the reason why so many organizations establish planning and intelligence divisions in independence from their action-oriented departments.

The normative effect of simple discrimination could be illustrated from the policy-making debates of any kind of governing body, but it is most clearly seen in the development of the common law, a process by no means so remote from policy making as might at first appear. So I will adjourn for a moment to the law courts, where a judge is hearing a case in which damages are claimed on the ground of the defendant's negligence. It is for the judge to say whether the defendant was negligent within the meaning of the law. What then is negligence? The law's only answer is to point to all those recorded instances in which negligence has been found to be present or absent. From these the judge must collect a gestalt, to which he must assimilate or from which he must distinguish the case before him. That act of his will alter the gestalt, however slightly, for the future, and this prospective effect is present to the mind of the judge *before* he gives his judgment and may well affect the judgment which he gives. For he knows that his decision is not only decisive for the case before him but also affects future decisions. His act of appreciation not only determines regulative action in the particular case but also changes, by its own activity, the appreciative system which it expresses.

Hence both the possibility and the importance of the dissenting judgment. In 1920 the Supreme Court of the United States heard an appeal by some men who had been convicted of sedition for publishing pro-Bolshevik pamphlets.[4] Seven members of the Court uphold their conviction. The eighth began his dissenting judgment thus:

'Sentences of twenty years imprisonment have been imposed for the publishing of two leaflets that I believe the defendants had as much right to publish as the Government has to publish the Constitution of the United States, now vainly invoked by them.'

It may seem strange that in a country where the simplest layman is supposed to know the law, the highest judges should be allowed publicly to disagree about it. It is strange, but no more strange than the fact which it so usefully recognizes, namely the power and not merely the power but the inescapable responsibility of men to choose what meaning the facts of life shall bear. To the other judges the publication was an act of sedition; as such the law required that it should be suppressed and punished. To Justice Oliver Wendell Holmes it was an expression of opinion; as such it was absolutely protected under the constitution.

Which was it 'really'? As well ask that question of the ambiguous figures with which psychologists illustrate their text-books; or better, those they use for your projective tests. It could be seen in either way, but not in both at once. Holmes was more prone to see threats to the free speech of men; the others more prone to see threats to the stability of society. They were at issue not on what to do but on how to see; and unlike most of us, they knew it. These are the divisions which have always rent and will always most deeply rend mankind. They are disputes about the architecture of our common appreciative system.

The dispute was not confined to the court room. A unanimous judgment would have comfortably confirmed the current setting of the country's appreciative system. Holmes' judgment made no difference to the appellants; but it released a strident mis-match signal in a field in which Americans, like other people, are sensitive to expressions of doubt and disunity. It thus contributed to the setting of the country's appreciative system, a process which, like the regulative segment of the same circle, can never be accomplished once for all. In 1920 the future Senator McCarthy was already a young man.

I wish I had time to extend these examples to show, in particular, the rigid upper limit to the rate at which the appreciative system can assimilate change. But these must suffice. I would summarize their lessons as follows. The policy-making process is a response to the conflicting and superabundant demands generated by appreciating a situation. It has two distinct results – the one an overt, regulative response; the other, a change in the setting of the appreciative system; that is, in the choice of what shall be noticed and how it shall be classified and valued. The second is often the more important and results from the mere exercise of appreciation, whether regulative action follows or not. When regulative action does follow, its claim to 'rightness' can be neither calculated before the event nor demonstrated afterwards. It can only be allowed or denied by a judgment similar to that which produced it. This judgment seems to involve some recognition and appraisal of form – which is why I have referred to it as in some sense a work of art.

## Some psychological implications

I want now to survey briefly the growing points in our understanding which may make this process less obscure and perhaps less inefficient than it seems now.

That the norms which control us, socially and individually, are created, developed and changed by the very act of recognizing them, odd as it sounds, is not psychologically news. The child *learns* to see, building up from repeated experiences the schemata by which future experiences will be classified. The medical student, learning to read a pulmonary radiograph, must go on looking until experience builds up in him the schema which alone can give the confusion meaning. In this process perceptual schemata seem to be only one example of all conceptualization. G. H. Lewes[5] expressed the general principle as long ago as 1879 when he wrote – 'The new object presented to sense, the new idea presented to thought must be *soluble* in old experience, must be *recognized* as like them; otherwise it will be unperceived, uncomprehended.'

Thus we have known for a long time that the world we live in is a mental artifact. Our knowledge of this artifactual world had grown since 1879 vastly but patchily. One of the least developed areas, as it seems to me, is our knowledge of the skills involved in making the artifact and of the ways in which these skills may best be developed. We can recognize, for example, in the research worker and others, the capacity to handle more numerous and refined schemata; to group observations and communications more ingeniously into complex patterns, displaying new relationships, and so to build up systems of schemata more complex, more self-consistent and more fruitful of further development. The importance of these skills is obvious. Even our most recent legislation on mental health, with it vigorous attempt to assimilate mental to physical illness, designed to displace some crude and ineptly valued schemata from the past, may itself seem crude to a later generation more ready and able to evolve for mental illness a schema, perhaps several schemata, of its own.

Again, if I am right, mental processes which produce *the correct answer* by applying specifiable procedures to given facts differ from those which produce *a good answer* by applying less specifiable processes of judgment to facts of which the relevance is itself a matter for judgment. The former, however complex, can be proved right or wrong; the latter, however simple, can only be approved as good or condemned as bad by a judgment of the same kind as that which produced them. I have stressed the ubiquity and importance of the second at all levels of executive responsibility; but both are needed, and we need to know more of the educative processes which develop them. Theoretically, this raises important issues about the value as educational disciplines of different fields of study in the arts and sciences. Practically, it is of great concern to, for example, all concerned with the education of engineers, surely destined to be both technologists and managers; and it has, I think, a corresponding relevance to medical education. I am sometimes surprised that university departments of psychology devote on the whole so small a share of their attention to the appreciative activities going on in the captive populations of which they are part.

We have learned, thanks to your profession, far more about the disorders of mental process which may distort the appreciative system; so much indeed, that a layman might suppose that freedom from disorder would produce uniformity of mental architecture. This would seem not to be so. Differences in the appreciative system are not necessarily evidence of disordered process. Studies of race prejudice, for example, have indeed shown psychopathological features from which children seem to be free; but children are also free from brotherly love, still more from the concept of the brotherhood of man. Studies of the origin of these more acceptable norms are less common in the literature; but it is clear that variety in the appreciative system is more than variety in pathology.

It is no more pathological to fear a threat to one's appreciative system than to fear bankruptcy or eviction. The biblical scholars of Tübingen who, a century ago, questioned the authorship of some of St. Paul's epistles were reviled by some of their professional colleagues with a bitterness which seems in retrospect more violent than the search for truth required; but the most hostile theologians of the day attacked them no more violently than many scientists at much the same time were reviling those who were trying to find room in the mansion of science for the facts of hypnosis. Need we criticize the 'two cultures' for being equally human? Need we describe as pathological the reluctance of either culture to embark on massive reorganization of its appreciative system, or even its stark inability to admit the new until room could be found for it without disrupting the whole?

Yet the redesigning of the whole to admit the new is equally a mental skill, not wholly unconscious, an object as well as a by-product of the policy maker's art; a skill of especial importance at a time when an appreciative system is unstable and under rapid change, as ours is today; most of all when many policy makers and others appear blissfully unaware that any appreciative system has an upper limit to its possible rate of change, which cannot be passed without disaster. This skill involves understanding the appreciative system as a system.

The appreciative system deserves to be taken seriously as a system;

neither a pale reflection nor a pathological distortion of the 'real world out there', but a semi-autonomous system in its own right. To do so is timely, since the system is being manipulated as never before; it is also timely because the understanding of systems is an active growing point in our understanding of the process of which we are part.

Ecologists have made laymen familiar with the idea of dynamic systems, in which change is due not to this cause or that but to the imbalance of forces in a field over a period. The idea gained ready access to lay minds, alarmed at the unintended repercussions of man's dealings with the land, from the first appearance of dustbowls to the latest extravagance of pest control. This ecological world is also the world of public health and largely even of clinical medicine. Is this epidemic due to a virus, to overcrowding, to bad sanitation or to failure in the supply of a vaccine? Did I catch my cold or succumb to it through fatigue or exposure? There is no answer to such questions. A combination of circumstances left the individual or the society vulnerable to an event which it would otherwise have withstood. For purposes of prevention and cure we may regard as the cause whatever variable we can most easily control, but it has no other claim to be distinguished as *the* cause.

The study of dynamic systems is changing our ideas of the way things happen. We tend to attribute happenings to some imbalance, whether in the population densities of the planet or the pressures of the barometric map or the endocrine system of a schizophrenic. We expect that change in any direction will breed its own limitations or reversals, so as to stabilize on some regular course, failing which it will spin off into chaos in oscillations of increasing amplitude or accelerating linear change. Continuity depends on regulation; stability, not change, requires explanation. Where once we sought causes to account for change, we now seek regulators to account for enduring form.

These regulators grow more complex with the emergence of new ways of mediating change. In a system as simple as the weather, change is mediated largely by pressure gradients. We can describe the behaviour of a meteorological system in terms of the earth's motion, the sun's heat, the existing imbalance of pressure and so on; and though we cannot control it or, save within narrow limits, predict it, we can understand it in terms of familiar mechanical laws. It is much less satisfactory to reduce all the varieties of human behaviour to some kind of tension reduction.

For even an ecologist, studying population densities and distribution in a rain forest or on the Arctic tundra needs a more complex model. He, too, is concerned with flows of energy, whether mechanically, as in the effect of rain-swollen rivers, or chemically through organic metabolism; but the organisms in his field also learn to respond to signals, and he may need to distinguish information flow from energy flow as a mediator of change.

The public health administrator deals with a system in which information plays a far more important part. Traffic accidents to men, as to hedgehogs, happen when information flow fails to keep up with energy flow; but policies to reduce road accidents only begin when these have been identified as a problem in the society's appreciative system, where they must compete for attention with all the other identified problems. To account for this he must credit his population – and incidentally himself – with power to generate and respond to symbols and to build therefrom a shared, symbolic system. This system serves not only to enable selective interaction, individual and collective, with the physical milieu, but also to mediate human communication and to organize individual experience; and it is this threefold function which gives it its partial autonomy. For the input of observation, dominant among simpler creatures, plays among men an ever smaller part relative to the input of human communication and self-generated speculation, and all these have their own feedback systems which do not always speak with the same voice. I have no time to develop this point here, but I note it as one example of what I believe to be a general tendency to underestimate the extent to which we live in and are confined to a communicated and communicable world.

That the appreciative system is semi-autonomous, is one of several possible worlds which may be developed as its dwelling place by an individual, a group, a sub-culture, a society, that it is not determined but merely conditioned by the world of objects and events which forms its physical milieu, and that it develops partly according to its own laws and its own time scale – all this will not surprise cultural anthropologists, sociologists or those psychologists whose chosen fields of study include behaviour in which this semi-autonomy is implied. It is possible, however, to choose fields of psychological study which exclude this troublesome variable, and there are two strong reasons for doing so. One is the wish to preserve the conditions of rigorous research method; the other is to avoid crediting the mind with a degree of autonomy which is still suspect. This second reluctance should by now have been lessened by the impact of yet another kind of system, the product of communication engineers. For these, with their theories and their hardware, have introduced and made respectable – are they not physicists? – a degree of dualism which psychology may be glad to borrow.

The regulative sub-systems of the communication engineer, such as the automatic pilot or the space rocket's control system, are physical systems no less than the systems which they control. Each is a part of the system which it controls; it probably draws such energy as it needs from the system's energy source. Yet how firmly it stands between the system and the real world out there! The ship's rudder responds not to any signal from without, but to the still, small voice of the pilot, which may be an artifact of any degree of complexity, derived by rules perhaps evolved by itself, from facts produced by its own processes and possibly stored for years. These controlling sub-systems illustrate vividly, at least up to a point, the semi-autonomous development of an appreciative system. The engineer devising the control system of a space rocket faces problems distinct from those of his colleague who is designing the rocket itself, and needs and uses a language equally remote from the language of metallurgy and fuel combustion. In the same way, I understand, a biochemist studying an enzyme system as a mediator of growth uses language equally remote from that of a colleague in the same discipline who is studying the same enzyme system as a link in the process of energy transmission.

It thus becomes possible to talk about the mind as a regulative subsystem with a separateness of concept and language which would have savoured of vitalism a few years ago. Indeed, in some seats of learning the word has already gone round the campus – 'There *is* a ghost in the machine. It's a mechanical ghost; we've made one.' This sounds too good to be true and I think it is; for if it were wholly true, two enigmas which have bedevilled psychology from the beginning, the 'mind-body problem' and the 'problem of consciousness', would dissolve without trace in the dualism of 'energy-information'. Parts of them have indeed so dissolved, but I think a residue will remain, which will be found to be inherent in the even more fundamental dualism of 'agent-observer'. As such, it may be far easier to state, but I expect it will remain logically incapable of solution so long as science speaks in the third person only whilst scientists sometimes use the first and second person also.

Be that as it may, system engineers and system theorists have vastly amplified our understanding of regulative behaviour. How far they will amplify our understanding of appreciative behaviour is not clear to me. There are two impediments. The first is practical. System engineers are usually employed to design *servants*; and no one would want to build into a servant discretion to vary the task set, as distinct from discretion to find the best way to do it. Dialogue is not encouraged between the engine room and the bridge about the competence of the helmsman or the wisdom of the course. This, however, is just what is encouraged in the making of policy. People argue incessantly about what most merits attention and how it should be regarded; and in doing so they reset each other's appreciative systems and their own.

The other impediment is theoretical. Information is an incomplete concept; for it tells us nothing about the organization of the recipient, which alone makes a communication informative. This reflects the fact that information as a concept was developed by communication engineers concerned with problems of transmission, who could make assumptions about the state of readiness of the receivers. But clearly the limitation of human systems of communication depends not only or chiefly on difficulties of transmission but on the organization of sender and receiver; and this not merely as terminals in isolated acts of transmission but as linked members in a reciprocal net of dialogue.

Thus assumptions and hypotheses about what I call the appreciative system are necessary to communication theory, and I look forward to the day when psychology will supply them. At present the word 'dialogue' is seldom, if ever, found in the index of a psychological textbook. The most ambitious attempt to fill the gap which is known to me is a series of papers by Professor MacKay[6] to which I am greatly indebted; but the main questions implied by my examples remain, I believe, unanswered.

I have no time, even were I competent, to review the contributions of system theorists and system engineers, on the one hand to the psychology of what I have called appreciation, on the other to the practice of policy making. There is much to their credit on both counts; there will surely be more. I will only insist on the nature of these contributions, their potential value and their potential danger.

Our ways of looking at things, what we notice and hence what we ignore, are greatly affected by the physical models we use. I have no doubt that the increasing use of electronic means of solving problems, including so-called policy problems, will affect both the way policy makers see their problems and the way psychologists see the behaviour of policy makers.

I have equally no doubt that none of our current conceptual models suffices to explain to ourselves the kind of appreciative and regulative behaviour which I have illustrated. This may be due simply to current inability to specify our problems with enough precision, inability which time may cure. We have abundant examples of science replacing art. It may also be due to the basic difficulty to which I have referred, of translating the language of the agent into that of the observer. Again it may be due to norm-setting tendencies of the human mind beyond those we have already charted. Almost certainly, in my view, it is due to all three causes. It is therefore of the greatest importance to keep the debate open, by insisting on the full complexity of the phenomena to be explained. For in this field, unlike the physical sciences, a theory accepted may limit or distort its subject matter. A mistaken view of planetary motion, held for centuries, made no difference to the planets, which continued in their ellipses, undisturbed by human preference for circular motion. But a mistaken view of human nature, once accepted, might easily provide its own bogus validation.

This is why I was at pains earlier to bring out the more enigmatic aspects of policy making, a process which I believe reflects common features of our individual mental processes. For the attempt to understand this process, now going ahead with powerful new conceptual tools, cannot fail to be architecture as well as exploration.

## Current social policy

I want in conclusion to refer briefly to one aspect of social policy which well illustrates the development of our appreciative system and which seems to me to have some special relevance to your profession.

The 19th century left us a society in which the individual's responsibility for himself had been increased and his practical and psychological support from his fellows had been diminished to an extent seldom paralleled in history. This state of affairs was supported by a legacy of ideas derived from the same period; that fantastic time when technologies, populations and material wealth were expanding in a world still so abundantly endowed with undeveloped space and resources that the idea of self-limitation was temporarily lost. Revolting against both the factual and the ideological legacy, we have come to accept that the individual's capacity to cope with life depends on three factors all largely beyond his control, namely his genetic heritage and early training, the experiences meted out to him by his milieu, and the support which he gets from his fellows; and that we have a social duty and a social interest to do what we can to influence all three factors favourably – a duty, because society owes all its members the chance of a viable life; an interest, because the individual's breakdown or deviance is not only a loss but a threat to his society. The assumptions which I have compressed into the last sentence represent a vast complex of new norms, which set a problem for policy, the problem not only of satisfying them but of reconciling them with a host of incompatible others which are equally a legacy from the past. In consequence our appreciative system is structured by norms more abundant in total, more varied in scope and more contradictory in content than can often have been brought together in one time and place.

These new norms create or colour a great volume of policy in health, education and welfare, in housing and town planning and in much else besides; policy which should form a coherent whole, though the executive departments concerned are many. Its aim is to support the individual, internally and externally, and to reintegrate him into a physical and social environment more suited to his needs than that which we inherited or that which, impelled by other norms, we are busy making now. I believe that this development will be to our age what public health was a century ago, though in conception it is different and far more ambitious. For its aim is to humanize life or at least to combat the dehumanizing tendencies inherent in other aspects of our development; to provide what might be called a public humanizing service.

The programme lacks a theoretic base adequate to its ambitions. Part of the lacuna is represented by the unanswered questions which I have posed about the development of our appreciative systems. This ignorance will not and should not stop the programme from proceeding. If history is any guide, the further understanding which it needs will emerge first from a jumble of empirical insights and practices, developed in action and transmitted by informal apprenticeship. The practitioners concerned will develop increasingly formalized professional training; these will fight their way into universities as applied sciences; and only then will they powerfully stimulate the pure sciences on which they need to rely. There were many doctors before there was much medicine and much medicine before there was much physiology; and I expect it will be the same again.

The process is already well advanced. Practitioners multiply. The humanizing services need a great variety of social workers. In politics and industry human relations develop their own professionals. Management consultants market new skills in organization. Planners, not least physical planners, make assumptions about the conditions best suited or least hostile to human life and sometimes ask social scientists to help in the task. Schools of social work, of business management, of public administration and of physical planning begin to root and grow in ever closer association with universities. New professions are emerging, based not on biological but on social sciences, on psychology, sociology, cultural anthropology and system theory applied to men and societies. I expect that some of them will soon equal medicine in their prestige and in their reliance on academic and professional training. When those days come, doctors, including psychiatrists, will no doubt be found working in inter-disciplinary teams led by social scientists, no less than the reverse, the appropriate pattern being decided by the nature of the subject matter. Today such associations in either form are even more rare than they need be.

Where, in the course of these new humanizing policies, stands the profession of psychiatry? The question is primarily for you and it may be no bad thing that you answer it at present in so many different ways. But perhaps I might venture in closing to point the question.

To humanize is a wider aspiration than to heal; and some psychiatrists, alert if not allergic to the tendency of laymen to expect too much of them, stress the difference between mental illness, even the mild neuroses which take so much of your time today, and the wear and tear of daily life. You may declare, as Professor Rümke[7] once declared that 'the understanding of the disturbances of the sick man hardly contributes to the understanding of the normal man'. You may claim a special disability in dealing with normal men on the ground that you see so few of them. You may thus seek to barricade yourselves within the safe confines of a medical speciality.

May I suggest that you should not overcall this hand? You assure us, for example, that you aim to make mental hospitals into therapeutic – or at least non-pathogenic – communities; but those responsible for other organizations, industrial plants, schools, barracks, are equally aware of some responsibility for the quality of the societies which they plan and administer. Is your experience irrelevant to these? Your success as therapists depends not only on hastening the recovery of your patients but on helping them, when well again, to re-establish themselves in the world from which they became displaced. Does not this require an understanding of the stresses of the world of the well? You must consider the effect of your patient's illness on his home and the strains which it, as well as he, can stand; and you will have to do still more, as domiciliary treatment increases. Does not this involve you in understanding the crises of the well? You sometimes advise parents who are not sick on the art of bringing up, and children who are not yet sick on the art of growing up. You are the best expert witnesses we have on criminal responsibility. You are potent influences in some juvenile courts. And what of your new responsibilities for and toward the psychopath? You teach those who are not psychiatrists what they need to know about mental illness and its preconditions. You are already educators, counsellors, planners and administrators in the field of preventive psychiatry, which is no frontier but a widening borderland. Moreover, you are today better qualified than others to do these things.

So I hope and expect that an increasing proportion of your (I hope) increasing numbers will be drawn into what I have called the public humanizing service. I hope so partly because your practical experience is necessarily so much wider than your professional claims; but at least equally because your presence will help to prevent the facile equation of wisdom and virtue with health. The fact that your patients read their experience awry does not mean that when well they will necessarily read it aright; for its rightness will be a matter for judgment. The sanest like the maddest of us cling like spiders to a self-spun web, obscurely moored in vacancy and fiercely shaken by the winds of change. Yet this frail web, through which many see only the void, is the one enduring artifact, the one authentic signature of humankind, and its weaving is our prime responsibility. It is the realization of this which makes our age an age of ideology and one which, I think, will turn men's attention increasingly towards the first, the norm-setting half of the regulative cycle, to study its endemic appreciative process, of which one half-conscious instrument is policy making and the total expression is social change.

## References

1. R.S. Peters, *The Concept of Motivation*, London, Routledge & Kegan Paul, 1958.
2. M. Polanyi, *Personal Judgment*, London, Routledge & Kegan Paul, 1958.
3. E. Jacques, *The Measurement of Responsibility*, London, Tavistock Publications Ltd., 1956, pp. 61 *et seq.*
4. Quoted in C.D. Bowers, *Yankee from Olympus*, London, Ernest Benn Ltd., 1949, p. 370.
5. G.H. Lewes, *Problems of Life and Mind*, London, Trubner, 1879. Quoted in M.L. Johnson Abercrombie, *The Anatomy of Judgment*, London, Hutchinson, 1960.
6. D.M. MacKay. 'Communication and Meaning' and the previous papers referred to therein. Published in *Cross-Cultural Understanding: Epistemology in Anthropology*, Helen Livingstone (ed), Harper & Row, 1964.
7. H.C. Rümke, 'Solved and Unsolved Problems in Mental Health' in W. Line and M. King (eds), *Mental Health in Public Affairs*. Toronto, University of Toronto Press, 1954, pp. 149, 150.

# 22

# Levels of human communication[*]

## I. The field of human communication

I want to talk about human communication in the restricted sense of exchanges between human beings primarily of words designed by each to affect the other. This is not the whole field of communication or even of communication which could be distinguished as human but it is a very important part of the field and it deserves separate consideration. It serves three major functions, each of which presents various levels of difficulty and calls for corresponding gradations of skill. I wish to contribute to a better understanding of the limitations which restrict communication between people and the ways in which these can be enlarged. For it seems clear to me that the governance of the contemporary world requires higher levels of communication than are now being achieved and requires us to raise our performance as communicators by every means available to us.

I shall of course be equally concerned with communication which takes place within and between institutions and between institutions and individuals. And I shall have something to say about the effect of our communications on ourselves. For we all know that what we say or write may change the state of our own minds, even when it has no effect on others.

I shall be concerned scarcely at all with the promises and threats of information technology. The possibilities and limitations with which I am concerned derive from the skills and limitations of the human mind in framing communications to other people and in interpreting and responding to communications by other people. The means by which such communications are conveyed across space and stored through time have multiplied explosively in recent decades. But this has not increased by one iota either the capacity of the human mind for receiving such communications or its facility for understanding what it receives. The change has overloaded our input channels, altered as well as diversified the character of what is offered and posed acute problems of screening and selection. These also I shall barely discuss. They are important but they are in danger of diverting our interest from the process itself – the process by which human beings change each other by exchanging words.

Still less shall I be concerned with the other branch of information technology, namely the transfer to machines of mental processes hitherto performed by human brains. These also are important in their own right, both practically, since their speed makes possible operations which were

*From *Communications*, Vol. 1, No. 1, 1974.

impossible before, and theoretically, since the task of specifying these operations fully enough to computerise them has thrown valuable light on what they are and how the brain performs them. But their practical effects do not alter the process which I am going to analyse and their contributions to theory seem to me to cast little light as yet on the way the process works, at least at the level which I am to consider.

The distinguishing mark of human communication is that it is interpreted by the receiver in the light of a huge number of assumptions about the meaning of words, the state of the subject matter and his concern with it and not least about the sender. Similarly, all communications are framed by the sender in the light of assumptions which he makes about the receiver and about the assumptions which the receiver is making. A large part of human communication is directed to discovering, confirming or changing the assumptions by which it is to be interpreted. So strange a process deserves to be looked at in its own right and with as fresh an eye as we can assume.

## II. The strangeness of human communication

Consider five of the outstanding oddities of human communication. First, men are capable of being communicated with and of being changed thereby. Let us forget for the moment the active aspect of communication. The obscurities, the possibilities and the limitations are best seen at the receiving end.

Secondly, we are not born with this capacity; and yet, if we do not develop it, we do not become recognisably human. This development is not simply an organic change. Although the brain and CNS develop, after as well as before birth, in ways which are necessary to full communicative power, the skills which they make possible can only be developed by using them. Biological development supplies the instrument but only human experience can supply a human programme.

Thirdly, these skills are extremely various. The new-born child, whose attention I cannot even attract, will be able, 10 to 15 years later, not only to understand nearly everything I say but also to derive from it much that I did not know I was conveying, including much about me, and very likely much that I had been careful not to say.

Fourthly, these skills are partly tacit. Even the words we use arise from a level inaccessible to consciousness. Sometimes they surprise us. If on reflection we are dissatisfied with them, we can only invite our unconscious servants to submit some alternative for our approval. And conversely, our unconscious organization is affected by our conscious utterances. We are changed not only by being talked to but also by hearing ourselves talk to others, which is one way of talking to ourselves. More exactly, we are changed by making explicit what we suppose to have been awaiting expression a moment before.

Fifthly, we know very little about how we carry on this extraordinary activity. We have not even a name for this state of affairs in our heads which is the fruit of past communication and which is both the target and the interpreter of present communication. This nameless state accounts for nearly everything which we and others do – and, more important, are. Our assumptions about it are basic to nearly all our explanations of the feelings, thought and doings of ourselves and our fellows. Its development has been the object of educators since the earliest time when anyone consciously tried to teach a child. Nearly all our communication is directed to changing its state in others or in ourselves. It is strange that neither scientific nor common speech should have a word for it.

I have taken to calling it an appreciative system,[1] because the word appreciation, as we use it when we speak of appreciating a situation, seems to me to carry with it those linked connotations of interest, discrimination and valuation which we bring to the exercise of judgment and which tacitly determine what we shall notice, how we shall discriminate 'situations' from the general confusion of ongoing event, and how we shall regard them. I conceive it as consisting largely of categories for classifying and criteria for valuing experience. I will return to it later. I call it a system, because these categories and criteria are mutually related; a change in one is likely to affect others. The actual state of this system at any time I will call its current setting. And I shall use these terms both for individuals and for those common settings which distinguish and give coherence to groups, societies and cultures.

With or without a name, this state of affairs in our heads which I call our appreciative system is the target for almost all our communication. We spend a vast amount of time and energy in informing and persuading others and in accepting, resisting or trying to understand the information and persuasion which comes to us from them. We spend no less time in assuring ourselves and others that we share common ways of appreciating matters of common concern and in repairing any divergencies which these exchanges reveal. For our appreciative systems are not only the targets for communication. They are our only means of interpretation and thus the basis of our power to communicate. Without it, we can only push each other about like bulldozers or frighten each other like cats. Human societies were not built and are not maintained by such crude arts.

## III. The functions of human communication

Human communication has two main functions. It contributes both to the parties' understanding of each other and to their understanding of contexts and situations which are of concern to them. It also has a third function in that it can contribute to their understanding of their own communication, monitoring its effectiveness, noting and correcting failures and enlarging limitations. The three are closely interconnected. A failure of any can affect the others. Each may call for skills of varying difficulty.

If someone tells me the address of a car park in the town of Coventry,

I am the wiser by a fact which is useful if I am going to Coventry by car. If not, I forget it; it adds nothing significant to my present state. If, however, he adds that this car park covers the roofs of several buildings, he may require me to revise my ideas of car parks, roofs, Coventry, city planning and even, slightly, of cars. If I have not previously met the idea that roof space is the only potentially flat, under-used open space in modern towns, I may long remember the occasion that first brought it to my notice but forget that it was in Coventry. Alternatively, it may awaken my interest in Coventry as an example of modern planning in matters other than car parks.

Thus the communication may simply add to the content of an existing mental file; or it may add to its cross-references; or it may even require a change in my mental filing system. It may do all three; equally, any or all three may be the intention of the communicator. The Buchanan report,[2] from which this example is taken, is almost wholly directed to showing that mental categories are conveniences which may grow out of date. The multi-purpose Great Hall of medieval times, for example, has long been subdivided into separate rooms for different purposes. How odd that we should still accept as natural the multi-purpose street, struggling to accommodate all its medieval uses, with parking added!

The effect of all this, however, is dependent on whether the recipient believes the good sense and the good faith of the sender. In this example the senders were professional men, sufficiently well known and not in a suspect relationship with the reader. Nonetheless, their report is persuasive only in so far as it confirms, rather than erodes, the tentative trust with which the reader begins reading. Where the sender is suspect, he must overcome the suspicion before any attention will be paid to his message. And in many communications this is the only point at issue.

In its first five years the British National Coal Board closed 275 pits. In nearly every case the need for closure was agreed in local discussions at pit level; but in five cases it was not. These were accorded very full consultation at national level, in the lively consciousness that the main issue was confidence in the authority which had taken the decision.

Everyone came to the consultation – the pit manager and the union representatives from the pit; district management and district union representatives; the national union and the national board. The district representative on the national mineworkers executive argued the whole case afresh with the Board's chief mining engineer and anyone else concerned. The rest sat and listened.

The people from the pit concerned learned, confirmed or corrected a number of facts about their own pit. More important, they learned how management appreciated the situation of which this closure was part, the interlocking variables, technological, financial, logistic and social, which they had defined as the situation. Still more important, they saw and heard the men who had made the decision and were able to form their own opinion of their competence and honesty and understanding.

They learned something from the simple fact that they had been invited.

In four cases what they learned made the decision acceptable. They did not need to agree that it was right. They needed only to conclude that it had been honestly made by competent men who adequately understood all the relevant aspects of the situation, including those which mattered most to the people on the spot. I think they were right in reaching that conclusion and I don't think they would have reached it if it had not been right.

In the fifth case the consultation altered the decision. The closure was postponed. The Board too learned something from the exchange of communication – perhaps even from making its own views explicit.

These two examples illustrate the three functions which I have distinguished and the interconnection between them. The first was in effect an educative exercise addressed by the authors to the world at large, as well as to those who commissioned their report. Its object was to spread a more rational and adequate understanding of the situation created by a crowded, urban environment; the extent to which it could be controlled and the relation between the different costs and benefits to be expected from different exercises in intervention or inertia. Readers of the report, comparing its 'appreciation' with their own, might reject it but they would at least be changed by knowing how the committee saw 'the situation'. And it is unlikely that their own view would be wholly unaffected by the comparison.

The second example was a mutual exchange between specific parties divided about specific proposed action. Yet the similarities are greater than the differences. It also was an exercise, in this case a mutual exercise, in education. The decision by one side whether to maintain or revise the decision and by the other whether to accept or contest it resulted from the changes generated by this process of mutual learning. Both sides were left changed or confirmed in the view of the situation which they brought to the meeting (and even confirmation is change). And what was learned in the specific case affected each party's appreciation of the whole industry, just as the generalisations conveyed by the Buchanan report had their application to every current problem of urban planning.

In each case some degree of mutual confidence was necessary to the intended function. In each case it was generated by the way the function was performed. And in each case, especially the second which allowed mutual exchanges, the process of communication itself was carefully designed and monitored with a clear understanding of the load which it was carrying, so as to further its two linked functions.

Each of the three functions deserves more detailed consideration.

## IV. The relevance and variety of human relations

The most basic function of human communication is to establish, change or maintain the relationship of the parties. All its other functions depend on this, though its importance varies with the situation.

The relation between the parties may vary along several dimensions.

Their attitudes to each other may vary from extreme hostility to extreme benevolence; and it may vary equally from extreme preoccupation with each other, whether friendly or hostile, to almost complete indifference, which may be unilateral or mutual. Their mutual intentions may vary from willed destruction, through coercion and bargaining to the highest levels of mutual support and cooperation. Not least the relations may vary in their relevance to the communication, which may require only a low or a very high level of mutual trust.

In achieving this function, communication is easiest when it involves no more than maintaining a low existing level of mutual trust which is undisturbed by the situation involving the communication. It is most difficult when higher levels of confidence need to be built up quickly, especially when it involves maintaining or even creating high levels of confidence in a situation calculated to breed doubt or distrust. In every case each party must confirm or alter his model of the other on which he bases his expectations. The more dependent he is on these proving reliable and the less confirmed they are by comparable past experience, the more difficult is the learning process which the exchange involves for him. And where he too needs to evoke similarly radical changes in the other, the more difficult for him is the teaching aspect of the same exchange.

These difficulties are due not only to the fact that either party may try wilfully to deceive the other but also to the fact that neither is wholly predictable or controllable even to himself. The expectations which we learn to entertain of other men are different in both nature and source from those which we entertain of the natural world. This difference is of fundamental importance to the study of communication, which is so largely devoted to creating a fabric of reliable expectations.

Herbert Simon[3] recently distinguished natural science from what he called the sciences of the artificial. The subject matter of natural science is the natural world which would be as it is if men were not here to observe it. But the environment in which we move is increasingly man-made. Even a tool is explicable only in terms of human purposes, much more an institution, a language, a culture. What kind of knowledge, asks Simon, can we expect to have about something which might be other than it is?

My answer is more extensive than Simon's and might not be acceptable to him. The expectations which we build from experience about the natural world assure us of regularities, invariant or statistical, which we cannot alter, though we can use our knowledge to manipulate the natural world. Our experience of other people, on the other hand, reveals regularities nearly all of which have been developed in them by what their society expects of them. If they are more reliable than the weather, it is because they are concerned to be reliable and their neighbours are concerned to keep them so in all those matters where each needs to be able to rely on his expectation of others. The laws of England are different from the laws of nature. They define not what will be but what ought to be. They are agencies which impose regularity, not observations which record it. And the regularities they impose are neither invariant nor statistical. They exemplify the net of mutual expectations which imposes on human life such regularity as it possesses.

This dual function of expectation in the human world is, incidentally, the reason why the distinction between pure and applied science, clear in the natural sciences, is so confused in the social sciences.

If confidence in the other were bred only by personal acquaintance and experience, even traditional societies would have fallen apart and modern societies could never have come into being. By far the most extensive body of mutual expectations on which we all rely is the body of expectations which we attach to the holders of positions, that they will act according to the responsibilities attached to those positions. We expect these role holders both to do what their positions require of them and to abstain from doing what the proper playing of their roles forbids. And they expect the same of us, in so far as we play roles which affect them. These mutual expectations have seldom been so reliable in human history as they are in Britain today, even though they are being eroded at an alarming rate. However strong or weak, they multiply trust between strangers which could not otherwise exist. I will return to the importance of these rules when considering institutional communication.

## V. Coercion, bargain and persuasion

The second function of communication is closely associated with the first. It is the function of changing the way in which one or both parties see or value some situation.

It may or may not also be intended to make another party do what he would not otherwise do, by coercion, bargain or persuasion. This is a dimension along which several levels of communication can be discerned. But they can all be reduced to a change of appreciation. The simplest formula of coercion – 'Do this or else' – introduces into the situation of the person addressed a new fact, the threatened contingency which awaits him if he refuses. Similarly the simplest formula of bargaining – 'If you do this, I will ...' – introduces into his situation a desirable contingency which alters the 'pay-offs' inherent in his situation.

Both depend on the ability of the person addressed to draw the logical conclusions and to be moved to action or restraint by contingent costs and benefits still in the future. Both therefore admit of levels of refinement dependent on the capacity of the person addressed to envisage and attach value to contingent future states. But neither of them requires of him any attitude towards the other party except the belief that he will perform what he threatens or promises if (but only if) the contingency arises. Nor does it require him to share or even understand that view of the situation which the other party holds.

Persuasion involves more radical changes in one or both parties. The Buchanan report invites the planned for, no less than the planners, both to recognise limitations and to believe in possibilities which, being unfamiliar, might not occur to them unless they allowed their minds to be led over the conceptual structure which the committee had created. The Coal Board, in my other example, invited those who their action would gravely hurt to examine the assessment of costs and benefits which commended it – costs and benefits which works in the particular pit would not normally take into account – and to agree that these were properly to be considered by those on whom the decision rested. The pitmen and their representatives were equally concerned to satisfy themselves that the costs *to them* were given their full value. In so far as either or both was *willing to consider* the views of the other the conditions of persuasion were present.

Thus the precondition of persuasion is willingness, in Mead's phrase, to 'take the role of the other'. It is a crucial condition which is not required in either coercion or bargaining. It need not result in either party being in fact persuaded. The essential factor is willingness to be led by the other to understand the other's appreciation.

Of my two examples the Buchanan report was an exercise in public education of the most general kind, whilst the Coal Board consultation was a confrontation between employers and union over specific action in a context of conflict. But the nature of the communication involved was essentially the same.

So in considering this function of communication I distinguish two dimensions, in each of which several levels of difficulty can be distinguished. One is the difficulty of envisaging and valuing costs and benefits increasingly subtle and remote in time and increasingly obscured by doubt and uncertainty. The other is the difficulty of taking the role of the other. The second is also part of the first, for in estimating the future course of events the behaviour of the other is an important component which can only be predicted however uncertainly by making assumptions about his motivations. But it is also important in its own right, because it is essential to building up wider and more commonly shared appreciations of a common situation which may in turn become the basis for more effective communication and greater mutual confidence.

## VI. Meta-communication

The third function of communication is important to the health and growth of the other two and is itself speeded by their growth.

As a lawyer it was at one time a familiar experience for me to seek agreement on documents drawn under English law with foreign lawyers whose domestic laws were different and who were not at home in English law or in the English language. I recall one occasion in particular when the only language common to all concerned was one which was native to none of us and which none of us spoke well. There were substantive points of difference between us on which agreement had to be negotiated. There were also countless misunderstandings due to differences of language and differences of legal concept. It was essential to distinguish the second, which were difficulties of communication, from the first, which were differences of interest; and to clear up the second before embarking on the first. This involved a great deal of meta-communication.

It might be expected that these difficulties of communication would have aggravated the difficulties of negotiation. In fact they had a dramatically opposite effect. In our efforts to understand one another our interests were wholly identical and the pursuit of this intellectual quest united us so closely that, although strangers when we first met, our negotiations, when we could at last begin them, were conducted as between familiar colleagues.

The example may seem too abnormal to be useful. In fact, it makes visible universal difficulties which are too often overlooked. Differences in the meaning of words and concepts constantly divide and confuse even those who communicate in their shared mother tongue. Moreover, these difficulties cannot and should not be eliminated. They are essential to the usefulness of language, which is creative only because it is imprecise.

Most people recognise that the content of most words develops with use. Those who compile dictionaries discover the current meaning of words by listing the ways in which they are actually used. And those who revise dictionaries, listing later usages, record changes and developments which have produced new words and changed the meaning of old ones. But it is not always realised that this open-endedness is essential to communication. Freedom, for example, denotes a universal human aspiration; but it is and needs to be open-ended, even ambiguous. It is worth endless discussion precisely because every age has to redefine its content.

The same is true of most factual categories. What is a house? When does a shack or shelter in which people live deserve to be regarded as a house? The qualifications change with time and illustrate the other aspect of creative imprecision and its practical importance.

In Britain today the standards to which any human dwelling is expected to conform are different from and much more exacting than those which were operative a century ago. They include, for example, indoor water and sanitation, which were relatively rare luxuries a century ago. The sources of these standards are many and disparate but they are all familiar. Urban density brought health hazards which growing medical knowledge turned into demands for pure water and sewage disposal. Industrial interests pushed the sale of pipes. Snobbery reinforced the convenience of the bathroom by making it a status symbol. Human sympathy then applied to the poor standards which had become the necessities of the rich; and even those not so moved observed that the widening franchise was making the favour of the poor more worthy of cultivation. In this and other requirements the standards of what a house should be grew and proliferated, producing in our day that significant expression the 'sub-standard house', to denote a dwelling which falls short of what a house 'ought to be'.

The example testifies to the growth of standards of expectation defining the limits of the acceptable and to the part of communication in this process. These standards are themselves basically tacit and specific; but they are partly developed by verbal argument appealing to principles which are general and explicit, such as justice, equality and compassion. Succeeding generations learned to be shocked at what did not shock their fathers; they redefined the limits of the acceptable. These new definitions become explicit in building codes and sanitary regulations. But these, expressed in words, are more general and more rigid than the tacit standards which give rise to them and which are constantly being changed by being applied to concrete cases.

There is thus constant interaction between the tacit and specific standards by which we make judgments and the explicit general words with which we justify them. And this is equally true whether we are arguing about what constitutes freedom or what constitutes a house. This distinction between tacit norms and explicit values is commonly overlooked. I believe it to be important; I shall return to it when dealing with intrapersonal communication.

## VII. Institutional communication

A great deal of communication takes place, to, from and between institutions, notably government departments, business corporations, trade unions and universities. Much of this is conducted by persons playing specified roles in the institution, a cabinet minister, a welfare officer, a bank manager, a shop-steward, a professor. Some of it is conducted on behalf of the institution by persons whose roles are minimised or made invisible. The recipient of a letter from a government department beginning 'I am directed to inform you ...' need not trouble to notice who signed the letter or in what capacity he signed. Where the signatory is minimised, the receiver must be guided solely by his understanding of the responsibilities which attach to the corporation as such. Where the signatory is significant, he can appeal also to his understanding of the responsibilities attaching to that particular role holder.

The distinction is masked today, because it has become fashionable to regard all our institutions, even every organization above the level at which its members can directly control it, as depersonalising and dehumanising environments, alien and threatening to individual men. Given such assumptions, communication with such bodies is bound to be suspect and those who represent them are likely to be regarded as diminished and distorted by their official roles. These assumptions, I believe, are false and mischievous, even lethal; but they are widespread and they demand to be understood. For our view of communication with and within institutions is bound to depend on our understanding of their nature and their relationship with the supposedly 'uninstitutionalised' individual.

We all belong to many human systems, some hierarchically arranged, some overlapping, all making partly inconsistent demands on us – as may, for example, the demands made on an individual who is a professional man, a member of a trade union, an employee of a public corporation and a citizen of the political society which includes them all. We all have roles to play in every system of which we form part, whether we are 'officials' or not; and our roles necessarily conflict. The management of these conflicts is the essence of the human condition. Human communication is the main agency by which these conflicts are resolved or contained. The limitations of our communicative skill is the main limitation on the level at which interdependent human life can be sustained.

Throughout human history the power of men over men has been controlled, as well as magnified, by organization and by the constraints and assurances implicit in organizational roles. And throughout nearly the whole of that history the quality of a man has been assessed by his success in performing his many social roles according to the criteria of his place and time.

So it is at first sight strange that institutions should have fallen into their present disrepute at a time when they are more competent and less corrupt than they have ever been before. The reasons for this change are too many to summarise but I will select three. First, the number and size of organizations of all kinds have greatly increased and so has their inter-relation. This has increased their conflicting demands on all who depend on them but hate to pay the price of their dependence. Secondly, the more recent of these bodies, business corporations and trade unions, are neither responsible to those most affected by their operations nor required even formally by their constitutions to have any regard for these unwilling victims of their activities. But the third and perhaps most far reaching reason is the radical and recent change in our concept of order itself.

For many centuries before the 18th the countries of the Judaeo-Christian tradition believed in a divinely appointed order, which was often invoked to support the existing politico-social order. A century before Darwin this began to give place to the idea of an evolving natural order. By the end of the 19th century biological and economic development had become weirdly coupled in a faith in 'automatic' progress, of which the political component was wholly negative. It required only the removal of constraints by the few, whether through monopoly of political power or through monopoly of the means of production, to allow order to evolve. Only in our day has it become accepted that human order is a human artifact, the supreme work of human art, and like all works of art, to be realised only by the sacrifice of many potential alternatives. Hence the fierce fight between rival forms of ordering and rival ordering forces. Hence, even more important, the decay of the legitimacy accorded to any of them. Hence the efforts of totalitarian regimes to impose on their members acceptance of the legitimacy of their own form of 'order'; and hence, equally, the growing anarchy of those regimes which do not yet do or do not succeed in doing the same.

It is easy to see why our age should draw an unreally sharp distinction between personal communication and communication which takes place within institutions and between institutions and those outside their ambiance. The analysis offered by this paper helps, I think, to reduce this gulf to its proper proportions. Within any institution the members may be expected normally to communicate better than they otherwise would in so far as the self- and mutual expectations which their institution embodies supply an appreciative system more commonly shared than it would otherwise be. Even in communication between the institution and those outside its ambiance, communication should be easier in so far as those outside can represent to themselves the frame of reference of its role holders. On the other hand, since multiplying institutions are the primary source of those conflicts which increasingly disrupt the human scene, it is natural that they should also draw lines of cleavage along which comprehension breaks. And this likelihood is increased where disparities of power engender fear.

No institution is entitled to the undivided allegiance of its members. Equally, no one is entitled to deny his membership of *any* human system of which he is in fact a part. The only stable form of human society is one in which every institution commands from its members enough loyalty to keep it working and in which every member is sufficiently aware of all his memberships to temper the demands of each of them. It is entirely possible, perhaps highly probable, that the developments of the past two centuries have created an institutional world too demanding for its members to manage. If so, polarised conflict will soon reduce it to the level of our limitations. But we cannot tell how great these limitations may be and we have a duty to enlarge them as far and as swiftly as we can. This is the most critical demand of our day on communication and on us as communicators.

## VIII. Intra-personal communication

I must deal even more summarily with the neglected subject of intra-personal communication.

We use the word 'consciousness' in at least four different senses. We use it to describe varying levels of *awareness*, from the liveliest activity to deep sleep. We use it to describe selective *attention*, as when our absorbtion in a game or a book excludes our awareness of anything else. We use it negatively to describe phenomena of *repression*, when unwelcome memories or appreciations are prevented from rising to consciousness. But its most common use is to describe the phenomena of *reflection*. When we say to someone, 'Think what you are doing!', we are inviting him to reflect on the nature and consequences of some course of activity; and we imply our belief that, if he does so, he may come to appreciate it differently and perhaps abstain from doing it.

This process of reflection produces what I have called appreciation of the contexts and situations in which we are acting. It is closely related to the use of words, and to their open-ended character. It is not surprising then that we sometimes learn more from what we say than from what we hear. Our words do more than make our thoughts explicit. In doing so they expose our tacit 'settings' to reflection. These are changed thereby and others are elicited. Our tacit and explicit components are capable of productive dialogue.

In this familiar personal experience we have the counterpart of that interchange between tacit norms and explicit values which I described and illustrated in the field of social policy. It seems to me to be the distinguishing mark of humankind. It enables us to enlarge the frontiers between 'I' and 'not-I' and between 'Now' and 'non-Now' and this is to enlarge the conscious living space which is the hallmark of human life. It has its dangers also; for it emphasises man the observer at the expense of man the experiencer and even distorts the character of man the doer. These dangers are the subject of a growing literature; I cannot pursue them here. But it is central to my theme to insist that these exchanges between the tacit and the explicit components of our minds are a form of communication characteristically human, vitally important and similar in character to other forms of human communication.

## IX. Conclusions

Although my reflections have ranged over wide areas, I do not think that they have at any point strayed outside the field which my subject demands. For I am saying nothing less than that the world we inhabit is made of words. The natural world, the human world and the personal world are built of expectations formed, nourished and monitored largely by verbal communication. Communication has built and constantly renews the appreciative system which is both its product and its interpreter. Each of us participates for good or ill or (usually) both in repairing and renewing this invisible fabric, on which human life subsists in dependence as complete as the dependence of biological life on the tattered robe of humus, inches thick, which surrounds our otherwise arid planet. This film of humus which supports biological life today and tomorrow is largely formed by the decay of vegetation accumulated through a million yesterdays. Similarly the cultural humus in which we grow, the fabric of our assumptions and expectations is the product of patient accumulation, won by men intent to preserve and develop their shared body of concepts and values which make their life human. The physical soil is a complex and vulnerable structure; the product of millennia can be poisoned or washed away in a night. Our cultural soil is an even more complex structure and even more vulnerable; and we depend on it no less.

I believe therefore that the ascending levels of communication which I have indicated along each of the three dimensions of communication represent a vector leading in the direction of developing humanity. It is the most fundamental dimension of human progress. And though it cannot be capable of indefinite expansion, it is the only form of progress which is unlikely to breed its own reversal.

# References

1. I have developed this concept more fully in *The Art of Judgment*, London, Chapman & Hall, and New York, Basic Books, 1965; and Methuen University Paperbacks, 1968; and in *Value Systems and Social Process*, London, Tavistock Publications, and New York, Basic Books, 1968; and Penguin Books, 1971.
2. Colin Buchanan (Chairman of Working Group), *Traffic in Towns*, London, HMSO, 1963.
3. Herbert Simon, *The Sciences of the Artificial*, Cambridge, MIT Press, 1969.

# 23

# Rationality and intuition*

## The causal and the contextual

Why not 'aesthetics in science'? Whence comes the implication that to find aesthetics in science is like finding poetry in a timetable? The answer lies in the sad history of Western culture which, over the last two centuries, has so narrowed the concepts of both Science and Art as to leave them diminished and incommensurable rivals – the one an island in the sea of knowledge not certified as science; the other an island in the sea of skill not certified as Art.

This debasement is relatively new. In medieval universities all fields of knowledge open to organized study were scientiae, and all fields of skill open to organized acquisition were Arts. Rhetoric and astronomy were equally scientiae; but the title accorded to the student who satisfied his examiners in these and in the other recognized scientiae was that of a Master of Arts. Similarly, Art was not separated from technology; there was an Art and Mystery of Bricklaying. Cellini made a splendid pair of front doors. Where was the boundary between art and architecture, mason, carver, builder and architect?

Moreover the two words 'Ars' and 'Scientiae' not only embraced virtually all skill and knowledge, but also overlapped each other's territory without offense. Everyone knew that knowing was a skilled *activity*, an *Art*. Both words connoted both product and process – on the one hand an accumulating store of knowledge and artifacts; on the other hand a growing heritage of transmitted skills and standards of skill and excellence in knowing and doing.

Science acquired its present limited meaning barely before the nineteenth century. It came to apply to a method of testing hypotheses about the natural world by observations or experiments which might give results inconsistent with the hypothesis to be tested. Thence it came to comprise the growing body of related hypotheses which had survived these tests. The method never explained wholly and often failed to explain at all how the hypothesis originally emerged. But this fact was not generally acknowledged until this century. Even now it courts opposition to describe a scientific

---

*From *Aesthetics in Science*, J. Wechsler (ed) 1978, based on a lecture given at MIT in April 1974, which was in turn based on *The Tacit Norm*, a paper prepared for a symposium on the Moral and Aesthetic Structure of Human Adaptation, held at Burg Wartenstein in July 1969.

theory as a work of *art*, largely because of the corresponding narrowing of the concept of Art.

Yet few would deny that a scientific hypothesis, a technological invention, a plan for a new city, a painting, a musical composition, and a new law are all human *artifacts*, skillful making by human minds of designs for ordering or explaining some aspects of what we experience as reality. And few would deny that all such designing involves the creation, imposition, and recognition of *form*.

Equally, few would deny that particular achievements such as these are episodes in a process of change which proceeds continuously, though slowly and often unconsciously, for example, in the kind of explanation which scientific minds find acceptable, in the kind of methods by which technologists approach their problems, in the aesthetic idiom in which artists express themselves, and in the ethical standards which lead societies to change their laws and customs. History reveals in retrospect the presence of standards in all these fields which guide those who work in them and those who criticize their work and which are themselves changed both by the creations which they guide and by the controversies which they provoke.

I am not denying in the least that there are differences between the different fields in which these 'arts' are practiced. Indeed, if I had space to pursue the theme, I would insist that these differences are much greater than are usually admitted either by scientists or by any of those who use the word 'science' as a generic term. I would insist that different fields of possible knowledge (scientiae) admit such different kinds as well as degrees of knowledge that it is confusing to class as 'science' even all those fields which aspire to the name. There are important differences between the natural sciences and the logical sciences which include all the branches of mathematics and symbolic logic. There are even more striking differences between the natural sciences and what Herbert Simon[1] has called the sciences of the artificial, by which he means the fields of knowledge of which the subject matter is partly man-made. Virtually our whole environment, he insists, is partly artificial in this sense. Not only tools, machines, and buildings but also institutions, languages, and cultures are human artifacts. What 'scientific' knowledge, he asks, is possible about a subject matter which might be other than it is?

I do not find his answer adequate, even on a very limited definition of 'science', but I warmly approve of the distinction which he draws. The regularities to be found in the 'artificial' world are different in origin, kind and reliability from those to be found in the natural world. The 'laws' of England are not 'laws of nature', and we have access to different means of knowing about them, notably a knowledge of human history which is open to us only because we ourselves are human.

I do not propose to pursue these differences here because I am concerned to explore the mental processes which are common to them all and especially the element connoted by the word aesthetics. My thesis is that the

335

human mind has available to it at least two different modes of knowing and that it uses both in appropriate combinations in its endless efforts to understand the world in which it finds itself, including its fellow human beings and itself. One of these modes is more dependent on analysis, logical reasoning, calculation, and explicit description. The other is more dependent on synthesis and the recognition of pattern, context and the multiple possible relations of figure and ground. The first involves the abstraction and manipulation of elements, irrespective of the forms in which they are combined. The other involves the recognition or creation of form, irrespective of the elements which compose it. Both are normal aspects of the neocortical development which distinguishes man from his fellow mammals. Both are needed and both are used in most normal mental operations.

They are often referred to as rationality and intuition, and the names would serve as well as any other, were it not that a difference in the character and function of the two capacities has attached to intuition, in our contemporary culture, a load of mischievous and misleading connotation.

The main difference to which I refer is that a rational process is fully describable, whereas an intuitive process is not. Because our culture has somehow generated the unsupported and improbable belief that everything real must be fully describable, it is unwilling to acknowledge the existence of intuition; and where it cannot avoid doing so, it tends to confine it to the area where the creative process is least constrained and most in evidence – namely the narrow contemporary concept of Art – so much so that when this ubiquitous faculty appears in the practice of 'science', it is greeted as a strange incursion from a foreign field called 'aesthetics'. But in my view this approach half accepts the cultural confusion which I wish to contest.

The theory of biological evolution is a convenient example. For a century before Darwin and Wallace the fact of biological evolution had been forcing itself into the consciousness of Western man. It was opposed by the strange belief, accepted for more than a thousand years, that each and every *possible* biological form had been specially created by a divine demiurge so obsessively creative that he could not leave any conceivable form unrealized. Lovejoy[2] has documented, in fascinating detail, the history of his theory and its eventual decay.

The main agent in its decay was the discovery of the fossil record. Here in sufficiently exact chronological order was a sequence of biological forms which exhibited continuity and discontinuity through change with time. Eohippus was a far cry from the favorite contemporary racehorse, yet the development of one from the other was clear enough.

Why was it clear? Measurement played no significant part in these acts of recognition. They were exercises in the human capacity of appreciating, comparing and contrasting *form*. They threw no light on how these developments took place or why some died out. That had to await a *theory*. But the apparent fact arrested human attention before there was a theory to explain it and provided the driving power to seek a theory. Without it there would have been no theory of evolution, for there would have been nothing to explain.

This intuitive sense of form entered also into the theory, the explication, no less that into the explicandum. The theory of natural selection implied a theory of particulate inheritance which did not exist in Darwin's day and would not exist for fifty years; indeed it seemed inconsistent with the view of biological inheritance then currently held. For if all inherited traits were mixed in a kind of general broth, no advantageous element could have survived long enough to develop its potential. Darwin was troubled when this was pointed out to him. His intuitive grasp of the way biological inheritance must work felt right. But ought he to trust it before theory had established its rightness by propounding and testing an explanation of *how* it worked? Happily he was already too deeply committed to withdraw. Time was to justify him.[3]

Are we to identify Darwin's intuition about the way inheritance must work with the intuition which asserted the fact of biological evolution? I think we should. If it strains the concept of 'aesthetics', even in the wide sense used in this book, let us widen that concept still further or choose some other term with less constraining implications.

It is, of course, perfectly reasonable to *mistrust* a faculty which is not fully describable (even though we cannot do without it), since its obscurity makes it hard to verify. We should expect then that the main function of the rational process would be to criticize and test so far as it can the products of the intuitive process. And this is, of course, precisely what it does, as the history of science so clearly shows. It can do so only in varying degrees and the less it can do so the more trust we have to repose in other tests by which we come to accept or to change the product of our intuition.

The history of the natural sciences is full of once accepted intuitions (such as the 'ether') which were later found to be unnecessary or wrong. Some of them held up the progress of science for centuries. Such was the intuitive belief that the paths of the planets must be circular. Some proved useful though wrong. Such was the original atomic theory. For two thousand years science proceeded on the unverified assumption that all material forms must be constructed of basic individual elements, capable of countless combinations but not themselves further divisible. Within a few years after the existence of atoms was first actually demonstrated, it was found that they lacked both the characteristics with which they had been credited. They were neither indivisible nor indestructible. Yet atomic theory, so far from receiving its death blow, took off into the new world of subatomic physics. One of the first dividends was an understanding of at least some of the forces which enabled atoms to combine, a fact predicated in the original theory, yet wholly inexplicable if atoms were, in fact, no more than elemental billiard balls.

I have therefore avoided so far as possible in this paper the use of the expression 'science and aesthetics'. I have chosen instead to concentrate on the relation between rationality and intuition. This is, indeed, well exemplified in the recent development of physics and mathematics to which this book is largely directed. But it is not confined to that context. I regard the creation and appreciation of form by the human mind as an act of artistry, whether the artifact be a scientific theory, a machine, a sonata, a city plan, or a new design in human relations. And I believe and seek to show that in all these acts of artistry, intuition and rationality are always involved, usually in the roles of creator and critic.

In the next section I explore the basis for this dualism. We know something about the processes of perception, cognition, and recognition. We know that we come to recognize repetitions and regularities in the physical world long before we have any theories about why these should be. We know that unsupported toys fall from our cots before we know anything about the law of gravitation. We know the reliability or otherwise of mother's behavior long before we know any psychology. Our knowledge is contextual before it extends to causality; and it grows in both dimensions half-independently. We learn to distinguish more subtly differentiated contexts, just as we learn to distinguish the operations of more generalized laws. And equally, we learn to envisage and create new contexts, just as we learn to detect new causal relations. The technological innovator is a creator of new contexts, just as the scientific innovator is a discoverer of new causal regularities often based on his discovery, or even creation, of new conceptual entities such as elements or particles. Synthesis and analysis, contextual and causal explanation are distinct though inseparable aspects of human mental process in all mental activities. It need cause us no surprise that they are equally manifest in physics and mathematics.

I stress the tacit nature of the standards which we develop to guide our intuitive processes because this has become a stumbling block to the 'rational' understanding of 'intuition', an aspiration which is obviously not fully attainable if the two are complementary capacities of the human mind.

In a later section I examine a process of design where the imposition of form on experience is more conscious and more obvious. I seek to show that in this case also the choice between possible forms is not governed by criteria which are fully describable and for the same reason.

In a brief last section I summarize the epistemological conclusions to which these reflections lead. They may not yet be orthodox, but they are far more constant with the thinking of our time than they would have been even a decade ago.

According to the view put forward here, knowing and designing are not separate or even separable activities, since our whole schema for knowing is a design, a model of reality consciously and unconsciously made, and constantly revised. Moreover it is a selective model made in response to our concerns which alone determine what we regard as relevant enough to be worth modelling. The design produced by the natural and the logical sciences is more conditioned by independent variables which it cannot 'redesign'. But it is a design for all that and a design that is intimately connected with the concerns that drive us to make it, concerns that notably include aesthetic satisfaction.

## Perception, cognition, and recognition

Professor Christopher Alexander, in his book *Notes on the Synthesis of Form*,[4] says, in effect, that design does not consist in the realization of form but in the elimination of 'misfit'. The designer approaches his task with a set of tacit criteria, which appear only when some specific design is found to be inconsistent with one of them. The norm is known only negatively, when it is infringed. For the state of 'fit' we have no evidence, except the agreeable absence of misfit. We have scarcely even a vocabulary for it – how vague and how numerous are all the antitheses to pain! Alexander observes that this elusive quality of the norm has been noted in other fields also; he instances the difficulty experienced by doctors when they try to define 'positive health', and by psychiatrists when they try to define psychological normality.[5]

I believe that Alexander's insight is of great generality and importance, and I shall develop it in ways which go beyond his statement and with which he might not agree. I shall postulate, as the basic fact in the organization of experience, the evolution of norms by which subsequent experience is ordered, and which are themselves developed by the activities that they mediate. I shall suggest that this evolution of norms is a fundamental form of learning; that it provides the criteria not only for ethics and aesthetics, but also for all forms of discrimination (including those used by the various sciences), and that the norms so developed are tacit by logical necessity.

Suppose, for example, that I say, 'That is an ash tree.' If you ask why I think so, I can only reply, 'Because it looks like one.' If you are not satisfied, we may approach the tree, examine its leaves and the character of its bark and its seeds, if it happens to be seeding. This analysis may or may not confirm my initial judgment but it played no part in making that judgment. The tree was too far away for me to see these details.

If I had said, 'That is a beautiful ash tree', you would have regarded my judgment as 'aesthetic' and we might have discussed the basis for my judgment that the tree was beautiful. Did I, for example, mean merely that it was an exceptionally fine specimen of its kind? It is less common to class as an exercise of aesthetic judgment the ability to classify it correctly as an ash tree, irrespective of my emotional response to it. This, nonetheless, is the wide sense in which I am using the words 'aesthetic' and 'intuitive'. The recognition of form is an exercise of judgment made by reference to criteria which are not fully describable because of the subtle combination of relationships in which they reside and equally because of their dependence on *context*.

I use the word 'norm' in an unusually wide sense, to cover the criterion for every judgment which classifies, whether it seems to involve a judgment of fact or of value. This distinction itself I regard as outmoded for more reasons than I shall have space to include. Professor Pitkin,[6] in her book *Wittgenstein and Justice*, has shown that the many different forms in which this antithesis is expressed (the 'is' and the 'ought', descriptive and normative, and so on) have different meanings. I shall stress that the *concern* of a human mind is necessary to define any situation and perhaps necessary to define even what we call a fact, since a fact wholly irrelevant to any human concern would not be knowable.

The norms which are best understood scientifically are those which turn visual sensory input into perception. The child learns to recognize and to name, partly by being often exposed to the same stimuli, partly by its own inner activity of ordering its experience, and partly by the persuasion of other human beings, exhorting, encouraging, correcting. In some way not yet fully understood, his central nervous system develops readiness to group together, attend to, and recognize aspects of his surround – faces, places, belongings, relations – which recur and are of interest to him and to organize his accumulating knowledge by classifying it in an increasing number of overlapping categories.[7]

These 'readinesses to classify' are commonly called schemata. The word 'schema' is important for my purposes because it is the only accepted word in a class much wider than that in which it is commonly used. We clearly develop 'readinesses to recognize' not only perceptual gestalten but also situations of great generality and complexity (such as illness and revolution) and concepts of great abstraction (such as entropy and the British constitution). We develop schemata, perceptual and conceptual, partly by being exposed to countless particular examples from which we abstract what they have in common for our purposes (as a doctor does in a hospital or a lawyer in the courts) and partly through the 'openendedness' of language, introducing us to abstractions which later examples make real (like a doctor with his textbook of physiology and a lawyer with his textbook of jurisprudence). It is commonly recognized that a combination of the two is the best way to develop those readinesses to recognize which it is the business of education to teach and of all ages to learn.

The duality of this process, though familiar to experience, has long been an offense to the Western scientific mind and has given rise to long-drawn controversy whether the mind *identifies* the familiar by checking a list of characteristics which define its identity or *recognizes* it by fitting some kind of perceptual gestalt to some kind of mental template. Adherents of either view can find plenty of weaknesses in the other,[8] but neither party, until recently, seems to have conceived the possibility that the brain might be capable of both processes and might use them in appropriate – or sometimes inappropriate – combinations. This, nonetheless, seems to be the fact. Brain scientists are much concerned with the neurological basis for this in the difference of function between the two hemispheres of the neocortex. I am not concerned with the problems of location which engage them, but I am intensely concerned with their finding that the human brain is indeed capable of what Dr Galin[9] calls 'two cognitive styles' of activity.

The child learns to see. So does the beneficiary of corneal grafting. So does the doctor learning to diagnose; the radiologist learning to read a radiograph; the stockbreeder and forester learning to distinguish a good specimen from a poor or sick one. So does the connoisseur of Chinese ceramics. All these people, later, can write books about the criteria they use, but they cannot express these fully in a rule which the inexperienced can apply. The future master must make these schemata his own by frequent use; and these schemata are also criteria, instruments by which specific misfits are detected, though they themselves cannot be specified.

Professor Woodger[10] instances the novice looking through a microscope for the first time. He has a visual experience, but he does not perceive anything because he has not yet built up the schemata by which to recognize the inhabitants of this elfin world. Cognition is the result, as well as the precursor, of recognition. G. H. Lewes[11] expressed this elegantly and generally as long ago as 1879. '... the new object presented to sense or the new idea presented to thought must also be *soluble in old experience*, be *recognized* as like them, otherwise it will be unperceived, uncomprehended.' (italics added)

Woodger has no use for the distinction between percepts and concepts. A percept is a concept. The link with the primary world of sensory experience is always tenuous and selective. A rabbit to an anatomist is a different bundle of abstractions from a rabbit to a cook – even if it be the same rabbit. Bruner, Goodnow, and Austin[12] agree with him that in perception, no less than in the most abstract thinking, the categories we use are our own invention; the order which we discover is imposed by ourselves and validated by its practical convenience to ourselves.

This is not to say that there is no order to be discovered in the natural world; on the contrary, the confirmation of experiment by the scientist and the less rigorous confirmation of the ordinary man's experience is taken as evidence that the order devised by the mind bears some valid relation to the order inherent in the 'real world out there'. We have at least constructed in our heads a viable analogue. But its viability is measured not only by its conformity with other experience of our own. It must also be sufficiently shared to mediate communication with others. Radical innovations in thinking take time to percolate into other minds and until they have done so, they are impotent and precarious.

Further, the validity of our chosen 'order' is measured also by its power to make our own experience acceptable to ourselves. For this it must be sufficiently concordant with the rest of our organizing concepts; and it must also create a world in which we can bear to live. Rokeach,[13] referring to 'belief systems' (which correspond closely to what I have called 'appreciative systems'), writes, 'Such systems ... serve two opposing sets of functions. On the one hand, they are Everyman's theory for understanding the world he lives in. On the other hand, they represent Everyman's defense network, through which information is filtered in order to render harmless that which theatens his ego ... a belief system seems to be constructed to serve both masters at once; to understand the world in so far as possible and to defend against it in so far as necessary.' This defensive function is not necessarily pathologic, though it always has a cost.

Thus, the world of reflective consciousness – I will call it the appreciated world – in which each of us lives, is structured by readinesses to conceive things and relations in particular ways, readinesses which are developed in our brains by experience, including experience received through human communication. I will extend the word 'schemata' to cover all such readinesses, since it is free from the normative implications of such words as 'standard', 'criterion', and 'norm' itself. None the less, such schemata do function as norms, standards, and criteria, even in the most purely factual acts of discrimination. Screening experience, they classify what 'fits' and reject 'misfits'. And they do so equally whether they define a state of affairs in my surround – 'That is a bull', or its implications for me – 'That is a threat', or a situation accepted by myself or others as requiring a particular response – 'That is an obligation.'[14]

## Some epistemological implications

I labor these familiar points because I want to rescue from their normal oblivion three facts which I believe to be highly important. First, facts are not data. They are mental artifacts, selected by human concerns and abstracted from experience by filtering through a screen of schemata. Second, this screen is necessarily tacit; we infer its nature only from observing its operations, but our inferences can never be complete or up to date. Third, the screen is itself a product of the process which it mediates and, though tacit, can be developed by deliberately exposing it to what we want to influence it. (This is the essence of education.)

These schemata do not exist in isolation. They develop within the multiple contexts of experience. I find it convenient to think of these contexts as ordered by a three-dimensional matrix. What we notice is selected by our concerns, and our concerns are excited by what we notice. I will call our concerns our 'value system' and call our organized readinesses to notice our 'reality system'.[15] I think of these as forming two sides of the matrix. The third is, of course, the dimension of time. Our reality system can represent the future and the hypothetical, as well as the actual present, and our value system can both evoke and respond to such constructions. Our most familiar mismatch signals are generated by the comparison of our expectations with our fears and our aspirations – that is to say, by comparing the constructions of our reality system and our value system when both are extended into the future.

I use and offer this simply as a convenient mental model. We are handicapped by lack of a realistic model of how our brains actually work, but communication science, by combining what we know of analogue and digital processes, can already provide us with a much more adequate picture than was possible even a few years ago, as Professor MacKay has shown.[16]

These schemata are systematically related; a chance in one will involve some change in others and will be resisted in proportion to the extent of change involved unless this resistance is offset by the perceived benefit promised by the change. The theory of biological evolution, for example, when first put forward, was perceived by some as a hugely liberating idea, by others as hugely threatening. Hence the intense controversy which it aroused among laymen as well as scientists.

The impact of change will also be affected by the ease with which the proposed change can be understood. Biological evolution, however acceptable or unacceptable, was widely understandable, at least in principle. The theory of relativity was not. This difference muted resistance in some quarters and increased it in others.

T. S. Kuhn[17] in *The Structure of Scientific Revolutions* has drawn a distinction between the normal course by which scientific knowledge grows by accretion and the periodic crises which call for a new 'paradigm'. He has pointed out that minds attuned to the 'normal' course seldom initiate the paradigm shift, though they unconsciously prepare the way for it. He has also observed that the same process is to be seen in art. So long as art worked within the paradigm of representation, its achievements were indeed cumulative. It progressively learned new ways to represent three-dimensional scenes on two-dimensional space. A new paradigm set new standards – not higher standards for the same kind of excellence but standards related to a different kind of excellence.

In fact, even what Kuhn calls 'normal' science does not proceed without minor shifts in 'tacit norms'. The simplest piece of induction is not explicable or even describable in the way in which we can describe and demonstrate the most complex deductive process. Nonetheless, paradigm shifts are most dramatically visible in the development of individual scientists and individual artists when they occur suddenly and make a major difference. Consider, for example, the story of Kepler, transported with excitement at suddenly seeing in Tycho Brahe's calculations what Tycho himself could not see – that they were consistent only with elliptical planetary paths, a concept banned from consideration by the authority of Aristotle. Most dramatic of all perhaps is the story of Kekule, seeing in a dream or vision as he dozed before the fire the benzene ring in the form of a whirling fiery serpent eating its own tail.

Wertheimer[18] claims that his discussions with Einstein showed how critical was the moment when it first occurred to Einstein to question the conventional concept of time. And although Miller[19] has criticized Wertheimer's reconstruction of Einstein's thought processes, his own well-documented account of those processes, not only in Einstein but in other leading minds who pioneered the amazing subsequent development of quantum theory, provides even more abundant examples of their paradigm shifts. It also reveals how closely these shifts are related to the personality and experience of the particular scientist involved. 'Making sense' of the world is, it seems, a highly individual activity, even where the subject matter of our enquiry is the apparently independent fields of the 'natural' and the 'logical' sciences. Why else should Heisenberg, fully at home in a nonvisualizable universe, call Niels Bohr's mathematics 'disgusting'.

Similar shifts are seen in the development of individual artists. The development of Picasso's art, as of many others, in other media as well as painting, illustrates the self-generated shifts of paradigm which a creative mind can achieve. The breakthrough comes sometimes after a spell of inactivity either willed or imposed by the artist's incapacity to produce. Sometimes it can be seen in retrospect as following a series of tentative struggles towards what, for the artist, was still a hidden goal. In either case, when it emerges it is unmistakable.

These dramatic shifts make visible with peculiar clarity the structure of tacit norms, previously taken for granted, which they assail and replace. I am equally concerned in this paper with the process by which a system of tacit norms changes gradually over time.

I will next examine an example of design of a different kind, the redesign of an urban environment. The effort is far more conscious. Nonetheless, the norms involved remain only half revealed both in the process by which the problem is, ultimately, defined and in the process by which one of many possible partial solutions is chosen. And the reciprocal effect of the effort on the norms by which it is guided, though not fully detectable even with the wisdom of hindsight, is no less important than in the example already examined.

## Design as the resolution of conflict between norms

Consider a problem of urban planning. Several criteria can be described in general terms. Buildings must have access to vehicular and pedestrian traffic appropriate to the activities which they generate; and the two types of traffic must be sufficiently separated to preserve an acceptable level of safety. Noise, air pollution, and interference with light must be kept within acceptable thresholds. And so on. But what in each case is the level of the appropriate and the acceptable? The policymaker may allot target values in each case but he can be sure that, if he pitches them high enough to be unquestioned, some at least, will not be capable of being realized. He cannot even make an exhaustive list, until an actual plan begins to emerge, so that its actual effect can be envisaged in each of the dimensions of success. He must wait for the planner before he can clearly define the problem that he wants the planner to solve.

What of the planner – in so far as his function can be separated? Each of the requirements which he has to satisfy (and which thus become his concerns) make relevant, as possibilities or limitations, features of the physical site; and these in turn suggest their relevance, for good and ill, to other requirements. Hypothetical solutions begin to shape themselves in his mind and in rough sketch plans; and these engender often unsuspected meanings as they intersect with the various requirements in which he is concerned or even suggest others with which he ought to be concerned. One cell after another in the matrix is activated by such intersections of concern and opportunity; and from each intersection streams of further activation resonate along all the dimensions of the matrix.

This exercise can easily lose itself in boundless complexity. The list of requirements and the facts relevant to each can be extended in number and time with no clear limit, and every extension multiplies their interactions with each other. Alexander, in the book already mentioned[20] makes some valuable suggestions for keeping these many-factored problems under control by identifying those variables which can be grouped together in relatively independent clusters. But in any but the simplest problem, it is, I believe, vain to hope for a solution which will produce for every requirement a 'fit' which would have been regarded as acceptable when the exercise began. Any solution will have to deal with some requirements in a way which will become acceptable only in the light of what it will make possible in other dimensions of success or, alternatively, of what is then seen to be the cost of making it any better, when this cost is measured in terms of the limitations it would pose on satisfying other requirements.[21]

The designer, then, like the scientist, is engaged in a synthetic exercise. He must produce a single design which will be judged by multiple criteria. Some of these reinforce each other; some conflict with each other; most compete with each other for scarce resources. All are affected in some degree by any change made in the interest of one of them. The number of possible designs, even within given costs, is unlimited and unknowable, for it depends on possibilities of innovation which cannot be known before they have been made. The comparison of one with another can be made only when both have been worked out and even then depends on the relative value attached to disparate criteria within the framework of a single solution.

However great the number of possible designs, the number submitted to the policy maker is seldom more than one. The resources demanded by large-scale planning are too great to permit detailed alternatives. Hence enormous importance attaches to the rapid and often obscure process by which the basic lines of the proffered solution are chosen, for these soon generate many vested interests, valid as well as invalid. Not least of these is that its sponsors, having grown familiar with its implications, can more confidently exclude the possibilities of unwelcome surprise, which would lurk in any alternative, until it had reached the same degree of elaboration.

The successful designer chooses what proves to be a viable approach by a process which is much better than random and which seems sometimes to be guided by uncanny prescience. So does the technological inventor, the scientific discoverer, the successful policy maker in government and business, and those apparently ordinary mortals whose human relations are at once richer, more varied, and more orderly than those of their neighbors. I do not postulate any unknown mental function – or, at any rate, any more unknown than they all are – when I describe these gifted people as having (like the artist) unusual sensitivity to form. But in thus grouping them together, I do suggest that they have something in common in terms of cerebral organizing capacity. I have no doubt that this something is a specially happy combination of the 'two cognitive styles' mentioned by Dr Galin in the paper already referred to – the one logical, analytic, and explicit; the other (and, in these cases, the more important) contextual, synthetic, and tacit.

## Giftedness in rationality and intuition

The tentative postulate seems to derive support from many sides. The capacity for sensory discrimination varies greatly between individuals. It is most easily charted in music because the sound patterns produced by musical instruments can be formally described,[22] even when they are immensely complex, as in concerted orchestral passages. It is demonstrable that people differ, not merely through differences in training, in their ability to recognize, for example, variations on a theme. It seems reasonable to suppose that this innate capacity for discriminating musical patterns sets limits both to musical interest and to musical achievement.

By discrimination in its most general sense I mean the ability to distinguish figure from ground, signal from noise.[23] It is the basic limitation of any information system. It is distributed between individuals not only unevenly but selectively. Those concerned with the study of gifted children distinguish at least four kinds of giftedness, each of which can be described as unusual power of discrimination. The most familiar are the intellectually gifted, who can be identified with some confidence by tests of ability to recognize logical, including mathematical, relations. Distinct from these are the inventive, whose ability for practical innovation can coexist with quite limited power to handle abstractions. The aesthetically gifted are again a class apart. They are often impractical and sometimes unintellectual; and their gift for appreciating sensory form is highly selective. Aesthetic appreciation of nature may be dissociated from the appreciation of the fine and applied arts; and within these last, sensitivity to one medium may not extend to others.

In the categories of conscious experience, these forms of giftedness cover a wide variety of gifts, but they are all mediated by the brain and central nervous system. They all involve discrimination, in some form, between figure and ground, signal and noise; and they all depend on tacit criteria developed by experience within the inherent limitations of the particular neural heritage.

Some students of human giftedness distinguish a fourth type – social giftedness. These are those who show unusual interest and ability in sensing, maintaining and creating relations with other people. These gifts too would seem to depend on unusually high capacity for discrimination. Students of human dialogue can show that it involves each party in setting up an inner representation of the other, and that the level of dialogue depends not only on the accuracy and refinement of this model, but also on the attitude of each to his inner representation of the other. G. H. Mead insisted on the social importance of a variable which he described as the ability and willingness to take the generalized role of the other. Communication theory begins to make this concept more precise.

I have distinguished two functions which in practice are never wholly separated but which are, nonetheless, logically distinct as two reciprocating phases in a recurrent process of mental activity. One is the creative process, which presents for judgment a work responsive to many explicit and tacit criteria. The other is the appreciative process, which judges the work by the criteria, tacit as well as explicit, to which it appeals, and finds it good or wanting, better or worse than another. The two phases of the process may alternate many times in the course of producing the work. The work may never be finished; in a sense it can never be finished, for it is part of an ongoing process. Even the individual works of an artist are part of his 'work', which ends only with his death, or when he has nothing more to say, and which continues even after that in the creative and appreciative minds which it quickens.

In the example last given, the form of the work was an urban design. An urban design may be viewed as a creation in any of the four fields in which we exercise judgment – scientific, technological, ethical, and aesthetic. It may be viewed as a work of art, appealing to aesthetic criteria, like a sculpture or a painting. It may be viewed as an invention, appealing to functional criteria of utility. It may be viewed as a social creation, appealing to criteria of social need and satisfaction. It may be viewed as an intellectual creation, and expression of abstract relations, like a scientific theory. Examples could be chosen which would more clearly emphasize any one of these aspects, rather than another. We may be right to distinguish sharply between these different kinds of knowing and their related criteria. Yet they have notable common features which are likely to correspond to common features in the working of the human brain or in the patterns which our culture imposes on it.

## The dynamics of change in normative systems

The common features I want to emphasize are the following:

1. The form is produced by the activity of a concerned mind structured by tacit norms as well as by explicit rules. This concerned mind abstracts for attention what I will call a *situation*, by which I mean a set of related facts relevant to its concern. Part of this situation is seen as not modifiable by the agent; I will call this the *context*. The rest of the situation is the area to which form is to be given. I will call it the *field*.[24]

2. The form is specific. It is to be realized in particular terms, by arranging the field in particular ways, in relation to the context.

3. Both phases of the process by which form is given to the field change the norms to which they consciously and unconsciously appeal. The appreciative phase changes them by the mere fact of using them to analyze and evaluate a concrete situation, for this may affect both their cognitive and their evaluative settings. The creative phase affects them by presenting new hypothetical forms for appreciation. The realization of the chosen form still further affects the norms involved, for it affects the situation, including its division between field and context. It would thus alter the stream of match and mismatch signals generated by the situation, even if it had not already altered the setting of the norms themselves.

This process of change is the focus of my attention, for I believe it is the key to our understanding of our predicament and of the scope of our initiative. I have argued that we know anything at all only by virtue of a system of largely tacit norms, developed by individual and social experience, which itself is structured by our individual concerns, and that this system has the threefold task of guiding action, mediating communication, and making personal experience meaningful and tolerable. It can change only at a limited rate, if it is not to fail in one or more of its functions. Its failures at the level of the individual can be studied in any mental hospital, and at the social level, in all the more disturbed periods of history, notably the present. Hence the importance of understanding the process of change, its possible patterns, and its inherent possibilities and limitations.

The system of tacit norms, which I call an appreciative system, tends to be self-perpetuating. Our mutual understanding and cooperation, our powers of prediction and effective action depend on its being widely shared and accepted. So any challenge to it awakes protective responses. Each generation has a powerful interest in transmitting it to the next. Representing as it does the accumulation of experience, it is supported both by authority and history.

In the social field it is also to some extent self-validating, since sanctioned mutual expectations tend to elicit the behavior which will confirm them. In the field of the natural sciences, where the variables are more independent, this conservatism is less likely to be self-validating though it may long inhibit change. Michael Polanyi[25] lived long enough to see the adoption in his lifetime of a scientific hypothesis formulated by him forty years before, but barred from acceptance in the meantime by its departure from the then most acceptable style of explanation. In his account of this experience he expresses his approval of this degree of inertia, even though it nearly cost him his scientific career.

On the other hand, such systems also contain within themselves the seeds of their own reversals. Each is a work of art, however unconscious, and, like all works of art, attains form only by a process of selection which excludes possible alternative forms. These in time clamour for realization. They are kept alive in the meantime in those individuals and subcultures which are least satisfied by the accepted systems; and they grow at the expense of the accepted system as soon as that system ceases to command the confidence and authority of its heyday.

Furthermore and more conspicuously, the accepted system is challenged by changes in the context, often brought about indirectly by its own development which renders that context no longer appropriate. These changes may be in the physical or the institutional or the social or even the intellectual context. All are abundantly illustrated in the recent history of the Western world. Physical exploitation has posed problems of pollution which turn growth from a promise into a threat. Market institutions, developing, have changed the nature of the market. Democratic political institutions, developing, have transformed the concept of democracy. 'Liberal' values have made a world which increasingly rejects liberal values. Styles of scientific thinking, pushed to their extremes, reveal their limitations and subsume or are overwhelmed by their rivals. 'Teleology', for example, a word wholly unacceptable to science even fifty years ago, attained respectability almost overnight as soon as it could be applied to manmade machines.

Finally, the accepted system may be challenged by collision with rival appreciative systems. This also is being illustrated by contemporary history as never before. In a world where interactions multiply on a planetary scale, inconsistent subcultures multiply by fission to attest the passionate need of each individual for an apt and shared appreciative system, however small the sharing group. It is in no way surprising that increased physical contacts across the world should have called into being not 'one world' but more mutually antagonistic worlds than ever before.

It may be objected that this, even though true in those fields of *scientia* which are affected by human culture, is not true of the natural sciences. The world's atomic scientists talk a common language, even though the world's politicians do not. I have argued that this is true only as a matter of degree.

## Conclusions

It seems to me possible, in the light of these ideas, to arrange the different fields of potential knowledge in an order which explains both the extent to which they are open to human knowing and the extent to which our acceptance of our knowledge rests on its survival of rational tests on the one hand and its congruence with tacit standards of form on the other. This 'order' does not involve sharp breaks between 'scientific knowledge' and 'unsupported beliefs'.

It is generally recognized today that even in the natural sciences the scientific method does not 'validate' its hypotheses. It can only test them and attach increased credence as they survive those tests. It is recognized also that credence develops at least as much from the congruence of theory with the existing body of knowledge and from its facility in explaining facts other than those which it was devised to explain and in generating further hypotheses which depend on it.

Less commonly recognized is the limited extent of the knowledge confirmed even to this extent and the status of the remainder. Even in the natural sciences theories rightly retain their power even though well established facts show that they must be at least incomplete. For example, the ascertained facts of what is now (perhaps mistakenly) called extrasensory perception show that our current ideas of sensory perception must be at least incomplete. But in the absence of a theory to link what we do not understand with what we do understand, these facts await incorporation in the general body of knowledge, just as the evidence for biological evolution had to await its explanatory theory. Even an adequate theory may have to wait long for acceptance, as Polanyi's experience showed, for no better reason than its departure from current fashions of explanation.

Equally often rival theories compete to explain the same set of facts, as did Ptolemaic and Copernican astronomy. The judgment that accepted the second was not the result of 'rational' resting. It was not even a preference for simplicity. For Copernicus, retaining circular planetary motion, had as much mathematical difficulty in accounting for his observations as did his Ptolemaic predecessors. Yet his theory, rightly in my view, bears his name, rather than that of Kepler who first gave the theory its manifest superiority in simplicity.

The situation is even more extreme in the field which Herbert Simon has called the 'Artificial'. For example, it is sometimes objected that most psychoanalytic theory is 'unscientific' because it cannot be disproved. This may be so, but we are not therefore irrational in accepting it in so far as we judge it to serve our need better than others or better than none. Human motivation is complex and culture-bound. Why should we expect to 'understand' it completely or once and for all?

The example is also a disturbing reminder of the relation between knowledge and design in the field of the 'artificial'. However unsupported these theories may be deemed to be, countless families in the past seventy years have made them *true for them* simply by accepting them. And more generally they have become part of Western culture to the extent that they have affected our basic assumptions about the areas in which they operate.

It is a minor example of this, for Western culture has been profoundly affected by the findings, the methodology, the attitudes, and the outlook of scientists. It is not wholly the fault of scientists that what has passed into the general culture is grossly distorted in two critical ways. One is the mistaken identification of science with rationality. The other is the exaggerated dichotomy between science and nonscience. These two errors are none the less a grievous threat to our understanding of our own mental processes, for they ignore two basic facts of human epistemology.

The first of these is that our basic knowledge of the world, our neighbors, and ourselves is a set of expectations based on exposure to the regularities of experience. Science has vastly amplified and refined these expectations, but what lies outside its reach is by far the greater part.

Second, the appreciation of form based on tacit standards is as basic to science as to the much wider area of our tacit and explicit assumptions. It emerges most clearly from a study of the great innovations in science, but it is equally important and far more common in conserving and securing general acceptance for the common assumptions on which all our cooperative activity proceeds, not least the cooperative activity of science.

# References

1. Herbert Simon, *The Sciences of the Artificial*, Cambridge, MIT Press, 1969.
2. A. O. Lovejoy, *The Great Chain of Being*, Cambridge, Harvard University Press, 1966.
3. In fact I understand that the theory of particulate inheritance has itself been so qualified by deeper understanding of the interactions of the gene pool that genetic theory today is more similar in its actual effect to that presumed in Darwin's day than the theory which emerged in 1905.
4. Christopher Alexander, *Notes on the Synthesis of Form*, Cambridge, Harvard University Press, 1967.
5. Christopher Alexander, op. cit., p. 198, note 21.
6. Hanna F. Pitkin, *Wittgenstein and Justice*, Berkeley, University of California Press, 1972.
7. The evidence on the subject of perception is conveniently summarized in M. L. Johnson Abercrombie, *The Anatomy of Judgment*, London, Hutchinson, 1960. The relation of cognitive capacity to neural development is, of course, the focus of most of the work of Piaget.
8. This was the focus of contention especially in the second decade of this century between gestalt psychologists (for example, Koehler, Wertheimer) and holistic philosophers (for example, Bergson, Smuts) on the one hand and traditional, analytic, reductionist science on the other. As so often occurs, the manifest facts on which the innovators were insisting were ignored because they were offered, or at least construed, as an 'either or' choice in which acceptance meant the rejection of equally valued insights on the other side. The debate continues to be bedevilled by the 'either or' disease even today when physics has blessed the concept of complementarity. Let us hope that neurophysiologists will prevail on the field on which psychologists and philosophers battled almost in vain.
9. David Galin, 'Implications for Psychiatry of Left and Right Cerebral Specialisation', *Archives of General Psychiatry*, October 1974, Vol. 31. This paper also contains an extensive review of the literature on this subject. For a special study of its implications for pattern recognition, see Roland Puccetti, 'Pattern Recognition in Computers and the Human Brain', *Brit J. Phil. Sci.* Vol. 25, 1974, pp. 137-154.
10. Professor Woodger, *Biological Principles*, London and New York, Harcourt Brace, 1929.
11. G. H. Lewes, *Problems of Life and Mind*. Quoted in M. L. Johnson Abercrombie's *The Anatomy of Judgment*.

12. J.S. Bruner, J.J. Goodnow, and G.A. Austin, *A Study of Thinking*, New York, Wiley, 1956.

13. Milton Rokeach, *The Open and Closed Mind*, New York, Basic Books, 1960.

14. Professor Rhinelander, in his book, *Is Man Incomprehensible to Man?*, expresses his opinion that this view is 'essentially accurate' even though it 'is at odds with much current philosophical theory and ... bristles with controversial assertions and implications', Portable Stanford, 1973, pp. 77, 78.

15. I have developed this concept of interacting reality and value system elsewhere, notably in *The Art of Judgment*, London, Chapman & Hall, and New York, Basic Books 1965, Ch. 4; and *Value Systems and Social Process*, London, Tavistock Publications, and New York, Basic Books, 1968, Ch. 9.

16. Notably in a paper 'Digits and Analogues', published in the proceedings of the 1968 AGARD Bionics Symposium, Brussels, which also contains the major references to his earlier works.

17. T.S. Kuhn, *The Structure of Scientific Revolutions*, Chicago, University of Chicago Press, 1970.

18. See M. Wertheimer, *Productive Thinking*, New York, Harpers, 1959, p. 214.

19. Arthur I. Miller, 'Albert Einstein and Max Wertheimer: A Gestalt Psychologist's View of the Genesis of Special Relativity Theory', *Hist. Sci.* XIII, 1975, pp. 75–103.

20. Chistopher Alexander, op. cit., Ch 5.

21. Well illustrated in the *Buchanan Report on Traffic in Towns*, London, HMSO, 1963, p. 16.

22. Jeanne Bamberger distinguishes the formal structure of music from the (much less describable) figural structure imposed by the performer and the hearer and has shown that young children impose a figural pattern even on a sound sequence from which the performer has eliminated all but formal elements. ('The Development of Musical Intelligence 1', July 1975, unpublished.) She is Associate Professor of Education, Division for Study and Research in Education, Massachusetts Institute of Technology and Associate Professor of Humanities (Music) at the same institution.

23. When I refer to 'distinguishing signal from noise' I do not wish to imply that there is necessarily only one distinction to be made. Many alternative divisions of figure and ground may be possible. Dr Hans Selye has described how, as a young medical student making his first contact with hospital wards, he was struck not by the variety of the patients' symptoms but by the similarity which distinguished them all from the nurses and doctors around them. They *all looked ill*. He learned his appointed lesson, which was to distinguish and diagnose their disease. But he did not forget his initial insight. It was later to inspire what was to be his predominant life work as a researcher – the study of the body's response to stress of any kind – which he was to call the general adaptation syndrome. Hans Selye, *The Stress of Life*, New York, McGraw-Hill, 1956, pp. 14–17.

24. I take this use of the word 'context' from Alexander (4).

25. Michael Polanyi, 'The Potential Theory of Adsorption', *Science* Vol. 141, No. 3585, pp. 1010–1013.

# 24

# Will and free will*

## Summary

1. The will is postulated in common speech only in relation to decisions involving the resolution of conflict between a response which is established and one which is (a) imperfectly learned, and (b) commended by criteria of necessity or obligation (or commitment). These are defined.

2. Thus to postulate the will as a mental faculty is to assert that a conscious process can expedite the learning of responses of this kind and the acceptance of the 'governors' (defined) by which such responses are dictated. Strength or weakness of will denotes greater or less facility for this kind of learning.

3. Freedom of the will is postulated only in relation to a class of decisions significantly different from the class described above; and, unlike strength and weakness, it does not admit of degrees. These facts suggest that it is predicated only of those responses and 'governors' which, in view of the predicator, could be and should be learned.

Thus the words 'will' and 'free will', as actually employed, have useful meanings, corresponding with common experience and carry psychological and neuro-physiological implications which deserve to be further explored.

I

The 'will' and 'free will' suggest primarily the theories, often inconsistent or discredited, which have gathered round the experience of human volition and responsibility; but behind the theories and independent of their validity lie the regularities of experience which the words were devised to denote. Theory designed to enrich and refine may sometimes obscure or distort the meanings of common speech; and some such fate seems to have befallen the unfortunate words 'will' and 'free will'. For when we enquire in what contexts these words are actually used, we find we can attach to them useful and precise, if unexpected meanings.

Not all decisions are supposed to admit of resolution by an act of will. Suppose (Case 1) that I take up the menu in a restaurant, hungry and unrestricted by money or digestion. What shall I choose? I have only to

---

*Unpublished paper prepared in 1979.

discover what I 'prefer'. The rival invitations of roast beef and roast mutton must be allowed to generate their respective responses in my head. The issue may not be trivial. If, I have been for years in a prison camp or for months at sea, the choice of my first meal may be hugely significant; for whatever I choose means saying 'no' to a host of delicious alternatives. Yet, however acute my quandary, my will cannot help me – unless, embarrassed by long hesitation, I call it in aid of 'choose something', as against remaining undecided, which is, of course, a different issue.

But suppose (Case 2) that I am dieting or economizing or training for a race. I should love to order lobster and champagne but my regime or my budget calls for herring and water. My will enters the lists in favour of herring; and if I choose herring, I shall explain my choice to myself and others in a way different from the way I should adopt if I had fallen for lobster.

What is the difference between Case 1 and Case 2? Common sense has no doubt about this and common speech reflects its certainties. Case 1 is a conflict between 'wants'. Case 2 is an example of the conflict which arises when the field of 'I want' is narrowed by 'I must (or must not)' or 'I ought (or ought not)'. These verbs imply governors of behaviour, assumed to exist and to be different from one another; and they would not have come into common use, if they did not reflect, however superficially or ineptly, facts of common experience. The psychologist, though he cannot define them professionally in ways which are wholly satisfactory, accepts and uses them in daily life, no less than the layman; for he cannot do without them. I too shall for the moment accept and use these categories at their face value. Later, I shall give them a more exact meaning.

So far it appears that the will cannot be involved in conflicts within the field of 'I want' and that it can be involved in conflicts between 'I want' and 'I must' or 'I ought'. Yet even in these latter conflicts it is not necessarily involved. The disciplined man need not struggle to avoid buying what he knows he cannot afford or eating what he knows he cannot digest. The athlete in training does not seriously contemplate an orgy of lobster and champagne. Once established, the governors securing these consistencies no longer require the reinforcement of the will, either because the inconsistent alternative ceases to be considered as a possible course of action or because the 'unwanted' behaviour becomes so closely assimilated to the 'wanted' course of action of which it is a constituent that it comes to share in the quality of being 'wanted', which bulks so large in common experience and is so elusive in theory – or even because it becomes 'wanted' for its own sake, as an athlete may come to enjoy his morning exercise.

So we must introduce a further qualification. The will is involved only where the response in the field of necessity or obligation is still imperfectly learned. It will be useful at this stage to collect some more examples.

The alternatives in Case 1 (beef or mutton) are closely comparable; but they might equally well have been disparate. Suppose (Case 3) that I had intended to go to a concert after dinner but I am late. Shall I bolt some food and go to the concert or cut the concert and have a comfortable meal? I have no idea how I choose between such incommensurables but it is not by an act of will. Suppose, however, (Case 4) that I would vastly prefer a comfortable meal but have promised A to meet him at the concert. Again there arises the kind of conflict that engages the will – unless the obligation to A is of a kind that I have accepted at least sufficiently to exclude the alternative, at most sufficiently to make it 'wanted' or its neglect 'not-wanted'.

The pattern of previous examples may be repeated at every level of complexity. Suppose that, as a professional man (Case 5) I am offered two commissions at the same time. Each attracts me but I cannot undertake both. Or suppose (Case 6) that I am offered an attractive commission at a time when I had planned to be on holiday (Case 7). No effort of will can solve these dilemmas. Suppose, on the other hand (Case 8) that I am offered an interesting commission just after I have accepted a dull one. To escape my commitment will involve breaking a moral obligation and perhaps some lying; and if I am well-disciplined in these matters, I shall not entertain it, whilst if I am unprincipled, I shall accept the attractive one and evade the other with an equal absence of inner debate. But if, for me, the situation poses a real choice, I shall feel my will engaged, successfully or otherwise, on the side of 'principle'.

Consider one further group of examples of the same kind. The judge (Case 9) sits on the bench, hearing a civil case of alleged breach of contract. Is his 'will' involved? 'Certainly not', says common sense. His duty is to apply legal rules to facts and this may involve legal doubts and perhaps conflicts of legal rules; but his will is neither needed nor relevant to decide such conflicts, unless he is under some duress or temptation – be it only the temptation to go to sleep – such that some action inconsistent with his duty becomes for him a real alternative.

This is true, however disparate the elements of his conflict. Suppose (Case 10) that the case is marginal. He would like to find that a contract exists, since otherwise the defendant will escape a moral obligation; but to do so will create a precedent which may unduly extend the scope of contractual liability. He weighs the claims of immediate justice, legal consistency, and social policy, conscious that his decision will not only declare but make law. Yet these conflicts call for no exercise of will. To resolve them is an accepted part of his judicial role.

The layman, on the other hand, required to act judicially, is more likely to be conscious of conflict involving the will. Suppose (Case 11) that I am rudely contradicted by a man I dislike and called on to admit that I am wrong. Wrong I am, but I may or may not need an effort of will to admit it. And if (Case 12) sitting on a selection board, I have personal reasons for wishing one candidate to succeed, it may require an effort of will to exclude these from the many other considerations which 'ought' to be taken into account.

In all these examples, the will is invoked only in a conflict between an established 'want' and an imperfectly learned response to commitment or perceived necessity, never in conflicts, however acute, within the field of established wants. The field of established want is curiously wide and easier to recognize than to define; I shall return to it later. It remains first to ask whether the will can be involved in conflicts within the field of necessity or commitment (i.e. accepted obligation).

The experienced explorer (Case 13) short of food, rations himself in the knowledge of his distance from his base and lies down, famished, beside a sack of food. Such conflict as he suffers through his immediate self-denial is resolved by an effort of will; but another conflict remains. If he eats enough each day to provide tomorrow's energy, he will run out of food before he reaches his base. If he reserves enough food for all his possible days' journeys, he will run out of energy before he reaches his base. He cannot afford to eat what he needs; but equally he cannot afford not to eat what he needs. How can he best budget his scarce resources so as to maximize his chances of survival? He *must* conserve his food; he *must* conserve his energy; yet he cannot do both adequately. As he weighs one possible compromise against another, none engages his will, except in so far as this is needed to exclude from the balance the craving for food now.

Similar problems await the adventurer whose goal is not set by biological necessity. The poor, ambitious student (Case 14) struggling in his spare time towards an academic qualification, needs books, leisure, food, a place to work, guidance – needs which in total exceed his resources of money and energy. They are necessities only because of his self-set goal; but while he holds to his goal, they are none the less necessities.

Conflicts within the field of obligation are equally common and equally remote from the intervention of the will. The politician (Case 15) whose situation requires him either to resign from the government or to share responsibility for a policy he disapproves, may by an effort of will exclude personal considerations; but he must still face a conflict of loyalties, which no effort of will can resolve.

We can now describe tentatively the circumstances in which the word 'will' is used in common speech and thus get a glimpse of its real meaning. Common speech accepts as given the existence of wants and aversions as governors of behaviour and recognizes that these are qualified by governors of necessity and commitment. Conflicts arise within each of these three fields and between them. Among these manifold conflicts, one class and one class only permits of being modified by the conscious act commonly called an effort of will; this is the conflict between an established 'want' and a response to necessity or commitment which is still imperfectly learned.

Will, then, has something to do with learning. The theory implicit in our current usage of the word would seem to be that the learning process involved in the particular class of conflict which I have identified can be reinforced and speeded by conscious activity of a particular kind. This activity is known as an effort of will. Strength and weakness of will denote greater or less facility in learning this kind of response.

## II

This conclusion, however, does not help us much, until we have attached a clearer meaning to the responses of necessity and commitment implicit in the verbs 'I must' and 'I ought'.

Common speech, following common experience, explains behaviour by dividing it, somewhat arbitrarily, into 'acts' and postulating a tendency to do acts which are felt to be agreeable, instrumental, or appropriate and to avoid their opposites. The category of the agreeable has as its central core the act which is psychologically satisfying in itself, in which common speech classes together a wide variety of experience, from the enjoyment of food, rest, and activity to the exercise of skill and the appreciation of beauty. The extent and validity of this class awaits our further examination.

The instrumental act is the act which is done for the sake of the state to which it is expected to lead. The 'appropriate' act is the act which the agent regards as the 'best' response to a given 'situation', a definition which, of itself tells us nothing of how situations are identified or how responses are matched with them.

The three kinds of motivation are usually present together, though one or other may be dominant. The behaviour of the footballer can be fully explained only by reference to the activity which he is enjoying, the success which he is seeking, and the rules which he is obeying; and the same is true of other activities.

Psychology need have no serious quarrel with these categories. Learning theory has been specially concerned with the category of the appropriate. Animal ethologists have analysed situations which evoke responses, innate and learned, and have shown how they depend on the presence both of recognizable spatio-temporal patterns in the environment, and of dynamic conditions in the organism. Learning experiments, on the other hand, have shown that patterns of response are reinforced or changed by 'results', retrospectively associated with them; so the instrumental element is also clearly present.

The validity of the category 'pleasurable in itself', is perhaps more doubtful. For a creature active by definition but of limited energy, both inactivity and over-exertion are in their extreme noxious, even lethal and it would be strange if these did not generate aversion; but within those quantitative limits it may well be that the direction in which appetite and aversion should flow can be explained simply by progressive impacts of learning on the innate dynamic structure. Nonetheless, no harm is done by leaving this category provisionally separate, in theory as well as in common experience, until it can be confidently resolved into others.

Common speech, following common experience, credits men with a notable extension of the power both for instrumental and for appropriate action and attributes this to increased power to foresee, to generalize, and hence to recognize relationships, spatial, temporal, and logical. We credit ourselves with the power to envisage long chains of instrumental acts leading to some desired future state; and likewise with the power to envisage relationships between ourselves and the environment, physical and social, extended in time and organized into coherent patterns, such as those which define our roles as parents, citizens or what not; or more generally, as human beings.

Instrumental and appropriate acts reflect the presence in human behaviour of governors making for consistency. Acceptance of a remote goal or of an enduring role involves the doing of long chains of instrumental or appropriate acts, mutually dependent, in that serious deviations vitiate the whole sequence; so the agent committed to a purpose or role acquires a kind of vested interest in it. I refer to these governors, whether of purpose or role, which are operative in the individual at any given moment as 'commitments'.

I do not wish to imply thereby that these governors are independent of each other and of equal validity. Manifestly they are not; but common experience tends to treat them so and an adequate enquiry into their relationship would take too long. I can only glance at two related difficulties which emerge as soon as we begin to compare them.

The first difficulty lies in defining their most obvious differences. The instrumental act derives its value from its expected result; it is directed to the future. The appropriate act derives its value from the current situation; it is required to maintain an ongoing relationship. It is significant in itself in a way which the instrumental act is not. This difference deserves analysis which I cannot give it now.

The second difficulty derives from the elusive meaning of the words 'present' and 'future'. On the one hand, the future is operative in the mind only in so far as it is presently represented. On the other hand this 'present' representation is an ongoing representation which has itself a time dimension. We have no conceptual model of the process by which the brain represents temporal sequence except that the process must itself be a temporal process. The implications of this tend to be concealed by the convention which treats the present as a point without temporal magnitude. Among the manifold confusions which flow from this, one is relevant to the central theme of this paper. The present representation of a projected action and its relevance to my commitments is an activity amply long enough to contain scope for learning.

In order that the agent may be moved to instrumental or to appropriate action, he must both recognize the contemplated action as being instrumental to some purpose or appropriate to some role and be set to realize the purpose or to maintain the role. Common speech, reflecting common experience, recognizes the function of conscious activity both in identifying the proposed behaviour as instrumental or appropriate and in presenting the purpose or role for revaluation. Psychology has not much to say about these conscious activities. It has usefully deflated the excessive claims of the will as a coercive function but it has considered it only obliquely as an instrument for reinforcing and speeding the process of learning.

It is now possible to give a clearer meaning to the categories of necessity and obligation distinguished in the first part of this paper. Broadly, they correspond to the categories of the instrumental and the appropriate; but the categories overlap.

I 'must' order herring (Case 2) to avoid the disasters which I have learned to foresee from overspending or rich living; but I am moved also by the sense that, having decided to diet or economize, I 'ought' to be able to maintain my self-imposed rule. The explorer (Case 12) must ration his food, if he is to survive; but his sense of what is expected of explorers will move him to do so, even when the will to live might falter.

That which is learned, then, is, first, the inescapable association of the contemplated act with the result or the role to which the agent is committed. Reluctance to accept the association as inescapable is part of the reluctance which an act of will can overcome. This, however, is not all that is learned during the inner debate which accompanies decisions of this kind. A step is taken in the process by which a 'commitment' is confirmed or displaced; and this also is a step in a process of learning.

The purposes and roles which give coherence to human behaviour are both the product and the governors of our day-to-day action. Together, they constitute the set of governors operative at any given moment. But, as already pointed out, the mental process in which a contemplated act is reviewed in relation to the immediate challenge which has evoked it and to the current set of governors to which it is relevant is amply long enough to modify the set of governors, no less than to modify the contemplated act – and this process of modification is the learning process.

It is now possible to give a clear meaning to the field within which the resolution of conflict neither needs nor permits an exercise of will. I will call it the field of the 'Established'.

The field of the 'wanted', even if it can be usefully distinguished in some contexts, is never found unqualified; human behaviour is structured from the beginning by 'rules' and 'purposes', which may become as deeply 'established' as more primitive 'wants'. So I will borrow a term which has perhaps been overworked in another context and describe as 'the Establishment' the complex of wants, structured by established rules and purposes, as it exists currently in the individual.

Within this Establishment there is endemic conflict. Common experience tells us nothing of how these conflicts are resolved, except that it is not by an effort of will. Like the judge with the marginal case (Case 9) the resolution of such conflict is part of our human role.

The Establishment, however, is not static. New entrants are forever knocking at the door. Specific decisions by implication admit new members of the Establishment and extrude old ones; and it is at this point, says common experience, that conscious activity of a special kind – the act of will – can make a difference.

The will, in other words, is the conscious process whereby we can influence the organization of our wants.

It would seem, then, that the categories implicit in common speech are neither meaningless nor oversimplified; but that on the contrary they imply a theory of behavioural development more refined than psychology has yet established but not inconsistent with anything we think we know about the interaction of conscious and unconscious processes and suggestive lines of further enquiry. Before turning to these, we can now seek a meaning for 'free' will.

## III

In which of the examples given in the first section of this paper is it possible to ask a sensible question about the freedom of the will? The agent in Case 1 may assert that he is free to choose either beef or mutton; but he only means that he is free to choose the one he prefers and however much he may assert that he is free to choose the other if he wishes, neither he nor anyone else can attach either meaning or importance to his protestations. The most ardent supporter of free will might agree that the agent's choice in such a matter is 'determined' by his own wishes and desires. The agent in Case 2, on the other hand, however great his passion for lobster and however weak his will, is by common consent deemed to be free to choose herring.

The explorer whose hunger drives him to premature inroads into his food, the student who gives up the course that tries him beyond bearing, will not raise metaphysical issues of free will. They reached their limit, a limit which waits somewhere even for the strongest will. But the explorer who eats more than his share, the student who steals to buy books, will not be excused the responsibilities of freedom because he has passed his limit.

Two distinctions thus appear between the will which is supposed to be strong or weak and the will which is supposed to be free. Firstly, questions about freedom do not arise in every case in which the will is involved; they arise only on ethical issues. Secondly, where they do arise, the freedom postulated does not admit of degrees. The will may be strong or weak along a continuous scale but its freedom is either present or not present. Clearly, it is determined not by reference to the individual will but to the situation in which that will is acting.

Thus far, it appears that the field of action in which the will is supposed to be free is narrower than the field in which it shows itself as strong or weak. There are, however, areas in which the reverse is true. Suppose (Case 16) that I impulsively interrupt a speaker in a way which is socially unacceptable; or (Case 17) that I forget to pay my neighbour some courtesy which society expects. No act of will is involved; I acted without deciding,

WILL AND FREE WILL

without even 'meaning' to be discourteous. Yet I shall not convince my neighbours or myself that I was not 'free' to act otherwise; and both they and I will regard my impulsiveness or forgetfulness as 'an explanation but not an excuse'. Clearly our conception of free will is built to the measure of our standards of personal responsibility and not vice versa.

The difficulty of reconciling the concepts of will and free will is greatly reduced by the conclusion already reached that the exercise of will is an exercise in learning. Is it absurd for my neighbours to deem me free not to interrupt, not to forget? By no means; they are saying that I can learn not to interrupt, not to forget; and by setting this standard of expectation, they are releasing the influence most likely to make me learn.

It would seem, then, that to assert the freedom of the will is to assert not that a man is free to do but that he is free to learn to do. The field of personal responsibility is the field within which people are deemed capable of learning the responses which a given society – or they themselves – expect.

By introducing a time dimension, this formulation makes sense of some familiar enigmas. Suppose (Case 18) that a man finds himself progressively unable to take alcohol. Long-established habits of drinking begin to lead to ever more unpleasant results. He comes to accept the fact that he had better stop drinking altogether; and this new response to situations which invite drinking begins to fight its way into the Establishment. The fight will probably be long and punctuated with reverses. For years, perhaps, the man's responses to the offer of a drink may be unpredictable. Yet, if and when the new behaviour becomes established, the whole course of the struggle is seen in retrospect as a single sequence of learning, in which failures, as well as successes played a constructive part and of which it was apt from the beginning to predicate the man's power to learn. And with the establishment of the new governor the need and the possibility for further acts of will is ended.

It is possible, of course, to regard the act of will as no more than a sense of discomfort, which disturbs the agent as he observes his inner conflict but which does not contribute to the result. It is possible but it is not logically defensible. For any change in the neural activity engaged in the conflict must involve the possibility of a change in outcome. It is most unlikely that within the neural milieu, there can be change without mutual interaction; and changes in conscious activity must be assumed to connote changes in neural activity.

I conclude, therefore, that to assert the freedom of the will may have either or both of two useful and precise meanings. It may be to assert that a particular individual or class of individuals is capable of learning a particular response or, more generally, of learning to adopt a particular purpose or role as a governor of behaviour. Alternatively, it may mean that the individual or class ought to be deemed to be capable of such learning and treated accordingly. (Since it cannot be known with certainty before the event what a given individual can learn, statements in the first form are bound to have some elements of the second; but the distinction between the two is obviously important and should be borne in mind.) In its second sense, it further implies that the assertion may in itself determine whether the power to learn is used or not.

The second sense may express the judgement of society or some normative group within society, or of the agent himself. The last is specially significant, as appears if we examine the curious way in which common speech uses the word 'determine'. Suppose (Case 19) that a successful doctor is describing his early struggles. 'Everyone', he says, 'advised me not to go in for medicine. They all said I would not be able to qualify, even if I could stay the course. But *I was determined. . . .*'

How comes it that this verb, technically used to describe the opposite of free choice, is proudly used in such contexts, by agents themselves, to describe the exercise of their own initiative? The agent is proud that his inner governor, self-discovered if not self-set, was justified by the event. 'Self-determination' spells freedom, in individual, no less than in collective political life. 'Determination' settles that our course shall be thus and not otherwise, whether it be our own determination or another's. The 'free will' which we implicitly claim in common speech is freedom to commit ourselves, to choose the governors by which we are to be 'determined' – or at least to influence that choice over however small an area and in however small a degree.

## IV

The model of human nature which tacitly underlies our common speech, so far as it appears from this brief analysis, seems to me to be of no small interest to psychology. It asserts that men can and do by a conscious act influence their choice of governors and speed the learning process by which these gain authority in the organization of behaviour; in other words, that men can and do in some measure choose what they shall be. It implies that this process is different from the process by which we resolve conflict between the inconsistent promptings of established governors. It thus directs attention to an obscure and critically important aspect of the organization of human behaviour.

All organisms are biological systems, dependent on maintaining a number of relationships, internal and external, such as the internal relations by which they assimilate food and the external relations by which they win food from the environment. They can be defined by the relations, inner and outer, which they are set to maintain, by the thresholds beyond which they cannot deviate from these without irreversible change and by the responses and skills available to them in pursuing the one and avoiding the other. Men differ from other animals not so much in their internal relationships (their physio-chemical balances and patterns of growth and decay) as in the range and variety – and hence the inconsistency and instability – of the external relations which they seek with their physical environment and with each other.

These normative relations are both the product of experience and the governor of behaviour; and we badly need a more adequate model of the circular process in which they thus figure as cause and effect. In this process common experience, reflected in common speech, assigns a limited but critical role to a special kind of conscious activity. It is at least a useful pointer.

Those to whom such speculations seem uselessly vague may be glad to conclude with an example which has undeniable physiological reality. Suppose (Case 20) that an ember from the fire falls onto a favourite rug. I pick up the ember and throw it back, ignoring the indignant protests of the burning tissue and inhibiting, by an effort of will, the reflex action which would otherwise drop the noxious thing at the first warning. Here the conflict is recognizably one between two nervous centres, anatomically distinct, which are in a position to interfere with each other but seldom do so. Suppose, on the other hand (Case 21) that I habitually listen to music in the company of those more musical than I. When I am bored and they are not, no major effort of will is needed to still those frequent, small reflex movements by which immobilized muscles would normally seek their own relief. In such matters the local authorities are accustomed to receiving their orders from above. I have already learned to keep still when this is required.

At this level the situation which evokes an effort of will and the process by which such efforts become unnecessary can be defined physiologically with some precision. The examples given in this paper show that the special class of conflict said to involve acts of will is far wider than the class in which cortical activity, occasionally but not regularly, interferes with reflex action. It may, none the less, have a physiological basis. It would be strange if it had not. In this, however, we must await a neuro-physiological theory of the organization of behaviour more sophisticated than anything yet in sight.

# Select bibliography

*This select bibliography is an updated version of Vickers' own, and retains his own reference numbers.*

## Books

1. **1959** *The Undirected Society*, Toronto, University of Toronto Press.
2. **1965** *The Art of Judgment*, London, Chapman & Hall; New York, Basic Books; Methuen University Paperbacks 1968; Harper & Row 1983.
3. **1967** *Towards a Sociology of Management*, London, Chapman & Hall; New York, Basic Books.
4. **1968** *Value Systems and Social Process*, London, Tavistock Publications; New York, Basic Books. Paperback by Penguin Books, London 1970, and New York 1971.
5. **1970** *Freedom in a Rocking Boat* (sub-title: *Changing Values in an Unstable Society*), Allen Lane, The Penguin Press. An original Pelican. U.S. hard cover edition by Basic Books. Paperback by Penguin Books, London 1971, New York 1972.
6. **1970** *Science and the Regulation of Society*. An occasional paper published and circulated by the Institute for the Study of Science in Human Affairs, University of Columbia.
7. **1973** *Making Institutions Work*, London, Associated Business Programmes Ltd; New York, The Halstead Press.
8. **1980** *Responsibility – its Sources and Limits*, Intersystems Publications, PO Box 624, Seaside, California 93955, USA.
9. **1983** *Human Systems are Different*, London, Harper & Row.
10. **1984** *The Vickers Papers*, Open Systems Group (ed), London, Harper & Row.

## Other publications

14. **1952** 'The Accountability of a Nationalised Industry', *Public Administration*, Spring 1952, based on a talk given at the Administrative Staff College in 1948, but much revised.
18. **1952** 'The Siege Economy and the Welfare State of Mind', *The Lancet*, 27 December 1952; also in slightly longer form under the title 'Background to Management', in *The Manager*, December 1952. (Republished in Book 3.)
19. **1953** 'Needs and Opportunities in Psychiatric Research', Epilogue to J.M. Tanner (ed) *Prospects in Psychiatric Research*, Blackwell Scientific Publications 1953.

20.   1953 'Collective Insecurity'. Address given at Annual Conference of BACIE in October 1953.

22.   1954 'Human Communication', *British Management Review*, Vol. 12, No. 2, 1954.

24.   1954 'Some Ideas of Progress'. The Wilde Memorial Lecture. Memoirs and proceedings of the Manchester Literary and Philosophical Society, 1954–1955. (Republished in Book 4.)

25.   1954 'Communication in Economic Systems', *Studies in Communication*, Communications Research Centre, Secker & Warburg.

26.   1954 'Lay Attitudes to Health and Health Services', *The Lancet*, 13 November 1954.

27.   1955 'Mental Health and Spiritual Values', *The Lancet*, 12 March 1955. Also in *Mental Health in Public Affairs*, proceedings of the 5th International Congress on Mental Health. William Lane and Margery Kind (eds), University of Toronto Press.

28.   1955 'The Pound of Flesh', *The Listener*, December 1955.

29.   1955 'Cybernetics and the Management of Men', *The Manager*, December 1955. (Republished in Book 3.)

30.   1956 'Man and Industry – a Round Table', *Canadian Welfare*, Vol. XXXII, No. 5, December 1956.

32.   1956 'Science and the Art of Living', *The Listener*, January 1956.

34.   1956 'Incentives of Labour', *The Political Quarterly*, Vol. XXVII, No. 3. July–September 1956. (Revised and republished in Book 3.)

35.   1956 'The Needs of Men', *University of Toronto Quarterly*, Autumn 1956. (Republished in Book 1.)

36.   1956 'Stability, Control and Choice', *The 9th Wallberg Lecture*, University of Toronto Press. Also in *General Systems Year Book*, Vol. 11, 1957, the annual publication of the Society for General Systems Research.

37.   1958 'Adaptation as a Management Concept', *Journal of the British Institute of Management*, Vol. 1, No. 3, January 1958. (Republished in Book 3.)

38.   1958 'Positive and Negative Controls in Business', *Journal of Industrial Economics*, Vol. VI, No. 3. (Republished in Book 3.)

39.   1958 'The Role of Expectation in Economic Systems', *Occupational Psychology*, Vol. 32, No. 3, July 1958. (Republished in Book 3. Article 15 in this collection.)

40.   1958 'What Sets the Goals of Public Health?', *The Lancet*, 22 March 1958. Also in the *New England Journal of Medicine*, 20 March 1958. (Article 8 in this collection.)

43.   1959 'Is Adaptability Enough?', *Behavioral Science*, Vol. 4, No. 3, July 1959. (Republished in Book 1.)

44.   1959 'The Concept of Stress in Relation to the Disorganization of Human Behaviour', in *Stress and Psychiatric Disorder*, J. M. Tanner (ed), Blackwell Scientific Publications. Also in *General Systems Yearbook*, Vol. IV, 1959. (Article 20 in this collection.)

46.   1961 'What Do We Owe the Children?', *New Horizons for Canada's Children*, B. W. Heise (ed), University of Toronto Press. The proceedings of the first Canadian Conference on Children.

47.   1961 'Judgment', the 6th Elbourne Memorial Lecture, *The Manager*, January 1961: (Republished in Book 3. Article 16 in this collection.)

48.   1963 'Mental Disorder in British Culture', *Aspects of Psychiatric Research*,

D. Richter, J.M. Tanner, Lord Taylor and O.L. Zangwill (eds), Oxford University Press.

49. 1963 'Appreciative Behaviour', *Acta Psychologica*, Vol. 21, No. 3, 1963. (Republished in Book 4. Article 10 in this collection.)

50. 1963 'Ecology, Planning, and the American Dream', *The Urban Condition*, L. J. Duhl (ed), New York, Basic Books. (Republished in Book 4. Article 9 in this collection.)

53. 1964 'The Psychology of Policy Making and Social Change', the 38th Maudsley Lecture, *British Journal of Psychiatry*, Vol. 110, No. 467, July 1964. (Article 21 in this collection.)

55. 1965 'Industry, Human Relations, and Mental Health', *Tavistock Pamphlet No. 9, Tavistock Publications*. Also in *Industrialisation and Mental Health*. Proceedings of the 17th Annual Meeting of the World Federation for Mental Health, 1964. Published by WFMH. (Republished in Book 3. Article 17 in this collection.)

56. 1965 'The End of Free Fall', *The Listener*, 28 October and 4 November 1965. (Republished in Book 4. Article 3 in this collection.)

57. 1965 'Medicine, Psychiatry and General Practice', *The Lancet*, 15 May 1965.

60. 1967 'The Multi-Valued Choice', *Communication: Concepts and Perspectives*, Lee Thayer (ed), Washington DC, Sparton Books. (Republished in Book 4.)

61. 1967 'Community Medicine', *The Lancet*, 29 April 1967. (Article 11 in this collection.)

62. 1967 'Planning and Policy Making', *The Political Quarterly*, July–September 1967, Vol. 38, No. 3. (Republished in Book 4.)

63. 1967 'The Regulation of Political Systems', *General Systems Yearbook*, Vol. XII, 1967. (Republished in Book 4.)

65. 1967 'What to Expect of a Doctor', *British Hospital Journal and Social Science Review*, 1 March 1968.

67. 1968 'The Uses of Speculation', *Journal of the American Institute of Planners*, January, 1968.

68. 1968 'Medicine's Contribution to Culture', *Medicine and Culture*. The proceedings of an international symposium sponsored by the Wellcome Trust and the Wenner-Gren Foundation, F. N. L. Poynter (ed), London, The Wellcome Historical Medical Library, 1969.

69. 1968 'The Promotion of Psychiatric Research', *British Journal of Psychiatry*, No. 114.

70. 1968 'A Theory of Reflective Consciousness', prepared for a Wenner-Gren Symposium.

71. 1968 'Individuals in a Collective Society', *Environment and Change*, W.R. Ewald Jr. (ed), Indiana University Press 1968. (Republished in Book 7.)

73. 1968 'Science and the Appreciative System', *Human Relations*, May 1968. (Republished in Book 4.)

76. 1969 'Two Streams of Medicine?', *Public Health*, Vol. 83, No. 6, pp. 270–274.

78. 1969 'A Classification of Systems'. Written for the Society for General Systems Research, London Chapter, based on a talk given at their first meeting. Published in *General Systems Yearbook 1970*. (Article 2 in this collection.)

79. 1970 Preface to E. Trist and E. E. Emery, *Towards a Social Ecology*. Published by the Plenum Publishing Co.

80. 1970 'Communication and Ethical Judgment'. A paper written for discussion at the Center for the Advanced Study of Communication, the University of Iowa, in May 1970. Published by Iowa in conference papers.

81. 1970 'Management and the New Specialists'. Commissioned by AMA for projected *Journal of Organisational Dynamics*. Published in Vol. 1, No. 1, 1972.

82. 1970 'The Containment of Conflict'. Commissioned for book to be published by Richter et al. (eds) called *Working for Peace*. Rewritten as item 90 below, 'The Management of Conflict'. (Article 12 in this collection.)

83. 1971 'The Demands of a Mixed Economy'. Based on a lecture given at the Wharton School, University of Pennsylvania, Philadelphia. Published in the *Wharton Quarterly*, Spring 1971. (Republished in Book 7.)

84. 1971 'Institutional and Personal Roles'. Based on a lecture given at University of California, Berkeley. Published in *Human Relations* 1971, Vol. 24, No. 5. Republished by the UC Berkeley. (Republished in Book 7. Article 18 in this collection.)

85. 1971 'Changing Ethics of Distribution'. Commissioned by *Futures* and published in June 1971. (Republished in Book 7.)

87. 1971 'International Organisations'. A paper given at a conference on the *Predicament of Man*, organized by the Science Policy Foundation in April 1971. Published in the proceedings of that conference.

88. 1972 'Levels of Human Communication'. A paper prepared for an International Conference on Communication in Barcelona in October 1972 and published in the proceedings of that conference, Lee Thayer (ed); and in *Communications* Vol. 1, No. 1, 1974 (No. 112). (Article 22 in this collection.)

89. 1972 'Incomes and Earnings – a Steady State?' An address published in Michael Schwab (ed.) *Teach-in for Survival*, London, Robinson and Watkins Books, 1972.

90. 1972 'The Management of Conflict', *Futures*, June 1972. (Republished in Book 7. Article 12 in this collection.)

91. 1972 'Towards a More Stable State', *Futures*, December 1972. (Republished in Book 7.)

92. 1972 'Commonly Ignored Elements in Policy Making', *Policy Sciences*, Vol. 3, 1972.

94. 1972 'The Emerging Policy Sciences', *Futures*, September 1972.

96. 1973 'Values, Norms and Policies', *Policy Sciences*, Vol. 4, No. 1, March 1973. (Republished in Book 7. Article 13 in this collection.)

97. 1973 'Motivation Theory – a Cybernetic Contribution', *Behavioural Science*, Vol. 18, No. 4, July 1973.

100. 1973 'Educational Criteria for Times of Change', *Journal of Curriculum Studies*, Vol. 5, No. 1, May 1973.

104A. 1973 'Educating for Planning'. A paper based on the preceding paper published in *The Planner*, Vol. 59, No. 10, December 1973.

106. 1974 'Projections, Predictions, Models and Policies', *The Planner* (Journal of the RTPI, Vol. 60, No. 4, April 1974.

106A. 1974 Experimental Education in Department Structured Universities.

107. 1974 'Population Policy, its Scope and Limits', *Futures*, October 1974. Based

on an address given at the invitation of the Population Council in April 1974. (Article 4 in this collection.)

109.   **1974** 'Policy Making in Local Government', *Local Government Studies*, February 1974.

112.   **1974** 'Levels of Human Communication', *Communications*, Vol. 1, No. 1, 1974. (Article 22 in this collection.)

112A. **1974** 'Changing Patterns of Communication'. (Article 14 in this collection.)

113.   **1974** 'The Uses and Limits of Policy Analysis'. *Futures*, Vol. 6, No. 4, August 1974.

114.   **1974** 'The Changing Nature of the Professions', *American Behavioral Scientist*, Vol. 18, No. 2, Nov/Dec. 1974. (Article 19 in this collection.)

116.   **1976** 'Problems of Distribution', *World Modelling: a Dialogue*, C. West Churchman and Richard O. Mason (eds), pp. 49–54.

117.   **1977** 'Practice and Research in Managing Human Systems', *Policy Sciences* Vol. 9, 1978.

117A. **1977** 'Learning and Institutional Culture'.

119.   **1977** 'The Future of Culture', *Futures Research – New Directions*, H. A. Linstone and W. H. Clive Simmonds (eds), 1977.

120.   **1977** 'Rationality and Intuition', *Aesthetics in Science*, Judith Wechsler (ed), MIT Press, 1978. (Article 23 in this collection.)

123.   **1977** 'The Weakness of Western Culture', *Futures*, December 1977. (Also in Book 8. Article 5 in this collection.)

124.   **1978** 'Some Implications of Systems Thinking'. A text prepared from a talk video-taped in England by the Open University and transmitted to SGSR for use at a Presidential Address at the Annual Meeting of the Society in Washington in February, 1978. Published in *SGSR Bulletin* for Winter 1978 and also in the first number of the *Nevis Quarterly*, published in October, 1978.

125.   **1978** 'Education in Systems Thinking'. A paper prepared for presentation at the first International Meeting of the SGSR in August, 1979, published in *Journal of Applied Systems Analysis*, Vol. 7, 1980. (Also in Book 8.)

126.   **1978** 'Settling Social Priorities'. A paper prepared at the request of Professor P. Checkland for publication in the *Journal of Applied Systems Analysis*. Published in Vol. 6 1979.

127.   **1979** 'Equality of Responsibility'. *Futures*, February 1979. (Also in Book 8.)

128.   **1979** 'Ethics, Patriotism and The State'. A paper written in preparation for a conference on The New Narcissism at the Architectural Association in March 1979. Published by *New Society*.

129.   **1979** 'The Ethical Criterion in Human Ecology', unpublished. (Vickers papers, Goring.)

130.   **1979** 'Stability and Quality in Human Systems'. A talk at Open University Summer School, Keele, 1979. (Also in Book 8.)

131.   **1979** 'The Future of Morality', *Futures*, October 1979. (Also in Book 8. Article 6 in this collection.)

132.   **1979** 'Autonomous Yet Responsible?' Published in *Long Range Planning*.

133.   **1979** 'A Sufficiently Stable Future.'

134.   **1979** 'Will and Free Will'. (Article 24 in this collection.)

135.   **1979** 'The Assumption of Policy Analysis', *Policy Studies Journal*, Vol. 9, No. 4. Special No. 2 1980–1981 to be published in a book and formed from that issue.

136.   **1979** 'The Ecology of Ethics'. Written for *The Ecologist*. Not published.

137.   **1979** 'Three Needs, Two Buckets, One Well', *New Directions for Teaching and Learning: Interdisciplinary*, No. 8, December 1981.

138.   **1980** 'Violence'. A paper prepared for conference organized by the Dag Hammarskjold Information Centre on the Study of Violence and Peace, held at Cumberland Lodge, Windsor, in January, 1981. Revised 19 January 1981 as 'Violence, War and Genocide'. May be published in the proceedings after the conference. (Article 7 in this collection.)

139.   **1980** 'Has Man become a Cancer? A review article covering the Brandt Report and the IUNC Report on the Conservation of Living Resources, published in *Town Planning Review*, April 1981.

140.   **1980** Alvin Toffler. 'The Third Wave'. A review article published in *Long Range Planning*.

141.   **1980** 'The Role of the Systems Analyst', published in bulletin of the *Society for General Systems Research* and *Complexity Management and Change, Conclusion*, Open University Press, 1984.

142.   **1980** 'The Poverty of Problem Solving'. A paper submitted to a conference of the NATO Advanced Research Institute on Systems Analysis in *Urban Policy Making and Planning*, held at Oxford in September, 1980. Later revised. (See 14.) Published in *Complexity Management and Change, Conclusion*, Open University Press, 1984.

143.   **1980** 'The Limitations of Systems Analysis'. A talk given to a Nato sponsored conference of systems analysts at Oxford in September 1980. (MS prepared for talk. Not used.)

144.   **1980** 'The Poverty of Problem Solving'. A revised version of 142 prepared after the conference and published in *Systems Analysis in Urban Policy – Making and Planning!* NATO Conference Series, Series 11: Systems Science, Vol. 12, Plenum.

145.   **1981** 'Systems Analysis – a tool subject or judgment demystified?', *Policy Sciences*, Vol. 14, 1981.

# Index